Militant Zionism in America

JUDAIC STUDIES SERIES

Leon J. Weinberger
GENERAL EDITOR

Militant Zionism in America

The Rise and Impact of the Jabotinsky
Movement in the United States, 1926–1948

RAFAEL MEDOFF

THE UNIVERSITY OF ALABAMA PRESS : TUSCALOOSA AND LONDON

Typeface: ACaslon

∞

The paper on which this book is printed meets the minimum requirements of
American National Standard for Information Science–Permanence of Paper for
Printed Library Materials, ANSI Z39.48-1984.

Library of Congress Cataloging-in-Publication Data

Medoff, Rafael, 1959–
    Militant Zionism in America : the rise and impact of the Jabotinsky movement in
the United States, 1926–1948 / Rafael Medoff.
        p.   cm. — (Judaic studies series)
    Includes bibliographical references (p.) and index.
    ISBN 0-8173-1071-1 (cloth : alk. paper)
    1. Revisionist Zionism—United States—History—20th century. 2. Zionism—
United States—History—20th century. 3. Jews—United States—Politics and
government—20th century. I. Title: Rise and impact of the Jabotinsky movement
in the United States, 1926–1948. II. Title. III. Series.
    DS150.R6 U654 2002
    320.54′095694—dc21

                                                                            2001006532

British Library Cataloguing-in-Publication Data available

Contents

Acknowledgments

Most factions of the American Zionist movement have been examined in detail by scholars, either as part of histories of the movement as a whole or in separate studies. The Jabotinsky movement is the major exception. The American branch of Jabotinsky's Revisionist Zionists has been almost completely ignored by historians, and the Revisionist offshoot known as the Bergson group has received only occasional and incomplete attention. One of the reasons Jabotinsky's American followers have received so little scholarly notice is the widespread assumption that they were not a force of political significance, either within the American Zionist movement or beyond. This book questions the validity of that assumption as it traces the rise of the Jabotinsky movement in the United States and assesses its impact, both within the American Jewish community and on American and British policy. It begins with the inception of the U.S. wing of Revisionism in 1926 and concludes with the attainment of the Zionist movement's primary objective, the establishment of the state of Israel in 1948. Because this study is primarily concerned with the political impact of American Revisionist Zionism and its role in affecting international events and policies, it does not focus on those segments of the movement that were not at the center of its political activity, such as its youth movement, Betar; that is a separate study which remains to be written.

I am grateful to the many institutions that granted me access to their collections during the course of the research for this book: the American Friends Service Committee Archives; the American Jewish Historical Society; the American Jewish Archives; the Central Zionist Archives (Jerusalem); the Hadassah Archives; the Jabotinsky Institute (Metzudat Ze'ev); the Jewish National Library at Hebrew University; the Library of Congress; the National Archives; the Public Record Office (London); the Franklin D. Roosevelt Library; The Temple Library; the United Nations Archives; the Special Collections Department of the University of North

Dakota Library; the Weizmann Archives; the Yale University Library; and the YIVO Institute for Jewish Research. Mordechai Haller, attorney and scholar, provided important research assistance at a number of these institutions, for which I am deeply grateful. A number of individuals graciously shared with me documents from their private collections, including Carl Alpert, Benzion Netanyahu, Harry Selden, and Baruch Rabinowitz. Professors Melvin Urofsky and David S. Wyman offered valuable suggestions concerning sections of an earlier version of this manuscript; I am grateful for their advice.

Portions of the research for this book were facilitated by the American Jewish Historical Society, which granted me a Sid and Ruth Lapidus Fellowship; the American Jewish Archives, where I served as a Marguerite R. Jacobs Memorial Post-Doctoral Fellow in American Jewish Studies during 1993 and 1994; the Melton Center for Jewish Studies at Ohio State University, which provided a research grant during 1991 and 1992; the Herbert Hoover Presidential Library Association, under whose auspices I served as a Hoover Scholar during 1988 and 1989; and the Lady Davis Fellowship Trust, which granted me a Graduate Fellowship at Hebrew University during 1986 and 1987. I thank these institutions for their generous assistance.

I am also grateful to Nicole Mitchell, Mindy Wilson, Jonathan Lawrence, and all those former or current members of the staff of the University of Alabama Press who were involved in the production of this volume.

This book is dedicated to my wife, Carin. As the Talmud teaches, "A good wife is like a beautiful gift from Heaven."

Militant Zionism in America

1 • Planting the Seeds of Militant Zionism in America

Snowflakes drifted gently across New York harbor as the SS *France* pulled up to the pier on January 27, 1926. Among its passengers was Ze'ev (Vladimir) Jabotinsky, orator, author, poet, and leader of the Zionist movement's maximalist wing. Ready to begin his first visit to the United States, Jabotinsky tightened his muffler, braced himself against the frigid morning air, and followed the walkway down to the dock. Considering the blustery winds and snowfall, he probably did not expect a large audience to greet him when he came ashore. But it must have been disconcerting to gaze about the pier and discover that the entire welcoming committee consisted of young Israel Posnansky, in his rumpled overcoat and earmuffs, teeth chattering, frantically rubbing his hands together as protection against the winter chill.[1] Although Posnansky was by no means Jabotinsky's only follower, the fact that he was the only one on hand to greet the Zionist leader upon his arrival dramatically illustrated the fact that activist Zionism had not yet taken hold in the American Jewish community. But when Jabotinsky returned to Europe, after five and a half months of lectures and organizing in the United States, he left behind the seeds of a movement that would one day profoundly affect the destiny of American Jewry.

Jabotinsky began his Zionist career not as a fiery dissident but as a mainstream Zionist orator and writer in turn-of-the-century czarist Russia. It was in Russia that the first modern associations for the resettlement of the Land of Israel, Bilu and Hovevei Zion, arose in the late 1800s. Responding to pogroms and governmental discrimination against Jews, these young activists pioneered some of the earliest Jewish settlements in modern Palestine, which was then under Turkish rule, and laid the foundation for the rise of a powerful Zionist movement in Russia. Theodor Herzl, the Viennese Jewish journalist who launched the World Zionist Organization (WZO) in 1897, was Zionism's political leader and foremost diplomat, but the Russian Jewish community provided the backbone of the movement and produced a steady stream of extraordinary orators and authors. Jabotinsky grew up in an intellectual milieu suffused with such stellar talents as Menachem Ussishkin, Nahum Sokolow, Shmaryahu Levin, Ahad Ha'am, Chaim Weizmann, and Nahman Syrkin.

One of the traits that set Jabotinsky apart from other prominent Russian Zionists was his determination to personally translate his ideals into concrete action. Well known in Russia for both his literary talents and his role in organizing armed Jewish self-defense groups, Jabotinsky gained international prominence through his successful campaign for the creation of a Jewish Legion that fought as part of the British army against the Turks in World War I and took part in the capture of Palestine. Jabotinsky and many of the other demobilized legionnaires settled in Palestine at war's end, expecting to witness the fulfillment of England's wartime promise, known as the Balfour Declaration, to facilitate the creation of a "Jewish national home" in Palestine.

But some British officials, especially those governing Palestine itself, thought a pro-Arab slant might better serve England's regional interests. Although the text of the Balfour Declaration was part of the terms of the Palestine Mandate granted Britain by the League of Nations in 1920, British policy on the ground was already evolving in a different direction. Jabotinsky's role in organizing Jewish defense militias to fight off Palestinian Arab rioters in 1920 aroused British disfavor. Arrested by the British for illegal possession of weapons during the riots and sentenced to fifteen years at hard labor, Jabotinsky was catapulted to martyr status in the Zionist world. An international outcry resulted in his release the following year.

During the early 1920s, Jabotinsky grew increasingly dissatisfied at the Zionist leadership's cautious response to the signs of a pro-Arab shift in Britain's Palestine policy. He urged WZO president Chaim Weizmann to fight London's opposition to the creation of a Jewish army in Palestine and to more aggressively oppose the English decision, in 1922, to bar Jewish settlement in the eastern part of Palestine, known as Transjordan. Weizmann, along with the growing Labor Zionist movement, favored quiet diplomacy and gradualist settlement activity as the way to slowly build a Jewish homeland. Jabotinsky, by contrast, preferred Herzl's approach of staging dramatic acts of public pressure. Jabotinsky thought in grand terms—creating a modern army, forming alliances with world powers, establishing a powerful sovereign state stretching across both sides of the Jordan River. Jabotinsky was a great believer in the power of ideas and the influence of public relations. His opponents ridiculed him for favoring "words over deeds," but in Jabotinsky's view, words would make it possible to accomplish deeds—that is, words were needed both to give Jews the sense of conviction that would motivate them to act for Jewish statehood, and to secure the international sympathy needed to move toward statehood without substantial outside interference.

Frustrated by what he regarded as the timidity of Weizmann and others in the Zionist leadership, Jabotinsky resigned from the Zionist Executive—the movement's ruling council—in early 1923. In the two years that followed, Jabotinsky established an activist Zionist youth movement of his own, Betar, as well as his own political faction within the WZO, known as the World Union of Zionists-Revisionists. The party's name signified Jabotinsky's conviction that Zionist policy urgently required revision. A more aggressive posture was necessary, he believed, to prevent Britain from completely embracing the Arab cause and altogether spurning Zionism.

Although it was not a major point of controversy during Revisionism's earliest years, Jabotinsky would also, by the early 1930s, emerge as a vociferous critic of the socialist economic theories promoted by the Labor Zionist movement and its powerful trade union, the Histadrut. Jabotinsky argued that in view of rising anti-Semitism in Europe and increasing Palestinian Arab hostility toward Zionism, the Palestine Jewish community (known as the *yishuv*) should seek greater unity by utilizing compulsory arbitration rather than strikes as a means of settling labor disputes. Tensions between Histadrut strikers and Revisionists who defied their strikes would often flare into violence.

In the cultural sphere as well, Jabotinsky's followers went their own way. The songs and literature of the Revisionist movement emphasized Jewish military achievements in biblical times, the bonds between Jewry and the Land of Israel, and the need for the territorial integrity of the Jewish national homeland, to be ensured by a Jewish military force. Labor Zionists, too, opposed Britain's severance of Transjordan from the Palestine Mandate, but whereas the Laborites gradually acquiesced in the decision and dropped the issue from their agenda, the Revisionists made the concept "Both sides of the Jordan" a centerpiece of their ideology and culture.

Revisionist, or maximalist, Zionism, then, came to represent a distinct worldview with well-defined perspectives on a broad range of political, cultural, and economic issues. It was not merely a political party, but a rapidly growing mass movement that hoped to direct the Zionist struggle and define the character of the future Jewish state.

The Revisionist message found especially receptive audiences in Eastern Europe. Jabotinsky's calls for a tougher stance toward the British, massive Jewish immigration to Palestine, and the quick creation of a Jewish state attracted sympathy among lower-middle-class Eastern European Jewish shopkeepers and artisans suffering from anti-Jewish discrimination and occasional persecution. Jabotinsky's militant posture also resonated among would-be emigrants who began considering Palestine as a possible destination once America's doors were nearly shut by restrictive immigration quotas imposed in 1921 and further tightened in 1924. The Revisionist platform contrasted sharply with the gradualist approach of mainstream Zionist leaders. Weizmann, expecting the British to remain true to the Balfour Declaration, advocated cooperation with the Mandatory rulers. He and his allies in the Labor Zionist movement, led by David Ben-Gurion and Berl Katznelson, preferred a "one more cow, one more *dunam*" approach to development of the country. To avoid antagonizing London, Weizmann remained deliberately vague as to whether he would be satisfied with something less than a sovereign state; he referred to the word "statehood" as "the *shem hameforash*," an ancient Hebrew term for the unmentionable name of God.

The sociological conditions in interwar Eastern Europe that bred sympathy for militant Zionism were not to be found in 1920s America. Attracting support for Revisionism in the United States posed a complex challenge. The political and social atmosphere in post–World War I America was not hospitable to foreign-based ethnic nationalist movements. The anti-German hysteria of the war years had generated strong pressure on all immigrants to "Americanize" by abandoning their native languages, old-world customs, and foreign political loyalties. The Communist revolution in Russia helped provoke a series of Red Scares in the United States in 1919 and 1920 that placed much of the blame for the Communist menace at the doorsteps of European immigrants. The Ku Klux Klan and other racist and anti-immigrant movements enjoyed a surge of popularity in the early 1920s; the Klan had 4 million members in forty-three states by 1924. A proliferation of anti-Semitic propaganda in the early and mid-1920s, including the serialization of the *Protocols of the Elders of Zion* in Henry Ford's *Dearborn* (Michigan) *Independent,* further intimidated the Jewish community. In such an environment, many American Jews feared that affiliation with a Zionist movement could be perceived as un-American.

Other factors, too, hampered American Zionism. The Balfour Declaration, the subsequent British conquest of Palestine, and the awarding of the

Palestine Mandate to Britain made it seem as if Zionism's central goal had been achieved. The need for a Diaspora Zionist movement was no longer obvious. While outbreaks of Palestinian Arab violence might normally have been expected to increase American Jewish interest in Palestine, the Arab riots of 1920 and 1921 were too brief and underpublicized to have a serious impact on American Jewish opinion. Furthermore, in 1921, the Zionist Organization of America (ZOA), the main Zionist group in the United States, lost its most attractive leader when Supreme Court justice Louis D. Brandeis resigned from its presidency in order to avoid a conflict of interest between his Court duties and his Zionist activity. Brandeis's departure deprived American Zionism of the prestige of having America's most prominent and respected Jew at its helm.

The atmosphere of the Roaring Twenties further hampered American Zionism. With their postwar prosperity and increased leisure time, Americans were enjoying dance crazes, provocative new fashions in clothing, national sports heroes such as Babe Ruth, and the introduction of movies. The newfound pleasures of American society beckoned, and American Jews were anxious to move up and fit in. Dramatic shifts were under way in the economic and professional profile of interwar American Jewry that made cultural integration and material advancement genuine possibilities. From a turn-of-the-century immigrant population consisting heavily of peddlers, sweatshop workers, and other blue-collar laborers, by 1930 most of the American Jewish workforce was white collar. About half of American Jews were involved in trade, and a significant number were now employers rather than employees. More than one-third of Jews were in commercial occupations, as compared to about 14 percent of Americans in general. Increasing numbers of Jews could be found in law, medicine, the entertainment industry, and journalism. Upwardly mobile children of turn-of-the-century Jewish immigrants were moving out of the ghetto-like Lower East Side and settling in suburban Brooklyn and the Bronx. Prosperous America, not impoverished Palestine, was the focus of American Jewry's attention.

Demographic patterns also affected American Jewish interest in Zionism. The rising tide of nativist sentiment in the United States had resulted in the enactment of restrictive immigration laws in 1921 and 1924, and these had drastically reduced the influx of Jews (among others). Between 1924 and 1931, 73,000 Jewish immigrants settled in the United States, as compared to the 650,000-plus Eastern European Jews who entered between 1907 and 1914. Jewish immigrants who had grown up in Russia and Poland, where they experienced anti-Semitism firsthand and generally had an affinity for Jewish tradition, were more likely to sympathize with Zionism than were native-born American Jews; with the tightening of the immigration laws, the segment of American Jewry that was born in the United States was rapidly increasing.

On the other hand, most American Jews still lived in heavily Jewish sections of a handful of major cities, even if many were branching out to satellite neighborhoods within those cities. During the 1930s, more than 40 percent of America's 4.3 million Jews lived in New York City. About 10 percent resided in Chicago; the rest could be found in cities such as Philadelphia, Baltimore, Boston, Detroit, and Cleveland. At least in theory, this pattern of self-segregation worked to Zionism's advantage by discouraging assimilation and encouraging a sense of Jewish ethnic solidarity.

Still, the numbers spoke volumes. American Jewish support for Zionism peaked with the issue of the Balfour Declaration and the subsequent British conquest of Palestine. At that point it seemed as if Zionism's major diplomatic goal had been attained, and the membership rolls of the ZOA plummeted. From a high of 149,000 in 1918, the ZOA had barely 18,000 members left by 1922. It had rebounded only slightly, to about 26,000, by the time Jabotinsky arrived in New York in early 1926.[2] If mainstream Zionism was having such difficulties, could the most militant and controversial faction of the Zionist movement take root in American soil?

If Jabotinsky's lecture tour was any indication, it was not going to be easy. His opening address, at the Manhattan Opera House on January 31, 1926, attracted an audience of some two thousand—but that meant just one-third of the seats were filled.[3] Elsewhere he spoke to "empty halls," he wrote his wife.[4] Sol Hurok's agency, Universal Artists, which had originally booked Jabotinsky for twenty lectures, reduced the number to ten because of "the unfriendly attitude of official Zionist circles," the Revisionists claimed.[5] Whether or not such direct interference took place is unclear, but two officials of the rival Labor Zionist movement in Palestine, David Remez and Avraham Harzfeld, who were also touring the United States in early 1926, repeatedly denounced Jabotinsky before American Jewish audiences.[6]

If there was indeed any deliberate effort by American Zionist leaders to undermine Jabotinsky's tour, it was not discernible in the pages of the ZOA journal, *New Palestine*. In February it allotted space for a substantial excerpt from the text of his Manhattan Opera House speech, and in March it ran a two-part series (each part a two-page spread) by Jabotinsky, explaining the Revisionist platform.[7]

Perhaps the most remarkable aspect of Jabotinsky's maiden American speech, and his *New Palestine* essay, was that his major points differed so slightly from the positions of the mainstream Zionist bodies. His calls for more Jewish immigration and for colonization of Palestine were standard Zionist fare. His hope for a Jewish army in Palestine was shared by American Zionist leaders, even if they were pessimistic about the chances of winning British approval. Although Jabotinsky criticized the Zionist leadership for negotiating to include a large number of non-Zionists in the Jewish Agency—Palestine Jewry's liaison to the British—that criticism was shared by many leading American Zionists. He did demand Jewish control of immigration, rather than reliance on England to permit increased immigration, but the difference between those two positions was not widely noted. Jabotinsky also differed from the Zionist leadership with his call for "a political drive in order to convince British public opinion and the British government" of the need for Jewish development, but he softened that demand by emphasizing that "the 'political drive' need not be hostile to England." Overall, the differences between Jabotinsky and the Zionist establishment were at this stage more a matter of tone than substance.

Sure enough, *New Palestine*'s March 19 editorial about the Revisionist phenomenon saw the new group as allies, not foes. The Jabotinsky group, it asserted,

> is part and parcel of the general Zionist grouping in the Zionist Organization. The revisionists may be said to belong to *our* party. They are merely a dissentient group that wants to impress upon the action of the movement the quality of their own views, but they do not form, in any real sense, a party as the term has been used in Zionist affairs heretofore. . . . [Jabotinsky's proposals are] not in principle at variance [*sic*] with the prevailing views in any of the existing parties or groups. [The only difference is that Jabotinsky] gives his program a characteristic nuance. He sings the same song in a higher key—with only slight variations. . . . [Any] Zionist, reading his complaints against the Zionist Executive, will come to the conclusion that the only difference that actually exists between Mr. Jabotinsky's advocacy of certain proposals, and the advocacy of the same proposals by others, with the exception of one or two, is a matter of emphasis.[8]

A number of prominent ZOA members, including author and lecturer Maurice Samuel, *New Palestine* editor Meyer Weisgal, and literary agent Joseph Brainin, urged Jabotinsky to refrain from establishing a U.S. wing of the Revisionist movement, since, they said, the June 1926 ZOA convention was likely to endorse "99 percent" of the Revisionist platform.[9] Even ZOA president Louis Lipsky seemed to agree "more or less" with Revisionist arguments, Jabotinsky found. Lipsky, returning from London in early April, confirmed to reporters that while he did not "endorse" Jabotinsky's platform, "we could adopt one or two points emphasized by the Revisionists; even the demand for Jewish military units in view of recent events in Palestine may receive justification which until now it did not have."[10] Jabotinsky, elated by what he saw as evidence that he was "conquering" the ZOA, canceled plans for a mass rally at Manhattan's Cooper Union hall to launch an American Revisionist movement.[11]

Jabotinsky's handful of devout followers in New York were instinctively suspicious of the ZOA officials' motives. These were the core of loyalists who made up the American Revisionist inner circle during its early years: Elias Ginsburg, veteran of Jabotinsky's World War I Jewish Legion as well as collaborator with Jabotinsky in the armed defense of Jerusalem's Jews during the 1920 Arab riots, now a banker in Brooklyn; Mordechai Danzis, a member of the editorial staff of the Yiddish-language daily *Der Tog*, remembered by his cohorts as witty and *heimishe;*[12] Johan Smertenko of the Jewish monthly *Opinion;* businessman Beinish Epstein; and Joseph Beder, owner of the Palestine Import Company, whose offices at 32 Union Square in lower Manhattan doubled as Revisionist headquarters. To these men, the nuanced differences between their leader and the Zionist establishment were ideological and political chasms that could not be bridged. They suspected that the ZOA's attempt to downplay the differences between mainstream Zionism and Revisionism was actually, in the words of one, "a skillful game intended to prevent the emergence of an organized Revisionist movement in the wake of Jabotinsky's successful lecture tour."[13]

The tour had, in fact, not been entirely successful. A more likely explanation for the ZOA's attitude was that its leaders genuinely believed their differences with the Revisionists were insignificant. But the Zionist leadership's attitude began to change in April, when the executive committee of the Order Sons of Zion, one of the ZOA's constituent organizations, endorsed Revisionism and called on the order's forthcoming convention to do likewise.[14] Suddenly the Revisionists looked more like rivals than potential partners.

Hardly a major force in the Zionist world, the order was a mutual aid society whose major accomplishment was the recent creation of a "Judea Insurance Company" in Palestine. But having lost nearly 90 percent of its national membership since 1918, the ZOA was not ready to lose the Order Sons of Zion and its five thousand members without a fight. When Jabotinsky delayed his planned April 10 return to Europe so he could canvass individual Sons of Zion lodges to woo their backing, the fight was on.[15] Nonetheless, the ZOA's arguments made little or no reference to any substantive ideological differences it had with the Revisionists. The themes of unity, discipline, and loyalty were invoked. "We are in need of common counsel, not of separation," a *New Palestine* editorial contended. "We are in need of understanding, not of the creation of new fractions or parties that build up artificial walls between Zionists, who are actually all interested in the attainment of the same object." Louis Lipsky's appeal to the order on the eve of its June 20–21 convention focused entirely on the order's contractual obligation to remain exclusively loyal to "its parent organization," the ZOA.[16]

Hoping that the endorsement of the Order Sons of Zion would serve as a stepping-stone to taking over the entire ZOA, Jabotinsky and his aides threw themselves into the campaign, visiting "scores" of Sons of Zion lodges and taking part in "six, seven sometimes eight meetings every week."[17] The normally placid Sons of Zion annual convention, held that year at the Hotel Scarboro in Long Branch, New Jersey, was transformed into a verbal battlefield. Lipsky and Jabotinsky, addressing the opening session, engaged in a "brilliant duel of words," the Jewish Telegraphic Agency (the only daily Jewish news service) reported. Yet Lipsky stressed the loyalty issue, making only passing reference to the danger that a Jewish army might harm Palestine Jewry's peace-loving image. Jabotinsky, for his part, stressed his devotion to the WZO, the right to dissent within the bounds of the Zionist movement, and Revisionism's commitment to the cause of Arab-Jewish peace. It may have been a brilliant duel of words, but the Sons of Zion delegates must have had trouble discerning any difference in the duelers' positions on political or ideological matters. Still, the Revisionists carried the day: the delegates voted 90 to 35 to endorse Jabotinsky's platform.[18] Lipsky got in a parting shot the next week, when the delegates to the ZOA's annual convention in Buffalo, New York, voted against permitting Jabotinsky to address them. At Lipsky's urging, the convention also passed a resolution condemning those who engaged in Zionist propaganda that "shouts reckless terms of expropriation and self-defence based upon exaggerated misleading and mischievous statements and employs the jargon of militarism"—an obvious jab at the Revisionists.[19]

Jabotinsky's "capture" of the Order Sons of Zion did not, however, translate into organizational growth for his movement in the United States. Two years after their leader returned to Europe, the U.S. Revisionists still had neither headquarters nor a functioning central committee. Three small Revisionist groups operated in New York City: in Manhattan, Brooklyn, and the Bronx; outside of New York, only Detroit, Cleveland, and Minneapolis had chapters of the movement. Part of the problem, according to Beinish Epstein, a member of the American Revisionists' inner circle, was that the Order Sons of Zion's interest in Revisionism had been skin-deep at best, and probably only "strategic," as he put it. The order's leaders were facing strong internal criticism, and possible ouster, because of their efforts to establish an American branch of the Judea Insurance Company. According to Epstein, they dabbled in Revisionism as a way of maintaining their power and diverting attention away from the insurance controversy.[20]

No doubt the Revisionists' difficulty in finding American adherents during the mid- and late 1920s was also due in part to the various factors that hindered all American Zionist groups, such as the rise of nativism and anti-Semitism in the United States, the perception that Zionism had already achieved its major goals, and the relative peace between Arabs and Jews in the Holy Land. An additional problem for Jabotinsky's followers was the similarity between their platform and that of the Zionist establishment. Why should someone join the Revisionists and endure all the unpleasantries of being associated with a small dissident group when its message hardly differed from that of the mainstream Zionist movement?

On the other hand, the Revisionists could at least take solace in the fact that their message was being heard. One could hardly pick up a Jewish newspaper in the spring or summer of 1926 without reading about Jabotinsky and his controversies. While there was plenty of criticism of Revisionism in the Jewish media, there was considerable sympathy, as well. "The most loyal Zionists could endorse most of his demands," wrote Shalom Rosenfeld in the Yiddish daily *Der Tog*. "What does Jabotinsky want? He wants more attention to facts, and less fear of consequences."[21] ZOA board member Abraham Goldberg, writing in another Yiddish daily, *Dos Yiddishe Folk*, declared: "I sympathize with Revisionism because it has vision, because it has a program, and because it is not afraid to criticize sharply and openly."[22] Jacob Landau, editor in chief of the Jewish Telegraphic Agency (JTA) was privately sympathetic to Revisionism, which helped ensure

Jabotinsky steady and often helpful exposure in the American Jewish press.[23] Israel Posnansky—the one-man welcoming committee when Jabotinsky's ship sailed into the New York harbor—knew they had a friend at the JTA when it reported that Jabotinsky was greeted upon his arrival in New York by "representatives of the American group of Zionist Revisionists, as well as a number of American Zionists."[24] The Revisionists also received more than a fair hearing in the pages of *Menorah Journal,* a leading Jewish periodical, which ran pro- and anti-Revisionist essays side by side in its October/November (1926) edition, and then in the next issue published a reply from the Revisionist, but not from his opponent.[25]

Jabotinsky could feel satisfied that his visit to America planted the seeds for a Revisionist future in the United States. His lectures and the Order Sons of Zion controversy stimulated a vigorous debate in the American Jewish press, English and Yiddish alike, that lasted long after Jabotinsky went home. His platform was a topic for discussion in sweatshops, delicatessens, and Lower East Side living rooms. Revisionist Zionism was now on the American Jewish map.

2 • Revisionist Zionism Takes Root in America

Elias Ginsburg surveyed the huge crowd marching through midtown Manhattan. For years, he and his colleagues in the American Revisionist inner circle had labored tirelessly and, it seemed, in futility, handing out leaflets on lonely street corners and issuing press releases that editors ignored. But when the moment of crisis came, when Arab rioters slaughtered 133 Jews throughout Palestine during the last week of August 1929, grass-roots American Jews responded as the Revisionists had hoped. More than thirty-five thousand angry protesters, organized in part by Ginsburg and other Revisionist veterans of Jabotinsky's World War I Jewish Legion, marched on the British Consulate in Manhattan. It was the largest Jewish demonstration in the United States since the parade marking the Balfour Declaration twelve years earlier.[1]

American Zionists, mainstream and Revisionist alike, would have preferred if positive impulses, rather than catastrophes, attracted Jews to Zionism. American Zionist literature during the 1920s was peppered with inspiring themes: restoring Jewish national pride, creating a new image of the Jews in Gentile eyes, and building a new kind of Jewish society in the Holy Land. But such messages resonated with only that small number of Jews for whom Zionism served as a substitute form of Jewish identity. Zionism offered a way for non-religious immigrants or children of immigrants to express their Jewishness.

But not for the majority. American Zionism, like its European counterpart, was primarily a crisis movement. Its numbers shifted as conditions facing Jews changed in Palestine and Europe. During periods of relative peace in the Holy Land and diminished persecution in Europe, few American Jews felt compelled to join the Zionist movement. Pogroms, on the other hand, whether in Palestine or Europe, created a sense of urgency and swelled American Jewish sympathy for Zionism. Sympathy did not automatically translate into dues-paying members, however. In the wake of the stock market crash of September 1929 and the economic depression that ensued, the six-dollar annual dues for membership in the Zionist Organization of America, and even the three-dollar dues charged by the Revisionists, became a luxury that some American Jews could no longer afford.[2]

Jabotinsky's American followers during the mid-1920s tended to blame their financial and membership problems on what they regarded as pressure by Zionist leaders on the Jewish media to ignore Revisionist activities and on local Zionist groups to refrain from inviting Revisionist speakers. While opposition from mainstream Zionist sources no doubt played a role in stymieing American Revisionism, the major obstacle to Revisionist growth in the United States was the same as that faced by all American Zionist groups before the 1929 riots: the absence of enough emotionally compelling reasons for American Jews to become active Zionists.[3]

The Palestine violence of August 1929 provided plenty of reasons: Arab rioters, Jewish victims, and indifferent British policemen. Now some heads were nodding in agreement when the U.S. Revisionists pointed to the Arab riots, as well as the weak English response, as vindication of their long-standing criticism of the British. "For years we have been warning the Zionist world of the danger which hovered over the heads of the Jews in Palestine," declared a statement issued by Revisionist headquarters in Manhattan. "Our persistent and long-lasting criticism fell on deaf ears until the bloody events in Jerusalem, Hebron and Safed opened the eyes of the blind and the ears of the deaf." The statement recalled previous Revisionist complaints about "the open and hidden animosity" of British officials in Palestine toward the Balfour Declaration, and pointed out that the *yishuv* would have been able to defend itself against the Arab rioters had the British heeded the Revisionist demand for a Jewish army in Palestine. The blame, in Revisionist eyes, was shared by "the criminal administration in Palestine" and the "weak, near-sighted and bewildered [Zionist] leadership" of Chaim Weizmann, president of the World Zionist Organization.[4]

The political demands made by the U.S. Revisionists in the aftermath of the riots clearly distinguished their movement from the mainstream American Zionist groups. The ZOA criticized the behavior of the British authorities in Palestine and spoke vaguely of the need to "discipline" the Arabs in the wake of the riots, but it made no specific demands.[5] The U.S. Revisionists, by contrast, called for the convening of "an extraordinary session of the Zionist Congress" in order to elect "a new Zionist leadership" that would demand "elimination of the present administration in Palestine," opening Transjordan for Jewish colonization, and the creation of a

Jewish military unit, under British command, to guard the *yishuv*.[6] For the first time, the U.S. Revisionists were offering American Jews a clear-cut reason to choose between mainstream Zionism and the more militant dissident faction.

The weeks and months following the riots saw a flurry of activity by the newly energized American Revisionists. First, there was the march on the British Consulate.[7] Then, the daily *New York World* published a lengthy defense of Revisionism and critique of the British.[8] And in what seems to have been the American Revisionists' first effort to influence American political figures, a number of U.S. senators, representatives, and governors were sent a Revisionist critique of Arab demands for the creation of a democratically elected legislative council to govern Palestine.[9]

The Arab demand for democracy in Palestine posed an embarrassing dilemma for American Zionists. As the editors of the ZOA journal *New Palestine* conceded, by "concentrating on a plea against 'taxation without representation,' which is bound to ring sincere in the ears of fair-minded men," the Arabs were presenting arguments "which form on the surface an irresistible plea, logical and just." Thus "the Zionist public was placed before the choice of having to agree that what the Arabs asked was just and logical and should be granted or of moving for its rejection on the ground that it would be injurious to our interests." Mainstream and militant Zionists alike did not hesitate to choose: Jewish national interests must come first. Although it meant risking the accusation that they were opposed to an American principle, U.S. Zionists across the board unequivocally rejected the idea of any sort of parliament or legislative council in Palestine so long as the Arabs were in the majority.[10]

Although the legislative council controversy never became a significant enough issue to compel large numbers of American Jews to take a stand, those Zionists who confronted the contradiction between immediate democracy and Zionism came down squarely on the side of Zionism. Ever conscious of how their stance appeared in non-Jewish eyes, American Zionists mustered a variety of public arguments designed to temper the image of Zionism as undemocratic: they argued that democratic experiments elsewhere in the Middle East had failed; that the Palestinian Arabs were not sufficiently literate to make proper use of democracy; and that the Arabs were not genuinely interested in democracy anyway, but merely hoped to use it as a weapon to thwart Zionism.[11] But it is significant that neither the mainstream American Zionists nor their Revisionist rivals ever wavered in their opposition to a legislative council. They strove to become Americans while remaining Jews; they worked hard to maintain the fragile balance between their Zionism and their Americanism; but when push came to shove, when forced to choose between an American principle and Jewish national survival, they unequivocally chose survival.

This ideological conflict between Zionism and democracy paralleled the many, and more difficult, choices Jewish immigrants faced in confronting the tension between their old-world ways and the realities of American life. Observance of the Jewish Sabbath and holidays conflicted with America's six-day workweek. The foreign languages the immigrants spoke impeded acculturation. Distinctive Jewish garb clashed with the dominant "melting pot" philosophy. A minority of Jews were hostile to Zionism because they feared that Jewish nationalism would be perceived as un-American; for the majority of American Jews who were sympathetic to Zionism, the question of democracy in Palestine had the potential to create similar concerns.

The dispute over democracy in Palestine seized American Jewry's attention anew in November 1929, when Hebrew University president (and former American Zionist leader) Judah Magnes proposed achieving peace in the Holy Land by establishing a binational Palestine, based on an Arab-Jewish parliament, instead of a Jewish state. The U.S. Revisionists blasted the Magnes proposal, charging that "the screen of democratic principle" was being exploited by the Arabs in order to "further oppress the Jewish minority and prevent the establishment of the Jewish national home in Palestine."[12] Mainstream Zionists, too, were critical of Magnes, but confined their protests to name-calling; the Revisionists went further, demanding that Magnes be forced to resign from office. The American Revisionists basked in the notoriety of media reports about their colleagues in Palestine disrupting Magnes's speech on the first day of the autumn semester.[13] When Magnes visited New York sixteen months later, the Revisionists staged a demonstration demanding his resignation, much to the aggravation of Stephen Wise, the longtime leader of the ZOA, president of the leading U.S. Jewish defense agency, the American Jewish Congress, and the most prominent Reform rabbi of his day. Wise told his ZOA colleagues, "I cannot imagine anything that could be much worse than to start a fight on Magnes and the Hebrew University now."[14]

There were numerous signs that the Jewish public's anxiety arising out of the Palestine riots was stimulating a period of organizational growth for Jabotinsky's American followers. In the wake of "the unfortunate events of last August . . . we at last obtained a respectful hearing," U.S. Revisionist secretary Emanuel Nagler recalled in 1930:

Zionists were sick and tired of the weak kneed and autocratic leadership of the movement . . . our policy of 100% Zionism began to appeal to them. They began to invite us to their centres and listen to us. Our membership from that time on has increased considerably. . . . Five years ago we had a small branch on the East Side of New York. Today we have districts in several sections of New York City, in Philadelphia, Cincinnati, Detroit, Indianapolis, Dallas, Los Angeles, Chicago and in Montreal.[15]

Fledgling Revisionist chapters typically were low on funds but high on idealism and commitment. Young activists would take to the street corners, employing simple methods to get their message out. A Revisionist newsletter described young militants in action in the Bronx:

The Bronx branch collects signatures for the petition by stretching a board upon two upright boxes placed on the sidewalk of a busy thoroughfare. Several sets of petitions are placed on the board. A few members secure the signatures and instruct the signatories; two or three others hold forth to the passing Jews, explaining to them the significance of the petition. The Jews invariably line up to do their duty. It is a splendid method. Other groups please do likewise.[16]

At the same time, an American branch of the world Revisionist fundraising arm, the Tel Hai Fund, was created in December 1929 with a sponsoring committee that included, in addition to the usual core of U.S. Revisionist veterans, Stephen Wise's son, James Waterman Wise; ZOA board member Samuel Margoshes; and Jacob de Haas, the longtime American Zionist leader and confidante of Justice Brandeis. The fund's declared purpose of financing the "physical training of Jewish youth" was especially appealing in the wake of the Palestine pogroms.[17] In mid-1930 an American wing of Jabotinsky's Betar youth movement was established, and a Betar summer camp opened two years later.[18] Although the first national convention of the U.S. Revisionists, in New York City in December 1930, was attended by only forty delegates, two of the conference's three day-long sessions were covered by the *New York Times,* a sure sign that the Revisionists were being taken seriously in the wider community.[19] The Revisionists' call for a boycott of British goods and services likewise earned a mention in the *Times,* even if it did not attract much public support.[20] Meanwhile, the centerpiece of the 1931 midwestern conference of Avukah, the ZOA's campus movement, was a debate on whether or not "Revisionism is beneficial to the Zionist cause." The phenomenon of maximalist Zionism was increasingly on the Jewish agenda.[21]

Nevertheless, the Zionist-Revisionists of America was a small organization—perhaps a thousand members nationwide at that point—with all the problems one would expect in a small organization, and those problems were exacerbated by the economic depression engulfing America in the 1930s. A group that possessed meager funds even before the 1929 stock market crash, and whose members were drawn primarily from the lower and lower-middle classes, found that even some basic necessities were unaffordable. Plans to purchase "a Jewish [Yiddish-language] typewriter and a mimeograph machine" had to be postponed for lack of funds.[22] There was so little money in the group's bank account that the $1,800 needed to finance a proposed visit to America by Jabotinsky in the spring of 1931 had to be borrowed.[23] The organization frequently operated on a deficit in the early 1930s, and although "the office rent and the girl [their secretary] were paid," executive director Elias Ginsburg sometimes went for months without remuneration. At one point, Ginsburg's family was "on the brink of starvation," as he put it, and he did not have sufficient funds to pay the medical bills for his seriously ill young son.[24] Another key activist, Beinish Epstein, was likewise "half-starved from lack of earnings." The bulk of the organization's work "was carried on by two and one half men," Ginsburg complained. "The older Chaverim [members] were either out of work or depressed or occasionally came to give *etzahs* [useless advice]," while "most of the younger element" were "trained to listen but not to work." Using his personal savings, Ginsburg briefly launched the first serious Revisionist journal in America, *Our Voice,* in early 1934. But it was not long before he ran out of patience (and money). Fed up with the organization's financial woes and what he called the "atmosphere of noxious jealousies, broken pledges, petty larceny and hypocrisy," Ginsburg resigned in disgust in the summer of 1935.[25]

There were other problems, too. The membership department had glum news to report to the board in early 1932 about its efforts to organize in Brooklyn: an initial meeting of the proposed Williamsburg district "was unsuccessful due to non-attendance of Revisionists," and attempts to organize an East Flatbush district had likewise flopped.[26] Betar, for its part, had its share of troubles during the early 1930s. At one point, Betar representatives were pleading with the Revisionist leadership "to do something, in order to re-organize [Betar]."[27] A frustrated Ginsburg described to Jabotinsky his experience with a Betar unit that had been instructed to assemble for a 10:00 A.M. meeting one Sunday: "I had to wait . . . till 11:30 A.M. before less than one half of the registered members reported for duty. . . . [They do not] understand either the seriousness or the depth of their tasks."[28]

Meanwhile, the accelerating tensions between the Revisionists and Labor Zionists within the WZO further complicated matters for Jabotinsky's American supporters. Although the delegates to the July 1931 World Zionist Congress ousted Chaim Weizmann from the presidency for saying that he did not share the goal of a Jewish majority in Palestine, the congress also rejected Jabotinsky's proposal to explicitly declare that the creation of a sovereign Jewish state was Zionism's aim. The Revisionist delegates marched out of the congress in protest, and many Revisionists began calling for withdrawal of their movement from the WZO. A mostly American faction of Revisionists opposed to secession from the WZO, led by the dedicated but irascible Meir Grossman, broke away in 1933 and established the Jewish State Party. The loss of the Grossman faction dealt a blow to the already small U.S. Revisionist group.

At the same time, relations between the American Revisionists and the ZOA deteriorated steadily during the early 1930s. In the summer of 1930, the Revisionists' hopes for a more activist American Zionist leadership had been briefly buoyed when supporters of Justice Brandeis ousted Louis Lipsky's ZOA administration. A triumphant Stephen Wise assured Jabotinsky, "We shall now have a militant organization prepared to stand against the American non-Zionists and the [Jewish] Agency, over whose minds Magnes and the Brith Shalom have a tragic dominance."[29] Revisionist sympathizer Jacob de Haas was among the key figures in the new administration, as was former ZOA president Julian Mack, who privately assured the U.S. Revisionist leadership after the convention that "much of the Revisionist platform has my fullest sympathy."[30] But the Revisionists' honeymoon with the new ZOA did not last long. Mack subsequently endorsed Chaim Weizmann's continued leadership of the WZO, and soon the American Revisionists were complaining bitterly to the new ZOA president, Robert Szold, that Jabotinsky supporters were being frozen out of various ZOA committees and treated "as a 'non-Kosher' element."[31] Szold did apologize for the "tone" of a 1931 New Palestine editorial criticizing both Magnes and Jabotinsky in equal measure, but the ZOA leader pointedly refrained from retracting its content and refused to publish a letter from the Revisionists on the subject.[32] At the same time, a local newsletter published by the ZOA's New York region denounced the Revisionists as "Fascisti, Hitlerites, Blackshirts."[33] The "Hitlerite" accusation was ironic, since the Revisionists were among the first in the Jewish world to warn of a coming tidal wave of fascist anti-Semitism in Europe. Over the opposition of mainstream Zionist leaders, Jabotinsky had urged European Jews to "liquidate the Exile before it liquidates you."

Indeed, the rise of the Nazis to power in Germany in early 1933 seemed to confirm the Revisionists' pessimistic worldview. Economic and social crises had propelled Hitler, through the democratic process, to the German chancellorship. German Jews would surely suffer; which European Jewish communities would be next? But while American Jews were reeling from the shock of Hitler's triumph and wondering what he had in store for German Jewry, the attention of the Jewish world was suddenly seized by startling developments in Palestine.

On a moonlit Tel Aviv beach in June 1933, the Labor Zionist leader Chaim Arlosoroff was shot to death. During the weeks preceding the killing, Arlosoroff had been sharply criticized in the Revisionist press in Palestine for defying the international Jewish boycott of Nazi Germany in order to negotiate an agreement to transfer Jewish assets from Germany to Palestine. In the wake of the assassination, Labor Zionist officials and publications immediately accused the Revisionists of "inciting" the murder. Three young Revisionists were arrested as suspects in the assassination, and a fourth was charged with inspiring the deed. Although the absence of serious evidence resulted in the acquittal of three of the suspects and the eventual release of the fourth, the Revisionists endured many months of intense criticism in the Palestine press, not to mention numerous physical assaults by enraged Labor Zionists.

American Revisionists endured only a small taste of what their comrades in Europe and Palestine suffered. The months after the assassination were "an ugly period," one young U.S. Revisionist recalled, but in America the ugliness consisted mostly of crude heckling of Revisionist speakers and occasional scuffles.[34] The weakness of the evidence against the alleged assassins raised hackles among those imbued with the American sense of justice, prompting a number of prominent mainstream Zionists, including Stephen Wise and former ZOA president Harry Friedenwald, to lend their names to the committee raising funds for the defendants.[35]

Still, the constant circulation of reports linking Revisionism to violence inevitably tarred the movement's image. "When a distracted Polish Revisionist, vainly waiting for years for a certificate to go to Palestine flings a stone at the window-pane of a British Consul, the news is spread on the front page, vehement articles and editorials or condemnation are written and once again Revisionists and Revisionism are dragged in the mire," Elias Ginsburg complained. "But when the Poalei Zion or Hashomer Hazair pacifists batter, wound and maim [Revisionists]—the Jewish press either does not know about it or at best reports a 'clash' between Revisionists and Poalei-Zionists."[36] Ginsburg and his comrades tried hard to combat "the Stavsky libel flood" (Avraham Stavsky was the main defendant) with their usual ammunition: leaflets, press releases, and lectures. But not all the damage could be undone, especially when "99% of our replies to attacks either went into editorial baskets or were returned to us."[37] When an American Zionist periodical accused the Revisionists of "singing obscene songs about the widow of the labor leader Arlosoroff," the Revisionists could only deny the allegation, knowing full well that even if the denial were published, some readers would still believe the accusation.[38] At one point, Ginsburg and his colleagues became so frustrated with Der Tog's "nasty drive" against Revisionism that four of them burst into the newspaper's office and demanded an immediate meeting with the editors, which was granted. They told the editors "frankly what we thought of them and their tactics," and "as a result, the attacks ceased" and Ginsburg was permitted to submit a reply to his critics. "My reply, however, was 'amputated,' despite my protests," Ginsburg complained to Dr. Joseph Schechtman of the Revisionists' Paris headquarters.[39]

Relations between the American Revisionists and the Zionist establishment were strained further by the growing conflict in Palestine between the Revisionists there and the Labor Zionists' trade union, the Histadrut. Rejecting the socialist class-struggle ideology of the Histadrut, Jabotinsky began calling for the creation of a new trade union that would be based on Jewish national solidarity rather than the concept of the Jewish working class fighting the Jewish bourgeoisie. Revisionist youths were hired to replace striking Histadrut workers, and Labor Zionist toughs responded with violent assaults against the strikebreakers. Jabotinsky's essay "Yes, To Break"—that is, to break the Histadrut's monopoly in the yishuv—in the Polish Jewish newspaper Haint in November 1932, brought Labor Zionist resentment of the Revisionists to a fever pitch.[40] The U.S. Revisionists embraced the anti-Histadrut theme with gusto, featuring it in their literature and meetings.[41]

This was not the sort of conflict that would serve the Revisionists well on the American scene. Although not necessarily wedded to socialist ideology, large numbers of working-class American Jews belonged to trade unions and through them had recently secured crucial advances in wages, hours, and workplace conditions.[42] In addition, a number of prominent American Jews had embraced the cause of union rights as part and parcel of the interwar progressive agenda. An antilabor image could only impair Revisionism's search for American Jewish support.

Perhaps the most important casualty of Revisionism's public-relations woes was Stephen Wise. During the early 1930s, the veteran ZOA leader had sympathized with much of the Revisionist platform. Ignoring anti-Revisionist appeals from WZO president Chaim Weizmann and Henrietta Szold, founder of the Women's Zionist organization Hadassah, Wise and his wife, Louise, carried on a friendly, even warm, correspondence with Jabotinsky. Wise frequently sought Jabotinsky's advice on Zionist matters. He lobbied American book publishers on behalf of Jabotinsky's history of the Jewish Legion. The Wises even repeatedly sent him donations ranging from $200 to $500—considerable sums in the midst of the Great Depression.[43] Wise told inquiring journalists that "there is nothing revolutionary or incendiary about the Revisionist movement," and he wrote to Revisionist activist Mordechai Danzis that "the time has come for a very significant revision of many things in the Zionist movement, beginning with much of our so-called leadership."[44] No wonder Louis Lipsky had accused Wise of being an "abettor of the Revisionists."[45]

By the autumn of 1934, however, the proliferation of negative reports about the Revisionists began to affect Wise's attitude. His old friend Irma Lindheim, a leader of Hadassah and committed socialist Zionist, returned from Poland in October with stories about Revisionists committing assorted "outrages" against other Polish Zionists, including allegedly denouncing their Jewish rivals to the Polish government as "communists."[46] Not long after that, another friend, Felix Frankfurter, the Harvard law professor and future Supreme Court justice, warned Wise that "the kind of a world that [Jabotinsky] wants is not, I believe, the kind of world that you and I want." A critic of big business, Frankfurter warned Wise that "the economic and social outlook" of the Revisionists was "precisely the same as that of the National Manufacturers Association in this country," which, he charged, would countenance "the abandonment of our liberties" for the sake of profits.[47] Meanwhile, Wise's son James ran a series of editorials in his journal *Opinion* criticizing "fascist" aspects of the Revisionist movement. Challenged by Jabotinsky about his son's rhetoric, Wise dissociated himself from James's broadsides but added: "I am just as deeply concerned and unhappy about the Fascist tendencies in Revisionism as Jim is." Wise often seemed to divide the world into fascists and liberals, militarists and humanitarians, union busters and progressives—and the Revisionists, with their martial style and distrust of the Histadrut, were looking more and more like the bad guys. The left in Palestine had its flaws, Wise conceded, but increasingly the right seemed to frighten him more: "Lamentable as may be certain tendencies in liberal or radical social Palestine movements," Wise wrote, "the real peril to civilization and human freedom and justice is to be found in Fascism."[48] Wise looked at Revisionism through the spectacles of an American social justice activist, and found it wanting. By the spring of 1935, he was ready to say so out loud. That March, in a highly publicized Sunday morning sermon at his Free Synagogue in Manhattan, Wise blasted the Revisionists' critique of the Histadrut as an attempt to bring about "a Palestinian duplication of all that is worst and most vicious in the practices of social exploitation." The Revisionists' "militarism" and alleged insensitivity to Palestinian Arab sentiment were further evidence that Jabotinsky's movement had become "Fascism in Yiddish or Hebrew," Wise charged. Citing the plight of southern sharecroppers, Wise asked, "Shall we have a share-cropper Palestine or shall we have a Palestine of Jewish freemen?"[49]

Wise's denunciation of Revisionism was followed within weeks by a public anti-Revisionist blast from Albert Einstein. A feature story in the *New York Times* highlighted Einstein's accusation that Revisionism was "the modern embodiment of those harmful forces which Moses sought to banish."[50] Meanwhile, editorials in the *Reconstructionist*, a leading Jewish monthly, warned that Revisionism would bring "the abuses of western capitalism" to the Holy Land and spoil the ideals "which have made Palestine a laboratory for social progress."[51] The Jabotinskyites also came under attack at the December 1934 convention of Avukah, the ZOA's collegiate arm, which strongly endorsed the Histadrut and expelled its own Manhattan Chapter, as well as the chapter's chairman, for having hosted a lecture by Jabotinsky.[52] When the *Menorah Journal* decided to publish a symposium on Revisionism, it titled the discussion "Is Revision-Zionism Fascist?," an indication of the extent to which the Revisionists had been put on the defensive. Elias Ginsburg was given space to address the issue, but Marie Syrkin of the Labor Zionists was given the last word a few issues later, where she insisted that Revisionism was indeed comparable to "German or Italian fascism," only it was now disguised with "freshly acquired Uncle Sam terminology."[53]

Understandably, the frightening rise of nationalist movements throughout interwar Europe and the escalating tension between the far right and the far left on the continent made it tempting for some in the Jewish world to see in Palestine the outlines of a similar conflict, but a closer look revealed significant differences. While the charge of "fascism" may have lent color and drama to the rhetorical assaults upon Revisionism, critics were hard-pressed to demonstrate that the accusation accurately reflected the principles of the movement or its leader. Those who read Jabotinsky's essays or heard him speak knew that he vigorously denounced totalitarianism and championed liberal democracy. He promoted the use of military force, not because he glorified violence per se but because he was convinced—as were many in the Zionist movement—that the establishment of a Jewish army was necessary to the creation and defense of a Jewish state. Jabotinsky's opponents made much of the light brown shirt worn by Betar members in the movement's early years, although the uniform's color had no connection to Mussolini, was designed long before the rise of Hitler, and was eventually replaced by a blue jersey. Critics of Jabotinsky also derived considerable ammunition from the writings of Abba Achimeir, the leader of a tiny but vocal faction within the Revisionist movement that expressed some sympathy for Il Duce in the early 1930s. But when the Achimeir line was put to a vote at the 1932 Revisionist world conference, it was overwhelmingly defeated, and Achimeir's faction as such faded into obscurity afterward.[54] Public opinion, however, is shaped in part by superficial impressions, and it was hard for the Revisionists to escape the impressions created by the constant publicity given to their clashes with Histadrut strikers, their military-style parades and uniforms, and the occasionally intemperate utterances of the Abba Achimeir faction.[55]

Jabotinsky's American followers took none of this lying down. "Hitlerism, ladies and gentlemen, is not determined by shirts and uniforms, nor by their color and insignia, nor by marches and the teaching of the art of marching," argued the U.S. Revisionist organ *Our Voice*. "Rotarians march, Communists march, and the Irish Catholics march. Doormen, bell-boys, nurses and members of the Salvation Army wear uniforms. That does not make them Fascists or Hitlerites. Some years ago all Russian high school girls were obliged to wear brown dresses. That did not make them Hitlerites."[56] Revisionist propaganda also blasted the excesses of the Zionist left, warning that "many teachers of the Palestine schools" were undermining Zionism by "propagating socialism and 'red flag' ideals among the children."[57] Jabotinsky's followers appealed to American Jewry's fear of anti-

Semitism, arguing that the Jewish left was creating "a wrong impression to the world that all Jews are Socialists or Communists . . . we cannot afford to be presented to the world as a people of 'revolutionaries' and radicals."[58] They established a U.S. League for National Labor in Palestine to finance alternative labor unions and propagandize against the Histadrut.[59] They even organized Revisionist sympathizers within the ZOA into a dissident faction, known as the "American 'B' Group of General Zionists," to combat what they said was the ZOA leadership's "surrender to the domination" of Histadrut–Labor Zionist ideas.[60]

Lobbying within the ZOA against the Histadrut was not necessarily a lost cause. The ZOA had never exhibited any special affinity for Labor Zionism as such. Traditionally, it had aligned itself with Palestine's General Zionist Party, a centrist movement whose "B" faction, as it called itself, was particularly critical of the Histadrut and Chaim Weizmann's leadership of the world Zionist movement. Stephen Wise, for one, had been at odds with the Labor Zionists over their support for including non-Zionists in the Jewish Agency hierarchy and their behavior in the Arlosoroff affair, among other matters.[61]

At the same time, however, significant segments of American Jewry simply could not be influenced by anti-Histadrut criticism. Ideological socialists, of course, were unapproachable on this topic, and there were more than a few of them in the Jewish community. Beyond the ideologues, there were many grassroots Jews who simply had benefited from union membership and could not be easily convinced that Palestine's premier union was harming the *yishuv*. Throughout the American Jewish community there was enthusiasm for the Roosevelt administration's New Deal policies, which were closely identified with labor rights. In addition, interwar American liberalism's "social justice" agenda, with its strong union component, had many adherents among American Jewish intellectuals, journalists, and the Reform rabbinate. It was hardly surprising that 241 Reform rabbis—some of them motivated by Jabotinsky's arrival in the United States in January 1935—signed a public statement endorsing the Histadrut and socialist ideals in Palestine.[62]

Still, for all the hostility Revisionism was generating in the American Jewish community, Jabotinsky's 1935 visit also demonstrated how far the movement had come. As it had in 1926, the Jewish Telegraphic Agency once again reported that Jabotinsky was greeted by a large welcoming committee upon his arrival—but this time it was true. The large crowd stood "for hours in the freezing temperature, impatient for a glimpse of this man whose last visit to the United States, in 1926, is still discussed as though it happened yesterday, so deep an impression did he make," the JTA asserted. More than one hundred Betar youths, standing at attention in crisp military style, waved American and Zionist flags, cheered, and sang as Jabotinsky disembarked from the SS *Manhattan* in what *Our Voice* called "a holy moment."[63]

The first to shake Jabotinsky's hand as he stepped ashore was Yeshiva College rabbinical student Baruch Rabinowitz. Recently returned from Palestine, where he had joined other young militants in tearing down the Nazi flag from the German Consulate in Jerusalem, Rabinowitz was overcome with emotion at his first encounter with the famed Zionist leader. "As I felt the firmness of his grip," Rabinowitz later recalled, "an emotion or a seeming electricity surged through me, similar in intensity to that which I felt the first time that my hands touched the Western Wall. . . . I raised his hand to my lips. It was the only time in my life that I have ever done this except to my father the Rabbi. Jabotinsky pulled his hand back, in shocked disapproval."[64] The Revisionist leader was notoriously uncomfortable with the level of adoration many of his followers felt for him.

The names that decorated the letterhead of the official reception committee that the Revisionists assembled for Jabotinsky's visit likewise testified to the increased stature that Revisionism had attained in the United States since Jabotinsky's 1926 tour. The most prominent Jewish congressmen of the day, Sol Bloom and Emanuel Celler, were among the nearly four hundred names on the committee, as were such ZOA stalwarts as Stephen Wise, Julian Mack, Abba Hillel Silver, Robert Szold, Richard Gottheil, and Horace Kallen.[65] Wise's son, James Waterman Wise, editor of the Jewish monthly *Opinion,* publicly urged those who had joined the committee to back out, and a U.S. Revisionist periodical charged that unnamed figures on the Zionist left had approached "the more influential" among those on the reception committee "with requests to withdraw," but to no avail.[66]

Revisionism's rising stock in America in the mid-1930s can be accounted for by many of the same factors that led to the significant increases in membership that the ZOA and Hadassah enjoyed during this time.[67] Arab massacres in Palestine and the rise of Nazism in Germany stimulated American Jewish concern for the safety of those Jewish communities. The spread of domestic American anti-Semitism, including the fiery radio broadcasts of Father Charles Coughlin, to which millions listened each week, stimulated a more militant and nationalistic mood in the American Jewish community that benefited all Zionist factions. As for the Revisionists in particular, the latest events in Europe and Palestine seemed to confirm Jabotinsky's pessimistic warnings. With their early role in the popular American Jewish movement to boycott German goods, their vocal anti-British rallies, and their forthright demands for Jewish statehood, the Revisionists were, at least in theory, well positioned to tap into new streams of grassroots support and carve out a niche for themselves in American Jewish life. By early 1936 there were new Revisionist chapters, or at least cells, in numerous cities far from the movement's New York base, including Pittsburgh, Cleveland, Minneapolis, Scranton, and South Bend, Indiana. Monthly newsletters in English and Yiddish were inaugurated by the national headquarters, and Beinish Epstein was hosting a weekly Revisionist radio show on New York City's WLTH.[68]

Jabotinsky's decision, in the summer of 1935, to formally secede from the WZO and become the "New Zionist Organization" was no boon to his American wing. Internal Jewish disunity in the face of external crises would not aid the newly renamed New Zionist Organization of America (NZOA) in its efforts to attract a substantial constituency in the Jewish community. But the damage caused by the breakaway from the WZO was offset by the addition to the Revisionist ranks, in late 1935, of two prominent mainstream figures: Jacob de Haas, the veteran American Zionist leader and Brandeis confidante, and Louis I. Newman, a Reform rabbi who had been ordained by Stephen Wise himself and had served as his assistant rabbi at Wise's Free Synagogue in New York City. What better way to rebut critics who called the Revisionists a fringe element, especially in the wake of Wise's recent public denunciation, than to point to Brandeis's right-hand man and Wise's disciple?

Reform rabbis were hard to find in any segment of the Zionist movement, much less among the Jabotinskyites. From its very beginning, in Germany in the early 1800s, Reform Judaism had rejected Jewish nationalism. In America, too, the Reform movement embraced universalism, and the Pittsburgh Platform, a prominent formulation of Reform Judaism's principles in 1885, specifically denounced the concept of a Jewish return to the land of Zion. Stephen Wise and the handful of other Reform rabbis who supported Zionism were a tiny minority. As the only Reform rabbi who supported Revisionist Zionism, Newman was a minority of one.

The passion and determination Newman exhibited in the rabbinate in the 1920s would serve him well as a leader of American Zionism's most controversial faction. During his six-year tenure as spiritual leader of the prestigious Reform temple Emanu-El in San Francisco (1924–30), Newman earned the nickname "battlin' Louie" for his adherence to principled positions even at the risk of his job. By refusing to perform intermarriages, instituting the Hebrew language as a requirement in the temple's Sunday School, and frequently denouncing the Reform movement's anti-Zionism, Newman angered congregants and board members alike, paving the way for his departure. His acceptance of a prominent New York City pulpit, Temple Rodeph Sholom, coincided with the aftermath of the 1929 Palestinian Arab pogroms. An active ZOA member in the 1920s and early 1930s, Newman grew disenchanted with what he regarded as the excessively cautious approach of the mainstream Zionist movement. At first he sought to change the ZOA from within, working with Jacob de Haas and a second Jabotinsky sympathizer, Isaac Allen, to create a U.S. wing of the "Group B" faction of the General Zionists that would lobby against ZOA endorsement of the Histadrut or socialist principles. When that project failed to gain ground, Newman joined the Revisionists. Less than a year later, he was elected president of the Revisionist movement in America.[69] A mainstream Zionist leader described Newman to a British Embassy official as "a fine man who has fallen into dubious company."[70] Hardworking, passionate, and "strong as an ox," Newman devoted long hours to both his congregation and his Zionist activities, but he frequently interrupted his workday to call his wife. On the Sabbath, he and his sons would relax with a stack of the latest Hebrew-language newspapers from Palestine.[71]

All of these developments were, not surprisingly, a source of considerable frustration for American Revisionism's ideological foes on the left. They vented their outrage with accusations—such as Marie Syrkin's charge that a Revisionist rally in Jerusalem "precipitated the Arab outbreaks" of 1929, or her warning that the Revisionist demand for statehood would be "dangerous to the political future of Zionism"—that found few takers. Blaming Jews for Arab violence and denouncing the calls for a Jewish state hardly seemed to suit Jewry's needs in the increasingly desperate 1930s.[72]

3 • Militant Zionism as a Response to Arab Terror and Nazism

A fresh round of Palestinian Arab attacks in 1936 rocked the Holy Land for six straight months and left American Zionists profoundly worried for Palestine's future. The Arab violence claimed eighty Jewish lives; hundreds more were injured. Sporadic assaults continued even after the British announced, in October, that they would dispatch a governmental commission headed by Lord Peel to formally investigate the Palestine problem. At the same time, the British sought to appease Arab sentiment by offering the Jewish Agency an unusually small allotment of immigration certificates for the month of May 1937—so small, in fact, that the agency rejected them as a matter of principle. It was an especially worrisome turn of events in view of the intensifying mistreatment of German Jewry. A series of laws stripping German Jews of their rights and restricting their livelihoods had been enacted during the first years since Hitler's rise, and the legal measures were increasingly accompanied by bursts of anti-Semitic violence.

With the threat of Arab violence in the air, immigration endangered, and the persecution of German Jewry accelerating, American Zionists waited anxiously for the Peel Commission's final report in the spring of 1937. In the context of the tense atmosphere that prevailed, it is perhaps no surprise that Jewish outrage exploded when New York City's municipal radio station, WNYC, broadcast speeches by three proponents of the Palestinian Arab cause inveighing against Zionism in June 1937. The Revisionists were prominent among the protesters.

NZOA president Louis Newman immediately fired off an angry telegram to Mayor Fiorello La Guardia, asserting that a municipal service should not be used for "anti-Jewish incitement" and predicting that leaders of the Arab riots in Palestine would "make capital of [the] fact that their agents here obtained facilities of [a] municipal radio station." The Revisionist rabbi urged Mayor La Guardia to help "correct as far [as] possible [the] harm already done" by "mak[ing] clear that the people of New York repudiate the provocative and inflammatory statements made against the great cause of Zionism."[1] Newman's protest was reinforced by a similar telegram from the National Council of Young Israel—the strongly pro-Zionist union of Americanized Orthodox synagogues[2]—as well as a "deluge" of angry phone calls to the WNYC switchboard and a flurry of critical editorials and news reports in New York's feisty Yiddish-language press.[3] The station's decision to broadcast speeches by four pro-Zionist speakers helped defuse the controversy, but the city official responsible for WNYC was nevertheless hauled before the Board of Aldermen (the equivalent of City Council) for a round of tough questioning.[4]

The WNYC controversy netted the Revisionists some useful publicity. It also strengthened the emerging sense of alliance between Jabotinsky's followers and the pro-Zionist segment of the Orthodox community in interwar New York, represented by the Young Israel movement. The two factions had much in common. Members of both groups were likely to be found in the lower economic strata, and both groups were strongest in the "second settlement" Jewish neighborhoods of Brooklyn, areas to which the children of immigrants frequently gravitated after leaving the Lower East Side of Manhattan, where their parents had originally settled.[5]

When Stephen Wise would privately make a derisive reference to grass-roots Jewish militants, he would complain about the "pesterers and preachers" of "a thousand Brooklyn street corners."[6] Wise knew his Jewish geography. By the late 1930s, Brooklyn was home to 860,000 Jews, 48 percent of New York City's Jewish population.[7] Although they had left the intensely Jewish environment of the Lower East Side,[8] Brooklyn's Jews had not left their Jewishness behind.[9] Rather, they brought with them to the outlying areas of settlement a vigorous sense of ethnic attachment and, in many cases, an Americanized but still intact Orthodoxy.[10] Zionist sentiment, too, flourished among Jews residing in these second-settlement areas. In Brooklyn's Jewish neighborhoods during the 1930s, Zionist lectures and concerts were a staple of the night life, stores frequently displayed Jewish National Fund collection boxes, and Eretz Yisrael studies were featured prominently in the curricula of the major "Modern Orthodox" day schools.[11] The Revisionists' emphasis on maintaining the territorial integrity of the Jewish homeland was particularly appealing to Orthodox Zionists, so it is no surprise to discover that in their contacts with the Young Israel movement, Jabotinsky's followers detected "strong Revisionist leanings among [Young Israel's] leadership."[12] There was also a certain degree of overlap among the memberships of the Revisionists and the U.S. wing of the religious Zionist movement, Mizrachi. A prominent example was the Epstein family: Rabbi Hayyim Fischel Epstein, a founder of Mizrachi, headed a pro-Revisionist faction in the movement, while his sons Beinish and David were two of the most prominent activists in Jabotinsky's American branch.[13]

Baruch Rabinowitz, a Yeshiva College rabbinical student and Revisionist activist, found strong sympathy for the Revisionist approach when he lectured in Pittsburgh's Orthodox community. At the conclusion of his impassioned speech, "half in English and half in Yiddish," urging the use of force against Palestinian Arab rioters, Rabinowitz found himself "moved to tears"

> as the revered Rabbi Ashinsky took out a crumpled five dollar bill from his pocket, laid it on the table, and in a tearful voice said, "I want the honor of being the first to contribute for such a purpose. It is *Kiddush HaShem*—a sanctification of God's name." . . . Behind him was a shriveled old lady, wearing a *shaytel*. She opened her worn purse, took out her change purse, and simply turned it over, emptying all of its contents on the table. Most of the others came forward too. These were the days of the worst depression of the 20th century. We raised a little over $300, a very substantial sum in those days for the size and type of audience.[14]

The U.S. Revisionists emphasized their movement's sympathetic attitude toward Jewish religious observance. Their newsletter made much of the fact that the Revisionist trade union in Palestine, "out of a decent respect to the Jewish religion," had pledged to "abstain from any act which may offend the religious sensibilities of our people" and therefore observed the Sabbath, holidays, and dietary laws in its public activities.[15] A full-page caricature in the March 1936 issue depicted the "Old (World) Zionist Organization" as a hybrid of two types, a bearded Orthodox Jew representing "Religion" and the "Jewish National Interest," and a secular Jew holding signs reading "Anti-Religious Stand of Hashomer Hatzair" and "Strike and Class Antagonism." This was contrasted with a representative of the New Zionist Organization: a stout pioneer, his head covered, holding in one hand a flag labeled "Jewish State on Both Sides of the Jordan," and in the other a parchment with the slogan "Social Justice in Spirit of Torah."[16]

The controversy over the WNYC broadcasts also illuminated some of the ethnic and social roots of the divisions within the New York Jewish community. While the Revisionists and the Orthodox were denouncing WNYC, the leaders of four mainstream Jewish organizations—B'nai B'rith, the National Council of Jewish Women, the American Jewish Committee, and the American Jewish Congress—were defending the Arab broadcast on the grounds of free speech.[17] To some extent, this division of opinion echoed the World War I–era disputes in the New York Jewish community between the forces of "uptown" and "downtown." Once again, the wealthier and more acculturated segments of the Jewish establishment, many of whom resided uptown in exclusive sections of northern Manhattan, were at odds with vocal, ethnically assertive, and politically militant grassroots Jews, many of whom lived downtown on Manhattan's Lower East Side or other heavily Jewish neighborhoods. When Jewish establishment leaders responded to the WNYC affair by embracing the American principle of free speech, they were making a point of their willingness to choose an American ideal over a narrow Jewish concern. Members of the Jewish leadership elite typically were active in American political and cultural life, enjoyed social and professional relationships outside the Jewish community, and were sensitive to non-Jewish perceptions of American Jewry. By contrast, the grassroots Jews who responded to WNYC with ethnic pride and public protest were part of a different world. Residing and interacting primarily among fellow Jews, often participating only peripherally in the broader currents of American society, they were less concerned about what non-Jews thought of the Jewish community and therefore less hesitant to speak out loudly and forcefully on such issues.

While there was evidence of grassroots Jewish sympathy for many of the U.S. Revisionists' positions, such sentiment did not easily translate into new members or money for the organization. The Arab radio broadcast dispute was a matter of small consequence on the Jewish agenda compared to the major Palestine-related events that seized American Jewry's attention in the summer and fall of 1937—and on many major issues, the NZOA was hard-pressed to demonstrate that its stance differed significantly from the positions of the mainstream Jewish groups.

When, for example, the Peel Commission recommended, in July 1937, the partition of western Palestine into separate Jewish and Arab states,[18] the NZOA was of one mind with most of the American Zionist leadership in denouncing the offer of such a small portion of western Palestine as unfair to the Jews. "Shameless arrogance" was how Louis Lipsky described the plan; Stephen Wise called it "the gravest betrayal of a most sacred trust."[19] The NZOA's Rabbi Newman assured Wise, his old friend and teacher, that at the forthcoming World Zionist Congress "you will find your strongest allies in the battle against partition in the Jabotinsky camp."[20] Indeed he did, but opponents of Peel were outnumbered at the congress, which voted to negotiate with the British on the basis of the Peel plan. In the end, however, Arab rejectionism doomed Peel's scheme and Arab violence resumed.

On the question of responding to Arab violence, too, the NZOA faced stiff competition from an increasingly militant American Zionist establishment. Accusations by the U.S. Labor Zionists—similar to the allegations of 1929—that the Arab violence was the result of Revisionist "provocations"[21] did not impress mainstream Zionist leaders, who were convinced that the culprits were Arab extremism and British tolerance of it. Stephen Wise criticized the British Mandate administration for "giving the Arabs too many chances already."[22] With the assent of prominent Zionists Brandeis, Julian Mack, Robert Szold, and Felix Frankfurter, Wise pressed Chaim Weizmann to refrain from making any new concessions to the Arabs and urged him to insist that the British return the Transjordan region to the Palestine Mandate.[23] The ZOA journal *New Palestine* had another idea on how to dispose of Transjordan: going even further than the Revisionists, a 1937 editorial in *New Palestine* proposed that "Jewish capital" be invested in the development of Transjordan in order to lure Palestinian Arab immigrants there and leave western Palestine to the Jews.[24]

On the subject of Jewish militancy, too, *New Palestine* was breaking new ground. Although it had previously published editorials excoriating the Revisionists for "speaking of expropriation and self-defense, breathing the spirit of aggression and violence, and expounding the blessings of militarism,"[25] it changed its tone in the wake of the latest crisis. When Revisionist militants in Palestine began to carry out retaliatory raids against Arab civilians, a *New Palestine* editorial found reason to sympathize with acts of retaliation. Although conceding that the attacks were not in line with the "Jewish national purpose in Palestine," the editorial contended that it was "hard to blame the hot-headed and hot-spirited young men who were involved in this violation of the national purpose. Those are to be blamed who, far from the scene, have used their moral influence to weaken the fiber of resistance at the Palestine front."[26] Stephen Wise, too, felt some sympathy for the Revisionist guerrillas. Even before the first of the Jewish retaliation attacks, he confided to a friend that perhaps Palestine's Jews had displayed "too much" self-discipline in the face of Arab violence, and "it would have been better for England to have had a taste of what these magnificent young Jews in Palestine could do if they finally took things into their own hands."[27] A year later, when the first Jewish reprisal raids took place,

Wise privately described the attacks as "regrettable but not inexplicable."[28] Nor was he alone in such sentiment. Hadassah board member Rose Halprin, visiting Palestine the following year, reported to her colleagues that while the phenomenon of Jewish retaliatory violence filled her with "horror and utmost condemnation," it was important to understand that Palestine Jewry's "self-imposed restraint has been strained to the breaking point under the continued lack of security and the inability of the Government to deal with the bandits."[29]

With prominent American Zionists opposing partition of Palestine and expressing understanding for Jewish retaliatory attacks, what was left to set the Revisionists apart from the rest of the American Zionist movement during the late 1930s? The answer was unauthorized Jewish immigration to Palestine—*aliyah bet.*

On a crisp, moonless night in the spring of 1937, a small boat approached the Haifa shoreline, out of view of British sea patrollers. Their leader, an adventurous Russian refugee named Moses Krivoshein, leaped into the ocean and swam ashore while the boat waited in the silent waters. William Perl, the Viennese Revisionist leader who helped organize the voyage, later recalled what happened next:

> There had been no prior arrangements in Palestine. In the middle of the night, Krivoshein, soaking wet, knocked at the doors of the Jewish settlers in nearby houses and whispered, "We have escapees from Hitler! They are offshore! Come and help us!" The next day, we had a telegram from one of the trustees in the group, announcing their safe arrival in Haifa, and several days later there came postcards with pictures of Mount Carmel from almost every one of the participants.[30]

It was the first of many boatloads of Jewish refugees that Perl and Krivoshein (who soon Hebraicized his name to Moshe Galili) sent to Palestine in defiance of British immigration restrictions during the 1930s. The program was known as *aliyah bet,* that is, the supplemental or parallel *aliyah* (immigration), illegally supplementing the limited immigration permitted by the British Mandate authorities. During the pre–World War II period, an estimated seventeen to twenty thousand such unauthorized immigrants reached Palestine by sea, of whom approximately two-thirds arrived on Revisionist ships, which were paid for in part by funds raised by Jabotinsky's

American followers.[31] The others arrived on ships sponsored by private individuals or the Labor Zionists, who belatedly joined the *aliyah bet* effort after initially opposing it because of their concerns about the ramifications of a conflict with the British.

Energized by the drama and success of the *aliyah bet* expeditions, NZOA activists began focusing their attention on ways to directly aid the project, especially in the aftermath of the March 1938 German annexation of Austria and the November 9, 1938, *Kristallnacht* pogroms, in which Nazi gangs destroyed hundreds of synagogues and Jewish homes and businesses, murdered dozens of Jews, and shipped thousands more to concentration camps. The intensified persecution of German and Austrian Jewry infused the *aliyah bet* organizers with an added sense of urgency and purpose. As one of the immigration activists put it: "This work we consider holy. Every life we save is a sacred mission fulfilled."[32]

The American efforts to aid *aliyah bet* were boosted by the arrival, in February and March 1939, of a delegation of Revisionist activists from abroad: Yitshaq Ben-Ami, one of the first Jews born in modern Tel Aviv, who had abandoned his agronomy studies at Hebrew University to join the Irgun Zvai Leumi, the Revisionists' militant underground in Palestine; his Irgun colleague Haim Lubinski; Robert Briscoe, a Jewish member of the Irish Parliament and veteran of the Irish Republican Army, who twenty years earlier had visited the United States to raise funds for the IRA; and Lieutenant Colonel John Patterson, a famous English lion hunter of Irish Protestant background, who had commanded the Jewish Legion that Jabotinsky had established during World War I. They were joined a few months later by Arieh Ben-Eliezer, an Irgun activist who had taken part in the armed defense of Jerusalem during the Arab riots of 1929 and 1936 and had then been sent to organize Irgun cells in Europe. Ben-Eliezer "was a handsome dark type and could have passed for Charles Boyer's twin brother, including the voice," a colleague later recalled.[33]

Shortly after their arrival, Lubinski and Ben-Ami paid a visit to the home of journalist-author John Gunther and his Jewish wife, Frances. "The Gunthers' home was one of only a few 'respectable' homes open to us," Ben-Ami later recalled. The four of them talked until the wee hours of the morning:

> Gunther did not feel personally involved in what we were saying or doing but he reacted to the problems of the Jews as he would to any other serious human problem and left the nitty-gritty of Jewish mat-

ters for his Jewish wife. They were sophisticated, worldly people. . . . They both knew so much about international politics that we could speak in a kind of shorthand, as if we were using headlines. In this way the Gunthers were unique. Americans were not well-informed about the world. In 1938, Senator Robert Reynolds of North Carolina, upon returning from "Hungria," announced that it was wrong for Hitler to have annexed the "Sudan."

But if Americans knew little about foreign affairs, the two Irgun "greenhorns" knew little about American Jewry until the Gunthers set them straight. "My image of a rich, generous Jewish community with a proud and strong ethnic consciousness was quickly deflated," Ben-Ami wrote. It was jarring for him to learn of the extent of anti-Semitism and nativism among the American public, the serious religious and political divisions within the Jewish community, and the phenomena of assimilation and anti-Zionism. The Revisionists truly had their work cut out for them.[34]

Colonel Patterson was the elder statesman of the group and often provided a shoulder to cry on during tough times. "I doubt whether we have another non-Jewish friend who takes as close a part in our sorrows and from whom we can always expect fatherly help," Lubinski wrote.[35] When another of the young activists confided to the lieutenant colonel that he was wearying of "the endless discussions with the Jews and the British" and the frequently frustrating "attempts to sell our views to the media" and would rather be "in the field, fighting Germans," Patterson advised him: "My young friend, the political fight is dirtier than the military one. Whoever is capable of it must do it. I did it, and I did it as an Irishman, because the cause was just and there are enough good people in the world to understand it."[36]

Working in conjunction with Louis Newman and the NZOA, the delegation addressed meetings in synagogues and private homes around the country, describing the perilous situation in Palestine and Europe and pleading for funds to sponsor *aliyah bet* transports. A series of meetings aimed at Orthodox donors, including a gathering at Brooklyn College, netted the *aliyah* operation "several thousand" dollars, by no means an insignificant sum for that time. Ben-Ami attributed their success among the Orthodox to the efforts of textile magnate Irving Bunim, the Young Israel movement's most prominent lay leader. The Revisionist emissaries were impressed by Bunim's insistence that the funds he raised "be spent on illegal immigration, not administrative, political or party expenses"; they reassured Bunim by providing a receipt for the money from the chief rabbi of Tel Aviv, Avigdor Amiel.[37] Bunim's friends were perplexed by his association with the Revisionists, a non-Orthodox group, when he had refused to accept a leadership position in the Religious Zionist group Mizrachi because of what he regarded as its excessive willingness to compromise on some religious issues. He responded by citing a parable about a plague that once struck the shtetl Jewish community of Brisk: "It raged throughout the High Holidays and endangered many people's lives. When Yom Kippur arrived, the great sage Reb Chaim Brisker told all the Jews that they should eat, lest they fall victim to the plague and die. Several zealots angrily asked how he could be so lenient about the laws of Yom Kippur. 'Oh, no,' Reb Chaim answered, 'I am not at all lenient regarding the laws of Yom Kippur. But I am very strict about the laws of *pikuach nefesh* [saving lives].' . . . The Jews in Brisk ate on Yom Kippur," Bunim concluded, "for the same reason that I work with Vladimir Jabotinsky—to save Jewish lives. I will work with anyone who saves Jewish lives, for that *mitzva* takes precedence over all others." In this context, Bunim was fond of citing a statement attributed to Rabbi Aharon Kotler, one of the leading sages of European-style Orthodoxy in America, when Kotler was challenged about his willingness to work with Stephen Wise, a Reform rabbi: "I would work with the Pope if it would save even the fingernail of one Jewish child!"[38]

With the exception of the Orthodox community, the illegal *aliyah* fundraising efforts stumbled initially.[39] Potential donors who asked mainstream Jewish groups about the Revisionists were frightened away by warnings of "Don't touch them," Ben-Ami recalled. "I wanted to grab the Jews and shout: 'It's almost too late! Help us! All we ask for are pennies. If every Jew in America gave us one dollar, we would build a bridge of ships over the Mediterranean.' . . . But we were never given a chance. A solid wall of indifference and hostility shut us out." Even after more than eight weeks in the United States, the delegation "had raised only pennies."[40]

The Irgunists were equally disappointed by the outcome of their political contacts in the United States, but perhaps only because they had somewhat naively expected that the minds of prominent American Jews "had finally been opened to our 'Jeremiahs' by the rise of Hitler." Briscoe's effort to secure an audience with President Roosevelt was unsuccessful, and he failed to make headway with Supreme Court justice Felix Frankfurter or New York governor Herbert Lehman, who feared that the Revisionists were "embarrassing England, which was already on the spot because of mounting German aggressiveness."[41] Briscoe enjoyed a somewhat more sympathetic reception from the eighty-three-year-old former Supreme Court justice and American Zionist leader Louis Brandeis. According to Ben-Ami, Brandeis was keenly interested in the details of the *aliyah bet* operation and told Briscoe, "If I were a young man like you, I would be with you."[42] Brandeis's colleagues in the Jewish leadership were troubled by his meetings—there were more than one—with Revisionist emissaries. "I wish the Great Good Man would be a little more careful about the people he sees," Stephen Wise complained to Frankfurter. "I think he could trust [ZOA president] Sol[omon Goldman] and [longtime ZOA official] Bob [Szold] and me sufficiently to let us decide not whom he is to see, but whom he is not to see."[43]

Wise could not control Brandeis's meetings any more than he could control the justice's changing views on Zionist affairs. Although Brandeis had been unsympathetic to the Revisionists during the 1920s and into the mid-1930s,[44] his attitude softened later, especially after the proclamation of the May 1939 British White Paper, which limited Jewish immigration to Palestine to fifteen thousand yearly through 1944, and thereafter subject to Arab consent. Brandeis became a defender of illegal immigration—an intriguing position for someone whose entire life was dedicated to upholding the law—at a time when the Revisionists were its best-known proponents.[45]

Brandeis's verbal sympathy was not what the NZOA was seeking. They needed practical assistance to make *aliyah bet* a success, and their initial inability to obtain that assistance was a source of mounting frustration for Ben-Ami in the spring of 1939. Deeply dejected at the thought that his appeals "were falling mostly on deaf ears," Ben-Ami seriously considered shutting down the office of their Revisionist front group, the American Friends of a Jewish Palestine (AFJP), and returning home to Palestine. He would have been pleasantly surprised to discover that in private, some mainstream American Zionist leaders were becoming increasingly concerned that England's Palestine policy and the plight of European Jewry were fueling American Jewish support for the Revisionists' militant brand of Zionism. Ben-Ami would have been equally pleased to know that the establishment's concern about Revisionist competition for the sympathy of American Jews was one of the factors influencing the American Zionist leadership to adopt a more aggressive political posture.

Already on the eve of the White Paper proclamation, some American Zionist leaders sensed that a political vacuum was developing in the Jewish community. "There are a number of Zionists unaffiliated with the [Zionist]

Organization [of America], who question what the Organization is doing in the emergency," Judge Morris Rothenberg, a former president of the ZOA, warned the ZOA Executive in May 1939. "They hear rumors and they wonder what action is being taken by the Zionist Organization." He called particular attention to the fact that the Yiddish press in New York had published little news about ZOA activities, convincing the ZOA Executive to hold a special press conference for the Yiddish-language media to explain to them "what is being done in the present emergency situation."[46]

Were the Revisionists beginning to fill the vacuum left by the mainstream American Zionist leadership? Jewish Agency emissary Georg Landauer wrote from New York to his friends back in Palestine that "the Revisionists are again rearing their heads" and launching "noisy" activities.[47] ZOA president Solomon Goldman worried about the "intensified activities of the Revisionists in this country," and his vice president, Dr. Israel Goldstein, circulated among their colleagues a detailed memorandum about the "headway" the NZOA and AFJP were making. The Revisionists were attracting "a good many names of 'respectables' such as women of prominence in Hadassah, well-known lawyers . . . and other unwitting laymen," Goldstein warned. In his own neighborhood, the west side of Manhattan, "the penetration has been considerable, [and] people of means and personal following have been attracted to one or another of these organizations and enthusiasm has been engendered chiefly by the claim that the Revisionists were the first to foster Aliyah Beth and have been responsible during the past two years for practically all of the illegal immigration."[48]

Goldstein contrasted what he called the "standard" and "routine" appeals made by the American Zionist leadership with the Revisionists' propaganda, which, by "concentrating on illegal immigration," is "dramatic, exciting and challenging to Jewish resistance." Furthermore, he noted, "the war emergency gives special edge to their activity." Within "a relatively short time," Goldstein warned, the Revisionists could succeed in establishing a base of American Jewish support that would be "very imposing." The danger was so great, according to Goldstein, that the Zionist leadership should—despite the legal complications and public-relations restraints—find a way to "make it clear to the public" that the mainstream Zionists, too, were involved in the smuggling of "uncertificated immigrants" to Palestine.[49]

An accelerated pace of attacks by the Jewish left was another indication that the American Revisionists were making waves. The U.S. Labor Zionist

journal *Jewish Frontier* blasted Briscoe and the NZOA for lobbying on behalf of "the fuehrer Jabotinsky."[50] *Hashomer Hatzair,* journal of the Marxist-
Zionist youth movement of the same name, denounced the Revisionists'
illegal boats as floating "concentration camps" filled with "a human element
so unfit for Palestine." Overcrowding and unsanitary conditions were actually typical of all ships carrying *aliyah bet* immigrants, although it may be
that the Revisionists, because they were weaker financially than many rival
Zionist movements, were compelled to purchase lower-quality boats and
fill them with more passengers than the normal capacity—not an entirely
surprising strategy given the desperation of the times. *Hashomer* called
for Revisionism to be "exterminated from the frame-work of the Zionist
movement."[51] A calmer critique was offered by the Emergency Committee for Zionist Affairs (ECZA), a recently established coalition of leaders of the major American Zionist organizations, which complained that
the AFJP was "seeking to duplicate or parallel the work of the Jewish
Agency."[52]

The publicity, even when it was negative, drew attention to the Revisionists' efforts and alerted potential supporters who had previously been
unaware of the *aliyah bet* project. In addition to the "nickels and dimes," the
Revisionists were soon attracting more substantial support. One activist recalls that the group received regular donations from "a variety-store owner
in Brooklyn, a retired East Side dentist, and an officer in a small bank,"
among others. The Tel Hai Fund, which had been dormant in recent years,
was revived to supplement the political and educational activities of the
AFJP. The funds were used directly to help rent the boats that smuggled
European Jews to Palestine. Much of the money was raised at parlor meetings hosted by a small but growing band of Revisionist sympathizers among
New York's writers and publishers and figures in the Hollywood entertain-
ment industry. Bernard Fineman, a Hollywood producer, latched onto the
Revisionist cause, and it was he who introduced it to his sister, Frances
Gunther; soon the Gunthers were hosting fund-raising and propaganda
meetings for the Irgun delegation in their living room. Writer Dorothy
Parker often joined them.[53]

Perhaps the best-known American supporter of Revisionism during
the 1930s was the prominent book-and-magazine publisher William Ziff.
Prior to his interest in Zionism, the colorful and adventurous Ziff had,
among other things, served as an officer in the army of Honduras and run,
unsuccessfully, for the United States Congress. The rise of Nazism in Germany provoked Ziff, who had previously remained aloof from Jewish com-

munal affairs, to embrace Revisionist Zionism. Jabotinsky's American supporters knew a good thing when they saw one; they persuaded Ziff to accept the presidency of the Zionist-Revisionists of America in 1935. Almost from the start, Ziff found himself uncomfortable in the role of Jewish organizational leader, and he resigned as president of the U.S. Revisionists after only a year. He remained active in Zionist politics, however, and in 1938 caused a considerable stir when he authored a stinging critique of British policy in the Holy Land called *The Rape of Palestine*. The British Foreign Office characterized it as "a violent and offensive book," and for years afterward the British monitored the pro-Zionist writings and speeches of this "unscrupulous gangster," fearful that his audiences were "lapping this poison up."[54]

It was Ziff who brought Harry Louis Selden, the gifted young managing editor of the humor magazine *Judge*, into the world of militant Zionism. Over lunch at Manhattan's posh Algonquin Hotel one day in early 1939, a few tables from where the *New Yorker* staff and others prominent in the local intelligentsia regularly dined, Ziff casually asked Selden if he had read *The Rape of Palestine*. An embarrassed Selden confessed he had not even heard of it, and on his way back to the office he stopped to get a copy, intending to skim it "just so I could say something intelligent about it the next time we met." Selden could not put the book down. He read the huge volume in one sitting and promptly volunteered to prepare a condensed version. The book was a staple of Zionist information efforts in the United States—both Revisionist and mainstream—for years to come. Selden also began showing up frequently at the office of the American Friends of a Jewish Palestine, "two dingy rooms in a rundown Madison Avenue building," helping to write and edit their brochures.[55]

The phenomenon of prominent intellectuals making common cause with the Revisionists irritated mainstream American Jewish organizations. The ECZA in 1940 established a special fund to finance the distribution of anti-Revisionist literature and resolved to compile a list of everyone publicly associated with the U.S. Revisionists and "find ways of cautioning the 'innocents' among them so that they know actually what type of organization they are aiding and abetting."[56] Those who publicly associated with the NZOA or AFJP often received letters from Jewish groups urging them to sever their ties with the Revisionists.[57] Some buckled under the pressure and withdrew from their Revisionist associations. Others, such as Selden, were inspired by the challenge and increased their involvement. In addition to having him write and edit Revisionist literature, the NZOA "loaned" Selden to the *American Jewish Chronicle*, an ostensibly independent monthly magazine edited by a veteran Revisionist, Dr. Benjamin Akzin.

Akzin, thirty-five, a native of Latvia, had the most distinguished academic record of any senior Revisionist. After completing doctorates in political science (University of Vienna, 1926) and law (University of Paris, 1929), he relocated to New England and completed a doctorate in juridical science at Harvard. While editing the *American Jewish Chronicle*, Akzin also taught comparative government and international relations at the City College of New York. As Revisionist "front" projects went, the *Chronicle* was unusually professional. Crisp, attractive, and well written, the *Chronicle* presented what were in effect Revisionist perspectives to readers who might not consider such views on their merits if they had known their source. Unlike the American Friends of a Jewish Palestine and the Tel Hai Fund, whose boards were filled with many of the same prominent Revisionist names as the NZOA itself, the *Chronicle* was circumspect about its agenda. It had no board of easily identifiable nationalists; its declared purpose was to present "all responsible points of view in Jewish affairs" without endorsing "any single one"; and Akzin, its editor, had indeed separated himself from Jabotinsky's movement in the late 1930s in frustration over the Revisionists' secession from the World Zionist Organization. The *Chronicle*'s main financial sponsor was the American Jewish philanthropist Edward Norman, a prominent non-Zionist, that is, a supporter of Palestine-related charities who did not subscribe to Zionist principles such as Jewish nationalism.[58]

Still, if one looked just a little below the surface, it was not hard to find the *Chronicle*'s Revisionist side. The British Embassy, which carefully monitored the militant Zionists, immediately recognized Akzin's name from the executive committee of the American Friends of a Jewish Palestine and, after perusing the first issue, concluded that it was "likely enough that it will in fact express the Revisionist point of view."[59] Israel Goldstein of the ZOA likewise understood the implication of Akzin's serving as editor; he knew Akzin as one of five individuals who constituted "the same common denominator of directorship" that ran all the Revisionist front groups.[60] Furthermore, the newspaper's office was at the same lower Broadway address as NZOA headquarters. And although the roster of contributing authors to the *Chronicle* was diverse, every one of the fourteen issues that appeared (it lasted only from 1939 to 1940) included articles by prominent Revisionists, including Frances Gunther, Lieutenant Colonel Patterson,

Jacob de Haas, Akzin himself (often under the pen name "Arnold Ben-son"), and Jabotinsky as well. As Akzin gradually returned to the NZOA leadership circle in late 1939 and early 1940, the contents of forthcoming issues of the *Chronicle* became a subject for discussion among the NZOA top brass.[61] The June 1940 issue was dedicated entirely to an exposition of the NZOA's platform and views.[62] Because of budgetary problems, how-ever, the June edition turned out to be the last issue of the *Chronicle* to be published.

A more urgent victim of the Revisionists' financial woes was the SS *Sakarya*, an old Turkish-owned coal carrier leased by Revisionist agents in Bucharest in November 1939 to carry illegal immigrants to Palestine. The ship's owners, learning at the last minute the true nature of the proposed voyage, demanded additional payments to guard against the danger that the *Sakarya* might be impounded by the British authorities. The twenty-three hundred passengers—the largest number of unauthorized immigrants ever brought on one ship to Palestine—were stranded on the freezing Danube River, braving a fierce winter and rationing their dwindling food supplies, while Revisionists in Europe and the United States scrambled desperately to raise the $10,000 needed to satisfy the shipowners.

Mainstream Jewish leaders were not receptive to the Revisionists' ap-peals. Stephen Wise spurned Louis Newman's request for assistance, insist-ing that "the Jewish Agency will deal with that problem as promptly and adequately as they can," while at the same time suggesting the Revisionists themselves would be to blame if the agency did not do so, since "[its] limi-tation in the matter of funds is still further narrowed by the competition which the new Zionist Organization has managed to set up!"[63] Harry Selden turned to the United Palestine Appeal (UPA), the major Jewish organizations' primary fund-raising agency for Palestine. The UPA, careful to avoid any connection to illegal activities, rebuffed the appeal, but the episode did yield a disturbing document when Revisionist activist Baruch Rabinowitz, by now serving in the pulpit of a small synagogue in western Maryland, wrote to the UPA to protest its refusal to help the *Sakarya*. Much to Rabinowitz's surprise, he received in return a long letter from UPA executive vice chairman Henry Montor that spelled out, in unusually frank language, the controversial basis of the Jewish leadership's rejection of the Revisionist appeal for aid:

> Selectivity is an inescapable factor in dealing with the problem of immigration to Palestine. By "selectivity" is meant the choice of

young men and women who are trained in Europe for productive purposes. . . . Sentimental considerations are, of course, vital and everyone would wish to save every single Jew who could be rescued out of the cauldron of Europe. But when one is dealing with so delicate a program as unregistered immigration, it is, obviously, essential that those people sent to Palestine shall be able to endure harsh conditions.

Montor informed Rabbi Rabinowitz that when the *Sakarya* problem first arose, an unnamed "responsible individual" offered to provide the necessary funds if Selden and the AFJP would cease raising funds for illegal immigration "and if it were to agree to 'selectivity' in immigration"; the AFJP refused the offer. Montor went on to accuse the Revisionists of exploiting the illegal immigration for monetary profit and claimed that "many of those who have been brought into Palestine by the Revisionists, on this purely money basis, have been prostitutes and criminals."[64]

Ultimately, the funds for the *Sakarya* were successfully raised from private sources and the ship set sail for the Holy Land. On February 10 it was intercepted by a British warship, which escorted the boat to Palestine and held the passengers—among them Dov Gruner, who later gained international fame when he was hanged for his role in the Jewish armed revolt against the British—in detention camps for several months. The immigrants were set free by midsummer, except for Ze'ev Jabotinsky's son Eri, who was held in prison for having organized the transport. Meanwhile, back in New York, the Emergency Committee for Zionist Affairs stepped up its attacks on the *aliyah bet* activists, issuing a strident twenty-six-page booklet titled "Revisionism: A Destructive Force." The pamphlet characterized Revisionism as "viciously Fascist" and claimed (although without documentation) that its ships "resemble concentration camps in that passengers were hung to the mast and were refused food in retaliation for criticism or complaints."[65] Ironically, the UPA—a leading member-organization of the ECZA—later circulated a fund-raising leaflet featuring a photograph of one of those Revisionist ships, the *Parita*, which had landed 850 unauthorized refugees at Tel Aviv in 1938.[66]

In the competition between mainstream Zionists and Revisionist dissidents for American Jewish support, the Revisionists' *aliyah bet* effort was a sure hit. Financially assisting the smuggling of European Jews through the British blockade of Palestine gave American Jews a practical way to respond to the Nazis, the English, and the Arabs. Zionist pioneers slowly building up the Jewish homeland still attracted American Jewish charity dollars, but saving refugees naturally had a special pull. Agricultural development "is excellent and commendable from a purely philanthropic standpoint," a U.S. Revisionist newsletter argued, "but [it] solves nothing for the millions of Jews who are being slowly but surely burned in the hellfires of Eastern Europe and ground between the millstones of striving parties and classes in most of those lands."[67]

While the Revisionists were undertaking daring and potentially life-saving activities, the mainstream Zionist establishment was mired in inertia. Germany's war with England, triggered by the German invasion of Poland in September 1939, stirred American isolationism to a fever pitch. Congress and public opinion were strongly opposed to American intervention in the European hostilities, and mainstream Zionists feared that any demands they might make upon the U.S. government with regard to Palestine might be perceived as dragging America into overseas conflicts.[68] Organized Zionist activity dwindled. "A feeling of dismay is spreading very rapidly among the friends of Palestine," Isadore Breslau found after assuming his new post as executive director of the ZOA in 1940. "Many people seem to feel 'what's the use.'"[69]

American Zionists were eventually jarred from their lethargy. The sinking of several boatloads of European Jewish refugees on their way to Palestine made a profound impact, which was supplemented by the incessant lobbying of Palestine Labor leader David Ben-Gurion, who visited the United States in 1939 and 1940 and pressed American Zionist leaders to take a more active posture.[70] The perceived competition posed by the Revisionists also played a role in prodding mainstream Zionists to become more active. At a meeting of the Hadassah National Board in December 1940, its chair, Bertha Schoolman, listed four factors that she said "called for greatly heightened Zionist political activity on the American scene": the suffering of European Jewry, Britain's immigration restrictions in Palestine, the wartime threat to Palestine Jewry, and "the temporary increase of Revisionist strength in this country."[71] What Schoolman hoped would be only a temporary rise in American Jewish sympathy for the Revisionist platform proved to be of considerably longer duration. As Nazi policy evolved from sporadic persecution of the Jews to systematic annihilation, and as British restrictions on Jewish immigration to Palestine consequently became a virtual death sentence for European Jewry, the Zionist maximalists found an even greater reception among American Jews and helped prod mainstream Zionist leaders to become more militant than ever before.

4 • Jabotinsky's Return to America

Jabotinsky's greatest diplomatic triumph had come in the midst of World War I, when he persuaded the British to organize a small Zionist army, the Jewish Legion, to assist in the Allies' Middle East campaign against the Turks. Beyond the legion's practical role in assisting the liberation of Palestine, Jabotinsky imagined—correctly, as it turned out—that its sacrifices on the battlefield would strengthen the Jews' postwar diplomatic claim to the Holy Land. He also hoped it would constitute the nucleus of the army of the Jewish state-to-be, a role that it realized on a small scale when former legionnaires led the defense of Jerusalem during the 1920 Palestinian Arab riots.

From Jabotinsky's point of view, the establishment of a Jewish army made as much sense in 1939 as it had a quarter-century earlier. If a Jewish fighting force aided the Allies against the Nazis, presumably England would be more favorable toward Jewish postwar demands for a state in Palestine. The Zionist fighters, toughened by their battlefield experience, would then become the core of the Jewish state's own army.

There was also a psychological angle to the Jewish army concept. Most Zionists, Revisionists included, expected the process leading to Jewish statehood to generate a new kind of Jew. Shorn of the burdens of anti-Jewish discrimination and the fears arising from living as an oppressed minority, the Jews of reborn Palestine would regain their long-lost pride as well as their physical prowess, forsake the "unproductive" occupations of Diaspora life, and take up the plow and gun. The American Revisionists delighted in a 1942 *Life* magazine cover story about a U.S. Army "guerrilla warfare expert" identified as "Bert 'Yank' Levy." A poem about Levy that the Revisionists circulated hailed "this son of warriors, of the Maccabees / Of David, of deep-thewed Samson, God-given Gideon / No banker this, no Doctor of German philosophy / This is the Fighting Jew."[1]

Yet London found plenty of reason to resist Jabotinsky's new army proposal. Mindful of the growing pro-Axis sentiment in the Arab world, the British feared that the creation of a Jewish army would push the Arabs closer to the Nazis and even lead to a renewal of Palestinian Arab violence. In addition, having distanced itself from the idea of a Jewish state, England could not be pleased at the prospect of the Jews having a full-fledged army at their disposal when they launched their inevitable postwar campaign for statehood. "A Jewish Army cannot be disassociated from Jewish Nationalism," an internal British Foreign Office report warned. "A Jewish nation supported by a Jewish Army under its own banner is only one step removed from the full realisation of political Zionism."[2] In this context, it is no surprise that Jabotinsky's initial appeal to the British for the creation of a Jewish army was quickly rebuffed.

As a Revisionist journal noted, "Zionists everywhere" had at first believed that active Jewish support for the Allies' war effort during 1939 and 1940, including the offer to create a Jewish army to aid England, "would cause Britain to at least suspend" the May 1939 White Paper. Instead, as 1940 dragged on, England's blockade of Palestine remained in force, and London would go no further than issue what the Revisionists derided as "vegetarian declarations" about equal rights for postwar European Jewry.[3] To make matters worse, from the Revisionist standpoint, mainstream Zionist leaders exhibited only a lukewarm interest in the Jewish army idea, for fear of appearing too demanding at a time when England seemed to be facing an imminent German invasion. The Zionist establishment's hesitancy dealt a serious blow to the Zionist cause, the Revisionists contended. "The physical blackout in the major part of Europe and the blackout of Jewish political wisdom everywhere are quite complete." Except, that is, for America—"The world's only beacon is this country and its great president," the U.S. Revisionist journal declared.[4]

It soon become clear to Jabotinsky that America would have to be the site of his Jewish army campaign. The major centers of Revisionist strength in Poland and elsewhere in Eastern Europe were now chafing under Nazi occupation. Palestine was no option for Jabotinsky personally—since the British refused to grant him entry—and it was in any event too far removed from the Western capitals where the future of Zionism would be decided. Nor was there much point in remaining in London, given England's waning interest in Zionism and its cool reception to the Revisionists' army proposal. The intensification of German submarine and bombing attacks on British shipping heightened the feeling among the Revisionist hierarchy in

London that there was precious little time left to get their leader to safer shores before the expected Nazi invasion.

Viewed from afar, the United States seemed to be the obvious choice for a major Revisionist campaign. It boasted the largest and wealthiest Jewish community in the world outside the war zone. It had a Revisionist movement, however small, already in place. Its government, as Britain's most important ally, was likely to have considerable influence with London on issues of concern to the Zionists. With the recent congressional repeal of legislation preventing Britain and France from purchasing American weapons, the United States was at last moving decisively away from its earlier isolationism.

America seemed to be Revisionism's—indeed, Zionism's—last hope.

On March 13, the SS *Samaria* arrived in New York, with Jabotinsky aboard. He was accompanied by two of his senior aides. One was thirty-four-year-old Aaron Kopelowicz, Jabotinsky's secretary. A Polish-born linguistic master who was equally comfortable in Polish, German, Russian, French, and English, "Kop" left his wife and young son in London while he accompanied his mentor to the United States; after the German bombing of Britain began that August, Kopelowicz's family joined him in America. Also joining Jabotinsky on the *Samaria* was Eliahu Ben-Horin, thirty-eight, who grew up in Russia and immigrated as a teenager to Palestine, where he spent seven years with a Zionist pioneer labor brigade, working in construction and agriculture. Daring and resourceful, Ben-Horin bribed his way across the Rumanian-Soviet border shortly after the Bolshevik Revolution to smuggle his family and a number of other Jews out of the USSR. Later, he smuggled weapons from Germany to Palestine for the Labor Zionist militia Haganah on the eve of Hitler's rise to power. Ben-Horin made his mark in Palestine as a Hebrew journalist, eventually rising to become, successively, editor of the dailies *Doar Hayom* and *Hayarden* and the "Palnews" news service before moving to London in 1937. With England as his base, Ben-Horin crisscrossed Europe between 1937 and 1939 on behalf of the Irgun's effort to bring unauthorized Jewish immigrants to Palestine. He played the key role in facilitating the dramatic voyage of the SS *Parita,* which brought eight hundred half-starved immigrants to Palestine after a harrowing eight-week journey in the summer of 1939. Ben-Horin's energy, devotion, and literary talents would prove to be formidable weapons in the arsenal of American Revisionist Zionism.[5]

Another rising young star of militant Zionism followed Jabotinsky to

America two weeks later. From London, Jabotinsky had cabled to Benzion Netanyahu, the thirty-year-old founder and former editor of the Palestine Revisionist daily *Hayarden*, to meet him in New York. Netanyahu's family was no stranger to America's shores. His father, the renowned Zionist orator Rabbi Nathan Mileikowsky, had traveled in the United States and Canada between 1925 and 1929 as an emissary of Keren Ha-Yesod, the fund for purchasing land in Palestine. During the Arlosoroff affair, Mileikowsky played a key role in persuading prominent rabbis, foremost among them Palestine's chief Ashkenazi rabbi, Avraham Yitzhak Kook, to protest against attempts to blame the Revisionist movement for the assassination. He also later helped arrange the nearly successful peace negotiations between Jabotinsky and Labor Zionist rival David Ben-Gurion. Mileikowsky changed his family name to Netanyahu, after one of the biblical "returnees to Zion" in the time of the prophet Ezra. It was a perfectly ordinary name for a Jew in twentieth-century Palestine, but presented unexpected difficulties for his son Benzion in the United States, from the comical phenomenon of receiving letters addressed to "Mr. Natan Yahu" or even "Mr. Hu," to the more irksome problem of being denied reservations at resort hotels during World War II because his name sounded Japanese.[6]

American immigration restrictions required every newcomer to arrange, in advance, for a U.S. citizen to act as a guarantor that he or she would not become a financial burden on the public. Netanyahu's guarantor was the veteran ZOA activist and former Jewish National Fund president Emanuel Neumann. While working for the Jewish Agency in Jerusalem during the 1930s, Neumann had grown fond of Netanyahu's writings. Privately sympathetic to the Revisionists but fearful of forfeiting his position in the mainstream Zionist movement, Neumann signed for Netanyahu at Ellis Island and would meet with him frequently in the years to follow, but he insisted that their relationship remain strictly a private matter. It was the first of what were to be many friendships that Netanyahu would enjoy with mainstream Zionist figures who quietly cheered for the Revisionist militants.[7]

Jabotinsky's inner circle in New York was shortly joined by the colorful Jeremiah "Irma" Halperin, son of the even more colorful Yehiel Michal Halperin, the man dubbed by the American Zionist press as "the Jewish Don Quixote" and the "Jewish Knight-Errant of Palestine." The elder Halperin, grandson of the famous Torah commentator known as the Malbim, helped establish some of the earliest Zionist settlements in late-nineteenth-century Palestine as well as the first Palestine Jewish militia, *Ha-Shomer*. He was also notorious for having demonstratively stepped into the lions' cage at the Jaffa Circus to challenge Arab allegations of Jewish timidity. His son Jeremiah, no less an adventurer, took part in the Haganah's fight against Arab riots in 1920 and 1929, then became director of military training for Betar, the Revisionist youth movement. A devoted man of the sea, Halperin established and directed a Betar Maritime School in Italy in the 1930s.[8]

There were two other important arrivals that spring. They were dispatched to America by the Irgun Zvai Leumi, the armed Palestine underground that had been born of the Revisionist movement but was increasingly asserting its independence from Jabotinsky. One was thirty-year-old Alexander Rafaeli (who would later adopt the surname Hadani), who had completed a Ph.D. in political science at the University of Heidelberg just as the Nazis were consolidating their rule, and then became an *aliyah bet* organizer for the Irgun in Europe. Rafaeli reached the United States on May 9 aboard the SS *Rex*, the last boat to reach America from Italy before the Italians joined the Axis. He was joined in July by another Irgun emissary, Hillel Kook, the shrewd but unpredictable twenty-five-year-old nephew of Chief Rabbi Avraham Yitzhak Kook. A senior Irgun activist in Europe, Kook sailed to the United States aboard the SS *Scythia*, right behind a ship that was torpedoed by the Nazis.

The arrival of Jabotinsky and his aides inspired a flurry of Revisionist activity. Within days, over five thousand Jews packed the Manhattan Center to hear the dynamic Zionist orator call for mass European Jewish immigration to Palestine (he used a figure of at least 300,000 annually), the establishment of a Jewish army to fight alongside the Allies against Germany, and the formation of a provisional Jewish government-in-exile, including all Zionist factions, for the duration of the war.[9] Jabotinsky's declared agenda posed a problem for mainstream American Zionist leaders because it was both popular among the grassroots and difficult to publicly oppose. The Zionist establishment might regard the Revisionists' goals as unrealistic, but who among them could say that he or she did not share the militants' desire for mass *aliyah*, an army, and Jewish unity? Frustrated ZOA veteran Louis Lipsky complained that Jabotinsky was essentially promoting the ZOA's own ideas, while a United Jewish Appeal official who attended the rally as an observer reported to the Labor Zionist leadership in Jerusalem that Jabotinsky's speech was "extremely moderate in form and in its whole conception."[10]

The Manhattan Center rally launched a series of meetings and rallies in New York in late March and early April 1940, with Jabotinsky as the centerpiece. He was received warmly at a Saturday night gathering of the Jewish War Veterans, and more than fifteen hundred Betar youths cheered their leader when he addressed their March 31 assembly. Although himself non-observant, Jabotinsky touched a responsive chord among religious Zionist audiences with his nationalist message. Several hundred "Orthodox rabbis and personalities" were on hand at one Brooklyn meeting. The leaders of the National Council of Young Israel, the association of modern American Orthodox synagogues, were likewise "very deeply impressed" when Jabotinsky addressed them, one aide reported.[11]

Who were Jabotinsky's most receptive audiences? Religious Zionists, with their strong sentiment for the Holy Land; Jewish veterans of the military, with their appreciation for the value of a Zionist army; and the less acculturated segments and lower socioeconomic strata of the Jewish community in general, with their stronger attachment to Jewish tradition, ethnicity, or simply the "old neighborhood." Many of them were drawn to the Revisionist themes of Jewish pride and Zionist assertiveness.

The call for a Jewish army also resonated strongly in urban areas with large numbers of Jewish immigrants or children of immigrants who had friends and relatives trapped in Nazi-occupied Poland. As it became clear that their loved ones were doomed to suffer, in the words of Stephen Wise, "a spectacle of daily torture and horror such as men have not beheld since the day of Gengis Khan,"[12] the idea of a Jewish army seemed increasingly appealing. As early as December 1939, three months after the German invasion, there were reports in the U.S. Jewish media of atrocities far beyond what might have been expected in the context of the travails of war. Stormtroopers in a village near Warsaw "forced all the Jewish men to dig a large pit and then lined them up before the ditch and shot them down from behind with machine-guns so that their bodies fell into the newly-dug grave," the Jewish Telegraphic Agency reported on December 8. Ten days later, the JTA informed its readers that "a quarter of a million [Polish] Jews have been wiped out by military operations, executions, disease and starvation . . . at least 80% of the remainder have been reduced to complete beggary."[13] After reading such reports, who could not feel some sympathy for the Revisionists' demand to create a Jewish army that would symbolize, as they put it, "revenge and survival"? Jabotinsky's literature spoke of "suicide squads engaging in desperate commando raids in to the heart of Germany . . . Jewish pilots bombing German cities in reprisals." A Jewish army "marching valiantly to the front would seem like an instrument of divine retribution to the Germans." The emotional appeal was undeniable.[14]

The large audiences and widespread media coverage that Jabotinsky initially netted irked mainstream Zionist leaders. New York mayor Fiorello La Guardia's decision to send official greetings to one of Jabotinsky's public meetings likewise irritated the Jewish establishment.[15] At an April 2, 1940, meeting of the Emergency Committee for Zionist Affairs, complaints were aired about "the hospitable attitude of the Yiddish press to the Revisionists." The ZOA's Louis Lipsky, fearing that the Revisionist leader was "making an impression on American Jews," urged his colleagues in the ECZA to take steps to "destroy the influence that Mr. Jabotinsky is exerting on the American public." The ECZA delegates responded by establishing a special fund to finance the production of anti-Revisionist literature.[16] The Revisionists' opponents also sometimes resorted to more unorthodox methods. "Anyone supporting us, even unofficially, is being subjected to concentrated attacks, and in some cases threatened to lose his or her livelihood if they do not disassociate from us," one senior Revisionist activist reported to a colleague.[17]

Attacks by Zionist rivals were only one aspect of the difficulties the Revisionists faced in their efforts to make headway in the United States in 1940. Unfamiliarity with the American scene was a serious handicap during the early months. Eliahu Ben-Horin found the American Jewish scene "a colossal field covering five millions of Jews spread over a very big country." He wondered how the Revisionists could succeed in the face of the "weak Zionist sentiment, Zionist faith and Zionist education of the Jewish masses."[18] Aaron Kopelowicz, who was delegated the task of reporting back to New Zionist Organization (NZO) headquarters in London on their work in America, conceded in mid-April that their mission was proceeding "very slowly" because of the prevailing political climate. He reported that despite the April 7 German invasion of Denmark and Norway, Americans in general still regarded the European conflict with disinterest—"a very dull affair"—and American Jews "have no idea whatever of what is going on in Palestine and not much of what is happening in Eastern Europe." Educational activity was desperately needed, but "all of us are very green" in "the methods of propaganda and organization here."[19]

Perhaps Jabotinsky and his colleagues erred by setting their initial goals too high. They arrived in the United States with what Kopelowicz called "planetary schemes"—huge plans for moving hundreds of thousands of Jews from one continent to another, creating an army, and laying the foundations of a Jewish state. Visionary but not yet attuned to American political realities, they mistakenly assumed that they would be able to move, with relative speed and ease, from the realm of ideas to the realm of serious political action, from speeches to deeds.

Within days of landing at New York, Ben-Horin was telling reporters that the Revisionists expected to create, within a year, a full-fledged "Jewish merchant marine" with "10 seaworthy liners" to carry unauthorized immigrants from Europe to the Holy Land.[20] Likewise, Jeremiah Halperin had barely stepped off the boat before he was announcing plans to organize a "Jewish Marine League" school to train crews for the would-be Jewish navy. Halperin's declaration was followed by some press releases and brochures announcing the league's aims, a wave of sympathetic inquires from potential Jewish sailors, and a campaign by worried ZOA officials to pressure the league's endorsers (including the chief rabbi of Great Britain) to dissociate themselves from the group.[21] But the lack of major financial backers prevented realization of the project, and an internal Revisionist assessment of the merchant marine campaign later termed it "a complete failure."[22]

The Revisionists' pursuit of major Jewish philanthropists usually ended in disappointment. "In all the circles of [Jewish] 'Society' we are under an absolute anathema," they found. "The old clique is still holding all the sources of money." When tensions mounted between Jabotinsky's aides and the American Friends of a Jewish Palestine group over dividing up funds raised from *aliyah bet* propaganda, Kopelowicz confided to the London office that "the trouble is not that we cannot come to an agreement as to the distribution, but that there is no money to be distributed."[23]

An additional complication was Jabotinsky's declining health. By early May 1940, Kopelowicz found his leader's "working capacity is next to nil and his nerves are so strained that it is absolutely impossible to think of any real work." Jabotinsky was homesick for the Jewish communities of his native Europe. He was also deeply dejected at his continuing separation from his family: his wife, Johanna, was stuck in England without an entry visa to the United States, while his son Eri was in jail in Palestine for *aliyah bet* activities. Under these strains, the Revisionist leader was functioning at only a fraction of his usual pace.[24] Unless Mrs. Jabotinsky's visa problem was solved soon, the Revisionists in America would face a financial "catastrophe," Kopelowicz grimly predicted in early May; their projects would "not stand the slightest chance if we cannot use to the fullest extent our main asset."[25] Nor was Jabotinsky the only one worried sick about loved ones abroad, especially as the Nazis swept across Europe in the spring of 1940. "Our souls are across the ocean," Kopelowicz wrote to a colleague in

London, "and our nerves, strong as they are, are nevertheless slightly shattered by this nerve-wracking speed of developments."[26]

Meetings of Jabotinsky's inner circle during the spring grew tense, even rancorous. Benzion Netanyahu pressed for an intensification of the Jewish army campaign, but Ben-Horin, Kopelowicz, and Benjamin Akzin—who had returned to the fold when Jabotinsky arrived in America—dismissed the proposal as impractical in view of the group's rapidly dwindling finances and their leader's black mood. Jabotinsky's despair was compounded when a Revisionist meeting targeting Russian Jewish immigrants attracted an audience of less than six hundred to a hall with a seating capacity of fifteen hundred. In the wake of that disappointment, the Zionist leader declared his refusal to give any further public lectures.[27]

Netanyahu had grown accustomed to working with a large, vibrant Revisionist movement in Palestine, a party stocked with talented and energetic speakers, writers, and activists. The Revisionist group in New York, by contrast, was "a shambles," in his view; its tired and pessimistic leaders had failed to capitalize on the initial enthusiasm generated by the first Jewish army rally. Frustrated by his colleagues' inaction, Netanyahu delivered an ultimatum: either revive the Jewish army campaign or focus immediately on an alternative issue—otherwise, he would return to Palestine on the first available boat.[28]

The next afternoon, Netanyahu learned by chance that Jabotinsky had agreed to speak at a forthcoming Betar memorial rally for Shlomo Ben-Yosef, an Irgun member hanged by the British in 1938 for his role in an unsuccessful retaliation raid against Arabs. Netanyahu made straight for Jabotinsky's hotel room, seeking an explanation for this apparent breach of the Zionist leader's recent vow to refrain from public speaking. Jabotinsky pleaded guilty; it was, he said, a previously scheduled engagement that he felt unable to cancel. Netanyahu sensed an opening. If Jabotinsky was willing to give one more public lecture, why not do so at a potentially influential Jewish army rally instead of an underpublicized Shlomo Ben-Yosef memorial? Betar leader Aaron Propes solved the problem by offering to turn the Ben-Yosef meeting into a Jewish army demonstration; Jabotinsky consented to speak.

Surprised by Jabotinsky's willingness to speak at the army rally, but doubtful that it could be organized in view of the lack of funds, the other Revisionist officials left the matter in Netanyahu's lap. He decided to gamble. Regarding the situation as "now or never" for militant Zionism in America,

Netanyahu reserved the Manhattan Center for June 19 and hired two publicists (one for the Yiddish media, one for the English) and a secretary on the promise of a deferred salary, to be paid for in ticket sales at three dollars a head. Others in the Revisionist hierarchy thought it preposterous that any significant number of tickets could be sold, but Netanyahu was banking on heightened community interest arising from events abroad—the Nazi invasion of Holland, Belgium, and France, which had begun on May 10; the constant reports of Jewish suffering in Europe; and the continuing British blockade of Jewish immigration to Palestine.[29]

As part of the rally strategy, Benjamin Akzin was dispatched to Washington, D.C., on a dual mission: secure a congressman or prominent foreign diplomat to speak at the rally, and establish the nucleus of a lobbying operation to advance the militant Zionist agenda in the halls of power. Akzin was not exactly the obvious choice for such a task; he was a brilliant political thinker, but with his professorial manner and occasionally squeaky voice, he was not the movement's most effective speaker. Still, the American wing of the Revisionists did not have a surplus of candidates for such work, and the dedicated core group of activists often assumed a variety of tasks outside their particular areas of expertise. At least Akzin's command of English would be an asset.

Akzin was not the first Zionist lobbyist in the nation's capital. In early 1939, ZOA president Solomon Goldman, with the backing of David Ben-Gurion, had convinced his colleagues in the U.S. Zionist leadership to set up an office in Washington, known as the American Zionist Bureau. Under the leadership of an activist rabbi, Isadore Breslau, the bureau scored some initial successes, such as persuading 192 members of the House of Representatives to sign a letter urging England to keep Palestine's doors open to Jewish refugees. Breslau's work was hampered, however, by a lack of funds, simmering conflicts between the rival Zionist groups that the bureau was supposed to represent in Washington, and increasing doubts among American Zionist leaders over how aggressive the movement should be.

With the eruption of war in Europe, many prominent American Zionists worried that vocal public activity on behalf of Palestine or European Jewry could provoke accusations that Jews were trying to drag the United States into overseas conflicts. This was a familiar dilemma for established Jewish leaders, torn between concern for their brethren abroad and fear that speaking out would somehow jeopardize American Jewry. Jabotinsky and his delegation, as foreign nationals who were only briefly sojourning in the United States, gave short shrift to acculturated American Jews' concerns about non-Jewish opinion, and viewed the shutdown of Palestine immigration and the plight of Europe's Jews as emergencies that should override all other worries.

American Zionist leaders soon lost interest in Breslau's Washington lobbying eruption; by mid-1940 it was sputtering, and by the end of 1940 it was officially shut down.[30] Akzin and the Revisionists hoped to move into the vacuum that the mainstream Zionists left behind.

Akzin boarded a Washington-bound train on the evening of May 4, intending to stay in the capital for "at least a month" to establish a "systematic watching and working post" that would help "put the Jewish question on the map of the world."[31] He brought a specific agenda to Washington: "to draw the attention of the makers of policy and of public opinion to the 'forgotten' Jewish angle of the war"—that is, the need to create a Jewish army to fight in the war, and the need for mass European Jewish immigration to Palestine.[32] The Revisionists correctly perceived that the United States was replacing Great Britain as the major world power and that the position of the American government on Zionist matters could force changes in Britain's Palestine policy. Akzin's contacts with Roosevelt administration officials were intended "to win sympathy which could eventually be advantageously utilized in our dealings with London."[33]

The complexities of Washington politics and society might have sufficed to bewilder a newcomer such as Akzin, but as he quickly discovered, the prevailing isolationist mood made progress particularly slow. A lobby that could be perceived as dragging America toward an unwanted foreign conflict would not quickly attract sympathy. "If you expect from me rapid and dramatic results, you'll be disappointed," he cautioned his NZOA colleagues, who anxiously awaited news of his expected political conquests. "All I can do, is gradually to get our ideas into them. This can be done, provided we have the means to keep in touch with them."[34]

Akzin was a devoted and seemingly tireless lobbyist. A glance at his daily appointments calendar for his second Friday in Washington reveals a veritable whirlwind of activity: a meeting with a State Department official at 10 A.M. and another at 11, the Czech ambassador at 12 noon, then over to the Latvian Legation for lunch at 1 P.M., back to the State Department at 4, space reserved in the midafternoon and early evening for a possible session with the Irish ambassador, and then off to catch a train to New York for a weekend of tending to personal business before returning to the nation's capital late Sunday night. An average day in Washington for Akzin usually also included one or two meetings with journalists and some time spent cultivating a social contact that might later lead to introductions to political figures.

The Jews with whom Akzin met during his first weeks in Washington were the most resistant to his Jewish army plan. He sarcastically referred to them as members of the "Society for Trembling Jews" because of their fear that the project would be seen as an attempt to enlist American Jews in a foreign cause and would thereby ignite "dual loyalty" accusations.[35] Representative Leo Sacks, a Jewish congressman from Pennsylvania, dismissed the Jewish army proposal out of hand. Akzin's meeting with Eugene Meyer, publisher of the *Washington Post,* was likewise "an absolute and unmitigated flop." Akzin soon became accustomed to the phenomenon of finding more sympathy for his views among non-Jews than among Jews. Of a Washington, D.C., appellate judge to whom he had presented his Jewish army arguments, Akzin wrote to his colleagues, "He is as gentile as you make them, and hence very sympathetic." Eventually Akzin formulated a line of argumentation to specifically address Jewish fears of anti-Semitism: since the Jews were worried about being accused of trying to drag America into Europe's war, Akzin asserted, the creation of a force of Jews who would fight could "offset the whispering campaign about this being a war in the interest of Jews, with Jews pushing everybody into it and not fighting themselves." He "tried it out first" on B'nai B'rith president Henry Monsky, "and it proved a 200% success," although Monsky kept his sympathy private. In any event, Akzin assured his colleagues in New York, Jewish support would be forthcoming once he managed to secure the Allies' endorsement. "Jews being what they are, if the idea has been *gutgeheissen* [approved] by the British they will flock to it."[36]

Meanwhile, events abroad gave the Revisionists some reason for hope. A government crisis in London, triggered by the German invasion of France, Belgium, and Holland, resulted in the replacement of Prime Minister Neville Chamberlain by Winston Churchill. "There are chances for better understanding with the new government," Ben-Horin exulted, noting that many of the new cabinet ministers were known to be pro-Zionist, particularly Duff Cooper, the new minister of information, who had previously written to NZO headquarters in London that he "fully endorses [the Jewish] army plans."[37] To the news from London, the NZOA leaders added an overly optimistic interpretation of Akzin's progress: "American statesmen and politicians were helpful and sympathetic" is how Kopelowicz characterized Akzin's early meetings, in a letter to his London colleagues. They came to the confident conclusion that their proposals "will soon become a public issue in the American press" and would thereby "put the Jewish problem on the map, on a wide scale."[38] Hoping to speed up the process, the NZOA dispatched Elias Ginsburg to Canada to sound out the Ottawa government on the possibility of establishing the Jewish army's training camps on Canadian soil so as to avoid infringing on American neutrality laws. Meanwhile, NZO operatives in London were peppering the new cabinet ministers with detailed memoranda urging a Jewish army. NZO cables to the New York group urged them to make a gesture that would arouse public interest in the scheme, such as offering to put a Jewish air force unit at England's immediate disposal.[39]

While the NZOA was waiting for further word from Akzin, he was finding during his initial lobbying effort that sympathy and influence do not always go hand in hand. Those among the Washington diplomatic corps who sympathized with the Revisionist agenda were not necessarily in a position to make a real difference. Irish ambassador Robert Brennan longed for Irish independence from England just as the Jews hoped for a Jewish Palestine independent of the British. "We share the same dislike and this created a strong mutual bond," Akzin found. Merchant Mahoney, chargé d'affaires at the Canadian Legation, was lukewarm at first, then "became frightened" when Akzin raised the specter of postwar European Jewish immigration to Canada; by the end of their talk, Mahoney was expressing sympathy for the Revisionist concept of mass Jewish immigration to Palestine.[40]

Eastern European diplomats were especially sympathetic. Nations that were occupied by, at war with, or threatened by the Nazis and uncomfortable with the size of their own Jewish populations were, not surprisingly, delighted at Revisionist plans to remove Jews from their countries and create an army that would aid their war effort. Officials at the Czech, Lithuanian, and Latvian Embassies were sympathetic and offered to pass on their views to the British; the Latvian ambassador even gave Akzin tips on which diplomats were likely to be receptive to his message and how best to approach them.[41] The Poles were supportive, although they became distressed in early May when Stephen Wise publicly criticized the Polish government for encouraging talk of a "mass evacuation" of Polish Jewry. Wise regarded the notion as a euphemism for violent expulsion and feared it would be cited by other countries as a precedent for the ejection of their own Jewish residents.[42] Akzin countered by telling his interlocutors at the Polish Embassy that Wise's statement was "proof that we are the only realistic group in Jewry."[43]

Isolationists in Congress likewise found it easier to understand the Revisionists than more liberal Jewish leaders. Senators Burton K. Wheeler (D-Idaho) and Gerald P. Nye (D-North Dakota), whose extreme isolationism and anti-foreigner sentiment made them anathema to mainstream Jewish leaders, seemed open to Akzin's arguments. "I set [Wheeler] thinking along the road that if he doesn't want us here, he must find for us a State somewhere," Akzin reported.[44] Nye even agreed to author an essay for the June 20, 1940, issue of Akzin's *American Jewish Chronicle*. It was not quite what *Chronicle* subscribers were accustomed to reading: Nye made the case for continuing tight U.S. immigration restrictions and keeping America out of the European conflict, although he also criticized Britain for breaking the pro-Zionist promises it made in the Balfour Declaration. Still, Akzin saw it in context: this was, after all, just the beginning of a relationship between militant Zionists and congressional isolationists, and beginnings are often rocky.[45]

For Akzin, the going was especially tough where it mattered most—among Roosevelt administration officials and British diplomats. State Department refugee affairs counselor Herbert Pell was cordial when Akzin called on him in early May, but he offered no specific support for the Revisionists' mass immigration plan. The European allies regard "shifting of populations [as] one of the methods of Hitlerism against which they fight," Pell noted. Certainly President Roosevelt disagreed, Pell said, but the Allies would not be budged from their stance. Still, Pell was cordial, even hospitable. He met Akzin repeatedly during the ensuing months and arranged for him to confer with other middle-level State Department officials, such as Herbert Feis (economic adviser to the secretary of state) and James Dunn (political adviser on European affairs).[46]

Akzin's first meeting with a British diplomat did not go well. Angus Malcolm, the British Embassy's secretary "in charge of the Jewish question," was "smiling and with friendliness oozing out of him put all obstacles in the way of Zionism."[47] Malcolm's attitude accurately reflected the prevailing view in British government circles, that acquiescence to Zionist demands such as mass immigration and the establishment of an armed force would harm London's relations with the Arab world—relations it was particularly keen on sustaining during wartime.

Unwilling to take "no" for an answer—even a "smiling" no—the persistent Akzin kept after the British Embassy staff until he finally secured a May 28 meeting with the ambassador, Lord Lothian. Akzin arrived at the embassy just hours after Belgium's surrender to Germany, and in the midst of the dramatic evacuation of over 300,000 British and French troops from Dunkirk. In view of the latest battlefield developments, Akzin opted to cast aside his previous caution and forcefully press the case for the creation of a Jewish army. Lothian listened with interest to Akzin's detailed exposition of the advantages to London of having a Jewish army fighting by its side. Although Lothian did not explicitly embrace the proposal, Akzin took it as a good sign when the ambassador referred him to an attaché to discuss some of the technical details involved in organizing a military force.[48]

The breakthrough came on June 5. Akzin was unexpectedly summoned to the Polish Embassy, where the ambassador, Count Jerzy Potocki, announced the good news: Lothian had told him that he supported the Revisionists' army plan and intended to cable London accordingly. The fact that Potocki and Lothian had also decided to decline the invitation to speak at the rally, "in view of the delicate neutrality situation," was a minor disappointment, entirely overshadowed by the blockbuster news that this senior British diplomat had agreed to promote the Jewish army scheme. Three days later, Lothian met with another Revisionist emissary, the just-arrived Lieutenant Colonel John Henry Patterson, famed British lion hunter, soldier, and commander of Jabotinsky's World War I Jewish Legion. Patterson came away from the meeting optimistic that Lothian was on their side.[49]

Lothian's apparent endorsement was all the more heartening in view of the latest disappointing news from NZO-London: replying to the Revisionists' inquiries about the position of the new government concerning a Jewish army, Prime Minister Churchill had dismissed the scheme as unfeasible and refused to meet with an NZO delegation to discuss it any further. At the same time, a senior aide to Information Minister Duff Cooper—presumably the leading Jewish army booster in the cabinet—suddenly insisted that the matter was not in his ministry's jurisdiction, and shunted it off to the Foreign Office.[50]

With Lothian on their side, the NZOA saw no reason to admit defeat. Who was to say that the prime minister's letter was final? Perhaps Lothian's influence would change his mind. On June 11, Akzin reported confirmation that Lothian had sent a cable to London endorsing the army plan. Akzin also revealed another powerful convert: Henry Monsky, president of the international Jewish social service organization B'nai B'rith, had privately declared his support for the army project. Three days later, there was more good news: Akzin had received a letter from the British Embassy saying that the ambassador had instructed the British consul general in New York to attend the meeting at Manhattan Center as "a sign of British appreciation of the Jewish offer."[51]

In New York, meanwhile, the lead-up to the June 19 army rally was gaining steam. Lothian met Jabotinsky in New York for a friendly luncheon on June 12 and promised to continue lobbying the cabinet on behalf of the army plan. Three days later, Jabotinsky held a press conference to discuss the rally and unveil Lieutenant Colonel Patterson as one of the speakers. The response of the media was "exceptionally encouraging," in the view of Jabotinsky's aides. The press conference with Patterson was attended by "all the big American and Canadian papers," resulting in "lengthy stories and photos in almost all the dailies," as well as an invitation to Jabotinsky and Patterson to take part in a broadcast to sixty-seven stations nationwide. "American opinion literally seething Jewish Army plan," the two cabled Churchill after the press conference; "Urge you to clinch matters by sanctioning [the army plan]." Kopelowicz could barely contain his excitement. The widespread media coverage, Lothian's embrace, and the "hundreds of cables, letters, and calls pouring in daily" to NZOA headquarters in support of the army plan—many of them personally volunteering to serve—was "creating a feeling of Messianic times," Kopelowicz telegrammed his London colleagues.[52]

A last-minute barrage of criticism and interference by mainstream Zionist leaders took some of the wind out of the NZOA's sails. A report from the New York Revisionists to London read: "When the Yahudim [wealthy, acculturated German-born Jews] and the O.Z.O. ["Old Zionist Organization," i.e., the established American Zionists] crowd saw [the NZOA's progress], they got busy at once and started sabotaging us." The former U.S. ambassador to Germany, James W. Gerard, agreed to speak at the rally— then backed down when his "Jewish friends" advised him to withdraw. Then the British consul general, who had been instructed by Lothian to attend, informed Akzin that he would not be there. After a delegation of mainstream Zionist leaders, led by Stephen Wise, visited Lothian on June 18 to urge him to stay away from the Revisionists, the ambassador decided to refrain from even sending greetings to the rally.[53]

A major reason for the Zionist leaders' plea to Lothian was their anxiety that the Revisionists were usurping their position as the spokesmen for American Zionism. "Stephen Wise will not tolerate any other Jewish organization working for Palestine and stealing honors and publicity from," the Revisionists complained.[54] Their barbed accusation seems to have contained a kernel of truth. Although World Zionist Organization president

Chaim Weizmann had called for the mobilization of Jewish armed divisions to defend Palestine against a possible Nazi invasion, the Revisionists had seized the issue by calling for a full-fledged Jewish army to fight in Europe as well as the Middle East, and dramatizing their position with colorful rallies and advertisements. Public endorsement of the Revisionist effort by the British ambassador would give the Jabotinskyites an added measure of credibility in their pursuit of grassroots Jewish support.

An additional concern of Dr. Wise and his colleagues was that the creation of an international Jewish army would provoke questions about whether Jews were loyal to the Jewish army or the armed forces of the United States. The proliferation of anti-Semitic "war-mongering" charges against the American Jewish community during the 1930s had Jewish leaders on edge. *Congress Weekly,* the organ of Wise's American Jewish Congress, openly worried that non-Jews would think "that the Jewish army is intended to be composed of Jewish citizens in America, thus raising questions which did not exist of the loyalty of Jews to their country."[55] The ZOA journal *New Palestine* likewise feared that any hints of American Jews joining a Jewish army would be "mischievous in their effect on the status of American Jews."[56] Thus the delegates who entreated Lord Lothian emphasized to reporters afterward that "American Jews would fight only when called upon to do so by their own country."[57] The British Foreign Office, hoping to exploit such American Jewish fears, at one point urged the British Embassy in Washington to circulate "the idea that the formation of a Jewish army might be contrary to American tradition."[58]

Breslau's own private account of the meeting with Lothian highlighted the Jewish leaders' concerns about "dual loyalty" accusations: "On Jabo's activities, we pointed out the danger of implicit Embassy support. . . . It would only throw into question loyalty of American Jews. Already in the press, American Jews because of Jabo's activities being called cold belligerents."[59] But the more limited army envisioned by Weizmann, Wise, and Breslau—a Jewish division of the British army based in Palestine to defend the Holy Land against an Axis invasion—found no greater sympathy at the White House than the militants' broader proposal for a full-fledged army that would fight in Europe as well as Palestine. President Roosevelt made it clear to Wise that Washington would defer to the British on the army question since a Jewish army might anger the Arabs and, after all, "in their Near Eastern campaign, the British must of necessity have the support of not only the Jews in Palestine, but also of a far greater number of Arabs in Transjordan, Sa'udi Arabia, and in the northern Arab states."[60]

The absence of any sign of official British sympathy was a blow to the Revisionists' rally, but the event was successful in other respects. An audience of over 5,000 jammed into the meeting hall (normal seating capacity: 4,600), including some 500 tickets sold on the evening of the rally. Neither the hot weather, the entrance fees, nor left-wing Zionist leafleteers branding the Revisionists "Mussolini's buddies" deterred the audience. Jabotinsky and Patterson delivered passionate speeches, and messages of endorsement from Czech consul general Karel Hudec, U.S. senators Claude Pepper (of Florida) and Frederick Coudert, Jr. (of New York), Polish consul general Sylwester Gruszka, and Yale University president Charles Seymour were read aloud.[61]

The excitement from the rally did not soon subside. Widespread media coverage helped spread the Jewish army message far beyond New York. Offers to serve in the prospective army flooded the NZOA offices from— among others—Jewish veterans of World War I, European refugees, idealistic young Zionists, doctors volunteering for the army's medical corps, and pilots ready to man the first Jewish air squadron in history. The Revisionist leaders, dumbfounded but delighted at young Netanyahu's successful initiative, determined to press ahead with the army campaign. Now they were convinced that if they could just secure a British statement of approval, "it would unchain a tremendous mass movement" among Diaspora Jews.[62]

The latest news from Canada gave the Revisionists additional reason for optimism. Two days after the rally, NZOA emissary Elias Ginsburg persuaded H. L. Keenleyside of the Canadian Ministry of External Affairs to approve the establishment of "transit training camps" where Jewish army recruits would receive temporary training before departing for the European battlefront. While reluctant to offer England unsolicited advice on the topic, Keenleyside promised Ginsburg that his government would endorse the army if asked by London for its view. Meanwhile, in Washington, Akzin convinced the head of the Polish government-in-exile, General Wladislaw Sikorski, to press the British for a Jewish army. And the NZO lobbyists in London appeared to be on the verge of a breakthrough when the Labor Party leader and Lord Privy Seal, Clement Attlee, told them he supported the army plan and would recommend it to the cabinet. Their hopes were soon dashed; in mid-July, Prime Minister Churchill reiterated his earlier rejection of the scheme. The NZOA campaign seemed to have reached an insurmountable roadblock. Stymied by England's refusal to consider the army plan, Akzin accepted a summer teaching offer at the City

College of New York, restricting his Washington visits to one day each week while the Revisionist leadership pondered its next move.[63]

It had been a whirlwind two months for Benjamin Akzin as militant Zionism's lobbyist in Washington. From the endorsement by the British ambassador to his sudden retreat at the insistence of the Zionist leadership, from the supportive reception by isolationist congressmen to the hostility of prominent Jews, and finally from the good news in Canada to the rejection by the government in London, Akzin's stay in the capital was an emotional roller-coaster ride. While he could not claim any specific diplomatic triumphs, Akzin had succeeded in establishing a militant Zionist presence in Washington for the first time. One step ahead of the mainstream Zionist movement in this respect, the Revisionists had recognized the need to present their case in a forceful and continuous manner in the corridors of power. Their efforts in 1940 would help pave the way for crucial lobbying efforts to rescue Jews from the Holocaust in the years ahead.

In the spring of 1940, at Benzion Netanyahu's behest, NZOA headquarters in New York launched a new organization, "Sponsors of the Jewish Army." It would be a vehicle for propaganda, fund-raising, and registration of potential recruits in anticipation of the day that the army would actually be created. Three grassroots organizers were selected to be sent into the field in early August: Benzion Netanyahu to New England, Eliahu Ben-Horin to the Pittsburgh-Cleveland region, and Benzion Hebrony, another recently arrived Revisionist from Palestine, to Detroit and Chicago. A first national convention of the group was tentatively scheduled for late September.[64]

As the preparatory work for the army campaign reached a particularly hectic pace at the end of July, Jabotinsky decided to get away for the weekend by visiting a Betar camp in upstate Hunter, New York. As he arrived at the camp on Friday afternoon, August 3, he found hundreds of anxious Betar youths lining the road in anticipation of his visit. "When Jabotinsky visited the camp previously, as he walked past our line-up, he would repeatedly pause to greet and speak with a number of the campers," Betar activist Sim Rosenberg later recalled. "It was as if he felt a personal bond to each and every one of us." But it was different that Friday. "He walked past us slowly, pale and exhausted, without the strength to stop and talk. We all sensed that something was terribly wrong."[65] When he reached his room, Jabotinsky collapsed, the victim of a massive heart attack. Attempts to revive him were unsuccessful. "His was a great heart and a strong heart," one of his followers would later write, "but it was not strong enough to stand the strain of the eclipse of humanity in the world and of the petty bestiality of Jewish politics."[66]

Needless to say, Jabotinsky's followers were devastated by his passing. "Losing him was, for all of us, like losing our father," Yitshaq Ben-Ami wrote. "I felt orphaned."

> Fate had taken Jabotinsky from our people at the most crucial time in our history. The Nazis had starved and dislocated entire communities in Poland and central Europe and hundreds of thousands of Jews were already dead. Jabotinsky was the one leader who could have injected pride and courage in the Jews around the world; despite the opposition and indifference he encountered, he could have rallied thousands of peoples to halls in New York, Philadelphia, Chicago and Los Angeles, sounding the alarm and awakening America's conscience. He could have reached the White House and represented the Jewish people not just as another pleader but as an acclaimed national leader. Young Jews from all backgrounds would have rejected their country's isolationism and joined Jabotinsky's Jewish army.[67]

Perhaps; but it was not to be. Instead, Jabotinsky's followers were left alone to carry the mantle of their fallen leader. But could they continue without him? At Jabotinsky's graveside, Kopelowicz remarked to Betar leader Aaron Propes, "In a few weeks we shall know who is buried here: Jabo or his work with him."[68]

The gargantuan problem that Jabotinsky's top aides immediately faced was how to keep their movement intact and energized in the wake of their devastating loss. The force of Jabotinsky's personality and the near-adoration that his followers felt for him had helped suppress most of the bickering and internal divisions beneath the surface in the Revisionist hierarchy. "As long as the *Nassi* [president] was with us he would bring us back to our senses every time we lost patience or courage, but at present the danger is very great indeed," Kopelowicz wrote.[69] The bleak news from the European front, including the collapse of France in June and the launching of Germany's air war against Britain on August 13, only intensified the mood of despair in the movement.

Benzion Netanyahu resigned from the NZOA shortly after Jabotinsky's death. Convinced that their cause was hopeless without the father of Revisionist Zionism and troubled at his NZOA colleagues' lack of enthusiasm for the Jewish army campaign, Netanyahu turned to freelance journalism, writing articles—sometimes under his own name, sometimes under the pseudonym "Nitay" that he had used years earlier, in Palestine—for the Yiddish weekly *Dos Yiddishe Folke,* the U.S. Hebrew-language *Bitzaron,* the American Jewish Congress journal *Congress Monthly,* and the ZOA monthly *New Palestine* (thanks to his Emanuel Neumann connection).[70]

At the same time, Jabotinsky's absence paved the way for long-simmering rivalries and personality differences to reemerge in the ranks of militant Zionism. Instead of appointing a successor to Jabotinsky, the NZOA leadership declared that New York would henceforth serve as the movement's interim world headquarters, with Akzin, Ben-Horin, and veteran Revisionist activist Dr. Stefan Klinger at the center of power. Kopelowicz, ill with heart problems, was unable to play a role; Ginsburg would remain in Canada. This plan may have been logical in view of the hazardous war situation in England and the newfound prominence of the American Revisionists, but it infuriated the British NZO leadership nonetheless. They were not calmed by Akzin's assurances that the concentration of power in New York was only temporary. The English Revisionists argued vehemently, but vainly, against New York's decision to reduce their branch to a small-budget lobbying and information office.[71]

In addition to the tension between the New York and London Revisionists, a split in the ranks was also emerging within the New York group itself. The Irgun Zvai Leumi emissaries who followed Jabotinsky to the United States, Hillel Kook and Alexander Rafaeli, never felt entirely comfortable working with the NZOA, just as the Irgun leadership in Palestine and Europe had become estranged from the Revisionist Party in recent years. Kook and Rafaeli remained on the periphery of NZOA activity, preferring the company of Yitshaq Ben-Ami and those Revisionists who were involved in Ben-Ami's American Friends of a Jewish Palestine. After Jabotinsky's death, the restructuring of the New York Revisionist leadership relegated Kook to a relatively minor role in the movement, further widening the rift between the Irgun group and the NZOA leaders. Jabotinsky's passing "severed our last links with traditional Zionism," Ben-Ami later recalled.[72] By the end of 1940, Kook, Rafaeli, Ben-Ami, and a handful of other key AFJP activists formally broke from the NZOA.

The Revisionists had also recently lost Rabbi Louis Newman, although for different reasons. In the wake of the 1939 British White Paper, Newman had increasingly used his pulpit as a forum to blast England's Palestine rule. "Munich and Palestine," he declared, were "shameful blemishes" on the

British record; London's Middle East policies were evidence of "her infirmity and unreliability."[73] Newman's strong words discomfited more than a few of his thoroughly acculturated—and in many cases, anti-Zionist—Reform congregants at Temple Rodeph Shalom. When his Revisionist colleagues needed to speak with him, Newman had to arrange to meet them on a bench in nearby Central Park rather than at the synagogue, where he knew they were not wanted. Eventually, a group of angry board members presented Newman with a stark ultimatum: leave the NZOA or leave Rodeph Shalom. Financially strapped and with no alternative job offers in sight, Newman stepped down from the NZOA leadership.[74]

Unity and revitalization were the goals of a New York conference of senior Revisionists from North and South America at the end of December 1940, but in some ways the gathering accomplished quite the opposite. Tensions flared as delegates hurled accusations at one another over the movement's inactivity since the death of Jabotinsky. Even the official U.S. Revisionist periodical *Zionews*, which sought to portray the convention in the most positive terms, could not help but acknowledge that during the first day's general debate, "Most of the speakers criticize[d] the outgoing Administration and some also sen[t] their arrows at Betar and the Presidency."[75] The conference's election of a new ruling Administrative Committee, replacing its London predecessor, further aggravated the rift between the American and British branches. By February, the London Revisionists had severed all communications with the New York group.[76] The South African NZO, the third-largest Revisionist group outside Europe and Palestine, was likewise peeved at the Americans' unilateral consolidation of power.

All of these problems were unceremoniously dumped in the laps of the NZOA's newly elected president, veteran activist Elias Ginsburg, and the new chairman of its National Council, Colonel Morris Mendelsohn, a one-armed hero of the Spanish-American War. "After he gave one arm for the liberation of Cuba, he decided to devote his second arm, his brain and his soul to the liberation of the Jewish nation," *Zionews* announced.[77] Overwhelmed by the enormity of the task at hand, Ginsburg resigned less than two months later; Colonel Mendelsohn was on his own. For better or worse, Mendelsohn was worlds apart from the typical European-born Revisionist ideologue. "It very seldom happens that people 'qui sont deja arrivee,' politically, socially, or financially, come to us," *Zionews* noted. Individuals of renown were more likely to "go the easy way and subscribe to the mediocre organizations headed by all the prominent and publicised personalities." Not so Mendelsohn, who, in addition to his distinguished service in the Spanish-American War, had until recently served as national commander of the Jewish War Veterans. He joined the Jabotinskyites despite the fact that "there is so little we can offer in the way of public honours, and so much abuse is to be expected by anyone who steps into Revisionist boots."[78]

Mendelsohn assumed the leadership of the militant Zionist movement in America at a time of mounting anxiety at home and abroad. The German bombardment of England had stalled, but the spring brought Nazi invasions of Greece and Yugoslavia as well as General Rommel's advances in northern Africa. Jewry might soon face the terrifying specter of "Nazi columns marching into the streets of Tel-Aviv" and of Palestinian Arabs collaborating with the Nazis to "surpass anything known in the history of human bestiality," *Zionews* feared.[79] Perhaps a Jewish army could help prevent such a tragedy—but England still refused to assent to its establishment, and the Roosevelt administration, restrained by isolationist public opinion and unwilling to clash with its British ally, was not about to press the issue. Mendelsohn also had his hands full with the NZOA's internal difficulties. Not only did he face the problem of dealing with the movement's rebellious overseas branches, but during the winter of 1940–41 the financial health of the American Revisionists hit rock bottom. In December, Kopelowicz described their situation as one of "extremely acute poverty"; even four months later, Ben-Horin was telling his colleagues, "we are penniless and without prospects to speak of," and when Mendelsohn "needed ten dollars, he had to borrow it from the Nessiut [the office of the presidency], which is no less penniless."[80] They spent many a long evening at their favorite lower Manhattan haunt, Trotzky's Restaurant, sipping tea, chain smoking, and endlessly debating ways to keep the movement from total collapse. Lacking the funds to undertake substantive projects, Ben-Horin was reduced to passing off the previous year's "Jewish merchant marine" scheme to journalists as if it were new; the recycled story netted the Revisionists a sizable article in the *New York Herald Tribune* in March 1941, but it hardly did wonders for the movement's credibility among those in the know.[81]

The financial woes led to other problems, as well. Benjamin Akzin, dejected by the infighting and lack of funds, resigned in January 1941 and took a position in Washington, D.C., on the staff of the Library of Congress. In desperation, Benzion Hebrony, who had been in charge of the Tel Hai Fund, was hired as an "experimental" replacement for Akzin. The experiment soon ended in "complete failure," with critics blaming what they called Hebrony's abrasive manner. Four more months were lost in wrangling over possible candidates and scraping together money for a salary. Finally, in April 1941, Kopelowicz was hired part-time; they still lacked the funds to pay him full-time.[82]

The situation in the field was equally dismal. Absorbed by the struggles over succession and reorganization in the wake of Jabotinsky's death, the New York activists could not make the time to focus on the movement's national structure. NZOA chapters in other parts of the country rapidly crumbled. Guidance, even supplies of literature, from the New York headquarters was sparse. Correspondence between New York and its branches consisted largely of requests for financial aid from NZOA headquarters that simply could not be met.[83] For the first time, the New York Revisionists tasted the bitterness of being one-upped by the American Friends of a Jewish Palestine; an attempt to establish a Los Angeles branch of the NZOA stumbled largely because AFJP emissary Alexander Rafaeli preceded them to the West Coast. The local Jewish community was not big enough to support two separate Revisionist organizations.[84]

As spring blossomed, there were fresh signs of life in the NZOA. Joseph Beder, formerly a leader of Betar in the United States and the Revisionist movement in Palestine, returned from the Holy Land to become the NZOA's new full-time executive secretary. Eri Jabotinsky was released from prison in Palestine and promptly sailed to New York, where two thousand Revisionists cheered him at a public reception that became a political rally. The participation of the Belgian and Czech consuls and Greece's military attaché at the rally indicated that the inroads Benjamin Akzin made in the Washington diplomatic corps the previous year could still produce dividends. Akzin himself, despite his resignation, continued to take part in occasional leadership meetings and privately offered guidance on organizational matters. By summertime, the veteran European Revisionist activist and Jabotinsky confidante Dr. Joseph Schechtman arrived and was quickly made a member of the ruling inner circle. With his thick Russian accent and studious manner, Schechtman was every bit the stereotypical European refugee intellectual.[85]

Under Beder's direction, the Revisionists, despite their meager finances, significantly upgraded the quality of their propaganda. Ten thousand copies of the NZOA's "Why a Jewish Army?" pamphlet were distributed; other new literature appeared as well. *Zionews*, a twice-monthly NZOA newsletter that had been prepared on an office typewriter and mimeographed, was upgraded with professional typesetting and printing. Phonograph records of Jabotinsky's speeches, in English, Yiddish, and Hebrew, were produced for sale. "Our main task has been in the field of public enlightenment and political education," Mendelsohn explained in a letter to potential supporters. "Ignorance of the Zionist problems and the situation in Palestine reigned and still reigns supreme among the Jewish and even Zionist masses in this country. We had to bring the facts home and to interpret them properly." At the same time, the NZOA launched a series of weekly public meetings on Sundays in Manhattan, typically drawing audiences of one hundred or more for discussions and lectures on Zionist topics. And with the advent of warm spring weather, open-air rallies were staged in various parts of the city.[86]

One of the NZOA's most impressive, if short-lived, projects that year was its ambitious Jewish Aviation League. On a frigid February afternoon in 1941, twenty-five uniformed Betarim were formally inducted into the league's "Jabotinsky Flying School" at the Rockaway Airport on Long Island. Master of ceremonies Aaron Propes implored the new cadets to be guided by their "obligations to those tens of thousands of Jews who have been plunged into concentration camps, to the millions of suffering Jews herded like slaves into ghettoes, to the thousands who have been mercilessly slaughtered and brutally massacred at the criminal hands of the barbarians." The young men were given basic aeronautical training throughout the spring, summer, and fall—without any substantial community backing, *Zionews* was quick to point out; "the scores of thousands of Jewish matrons who get wildly enthusiastic every time they are requested to knit woolens for the soldiers of any army fighting in the Sahara, did not deign to notice the existence of this worthy Jewish enterprise."

By August, the cadets had learned enough to fly overhead in military formation, and dip their wings in salute, during a *yahrzeit* assembly at Jabotinsky's grave. They were formally introduced to the press at a dramatic graduation ceremony in November. The new pilots marched in file past a group of saluting dignitaries that included, among others, Eri Jabotinsky; his mother; the widow of Zionist leader Max Nordau; and a leader of the patriotic "Minute Men of America" group. The ceremony netted generous local media coverage, featuring statements by students such as twenty-year-old Herman Juster of Brooklyn, who said he wanted to become a pilot in order "to do my bit to lick the dictator menace."[87] One of the graduates, Eugene Stein, was later twice decorated for "courage, coolness and skill" in shooting down German planes.[88]

Literature about the Jewish Aviation League made no mention of its

Revisionist connection; not many readers would have recognized its address as identical to that of NZOA headquarters. By stressing the project's patriotic implications and obscuring the political affiliations of its sponsors, the Revisionists were able to persuade thirteen congressmen and nine senators, as well as an assortment of Christian clergymen, journalists, and state officials, to serve on the league's "Sponsoring Committee."[89]

The Revisionists were beginning to realize that some of their ideas could be more effectively marketed under the rubric of other groups. Benzion Netanyahu, an advocate of this approach, later explained to a colleague that openly using the NZOA name meant having to "take a great deal of time to disprove and wipe out the false accusations with which our Zionist opponents have labelled us for almost twenty years. . . . It seems to me that the only effective method to break the propaganda blockade of Official Zionism would be the creation of American Front Organizations that would become the exponents of our ideals, undertake to support them actively, and finally draw many sympathizers and followers to our ranks."[90]

This philosophy guided Netanyahu's efforts, in the spring of 1941, to convince Hillel Kook and the other Irgun emissaries to create a front group for promoting the Jewish army cause. Kook, a dynamic and tireless activist, emerged as the natural leader of the Irgun delegation. "We accepted his suggestions as the next thing to commands," recalled Yitshaq Ben-Ami, a key member of Kook's inner circle. "Though we were on a civilian mission involving public relations and political activities, we still considered ourselves a unit of a liberation army, and we kept a strict hierarchal discipline within our ranks just as we had in Eretz-Israel."

> It was the ultimate source of our strength. Our attitude was the same as that of all nations in time of war—accept discipline or accept defeat. Not that everything went smoothly among us. We never lacked for arguments. We disagreed, sometimes vehemently, about policies, tactics, and specific courses of action. But eventually a consensus always emerged, and when it did, we all adhered to it regardless of whether or not it led to bruised egos. It enabled our small disciplined group to achieve the impact we eventually had.[91]

Already expecting that notoriety was just around the corner, Kook had adopted the alias "Peter Bergson" so that his controversial activities would not embarrass his family in Palestine, among them his uncle, Chief Rabbi

Avraham Yitzhak Kook. Samuel Merlin, an Irgun emissary who had recently arrived from Rumania, emerged as Bergson's right-hand man and chief propagandist. Although initially hesitant to embrace an issue he thought would meet with stiff British and Jewish resistance, Bergson relented when Netanyahu's efforts brought in a best-selling author, the Dutch expatriate Pierre van Paassen, as chairman of the army campaign. Kook was convinced that having a prominent non-Jew as chairman was the key to success.[92] Van Paassen's leadership would demonstrate to Washington and London that the army idea had significant support beyond the narrow confines of the American Jewish community.

Netanyahu then helped broker a truce between the Revisionists and the Bergson boys, resulting in a joint NZOA-AFJP rally that drew four thousand people to the Manhattan Center in June 1941. Ignoring an appeal by the Emergency Committee for Zionist Affairs to boycott the rally, Van Paassen delivered an impassioned keynote address, which Michigan congressman John Dingell later entered in the *Congressional Record*.[93] The success of the rally inspired Bergson to set aside the AFJP and establish the "Committee for a Jewish Army of Stateless and Palestinian Jews" in its place. The name was cumbersome, but the concept was precise: the Allies should establish a Jewish army, composed of European Jewish refugees and Jewish citizens of Palestine, that would help fend off a Nazi invasion of the Holy Land and undertake retaliatory raids against Axis targets in response to anti-Jewish atrocities.[94]

To get started, Bergson used Van Paassen's name to attract a host of prominent supporters. Each new celebrity endorsement in turn brought in others; during the early months, the committee was printing up new letterhead every four days. The VIPs included two leading theologians, Reinhold Niebuhr and Paul Tillich; a number of Hollywood stars, such as Eddie Cantor and Melvyn Douglas; the renowned journalist and playwright Ben Hecht, whose credits included such blockbusters as *Scarface* and *Wuthering Heights;* and a handful of U.S. senators and representatives. One of the most enthusiastic was Senator Claude Pepper of Florida, who agreed to address one of the first Jewish army meetings during a visit to California. When Bergson and Hecht went to pick up the senator at the Lakeview Country Club to take him to the meeting, they had to wait in the lobby while Pepper finished his dinner because of the club's prohibition against Jews in the dining room.[95] At their first major public rally, in Washington on December 4, 1941, the Jewish army campaigners read aloud messages of support not only from Senator Pepper but also from his colleagues Guy Gillette, Edwin Johnson, and Styles Bridges and, most significantly, Secretary of War Henry Stimson.[96]

The Japanese attack on Pearl Harbor three days later further galvanized the Jewish army activists. Now that America had shed its neutrality, Bergson's opponents could no longer claim that the project was an attempt to drag the United States into foreign wars. The Jewish army campaign could be seen as a patriotic endeavor, a way for Jews in Europe and Palestine to contribute to the American and Allied war effort. The Bergson boys were ready to shift into high gear.

5 • "Words Are the Most Effective Means of Political Warfare"

"JEWS FIGHT FOR THE RIGHT TO FIGHT" declared the headline of Bergson's full-page advertisement in the *New York Times* on January 5, 1942, employing a phrase coined by Netanyahu in one of his *Bitzaron* columns. The ad boasted 133 signatures, including 3 U.S. senators, 14 members of the House of Representatives, 11 rabbis, 5 Christian clergymen, and an assortment of well-known authors, journalists, and entertainers. Additional ads demanding a Jewish army would follow, in the *Times* and elsewhere, each generating enough contributions to sponsor the next.[1]

Jewish political advertising of this sort was an innovation. Jewish organizations usually resorted to newspaper ads only to announce specific events, and even then only in the Jewish press. The Bergson group was venturing into unknown territory, splashing a controversial political message across the pages of America's largest daily newspaper, where it would be read primarily by non-Jews—"just as you would advertise Chevrolet motor cars or Players cigarettes," Eri Jabotinsky marveled.[2]

Although newcomers to the United States, Bergson and Netanyahu had quickly grasped the most basic principle of American political advocacy: a controversial cause is not likely to be embraced by the White House or Congress unless it has first gained substantial public acceptance. The Jewish army issue had to be taken out of the back pages of the Yiddish press and brought to the attention of large numbers of Americans. The *New York Times* ad was a first important step in that direction, followed one month later by the introduction of a congressional resolution, authored by Representative Andrew L. Somers (D-Brooklyn), urging the creation of a Jewish army. That was another innovation for Jewish activists: seeking congressional action despite the opposition of the Roosevelt administration. The administration, anxious to avoid irritating the British, declined to support the Jewish army idea, although several officials, most prominently Secretary of War Henry Stimson, expressed their personal sympathy for the proposal.

Although the Somers army resolution never came to a vote, it fired a warning shot across the administration's bow: militant Zionists were ready to press their agenda on Capitol Hill, with or without the approval of the White House.

The *Times* ad and the Somers resolution ignited a public discussion, which the *Times* itself further fueled by publishing an editorial condemning the army proposal, to which its rival, *PM*, responded with an editorial heartily endorsing the army idea.[3] The top brass at the *Times* feared that talk of a "Jewish army" would arouse Gentile suspicions about Jewish separatism and nationalism. Taking the same point to an extreme, the *New Republic* would later editorialize that "the idea of putting the Jews into a separate army and making of all the Jews a separate people . . . is precisely what Hitler and Goebbels say."[4]

Representative Somers, Bergson's earliest and most enthusiastic supporter in Congress, was the son of a militant Irish nationalist and felt a natural kinship with Jewish opponents of England. The British Foreign Office derided him as "the less happy type of Irish-American Catholic demagogue."[5] Given England's troubles administering Ireland, the British were understandably jittery about the possibility of Irish Americans and Jewish Americans uniting against their common enemy. Internal British government correspondence during the 1940s made repeated reference to indications of Irish-American support for maximalist Zionism. In a typical expression of such concerns, a report sent to the British Embassy in Washington by a British consular official in New York who attended a Revisionist rally made much of the fact that one of the speakers, a U.S. army major, had "suspicions of an Irish accent."[6]

When the Bergson group decided, in 1941, to assign a full-time lobbyist to Capitol Hill, Congressman Somers volunteered the use of his office and secretarial staff. The man chosen for the mission was Rabbi Baruch Rabinowitz, who had recently resigned his Maryland pulpit to work full time for the Bergsonites: "Day after day I visited members of Congress of both Houses. I saw an average of six Congressmen a day, five days a week. I spent the days keeping my appointments and speaking with members of Congress. A good part of my nights I spent preparing speeches for those of them that agreed to deliver them."[7] Rabinowitz also delivered public lectures and radio addresses, "talked up" Bergson's issues with influential journalists, cultivated sympathizers among the international diplomatic corps, and supervised fund-raising activities.[8]

Mainstream Jewish leaders were of two minds with regard to the Jewish army activists. On the one hand, they were instinctively distrustful of any intrusion onto the American Jewish scene by previously unknown foreigners who were associated with a controversial minority faction in the Zionist movement. Thus, when visiting Labor Zionist chief David Ben-Gurion appealed to the American Zionist leadership, in mid-December 1941, to boycott the Bergsonites because of their Revisionist background, the Zionist leaders consented.[9]

Yet at the same time, many American Jewish leaders personally sympathized with at least some version of the Jewish army idea. Furthermore, the differences between the Bergson proposal and the more limited armed force advocated by the Jewish Agency were not substantial, nor could those differences be easily explained to the public. Since many of the attacks on the army idea assailed the entire concept of Jewish nationalism or Zionism, mainstream leaders often had little choice but to respond to the anti-army attacks. Stephen Wise's eighteen-hundred-word reply to the *Times* editorial, on behalf of the Emergency Committee for Zionist Affairs, offered a resounding defense of the Jewish army concept. No wonder the British Embassy in Washington reported to the Foreign Office in July 1942 that the Committee for a Jewish Army "is officially frowned upon by orthodox Zionists on accounts of its Revisionist connexions and objectives, but its activities naturally are not entirely unwelcome to them and they tend more and more to take up the Army cry."[10]

Another factor deterring mainstream Jewish leaders from publicly opposing the Committee for a Jewish Army was the leadership's perception that Bergson was winning widespread grassroots support in the Jewish community. As evidence of the Jewish army group's popularity mounted throughout 1941 and 1942, American Zionist attitudes toward the Bergsonites began to soften. Hadassah board member Bertha Schoolman was alone when she first proposed to her colleagues in January 1942 that in view of grassroots support for a Jewish army, the Zionist leadership should either cooperate with Bergson or "create a Jewish Army Committee of its own."[11] Yet at the next Hadassah board meeting, just two weeks later, several veteran Hadassah leaders praised the Bergson group for having "brought in new ideas and taken the initiative" and "acting quickly and well in this instance." Former Hadassah president Rose Halprin charged that the Jewish Army agitation "had come about because the Emergency Committee [for Zionist Affairs] did not work fast enough. . . . The public is stimulated on the question of the Jewish army and questions are being asked." The Hadassah leadership proceeded to pass a resolution urging the ECZA to seek a rapprochement with Bergson.[12] That same month, the ZOA Executive decided that "inasmuch as there seems to be a sentiment in the country in favor of a coming to terms with the Jewish Army Committee, and since the Jewish press in particular was pressing for unity and cooperation," the ZOA would seek a deal with Bergson.[13] Soon Nahum Goldmann of the World Jewish Congress, the international Jewish defense agency founded by Stephen Wise and Goldmann, who was one of the Revisionists' staunchest foes, was telling his colleagues that "in view of the growing strength of the Jewish Army Committee and the participation of many Zionists and important local persons in the public meetings and dinners held under its auspices," the ECZA should speak to Bergson's group "and try to amalgamate with it under certain conditions."[14]

Those conditions, however, proved onerous. In a series of quiet negotiations between the ECZA and the Jewish Army Committee, the ECZA insisted as a precondition to any merger that it be granted the right to appoint a majority of the army committee's board members. As a compromise, Bergson offered to allot 50 percent of the seats on a joint Committee of Policy to ECZA appointees, but he was not prepared to surrender total control. The peace talks fizzled.[15]

The Jewish army activists were not exactly brokenhearted over the failure of the negotiations. Unity with the Jewish establishment would have enabled them to enjoy the mainstream leadership's access to the centers of Washington political power, but it also might have entailed substantially watering down their agenda. Independence enabled the Bergson boys to remain true to their maximalist agenda and gain grassroots support by offering American Jews a concrete way to respond to the news of tragedies abroad. Throughout the previous summer and fall, stunned readers of the Jewish press learned of massacres of unprecedented dimensions in the Nazi-conquered parts of the western USSR, including a November 16, 1941, report by the Jewish Telegraphic Agency that fifty-two thousand Jews in Kiev had been "systematically and methodically put to death following the Nazi occupation." In February 1942, *Life* magazine ran a two-page photo spread documenting what it described as the "methodical massacre" of Polish Jewry.[16] Two days after *Life* hit the stands, a German submarine torpedoed the SS *Struma*, a refugee ship that was stranded in the Black Sea by England's refusal to permit passage to Palestine. All 769 passengers drowned. In the face of the ever-widening European catastrophe, it was no wonder that larger numbers of American Jews were attracted to the Bergsonite message of Jewish armed resistance.

These developments also had an impact on the mainstream Zionist groups. Shaken by the news of Nazi massacres in Europe and prodded by the visiting Labor Zionist leader David Ben-Gurion to adopt a more activist approach, the member-organizations of the Emergency Committee for Zionist Affairs convened an "Extraordinary Conference of American Zionists" at the Biltmore Hotel in New York City in May 1942. In language strikingly similar to what the Revisionists had been saying for years, the six hundred delegates adopted resolutions denouncing the 1939 British White Paper as "cruel and indefensible," urging "that Palestine be established as a Jewish Commonwealth," and endorsing the creation of "a Jewish military force fighting under its own flag" alongside the Allies. It was the first national Zionist gathering in the United States since Pearl Harbor, and represented a break from the cautious attitude that had enveloped American Zionists during the first months following America's entry into the war. The wording of the Biltmore resolutions constituted a clear triumph of Ben-Gurion's more activist line over the more conservative approach of Chaim Weizmann and his followers. In the months after the conference, the Biltmore resolutions became a sort of touchstone of Zionist commitment, with all of the major American Zionist organizations specifically pledging themselves to promote the Biltmore program.

The differences between the U.S. Revisionists and the Zionist mainstream were further blurred by Bergson's decision to avoid any direct public criticism of the British during the Jewish army campaign. The Jewish Army Committee's newspaper ads extolled the virtues of a Jewish fighting force and the contributions it might make to the Allied cause. The ads carefully refrained from challenging England's refusal to create an army or its ongoing blockade of Palestine. Bergson was hoping to attract a broad variety of supporters. He feared that attacks on Great Britain, an American ally fighting valiantly against the Nazis, might alienate potential backers. He also believed that his more moderate approach stood a better chance of influencing British officials.

The British, for their part, were indeed concerned that Bergson's approach was gaining supporters. Lord Halifax, who in 1941 replaced Lord Lothian as ambassador in Washington, was becoming increasingly irritated by the ability of the "nucleus of extreme revisionist Zionists" to "conceal [themselves] from view by the outer rim of misguided humanitarians of every stripe and colour who form the bulk of the membership of the movement." The Jewish army campaign "appeals to the average American, Jew and Gentile alike, with the apparently simple and moving plea that many thousands of Jews, anxious to fight and die in the war against Hitler, are being denied that elementary right by His Majesty's Government." Bergson's line resonated among Americans who already harbored negative feelings about England, Halifax reported to Foreign Minister Anthony Eden, and "I need not remind you that anti-British grievances still find fertile soil in American public opinion." While Bergson's supporters "may be ignorant of the specific facts of the case [they] are prepared to believe the general thesis that His Majesty's Government is liable to deal unfairly with minority groups, be they Indians, Jews or anyone else, who are regarded as an obstacle to some open or secret Imperialist scheme being hatched in London at a given moment."[17]

As a result, the campaign "has thus far been received sympathetically both by the American press in general and by the large collection of eminent Americans whom it has managed to persuade to sign its proclamations," Halifax complained to Foreign Minister Eden. "Such opposition as it has stirred up against itself has not been sufficient to offset its general progress." And things were likely to get worse. "The impressive list of names" on Bergson's advertisements "and the cumulative effect of the repetition of such manifestos over a period of many months, is bound to sink in."[18] The State Department, too, was annoyed by the large number of congressmen and other VIPs signing the Jewish army broadsides. Wallace Murray, one of the State Department's central Mideast policy makers, feared that the "agitation for the formation of a Jewish army" was already having an "alarming effect" by arousing anti-American feeling in the Arab world. Still, it was thought in the State Department that granting the Bergsonites a meeting with the Foreign Office or Colonial Office might slow down their momentum. But the British would have none of that; giving the Bergson group an audience would mean publicly recognizing its significance or legitimacy.[19]

At the same time, Bergson's reluctance to criticize the British cost him the support of one of his most important partners. Benzion Netanyahu perceived England as weak and desperate, susceptible to Jewish pressure if it feared losing American public opinion. He regarded the Bergson line as an unnecessary and inappropriate deviation from the principles of militant Zionism. Bergson and his loyalists rejected such criticism, insisting that their approach was a legitimate tactic that was completely consistent with the principles of Jabotinsky. "Merlin often solved our internal debates by saying, 'If Jabotinsky were alive, he would do it this way.' . . . The teacher was not with us, but his teachings were," according to Ben-Ami.[20] Netanyahu believed that Bergson and company were misinterpreting Jabotinsky's teachings, and he defiantly provoked Bergson's ire by openly criticizing the British in his own speeches at Jewish army rallies. At Jewish Army Committee board meetings, however, Bergson's approach consistently won out over Netanyahu's. Finally, in frustration, Netanyahu resigned from the Jewish army group in the spring of 1942.

Netanyahu had no way of knowing that the British themselves interpreted even Bergson's moderate approach as an attack on His Majesty's Government's Palestine policy as well. Halifax warned Eden that the Jewish army campaign was becoming "a source of Anglo-American irritation." He worried—and told Eden—that the endorsement of the Jewish army effort by so many "Congressmen, bishops, generals and serving officials [of the U.S. government]" was "bound to suggest to the public that the Palestine policy of His Majesty's Government is condemned or at any rate regarded with doubt by a great many eminent Americans in every sphere of public life." The embassy even appealed—unsuccessfully—to U.S. undersecretary of state Sumner Welles to take action against American government employees who signed Bergson's ads.[21]

The loss of Netanyahu was quickly overshadowed by the deepening involvement of Bergson's prize "catch," Ben Hecht. "Our mission in the United States would not have attained the scope and intensity it did if not for Hecht's gifted pen," Yitshaq Ben-Ami later recalled. "He had a compassionate heart, covered up by a short temper, a brutal frankness, and an acid tongue. Once he decided right from wrong on any issue, he mobilized all his faculties to fight for his beliefs with righteous fury."[22] Hecht's first meeting with Bergson was a memorable event for both men. "I was an honest writer who was walking down the street one day when he bumped into history," Hecht recalled. A thoroughly assimilated Jew whose ethnic consciousness had been roused by the ravages of Nazism, Hecht wrote a column for *PM* in April 1941 that caught Bergson's eye. In it, Hecht blasted prominent American Jews who hesitated to speak out against the Nazi persecutions for fear of calling attention to their Jewishness. Bergson immediately called for an appointment. They met at Hecht's favorite hangout, the Twenty One Club in Manhattan. The "tall, sunburned" Jeremiah Halperin, "who had recently created a Hebrew Navy for the nonexisting Hebrew Republic of Palestine," came along with the man with the "small blonde mustache, an English accent and a voice inclined to squeak under excitement. He was Peter Bergson of Warsaw, London and Jerusalem."[23] Hecht and Bergson were a perfect match from the start. Both men were fired by a determination to shatter the image of the Jew as weakling, and replace it with the image of Jew as soldier. Hecht's flair for catchy slogans and eye-grabbing headlines precisely suited the Bergson activists' new emphasis on newspaper ads as the medium for communicating their message to the world.

As soon as the Revisionists heard that Netanyahu had left the Committee for a Jewish Army, they were knocking at his door. By early 1942, the NZOA was, in Colonel Mendelsohn's words, "deteriorating in influence and strength, almost to [the] vanishing point."[24] The financial situation was so bleak that "there was not even enough to pay the girl's wages," Mendelsohn told a colleague, referring to the NZOA's lone secretary.[25] Soon the lack of funds forced their office to close down altogether. When board member Samuel Katz showed up on Netanyahu's doorstep one May evening, it was to ask him to, in effect, resurrect the dead. At first glance, the offer was hardly tempting: he would be assuming leadership of an organization with no office, no staff, and no funds. On the other hand, he was accustomed to poverty; despite its initial propaganda successes, the Committee for a Jewish Army had been constantly "on the verge of bankruptcy" during its early months. More often than not, lunch was a nickel bag of peanuts and dinner was the hors d'oeuvres at that night's parlor meeting.[26] "I remember coming to the office early one morning," Ben-Ami later wrote, "and finding Arieh Ben-Eliezer there—he had arrived from out of town the day before and was too embarrassed to mention to the secretary that he had no money for a hotel room. He had slept on a desk."[27]

To make matters worse for Netanyahu, the Revisionist ranks had been severely depleted during his absence. Kopelowicz had left; so had Akzin. Ben-Horin had returned from a long stay in South Africa—surviving an injury suffered on the way home when his ship was torpedoed by a German submarine in the Caribbean—but he resigned as editor of *Zionews* in June in order to pursue freelance journalism full time. If *Zionews* were to continue, the burden of editing the journal would be upon Netanyahu's shoulders alone. The situation was, in short, dismal. There were only two reasons for Netanyahu to return. First, he was promised a free hand in deciding what should be on the U.S. Revisionist agenda and how it should be implemented. Second, Netanyahu understood that he was the NZOA's last hope; if he did not take the job, Jabotinsky's movement in America would be dead, possibly forever. He took the job.[28]

Back in June 1940, Netanyahu had gambled on the first Jewish army rally, betting the house on the hope that he could sell enough tickets to cover the rally's costs. He won that bet. Two years later, he was ready to gamble again. Renting an office and installing a telephone required no advance payments; they were quickly secured. A secretary was found who was willing to begin work on the promise of a deferred salary. A printer agreed to extend temporary credit to publish the first glossy, professionally designed issue of the new *Zionews*. Ads in the journal, parlor meetings, and fund-raising forays by NZOA board members netted barely enough revenue to keep the organization alive during Netanyahu's first grueling months as executive director. November 17 was chosen as the date for the revived NZOA's first major public rally. The theme: a demand that the Jewish people be granted recognition by the Allies as a partner in the war against Hitler and in postwar deliberations.

In the months preceding the rally, Netanyahu revived the Revisionist lobby in Washington, traveling to the capital twice each month, for several days at a time, to explain the NZOA's perspective and—especially—to secure two senators, one Democrat and one Republican, to speak at the November rally. Bipartisan support would boost the credibility of their cause.[29]

Netanyahu set his sights first on Senator Elbert Thomas of Utah, a devout Mormon. Instinctively sympathetic to the Jews as the people of the Bible ("Your heroes are my heroes," he would tell Netanyahu), Thomas became attracted to the Zionist cause after an emotional visit to Palestine in 1912. Although a Democrat, he criticized the Roosevelt administration's tight immigration restrictions during the 1930s. Netanyahu had also read about Thomas's April 1942 speech to the National Labor Committee in New York, in which the senator declared that the administration had a "responsibility to the Jews to support the establishment of the Jewish state."[30] Nervous but hopeful, Netanyahu began his meeting with Thomas with a long discourse on the origins and goals of Zionism, the current situation in Palestine, the conflict with the British, and the travails of European Jewry under the Nazis. After forty minutes, the Senator cut in: "You've been talking for forty minutes, but you got me after the first ten." Thomas agreed to speak at the rally—and even asked Netanyahu to draft the speech—so long as there were no objections from the White House; there were none.[31] Netanyahu had his Democrat. Now he needed a Republican.

Flirting with controversy, he sought out Senator William Langer of North Dakota, whose image in the Jewish community had been tarnished by his recent defense of the civil rights of an American Nazi activist. To Langer, the same principle of equal rights that had moved him in that episode required him to speak out in favor of the Jewish right to statehood in

Palestine. He immediately agreed to address the NZOA rally and to deliver a pro-Zionist speech on the Senate floor, ghostwritten by Benjamin Akzin.[32]

Akzin was dumbfounded by Netanyahu's quick success on Capitol Hill. Two years earlier, he had spent long hours trying, in vain, to find one member of Congress to address a Revisionist rally; here Netanyahu, on his first day out, landed two senators. Emanuel Neumann, of the mainstream Emergency Committee for Zionist Affairs, was likewise shocked by Netanyahu's accomplishment. Two days before the rally, Neumann called Netanyahu with a request: considering how difficult it was for any Zionist group to find a U.S. senator to participate in a public rally, and in view of the fact that the ECZA was about to hold its own rally, which he felt was certain to be "much more important and influential" than that of the Revisionists, would Netanyahu be willing to "give" Thomas to the ECZA? "Not in a million years," the Revisionist leader replied.[33]

Neumann would soon discover that, in fact, congressional sympathy for the Jewish plight had grown substantially during 1941 and 1942, and finding a senator to address a rally was not nearly as difficult as it had once been. When Benjamin Akzin first roamed Capitol Hill in the summer of 1940, his appeals did not resonate strongly because news reports about the Jewish plight in Europe were sporadic and because many congressmen feared association with causes that could be seen as dragging America into overseas conflicts. In the two years that followed, reports of intensified Jewish suffering under the Nazis reached the U.S. media with increasing frequency; the widely publicized sinking of the refugee ship *Struma*, with 769 passengers aboard, in early 1942 grimly demonstrated the plight of Jews trying to reach British-blockaded Palestine; and America's entry into World War II undercut isolationists' objections to the Zionist cause. These and related developments helped pave the way for Netanyahu's success as a Zionist lobbyist in Washington.

The November 17 rally was a success by any standard. More than three thousand people filled the Manhattan Center, a substantial audience considering the long months that had passed since the last major Revisionist event in the city. Senators Thomas and Langer kept their promises to speak at the rally, an impressive statement of congressional support for the militant Zionists. Each of them was interrupted by prolonged standing ovations. International sympathy was also in evidence: Greek consul general Nicholas Leli and Polish representative Count J. K. Krasicki rose to extend their greetings and read statements of support for the rally's aims; Dutch royal consul Teixeira de Mattos and Yugoslavian consul Oscar Gavrilovitch were also on hand to express their solidarity. The speeches were broadcast over WBYN and WEVD, and the rally netted good coverage in New York's Yiddish and general newspapers. It was an auspicious beginning for the revived Revisionist movement.[34]

The escalating tragedy of European Jewry cast a long shadow over Netanyahu's November rally, and over Bergson's Jewish army activities as well. Revisionist speakers, press releases, and advertisements now constantly referred to the suffering of the Jews in Europe. Their plight underlined the demand for a Jewish army and gave urgency to the calls for a Jewish role in the Allies' decision-making councils. Yet, until late 1942, the immediate problem of rescuing European Jews from Hitler did not figure on the agenda of either the NZOA or the Bergson group. Like most Jews in the Diaspora, the Revisionists did not quickly grasp the enormity of the Nazi slaughter. Although Jabotinsky had spoken of the need for "emergency evacuation" in the 1930s, and warned European audiences to "liquidate the exile before it liquidates you," he did not foresee genocide.

Netanyahu and his colleagues did read the fragmentary reports of Nazi massacres that appeared in the Jewish and general press during the latter months of 1942, and they reprinted or summarized at least several of them in every issue of *Zionews*. In fact, a headline in the December 1 issue, "European Jewish Holocaust Fails to Arouse Nations," represented one of the earliest uses of the term "Holocaust" in connection with Hitler's slaughter of the Jews. But, like most Jews in the free world, the NZOA activists did not recognize the reports from Europe as pieces in a single, huge, horrifying puzzle. They did not use or understand the term "Holocaust" in the same sense that it would later be understood. Knowledge did not immediately lead to comprehension. Nor did it lead to a change in the NZOA's agenda. In late 1942, its press releases, leaflets, and occasional public meetings still focused primarily on the demand for official Jewish representation among the Allies. Bergson's propaganda still trumpeted the creation of a Jewish army as the way to respond to Hitler.

Netanyahu considered this two-pronged campaign, with the NZOA and the Jewish Army Committee operating independently but simultaneously, each in its own territory, as a particularly effective strategy for advancing the militant Zionist agenda and chipping away at the domineering role of the Jewish establishment. "It is only regrettable," he wrote to a colleague in November 1942, "that our friends in the Committee for a Jewish Army do not understand, for the time being, the value of this double-front idea."[35]

By late autumn 1942, Bergson's attention began shifting away from the Palestine conflict, and away from his own Jewish army campaign as well. In early December, the Roosevelt administration publicly confirmed that 2 million Jewish civilians had been massacred as part of a systematic Nazi annihilation plan. The news of the extermination, and the apathetic international response to it, jarred Bergson and his colleagues. Two million Jews "had been butchered" and 4 million more "were yet to be fed to the lime kilns and bonfires," Hecht later recalled. "Yet there was no voice of importance anywhere, Jewish or non-Jewish, protesting this foulest of history's crimes."[36]

The Bergsonites rearranged their agenda. The rescue of European Jewish lives became their top priority, and Ben Hecht their most powerful weapon in trying to make it America's concern as well. "For Sale to Humanity: 70,000 Jews," blared the shocking headline of Bergson's full-page ad in the *Times* on February 16, 1943, his debut as a rescue activist. The advertisement cited media reports of a Rumanian offer to permit its Jewish residents to emigrate—and thereby escape Nazi persecution—for the cost of transportation, estimated at fifty dollars per person. Bergson's purpose was not to raise the funds for a Rumanian Jewish exodus—he had no connections to the Rumanians or anyone else who was actually involved in such a project—but rather to publicize the idea that large numbers of Jews could be saved, in Rumania and elsewhere, if the Allies would take advantage of opportunities to do so.[37] It was a deliberate and forceful rebuke to the Roosevelt administration's contention that an Allied victory over the Nazis was the only way to rescue the Jews. The advertisement also raised more than enough money to pay for Bergson's next ad, setting in motion a self-sustaining torrent of militant Jewish messages for years to come.

Mainstream Jewish leaders, stunned by the magnitude of the slaughter in Europe but fearful of taking issue with a popular president in the midst of a war, initially accepted the administration's "rescue through victory" approach. An editorial in the B'nai B'rith journal *National Jewish Monthly* in early 1943 put it this way: "There is only one way to stop the Nazi massacres, and that is by crushing the Nazis in battle." The Jewish leadership sponsored a day of nationwide fasting and prayer, but hesitated to take further public action, prompting criticism from some in the Jewish media. The *Jewish Spectator* asked, "Is one day of mourning an adequate expression of the horror and despair that clutch at the hearts of all true Jews? It is shocking and—why mince words?—revolting that at a time like this our organizations, large and small, national and local, continue 'business as usual' and sponsor gala affairs, such as sumptuous banquets, luncheons, fashion teas, and what not. . . . How shall we feast while our brothers and sisters are perishing?"[38]

As further details of the genocide reached the West, as the spring of 1943 wore on without evidence that Allied victory was imminent, and in the face of criticism from some segments of the Jewish media, a number of Jewish leaders grew increasingly uneasy with the administration's position. Eleven mainstream Jewish groups cosponsored a March 1 anti-Hitler rally in New York City's Madison Square Garden at which they called for, among other things, modest adjustments in America's strict immigration policy to permit some refugees to find haven, a position they had previously been reluctant to advocate.

At the same time, the Bergsonites, adopting a more dramatic approach, organized a pageant, *We Will Never Die,* to publicize European Jewry's plight. Striking a chord of humanitarian sympathy among the Hollywood elite, Hecht used his connections to recruit an array of prominent actors for the pageant's cast, including Paul Muni, Edward G. Robinson, and Stella Adler, with a score by Kurt Weill. In three acts, lasting ninety minutes in total, *We Will Never Die* dramatized the major events of Jewish history, Jewry's contributions to civilization, and the Nazi massacres. Its two opening performances at Madison Square Garden on March 9 were viewed by audiences of more than forty thousand. When it was staged the following month in Washington, D.C.'s, Constitution Hall, the audience included First Lady Eleanor Roosevelt, hundreds of members of Congress, cabinet members, Supreme Court justices, and members of the international diplomatic corps. *We Will Never Die* struck the first major blow at the wall of silence surrounding the Nazi genocide. At the same time, the rivalry between established Jewish groups and the Zionist dissidents was escalating. Sponsors of the show in upstate New York, Baltimore, and Gary, Indiana, reported pressure by local mainstream Jewish organizations to cancel their showings. Some media reports alleged that Stephen Wise had even urged New York governor Thomas Dewey to cancel plans to declare March 9, the date of the show's Madison Square Garden debut, an official day of mourning for European Jewry.[39]

Bergson shrugged off the Jewish establishment's opposition and moved on to his next project, but other members of his inner circle were more troubled by the intra-Jewish fighting. "I can easily say that my struggle during those years was often harder, more tense and more depressing than the battles I was to know on the beaches of Normandy, in the flatlands of southern Holland and in Bastogne in Belgium," Alexander Rafaeli later recalled. "We fought against narrow minds. . . . The Jews were scared to demand help for European Jews and were frightened to fight against anti-Semitic politicians, primarily in the State Department." Rafaeli was amazed to encounter such fears among American Jews "in the middle of the 20th century, after the Jewish community had attained significant achievements and made an important contribution to the strength and welfare of the American republic."[40]

Although *We Will Never Die* refrained from directly criticizing FDR, it reinforced the growing public perception that the Allies were doing less than they could to aid Hitler's Jewish victims. Certainly the British understood it that way. Ambassador Halifax complained to Foreign Minister Eden that the Hecht pageant, which was "by implication anti-British," was "produced with great skill by Hollywood actors of the first order" and enjoyed "a highly successful tour of New York, Washington, Chicago, and other large towns."[41]

Meanwhile, the British Foreign Office, under pressure from members of Parliament and church leaders, had been prodding the State Department to make some superficial gesture on the refugee issue. Faced with the new stirrings in the Jewish community, combined with murmurs of discontent in Congress and the media over Allied indifference toward the Holocaust, the State Department moved to head off further public controversy by agreeing to an Anglo-American conference on the refugee problem. The twelve-day gathering, in Bermuda, simply reiterated existing U.S. and British policy: no changes in their own immigration laws, no possibility of opening Palestine, and some additional exploration of remote locales where small numbers of refugees might settle. The results of the Bermuda conference were so meager, in fact, that the conferees decided to keep the minutes of the proceedings secret to avoid risking embarrassment.

The Roosevelt administration underestimated the anger and disappointment that the Bermuda fiasco would generate in the Jewish community and beyond. Bermuda had raised hopes of Allied action to rescue Jews; the disappointment was all the worse because of the expectations it had created. The Bergson group set the tone of the public's response. On the day the conference opened, a Bergson ad in the *Washington Post* had demanded that "the gentlemen at Bermuda" take "ACTION—not 'exploratory' words."

When the gathering ended, the headline of a Bergson group advertisement in the *New York Times* declared: "To 5,000,000 Jews in the Nazi Death-Trap, Bermuda Was a Cruel Mockery."[42] As a member of the U.S. delegation to Bermuda, Senator Scott Lucas (D-Illinois) was particularly stung by Bergson's criticism. From the floor of the Senate, he angrily denounced the militant Zionists as ungrateful "aliens" who were enjoying hospitality better "than they can get at any other place under God's shining sun," yet were "taking advantage of the courtesy and kindness extended to them" by criticizing U.S. government policies. Lucas subsequently pressed the State Department and the FBI to investigate if Bergson could be drafted and how he was raising funds for his newspaper ads.[43]

Bergson was not alone in his criticism of the Allied response to Nazi atrocities, nor was he the first to denounce the Bermuda conference. Dr. Israel Goldstein, now president of the Synagogue Council of America, blasted Bermuda as "not only a failure, but a mockery." Even Stephen Wise, who cherished his personal friendship with FDR and was therefore particularly reticent to take issue with Allied policy, called the gathering "a woeful failure."[44] But the Bergsonites were splashing bold demands across full pages of the nation's major daily newspapers, while mainstream leaders still preferred a more cautious approach, issuing their statements in measured tones and utilizing stock methods.

Dissatisfaction with the Jewish leaders' caution gradually intensified during the spring and summer of 1943. The U.S. Mizrachi journal *Hamigdal* decried the Jewish establishment's "'sha-sha' policy," while the Independent Jewish Press Service urged Jewish leaders to "scrap our hush-hush mufflers and get ourselves a loud-speaker."[45] Even Bergson's political foes acknowledged that Jabotinsky's followers had a better understanding of the needs of the hour and the sentiments of the Jewish masses. "They focused attention on the problems," the Labor Zionist journal *Furrows* would write of the Bergson activists in a year-in-review essay at the end of 1943. In contrast with "the vacillations and temporizing of official Jewish leadership," the Bergson committees engaged in nonstop "advertisements and political agitation" to rescue European Jewry. "Their work succeeded in catching the legitimate Jewish organizations off guard and in demonstrating the inadequacy of Jewish leadership."[46] An internal ZOA survey of American Jewish political affairs in 1942 and the first half of 1943 likewise concluded that the cautious tactics of the American Zionist establishment had created a vacuum that "the irresponsible Bergson committees" were rapidly filling. "The popularity of these young men from abroad zoomed during this period of Zionist political inadequacy," it reported.[47]

The Bergson boys were also one step ahead of the Jewish establishment in their recognition of the fact that an issue of Jewish concern would not be addressed by those in power unless it was first thrust before the general public. Administration officials were unlikely to be troubled by an editorial in a Jewish monthly, but they sat up and took notice when a Jewish critique of U.S. policy was dramatically unveiled before the readership of the *New York Times.* Jewish political power in wartime Washington depended on the extent to which the broader community took interest—or at least was perceived to be taking interest—in issues of Jewish concern. Ironically, this simple principle was grasped more quickly by the handful of European-born Revisionists who had come to the United States just three years earlier than by seasoned veterans of the American political scene such as Stephen Wise.

Bergson's committee and Netanyahu's Revisionists provided a powerful one-two punch. The Bergson boys focused on the need for U.S. rescue action, downplaying the Palestine issue in order to broaden their base of support, while the NZOA focused on Jewish statehood as the ultimate answer to the persecution in Europe. In the Revisionists' view, the plight of the Jews under Hitler demonstrated the folly of the mainstream Zionists' gradualist approach to building a Jewish national home. Chaim Weizmann may have imagined that a Jewish homeland would be built with "a dunam and a cow, and then another dunam and another cow," one Revisionist activist noted in 1942, "but history does not move with that tempo, and has not moved with that tempo of Dr. Weizmann's for a long time." He added:

> In the last ten years it was not one Jewish home here and one Jewish home there that has been destroyed. It was not one Jew now and another Jew then, but the entire Jewish community of Austria, and then of Czechoslovakia and then of Poland, and then of Holland and then of France and of Rumania, and now Lithuania and Morocco, and God knows what other Jewish community tomorrow. Not house by house and cow by cow and Jew by Jew, but entire Jewish communities, old established communities were wiped out, crushed, smashed beyond repair in one day at the stroke of a pen in the Wilhelmstrasse. . . . And for that fantastic and cruel pace, Dr. Weizmann's tempo of a cow now and a dunam tomorrow, one Jew this week and another Jew next month, is no match.[48]

Seeking to capitalize on the momentum created by the NZOA's November 17 (1942) rally, Netanyahu wanted to place a full-page ad of his own in the *Times*, announcing a Revisionist campaign "to save the persecuted and uprooted Jews of Europe through the formation of a Jewish State in Palestine." He headed for Washington in search of congressional endorsements for the ad. Senator Thomas assented. So did Clare Booth Luce, a prominent Republican congresswoman from Connecticut who found Chaim Weizmann's reluctance to criticize the British puzzling; a downtrodden people fighting for its freedom should pull no punches, she told Netanyahu.[49]

Netanyahu expected that the ad would attract enough donations to cover its cost. But how could he come up with either $1,800 in advance to pay the *Times*, or an advertising agency that would serve as guarantor of the payment? Emanuel Neumann had the answer. Unbeknownst to his boss, ECZA chair Stephen Wise, Neumann maintained a secret friendship with Netanyahu and periodically gave him helpful advice. Neumann sent Netanyahu to a wealthy former department store owner, Louis Germain, whom he knew to be a Revisionist sympathizer. Germain served as guarantor of the ad, which brought in enough contributions in the twenty-four hours following its appearance to cover the initial cost. Future NZOA ads were guaranteed by Jacob Ribakov, the owner of a New York advertising agency, who met Eliahu Ben-Horin at their weekly poker game and became enthralled by the cause of Revisionist Zionism. Each Revisionist ad brought in enough money to reimburse what Ribakov had advanced. Then, when new projects arose, Netanyahu would send telegrams to the largest donors from the recent ad, most of whom would consistently respond with new contributions; "each ad was like spreading a net in the sea." Netanyahu's group soon found itself able to mount a self-sustaining flood of political ads comparable to Bergson's.[50]

More often than not, the NZOA placed its ads in the *New York Post*, which had adopted a strongly pro-Zionist stance and emerged as the newspaper of choice for a significant portion of the Jewish community. They also branched out, sometimes to the *New York Times* but also to the less expensive *Washington Post*, Chicago's *Daily News* and *Daily Sun*, Yiddish dailies such as *Der Tog*, and the prominent liberal political weekly *New Republic*.[51] A number of the earliest NZOA ads, in 1943 and 1944, sought to attract readers by appealing to their humanitarian instincts with headlines such as "Massacred by Foe, Ignored by Friend, a People Appeals to the Conscience of America" and "The White Paper Must Be Smashed, If Millions of Jews

Are to Be Saved!" The tone soon changed, however, because Bergson's ads were cornering the market on humanitarian rescue and because Netanyahu, who drafted the NZOA's ads, was becoming increasingly cognizant of the need to appeal to America's political or military self-interest. By 1944 and 1945, typical NZOA ad headlines read "Is an American Treaty, Too, Just a Scrap of Paper?" (referring to the 1924 Anglo-American Convention on Palestine, which prohibited unilateral changes in the British administration of the Holy Land), "No American Army Needed to Protect a Jewish State," and "Is America to Be a Party to the Palestine Betrayal?" If it could be demonstrated that American credibility, honor, or lives were at stake, the NZOA assumed, Americans would be more likely to take an interest in the Palestine crisis. The British, too, were taking notice. By the spring of 1943, worried British Embassy officials in Washington were literally counting the number of militant Zionist ads that appeared in the American press and reporting back to Foreign Minister Eden on their frequency.[52]

Netanyahu was a great believer in the power of the written word. "Statesmen here know that words are the most effective means of political warfare," he once wrote to a colleague:

All governments invest millions in this country to spread "words"—the Russians, the British and the Chinese, and down to the smallest nations like the Poles, Czechs and the Dutch. Only we fail to understand that "words" are the beginning of everything, and if we spend $50,000 on propaganda we believe we have done the maximum in this direction. *Millions,* my dear friend, must be spent on enlightening propaganda before you can begin to expect results. *Millions*—and not a few dollars here and there, as old Zionists do.[53]

In addition to their general educational value, advertisements could be used as political weapons for specific occasions. Thus when Prime Minister Winston Churchill visited Washington in May 1943, he opened his morning paper to read a full-page NZOA broadside headlined, "Mr. Churchill, DROP THE MANDATE!"[54] The Revisionists argued that since the English had failed to fulfill their pledge to facilitate the creation of a "Jewish National Home" in Palestine—a promise included in the text of the actual League of Nations Mandate—they were obliged to surrender the Mandate. At the time, the idea of Britain dropping the Mandate was inconceivable—to the British, to mainstream Jewish leaders, to just about everybody except

Netanyahu and his colleagues. Nobody could imagine that within four years the British would be doing exactly that.[55]

The Jewish monthly *Reconstructionist,* which usually showed little sympathy for Revisionism, praised the "dignified" tone of the Churchill ad and applauded the NZOA for "quoting chapter and verse of British official statements revealing the cruel *volte face* of England's present wartime leader." Ironically, another *Reconstructionist* editorial on the subject credited "the New Zionists" for "having stimulated a wide interest in the problem of a Jewish army for Palestine and in the plight of European Jewry"— evidently a reference to the ads and other activities of the Bergsonites, not the New Zionists.[56] This sort of blurring of the Revisionist factions in the minds of the wider Jewish community would occur frequently in the years to follow, usually to the NZOA's advantage.

Netanyahu undoubtedly would have been delighted to hear a frantic Stephen Wise telling his colleagues that the NZOA's "hideous" "Drop the Mandate" advertisement had "deeply shocked" Roosevelt and Hull and "sticks in their craws." FDR told Samuel Rosenman, one of his closest Jewish advisers, that both he and Churchill were "incensed" by the ad, and instructed Rosenman to speak with Zionist leaders to see if they could put a stop to the militants' outbursts. Rosenman quickly relayed all of this to Wise and recommended a meeting between mainstream Jewish leaders and the Bergsonites; Wise, appalled at the idea of treating Bergson as a serious political player, vetoed that idea.[57]

Meanwhile, the Revisionists spent part of the spring of 1943 seeking inclusion in the American Jewish Conference, a gathering of leaders of all major U.S. Jewish organizations planned for the summer. The NZOA leaders were outraged that they were not among the groups invited to take place in a January meeting of Jewish leaders in Pittsburgh, at which the agenda of the conference was planned. Benjamin Akzin reminded B'nai B'rith president Henry Monsky, initiator of the Pittsburgh meeting, that it was Jabotinsky who, in 1939 and 1940, had repeatedly urged the mainstream Zionist leaders to join hands in planning a united postwar Jewish agenda.[58] Akzin's appeal was in vain, as was the flurry of protest letters and telegrams sent by NZOA officials, members, and sympathizers to the conference organizers. Stephen Wise and other political opponents of the NZOA were determined to keep the militants out. At one point they argued that the NZOA did not have a sufficiently large membership to qualify as a "major organization"; at another, they claimed that the NZOA's name was too similar to that of the ZOA and would have to be changed as a precondition to joining the conference, so as to eliminate confusion between the identities of the two organizations. To defuse accusations of political blackballing, the conference organizers also banned participation by Jewish Communist groups—a "balanced" exclusion of "extremists" on both ends. The Revisionists' protest that they represented a significant portion of Zionist opinion, in no way comparable to the tiny Communist factions, were to no avail.[59]

Four weeks before the American Jewish Conference opened, the Bergson group again stole the Jewish establishment's thunder by sponsoring their own "Emergency Conference to Save the Jewish People of Europe" in New York City. The impressive list of sponsors included Secretary of the Interior Harold Ickes, numerous members of Congress, Hollywood celebrities, prominent newspaper editors such as William Randolph Hearst and William Allen White, and leading intellectuals, among them the black author Langston Hughes.[60] Fifteen hundred delegates endured New York's sweltering summer heat to hear panels of experts detail practical plans for rescuing Jews from Hitler—a frank rebuff to the administration's claim that rescue could be achieved only through Allied military victory. The participation of prominent congressmen and labor leaders, plus addresses by former president Herbert Hoover and New York mayor Fiorello La Guardia, helped net the conference nationwide media coverage. In addition to publicizing the rescue issue, the gathering produced a new organization, the Emergency Committee to Save the Jewish People of Europe. It replaced the Committee for a Jewish Army as the primary focus of Bergson activity.

The British Embassy in Washington, which kept a watchful eye on Jabotinsky's American disciples, was convinced that the various factions were all part of a single anti-British conspiracy. "The Emergency Committee, like the Jewish Army Committee and the Revisionists (New Zionists) are, in fact, different 'fronts' for the same group," the embassy reported back to the Foreign Office; the only difference between the Emergency Committee and the Jewish army group was that "the outer husk of well known names is somewhat altered." What worried the embassy was that by focusing on "the general subject of the necessity for rescuing the Jews of Europe" instead of "the original emphasis on Palestine and Zionist claims," the Bergsonites may have hit upon "a technique [that would] not merely widen the appeal of the Committee and obtain support which might not be given to a purely political programme," but also provide "an alternative means of arousing feeling against the policies of the United States Government and His Majesty's Government."[61]

Bergson's penchant for creating new groups—and there were more to come—was not shared by all of Jabotinsky's disciples. Benjamin Akzin, for one, had previously complained about the proliferation of Jewish nationalist front groups, "with the tiny membership of these associations just as interlocking as their directorate" and "with each one of us a member of more boards of directors than J. P. Morgan."[62] Netanyahu and others, by contrast, saw value in the establishment of new organizations. Multiple-issue groups were often spread too thin. Single-issue organizations, by focusing on a narrow topic, attracted a constituency deeply devoted to that issue and communicated a simpler message to the public, the media, and Congress. A variety of groups making noise on different but related aspects of "the Jewish problem" also conveyed the impression—and it was not an inaccurate impression to convey—that a significant segment of the Jewish community felt strongly about those issues.

Perhaps even more important, each of these Zionist activist factions attracted its own following of prominent non-Jewish Americans, whose signatures on their advertisements demonstrated that their causes enjoyed significant support beyond the Jewish community. This was especially true of Bergson's Emergency Committee to Save the Jewish People of Europe, which garnered sympathy by appealing strictly to the public's humanitarian instincts and deliberately avoiding political controversies such as the future of Palestine. Although Revisionists and mainstream Zionists alike chided Bergson for downplaying Zionist principles, Bergson understood that finding the lowest common denominator was the key to attracting the support necessary to effect change. The Emergency Committee's simple plea to rescue the downtrodden resonated across a broad spectrum of Americans, and that impressive range of support, in turn, increased the pressure on the Roosevelt administration to respond. A columnist for the left-wing political journal *New Leader* "nearly fell through the floor" when he "took a gander" at the Emergency Committee's list of sponsors. "Nestling cheek by jowl on one piece of paper," he marveled, were "Congressman James Domengeaux, bitter Southern reactionary" and "Erwin Piscator, left-wing producer," as well as "Lowell Thomas, Big Business propagandist" and "Mary Van Kleeck, leading Communist Party fellow traveller," among other odd couples.[63] A cause that could cut so far across ordinary political lines was one that a president could not afford to ignore on the eve of an election year.

While Bergson was capturing headlines with his campaign for Allied rescue action during the summer and autumn of 1943, Netanyahu and his colleagues were quietly preparing the groundwork for a major new political initiative concerning the Palestinian Arab issue. All factions of the Zionist movement in Palestine and in the United States publicly pledged equal civil and religious rights for the Arab residents of the Jewish state-to-be. Although the Arabs were still a majority of the population—in 1941, there were approximately 1 million Arabs and 500,000 Jews in Palestine[64]—Zionists expected that once Britain relaxed its immigration restrictions, a massive Jewish influx from Europe would give the Jews a majority. On occasion, however, individuals in various factions of the movement had raised the idea of encouraging Arab emigration in order to facilitate the creation of a Jewish majority and statehood. The author and early British Zionist Israel Zangwill first advocated encouraging Arab emigration in 1905, and he continued to periodically raise the topic until his death in 1926. Benzion Netanyahu became interested in the idea while editing a Hebrew-language collection of Zangwill's essays. The volume, published in 1939, began with an introduction by Netanyahu reflecting sympathetically on Zangwill's view of the Arab issue. He also discussed the Arab question with a number of colleagues, among them Emanuel Neumann, who shortly afterward authored an op-ed for the Hebrew-language *HaBoker* and the English-language *Palestine Review* urging that "the masses of Palestinian Arabs be transferred peaceably and in orderly fashion to Iraq."[65]

After relocating to New York, Netanyahu discussed the Arab issue with his NZOA colleagues, and Eliahu Ben-Horin authored a plank in the NZOA's February 1942 platform recommending that those Palestinian Arabs who would "not be willing to live in a Jewish state" should be offered "full compensation for the immovable property left behind by them" if they would emigrate. Ben-Horin later made a similar suggestion in his 1943 book, *Middle East at the Crossroads.*[66] By the summer of 1943, expecting the victorious Allies to redraw borders and rearrange populations during the postwar reconstruction of Europe, Netanyahu was convinced of the need for a front group advocating population transfers as the key to Middle East peace. Palestinian Arab farmers would make underdeveloped Iraq bloom, and European Jews would come to Palestine to help build the Jewish state.

The new group was to be called the American Resettlement Committee for Uprooted European Jewry, and Ben-Horin was named its executive director. Netanyahu's first task was to recruit a large number of prominent endorsers, preferably non-Jews so as to demonstrate a broad range of support for the Arab transfer concept. He spent much of the summer shuttling back and forth between New York and Washington, lobbying congressmen to join the new committee. Ben-Horin's first task was to persuade a major political figure to accept the chairmanship of the Resettlement Committee. His first choice, former president Herbert Hoover, declined. Hoover suggested he try the Republican presidential candidate of 1936, Alf Landon, and Ben-Horin traveled to Kansas to see him. Landon, too, said no, although he expressed sympathy for the militant Zionists and later spoke at NZOA meetings. Ultimately, the Resettlement Committee's first and only public activity was its placement of a large advertisement in the *New York Times* on October 5. Twenty-four congressmen signed the ad, as did seventeen Christian clergymen, twenty-five presidents of American colleges and universities, and a wide assortment of public officials, authors, artists, and journalists. But Colonel John Henry Patterson was listed as chairman.[67] Without a prominent political leader as chair, the Revisionists were convinced that the committee would never attract sufficient funds to make an impact. It elicited little public comment, aside from a predictable condemnation by U.S. Labor Zionist leader Hayim Greenberg and a two-part series in the U.S. Mizrachi journal, authored by Meir Grossman of the Revisionist breakaway Jewish State Party, endorsing the Resettlement Committee. Mainstream Zionist leaders preferred to keep discussion of the volatile population transfer notion behind closed doors. The committee was disbanded almost immediately after the *Times* ad appeared. The Arab transfer concept, however, was destined to resurface.[68]

Meanwhile, unbeknownst to either Bergson or the NZOA, a seismic shift in the mainstream American Zionist leadership was under way. Dissatisfied activist elements within the ZOA had been pressing Abba Hillel Silver, a dynamic Zionist orator and Reform rabbi from Cleveland, to seek the presidency of their organization. Shaken by the Nazi persecutions and the Allies' apathy—as symbolized by the Bermuda conference—many Jewish activists were growing disillusioned with Stephen Wise's cautious approach and now embraced Silver's more militant style and agenda. Fearing a Silver triumph in the forthcoming 1943 ZOA presidential election, the ZOA leadership agreed to a last-minute compromise: Silver would refrain from competing for the ZOA presidency in exchange for co-chairmanship—along with his archrival Wise—of the American Zionist Emergency Council (AZEC), previously known as the Emergency Committee for Zionist Affairs.[69]

Unfortunately for Wise, the deal was struck just prior to the American Jewish Conference, providing Silver and his forceful brand of Zionism with a major platform just when Wise was hoping to appease the State Department by toning down vocal Zionist fervor in the Jewish community. Just at that moment, the State Department and the British Foreign Office were urging their respective governments to issue a "sedative joint statement" banning all further public discussion of the Palestine issue until the end of the war, in order to placate the Arab world.[70] U.S. Major General George V. Strong, in a memo to the army chief of staff, argued that such a statement was especially imperative in view of what he called the American government's "policy of winking at the practice of high ranking military officers and government officials as well as prominent citizens sponsoring Zionist propaganda. This official 'silence' is interpreted by Arabs as official approval of Zionist aims"—hence only an official statement which "insists that all partisan groups interested in Palestine cease propaganda activities for the duration" would allay Arab suspicions, Strong counseled.[71]

Administration officials threatened Wise and Nahum Goldmann, head of the Jewish Agency's Washington office, that the declaration would go forward unless the American Jewish Conference was postponed—the State Department feared the conference would issue pro-Zionist statements that would upset Arab opinion. But given the increasingly militant mood in the American Jewish community, and especially now with Silver literally looking over his shoulder, there was no chance Wise could cancel the conference. Neither Wise nor Goldmann mentioned the demand for a Palestine homeland in their speeches, but those glaring omissions only served to further energize the grassroots delegates.[72] Activists within Wise's own American Jewish Congress engineered a last-minute schedule revision that permitted Silver to address the conference. He delivered an emotional and electrifying appeal for statehood, prompting prolonged, thunderous applause and resulting in the overwhelming adoption of a resolution demanding the creation of a Jewish commonwealth. Almost overnight, Silver was transformed into the undisputed leader of the increasingly militant grassroots Jewish community.

At first, the Revisionists were not quite sure what to make of Silver's rise. The Bergson group's Alexander Rafaeli recalled that while serving as a young Irgun emissary to the 1939 World Zionist Congress in Switzerland, he had attended a private meeting in which Silver said he "supported" and "encouraged" the Irgun's illegal immigration activities. Silver "was the only American delegate to speak up in this spirit and to support outright the Irgun's activities," according to Rafaeli. Yet the day after that meeting, Silver delivered a speech before the Zionist Congress in which he urged cooperation with the English and denounced extralegal immigration to Palestine. After witnessing the contradiction between the "warm compliments" he showered on the Irgun in private and his denunciations of Irgun activity in public, Rafaeli concluded that Silver's relationship with the Zionist right was one of a "platonic love."[73] But the relationship between Silver and the Revisionists would take some surprising turns now that Silver had taken over the mainstream Zionist movement.

In determining how to deal with the Zionist right, Silver had to take into consideration the mood in the American Jewish community in the autumn of 1943. The news of Nazi atrocities in Europe, the refusal of the Allies to take meaningful action to aid Jewish refugees, and the British ban on almost all Jewish immigration to Palestine infuriated American Jewry and sparked growing sympathy for militant positions. The same mood of militancy that paved the way for Silver's ascent in the American Zionist hierarchy had led to increased support for the groups further to the right, especially the Bergsonites.

Bergson, by virtue of his high public profile, was the primary competition. Silver hoped to neutralize his competitor by co-opting him. Cooperation with the Bergsonites may have seemed feasible to Silver because of the fact that two years earlier, Bergson had engaged in serious discussions with Silver's predecessors at the AZEC about a possible merger. As Silver would soon discover, times had changed. At the time of the 1941–42 negotiations, Bergson's Jewish army group was new, relatively small, and prepared to make substantial concessions to the established Zionist leadership, only to find that the establishment was not willing to compromise.[74] In the autumn of 1943, however, Bergson's boys were negotiating from a position of strength—so strong, in fact, that they had relatively little incentive to negotiate at all. Bergson followed up on the Emergency Conference with a series of attention-grabbing newspaper ads and rallies during August and September, climaxing in a Bergson-organized march on Washington by more than four hundred rabbis to demand U.S. intervention to rescue European Jewry. The dramatic October 6 march, just two days before Yom Kippur, garnered substantial media coverage, particularly when Roosevelt (acting partly on Stephen Wise's advice) refused to meet the protesters. The Yiddish press brimmed with unprecedented criticism of FDR, and the Bergson group harvested substantial new support both among grassroots American Jews and in Congress. British Embassy officials sarcastically dismissed the protest as "a 'March on Washington' in Pullman [train] cars," but they could not hide their growing annoyance over the activities of "the indefatigable Mr. Bergson."[75]

No wonder, then, that Bergson was in no rush to cut any deals with Dr. Silver. As far as Bergson was concerned, he had no need for the Zionist establishment; it would tie his hands. The first Silver-Bergson meeting, in mid-October, served only to illustrate the gap between their perspectives. When Silver spoke of the need to "integrate" Bergson's work with that of the AZEC, Bergson did not even respond, "except in a general expression of good will and desire to avert controversy and conflict" between the AZEC and the two new organizations he was planning to launch (one Jewish and the other predominantly non-Jewish) to lobby for Jewish statehood.[76]

Evidently adopting the "If you can't join 'em, fight 'em" approach, Silver gave up hope of joining forces with Bergson and opted to let the AZEC staff continue its policy of occasional public attacks on the dissidents. It may be that because he had so recently assumed the leadership of the AZEC, Silver was reluctant to make too many waves with a drastic step such as trying to reverse the existing AZEC policy of publicly criticizing Bergson. Or it may be that Silver gauged—no doubt correctly—that his more moderate and cautious co-chair of the AZEC, Stephen Wise, would never have agreed to lay off the Bergsonites. Still, it is noteworthy that Silver himself generally refrained from initiating or lending his name to attacks on the Bergson group, with a few notable exceptions.[77] He left that task to the AZEC staff members who normally carried out anti-Bergson activities: Harry Shapiro, Arthur Lourie, and Harold Manson (who regularly infiltrated Bergsonite meetings).[78]

At the same time, Silver would not tolerate direct competition from the Bergsonites. When, at the end of 1943, they launched their American League for a Free Palestine (ALFP), which competed for much of the same constituency as the mainstream Zionist movement, Silver did not hesitate to blast it as a "paper organization" that has "hurt our cause in Washington."[79] Silver was following the advice of Arthur Lourie, who had pointed out that it would be "far easier to attack the Bergson group on the basis of this new organization than with reference to the Emergency Committee to Save the Jews of Europe," since the Emergency Committee really did have widespread support and was filling a vacuum in the Jewish community, while the ALFP could be accused of duplicating the AZEC's work and—at least for the moment—lacking a significant constituency.[80]

Ironically, Silver's opponents within the Zionist establishment saw little difference between Silver and the groups to his right. Stephen Wise was furious at Silver's willingness to criticize the Roosevelt administration's Palestine policy and his insistence on pressing ahead with congressional resolutions that the administration opposed. As far as Wise was concerned, Silver and his followers were "representatives of American Irgunism and ZOA Sternism."[81] Wise's ally, Nahum Goldmann, likewise sought to discredit Silver by associating him with the Zionist maximalists, charging that Silver's willingness "to fight the President and the administration" was "Revisionist tactics." Goldmann warned: "What may be good for other peoples is not good for us. We cannot throw bombs, and we cannot fight against all the powers of the world, [we cannot] antagonize everybody."[82] Wise, unlike Silver, hesitated to criticize the British, privately acknowledging that he was "an Anglophile almost to the point of Anglo-mania."[83] He was also a devoted Democrat and Roosevelt supporter, prompting Silver's supporters to accuse him of kowtowing to "the Politics of the Green Light [from the White House]."[84] Silver's right-hand man Emanuel Neumann characterized the difference between Silver's approach and Wise's as "vigorous public action as against timidity and a reversion to *Shtadlanut* [quiet diplomacy]."[85]

The political differences between the two AZEC co-chairs soon degenerated into extreme personal animosity. Silver accused Wise of suffering from an "hysterical-prestige complex" and branded Goldmann a "political gigolo" who was "pulling shyster tricks" to undermine Silver's work in Washington.[86] Wise, for his part, called Silver a "gangster" and labeled Silver's aides "henchmen," "creatures," and "pet assassins." At one point, Wise even asked former ZOA president Rabbi Solomon Goldman—perhaps facetiously—to pray for Wise to receive "divine protection" to prevent Silver from assassinating him.[87] Twenty-five years later, Goldmann still brimmed with anti-Silver animosity, asserting in his memoirs that "there was something of the terrorist in [Silver's] manner and being."[88]

Such attacks by the more cautious elements in the Zionist leadership did not deter Silver from cooperating with the Jabotinskyites. Although his efforts to work with the Bergson group failed, Silver had more success in his efforts to bring about cooperation between the AZEC and the NZOA. The U.S. Revisionists had followed Silver's rise to power "with interest and satisfaction," and in October 1943 they suggested to him "a collaboration between our organization and your Committee." Together, they hoped, this "united Zionist effort" would be "strong enough to smash the White Paper of 1939."[89] Silver telephoned Netanyahu in October to propose that the Revisionists formally apply for membership in the AZEC. Intrigued, Netanyahu and NZOA board member Samuel Katz grabbed the next train to Cleveland. "We sat down with Silver in his living room at 6:30 in the evening and didn't get up until 1:30 in the morning," Netanyahu recalled. Silver expressed agreement "with almost everything we said" and promised that the AZEC would refrain from interfering in the Revisonists' political activities.[90]

The NZOA board unanimously recommended joining the AZEC. The AZEC leadership, however, was not so sure about the idea. Silver "pleaded" (as Hadassah officials characterized it)[91] with his AZEC colleagues to accept the Revisionists' membership application, emphasizing that "Zionists all over the country feel that unity must be established." Silver also "made clear that this section of the Revisionists does not include the Bergson Group" and offered the interesting argument that "if the Revisionists come into the Emergency Council they may be able to help us destroy the [Jewish] Army Committee." Needless to say, Silver did not mention his own recent effort to secure an alliance with the Bergsonites.[92]

Several of the AZEC delegates objected to admitting the NZOA on the grounds that so long as the NZOA was affiliated with the world Revisionist movement, it would not be completely loyal to the World Zionist Organization, and might even pass confidential AZEC information to their colleagues abroad.[93] Nahum Goldmann, for his part, argued that the Revisionists could be admitted only if they accepted that they could "not [enter] on the basis of recognizing them as equals."[94]

The AZEC conferees resolved to send a telegram to Moshe Shertok, director of the Political Department of the Jewish Agency in Palestine, explaining the issue and—no doubt at Silver's insistence—emphasizing both the "necessity [of] creating [the] broadest possible frontier [in the American Zionist movement]" and the "desirability [to] checkmate [the] Ber[g]son Group."[95] They reported to Shertok that the Revisionists assured them they had "neither a cause nor common endeavor" with the Bergsonites, are "not members [of the] Ber[g]son group," and had even agreed "to go along with the Emergency Council in its future attitude towards [the] Ber[g]son group." Silver's arguments were not sufficiently persuasive. So long as the NZOA was tied to the Revisionist movement abroad, Silver could neither win the assent of the Jewish Agency leadership to accept the Revisionists into the AZEC nor muster a majority in the AZEC to admit them. A dejected Silver conceded to Benjamin Akzin that the Jewish

Agency leadership was "making difficulties" about Revisionist participation in the AZEC. Unable to grant them entry, Silver expressed his hope "from time to time, to sit around the table with NZO leaders and informally discuss points of view and needed action." Unofficial cooperation was better than none, and Netanyahu and his colleagues continued to meet with Silver occasionally, in New York, Washington, or Cleveland, until finally, three years later, the Revisionist movement as a whole rejoined the World Zionist Organization and the U.S. Revisionists were allowed to join the AZEC.[96]

6 • Wooing the Republicans

The affection most American Jews felt for Franklin Roosevelt is summa-rized by a 1940s-era quip that, playing on the Yiddish word for world, *velt*, describes a Republican politician as complaining that the Jews seem to have three such "velts": this *velt*, the *velt* to come, and Roosevelt.[1] The first Democratic presidential candidate to win a majority of Jewish votes had been Alfred E. Smith in 1928. As victims of bigotry, Jews identified with Smith, a frequent target of anti-Catholic barbs. The Democratic Party worked hard to attract ethnic and religious minorities to its ranks, and the Democrats' efforts to portray themselves as the party of immigrants and the working man made them far more attractive than the Republican Party, with its fervent opposition to immigration and unsympathetic view of labor rights. The vehement opposition of the extreme right to FDR made Jews even more comfortable in the Democratic camp. FDR's unprecedented ap-pointment of a number of Jews—however tenuous their connections to Judaism—to senior positions in his administration won him many fans in the Jewish community. Roosevelt's support for social welfare legislation and his sympathy for labor rights appealed to a substantial number of working-class Jewish labor union members. His criticism of Hitler, in the 1930s, even if it was not backed up by concrete steps to aid Hitler's victims, further endeared Roosevelt to Jewish voters. More than 80 percent of American Jews voted for FDR in 1932, and more than 90 percent supported his re-election in 1936 and 1940.

Stephen Wise's close relationship with Roosevelt seemed almost the embodiment of American Jewish sentiment. When a matter of Jewish con-cern arose, Wise would address it behind the scenes with an adoring "Dear Boss" note or, on occasion, a private meeting at which the president would set Wise at ease with vague assurances. Because of his admiration for Roosevelt and his eagerness to preserve his access to the White House,

Wise hesitated to challenge FDR's refusal to aid European Jewry or press the British on Palestine.

But sentiment in the Jewish community at large was beginning to diverge from the Wise line. American Jewish doubts about Roosevelt began emerging in the spring and summer of 1943. First there was the disappointment of the Bermuda conference. Shortly thereafter came a flurry of media reports of a planned Anglo-American declaration banning public discussion of Palestine. The scheme was defeated at the last minute by the intervention of FDR's Jewish advisers, but the episode raised questions in the Jewish community about the Roosevelt administration's sensitivity to Jewish concerns. The author and critic Melvin Lasky spoke for many in the Jewish community and beyond when he wrote, in October 1943, that when it came to the plight of European Jewry, "the United Nations [as the Allies were informally called, prior to the establishment of the United Nations organization] appear to be united in a program of sympathetic mumbo-jumbo and do-nothingism."[2]

"We all thought that Roosevelt was the greatest friend the Jews had," recalled Irving Bunim, a leader of the U.S. Orthodox rescue group Vaad Ha-Hatzala. Bunim's disillusionment with FDR began in 1943, after he and his colleagues received a report that the Nazis were singling out and murdering the Jewish soldiers among their Allied prisoners of war. Rabbi Aharon Kotler, a prominent Orthodox rabbinical scholar active in the Vaad Ha-Hatzala, "woke me up in the middle of the night and gave me the report. . . . We took the midnight train to Washington." Bunim drafted a memorandum that they would deliver to Roosevelt aide David Niles. The final paragraph referred to the Nazi persecution of European Jewry as "a very sad drop of the curtain of two thousand years of murdering our people." Rabbi Kotler insisted that Bunim delete that line, because "If Roosevelt will see that it has been done for two thousand years, he will say, let it be another year." Startled to hear a prominent rabbinical sage speak so critically of FDR, Bunim began to rethink his former assumptions about Roosevelt's presumed sympathy for Jewish concerns. His subsequent encounters with administration officials who declined to intervene on behalf of European Jewry further eroded Bunim's earlier affection for FDR.[3]

The U.S. Revisionists, whose leaders were, for the most part, not even American citizens, much less loyal Democrats, felt no special affinity for FDR and recognized the risks inherent in Wise's relationship with the president. After all, they reasoned, what could possibly motivate Roosevelt to take action requested by Jews if he felt that he had the Jewish leadership in his pocket? The Revisionists also realized that grassroots Jewish support for FDR was not invulnerable. Jabotinsky's followers had their fingers on the pulse of the grassroots and closely monitored signs of Jewish disenchantment with the administration. They were perceptive analysts of the "Jewish street" because they tended to live in working-class neighborhoods, attend European-style synagogues, and read the Yiddish-language press, where criticism of FDR's positions on European Jewry and Palestine appeared with increasing frequency in the second half of 1943.

The Bergson group was responsible for generating, or at least accelerating, some of the criticism of the Roosevelt administration. Ben Hecht penned a November 1943 full-page ad about the ghost of his Uncle Abraham, a victim of the Nazis, "sitting on the window sill two feet away from Mr. Roosevelt," waiting in vain for the president to do something for Europe's remaining Jews. The silence of the Allies was a death sentence for the Jews, the ad warned: "The Germans will think that when they kill Jews, Stalin, Roosevelt and Churchill pretend nothing is happening." According to Hecht, two days after "My Uncle Abraham Reports . . ." appeared, financier Bernard Baruch, adviser to the president, complained to Hecht that FDR was "very upset" about the ad and pleaded for a moratorium on such attacks.[4]

The Bergson boys understood that if the president was upset, he was paying attention to their protests, and if he was paying attention, they were probably on the right track. "The administration was feeling our pressure," Ben-Ami concluded.[5] They forged ahead with the next stage in their rescue campaign: congressional intervention. At Bergson's behest, Senator Guy Gillette ("a simple, confused but very honest Presbyterian," according to the British Foreign Office)[6] and Representative Will Rogers, Jr. (whose Native American heritage sensitized him to the suffering of ethnic minorities, arousing his interest in the Jewish plight), introduced a resolution asking the administration to create a special governmental agency to rescue Jews from Hitler. "The Jewish problem has entered the realm of national American politics," a U.S. Labor Zionist journal noted on the eve of the hearings on the Gillette-Rogers resolution. "It will be discussed when the resolution will be placed before Congress. The Revisionist group which won over a group of Congressmen may rightly take credit for it."[7] The hearings exploded into a national controversy when State Department official Breckinridge Long, in his testimony, presented wildly exaggerated statistics about the number of refugees who had been granted entry to the United States.

Mainstream Jewish organizations now joined the militants in denouncing the State Department.

Assessing the administration's approach to the rescue resolution, Eri Jabotinsky, who was then active in Bergson's Emergency Committee to Save the Jewish People of Europe, wrote in December 1943: "It is felt in Democratic as well as in Republican circles that the issue involved, if not handled carefully, may lose for the Administration a good million of Jewish votes, especially in New York City. . . . The debate around the Resolution," he continued, "has certainly succeeded in awakening widespread Jewish interest, and the failure of this Resolution to be adopted by Congress would certainly create a deep rift between the Jews on the one side and the State Department, even the President, on the other side. It is typical today to hear public orators at Jewish public gatherings saying that Jesus was not the Messiah nor apparently is Mr. Roosevelt."[8]

It was at this point that Bergson's publicity campaigns and the controversy in Congress over Bergson's rescue resolution intersected with the Roosevelt administration's political interests. Treasury Secretary Henry Morgenthau Jr. and his aides had recently become aware of the State Department's behind-the-scenes obstruction of rescue efforts. With another potentially explosive round of Senate hearings in the offing, and with public criticism of the administration reaching a crescendo, Morgenthau and his staff set to work on a memorandum to FDR that would urge him to preempt Congress by establishing the rescue agency that the resolution was seeking. Shortly before presenting the memo to FDR, the Treasury Department staff met with Roosevelt adviser Ben Cohen to discuss how best to approach the president. Cohen told them "there is also a factor which you don't want to put in the memorandum [to FDR] which will influence the President and influence [Secretary of State Cordell] Hull. We all know that during this political year minorities are being exploited . . . all the politicians are trying to exploit the value of minority groups, and the situation has gotten to the point where something has to be done."[9]

There could be no doubt which American "minority group" might be "exploited" by politicians with regard to the persecution of European Jewry. By the autumn of 1943, the leading undeclared candidates for the Republican presidential nomination, Wendell Willkie and Thomas Dewey, were already wooing Jewish support. Willkie publicly endorsed the goal of Jewish statehood, while Dewey appeared at a Zionist rally in New York in November 1943 and called for the opening of Palestine to all Jewish refugees. In his diary, Vice President Henry Wallace worried about "how vigorously Willkie is going to town for Palestine." Wallace also noted the advice Winston Churchill had offered earlier that year when FDR had spoken of the need to maintain good relations with the Arab countries in order to have a bloc of friendly states in the Mediterranean region; Churchill replied that "there were more Jews than Arab votes in the Anglo-Saxon countries and we could not afford to ignore such practical considerations."[10] Morgenthau and his aides may have been motivated by humanitarianism, but the president was more likely motivated by the election-year danger of the congressional rescue resolution becoming, as Morgenthau put it, a "boiling pot on [Capitol] Hill" that could "explode into a nasty scandal."[11] Such a scandal would have publicly revealed the State Department's months of intentional obstruction of rescue. Heeding Morgenthau's advice, FDR preempted congressional action by establishing the War Refugee Board in January 1944.

Morgenthau and his staff, as well as several leading newspapers, acknowledged the link between the militant Zionist lobbyists, the rescue resolution, and the creation of the War Refugee Board. "The tide was running with me. . . . The thing that made it possible to get the President really to act on this thing was the Resolution which at least had passed the Senate to form this kind of a War Refugee Board, hadn't it?" Morgenthau remarked at a Treasury Department staff meeting not long afterward. "I think six months before [the resolution], I could not have done it."[12] The *Christian Science Monitor* reported that the establishment of the War Refugee Board "is the outcome of pressure brought to bear by the Emergency Committee to Save the Jewish People of Europe, a group made up of both Jews and non-Jews that has been active in the capital in recent months," and an editorial in the *Washington Post* noted that in view of Bergson's "industrious spadework" on behalf of rescue, the Emergency Committee was "entitled to credit for the President's forehanded move." Despite limited powers and meager funds, the War Refugee Board rescued an estimated 200,000 Jews during 1944 and 1945.[13] Bergson was no longer merely someone who had "made himself a nuisance in Washington"; the self-styled "nuisance diplomat" had emerged as a significant political force, playing a central role in facilitating the Roosevelt administration's only meaningful response to Hitler's annihilation of the Jews.[14]

In March 1944, as the British White Paper approached its five-year expiration date, Roosevelt met privately with Silver and Wise to assure them of his eventual support for Zionist aims. Wise's description of their talk no doubt impressed his Jewish listeners, but he stretched the truth somewhat when he claimed the president strongly opposed British restrictions on Jewish immigration. The White House, aware that Wise's exaggeration would help cement Jewish support for FDR's reelection, did not go out of its way to distance itself from Wise's claim. Vice President Wallace's diary entries for that week noted the contrast between FDR's anti-Zionist remarks to Wallace and his pro-Zionist remarks to Silver and Wise. "The President is certainly a waterman," Wallace wrote. "He looks one direction and rows the other with the utmost skill."[15]

Although FDR's gestures mollified many of his Jewish critics, the Revisionists had glimpsed the potential for exercising election-year leverage on the administration. Netanyahu and company also took note of the early efforts by two of the leading undeclared candidates for the 1944 Republican presidential nomination, Thomas Dewey and Wendell Willkie, to seek Jewish support. Dewey appeared at a Zionist rally in New York in November 1943 and called for the opening of Palestine to all Jewish refugees. Willkie publicly endorsed the goal of Jewish statehood. Indeed, Vice President Wallace, in his diary, expressed concern about "how vigorously Willkie is going to town for Palestine." The following April, the Capitol Hill correspondent for the *New Republic* reported that the Republicans expected that a significant number of Jewish voters might support the GOP in the 1944 presidential election.[16] Although Jews constituted just 3 percent of the national population, they were 14 percent of the population in New York State. With its forty-seven electoral votes—the most of any state—New York played a decisive role in presidential campaign politics; indeed, with one exception, no candidate had been elected president since 1876 without winning New York.

From the perspective of Jabotinsky's followers, the problem with the traditional lopsided support for the Democratic administration was that FDR and the Democratic Party might assume they were assured of Jewish votes and would therefore feel no need to address Jewish concerns. In the NZOA's view, the time was ripe for an entirely new approach to Jewish involvement in American politics: to promote Jewish interests by forcing both parties to compete for Jewish electoral support.

Benjamin Akzin had already planted the seeds for this effort when he courted Republicans and isolationist Democrats on Capitol Hill back in 1940. His successors at the NZOA reaped what he had sown. In the summer of 1942 and again in the summer of 1943, Netanyahu had enjoyed considerable success recruiting congressmen to endorse specific Revisionist projects. In late 1943, Netanyahu began making regular visits to Washington to acquaint members of Congress with the militant Zionist agenda. In between his trips, the Revisionist leaders "kept in touch unceasingly with our Washington grinds, outlining our viewpoint" to key congressmen— especially Republicans—and their aides.[17] Netanyahu was surprised to discover that some prominent members of Congress seemed to know relatively little about the Palestine situation. Under Stephen Wise's administration, American Zionist Emergency Council (AZEC) officials had made only sporadic contacts on Capitol Hill; "the old Zionists have not even given [congressmen] the most elementary information," Netanyahu complained.[18] He pressed congressmen to support abolition of the White Paper, unrestricted immigration to Palestine of refugees from Hitler, and eventual Jewish statehood.

By the spring of 1944, with the June Republican national convention just around the corner, the NZOA began focusing its attention on those party officials and Republican congressmen most likely to shape the platform's foreign policy planks. Those singled out for special attention included former president Herbert Hoover; former presidential candidate Alf Landon; Senators Robert Taft (Ohio), Albert Hawkes (New Jersey), Ralph Brewster (Maine), Styles Bridges (New Hampshire), and Claude Pepper (Florida); and Representative Clare Booth Luce (Connecticut).[19] Luce was especially warm to the Revisionist agenda; on the eve of the convention, she called Netanyahu to say, only half-kidding, "I'm going now, to do your work at the convention."[20] As for Hoover and Landon, Ben-Horin had already established a friendly rapport with both when he tried to woo them for the chairmanship of the Resettlement Committee in 1943. A year later, Ben-Horin's spadework began to pay off, as Netanyahu and his colleagues now found they had relatively easy access to the two influential elder statesmen of the party. In round after round of personal meetings, telephone calls, letters, and telegrams, the militant Zionists pleaded with the Republican leaders for the adoption of a convention plank endorsing Palestine immigration and statehood. The lobbying barrage was, as a Revisionist newsletter noted, an important "departure from the Old Zionist policy of counting on the support of the Democratic Party only." Indeed, it was no small matter that an influential Republican figure such as Landon was "now in close association with the NZO, although he, like other Republican leaders, previously had no connection with the Old Zionists."[21]

Netanyahu and his cohorts were hardly the only ones to realize that Jewish political power could be augmented by courting the Republicans. Abba Hillel Silver, although himself not a Republican, had publicly endorsed

Wendell Willkie for president in 1940 and enjoyed access to Republican leaders, particularly Senator Taft, who represented Silver's home state of Ohio. Beginning in April 1944, Silver and his aides met repeatedly with Taft, Governor Thomas E. Dewey of New York (the expected Republican presidential nominee), and members of the Republican convention's Drafting Committee and its Committee on Foreign Affairs. Silver and his colleagues were consulted on drafts of the Republican plank on Palestine, enabling them to improve the wording.[22] Behind Silver's back, however, the Revisionists won key Republicans to a maximalist Zionist position that employed language even stronger than Silver wanted. In addition, Netanyahu sent the Revisionist and Republican activist George Sokolsky to the convention to look over the shoulders of those who were drafting the Palestine plank.[23] The final text not only endorsed statehood but also directly criticized Roosevelt:

In order to give refuge to millions of distressed Jewish men, women and children driven from their homes by tyranny, we call for the opening of Palestine to their unrestricted immigration and land ownership, so that in accordance with the full intent and purpose of the Balfour Declaration of 1917 and the Resolution of a Republican Congress in 1922, Palestine may be constituted as a free and democratic Commonwealth. We condemn the failure of the President to insist that the mandatory of Palestine carry out the provisions of the Balfour Declaration and of the mandate while he pretends to support them.[24]

Silver, believing that an open attack on FDR might backfire, sought unsuccessfully to have the anti-Roosevelt sentence removed. The fact that Silver tried to tone down the Republican plank did not impress Stephen Wise and other Democrats in the AZEC, who accused him of embarrassing the president by supporting even a milder version of the Republican resolution. Instead of extending the normal courtesy of praising the Republican plank, the AZEC executive committee would only agree to publicly praise "the section of the Palestine plank" that referred to immigration and a commonwealth, lest they be suspected of praising the anti-Roosevelt portion of the plank as well. Silver was shocked to discover that "many of the members of the [AZEC Executive] Committee are far more involved and committed in one way or another to the Democratic Party than they are to Zionism, and that in the case of a conflict of loyalties, they will sacrifice Zionist interests."[25] The Revisionists, by contrast, rejoiced at the Republican platform and regarded the response of the Wise faction of the AZEC as predictable. In their view, the latest developments proved that with a little political savvy, militant Zionism could produce concrete political results, leaving the advocates of old-style *shtadlanut* sputtering in frustration.

The Democratic national convention in Chicago loomed just over the horizon, barely a month away. During the weeks preceding the convention, Netanyahu repeatedly consulted with Congressman Emanuel Celler, the feisty Brooklyn representative who was expected to have a hand in shaping the 1944 platform planks on foreign affairs. Celler was the most outspoken of the seven Jewish members of Congress and a strong critic of the Roosevelt administration's policies toward Palestine and European refugees. A frequent endorser of NZOA and Bergsonite projects, Celler was "as friendly and supportive as if he were a member of the organization," Netanyahu recalled. "There were even times when the language he recommended for a resolution or an advertisement was stronger than the language that we intended to use."[26]

On the eve of the convention, Celler warned the Democratic leadership that they could lose the Jewish vote in the November presidential election if they failed to match the Republicans' stance on Palestine. The Democrats heeded his warning, endorsing "unrestricted Jewish immigration and colonization" to be followed by the establishment of "a free and democratic Jewish commonwealth."[27] Stephen Wise believed that his relationship with the administration and leading Democrats was responsible for the resolution. The NZOA, however, claimed that its friendship with Celler helped prompt Celler's energetic efforts on behalf of a strong Palestine plank. Perhaps the most significant factor was the simple political reality that the Democrats did not want to be usurped on Palestine by the Republicans. To the extent that the Revisionists could claim credit for influencing the Republicans, they could feel, with some justification, that their actions had indirectly influenced the Democrats as well. It was not unreasonable for Netanyahu to conclude that while the "extremely valuable contribution of Dr. Silver" had played an important role wooing the GOP, "if not for the systematic spadework and the general effects of the campaign carried out by [the NZOA] in this country before, during and after Dr. Silver began his valuable work, a favorable political attitude by the [two major parties] would not have been effected . . . our work among the Republican Party leaders, ranging from Hoover and Landon down to the officials of the party machine, began long before the [mainstream] Zionists undertook any action in this direction."[28] The ramifications of the two parties' resolutions extended beyond the American political scene. The ability of Zionist lobbyists to convince both major parties to go on record in favor of Jewish statehood also sent a powerful message to London. England would need America's help after the war, and American Jewish political power was emerging as a factor in the shaping of America's postwar Middle East policy.

Three weeks after the Democratic convention concluded, Jabotinsky's disciples could point to another success: the Jewish army campaign. Although the Bergson group had largely dropped the Jewish army issue in order to focus on rescue as of early 1943, Jewish Agency officials in London had continued to periodically lobby for the proposal in their meetings with British officials. Finally, in August 1944, Prime Minister Churchill, moved by the slaughter of Hungarian Jewry and hoping to impress American public opinion, consented to the creation of a Jewish fighting force. The Jewish Brigade, which reached a strength of five thousand soldiers, saw action during the final months of the war and then played an important role in helping survivors immigrate to Palestine at war's end. The Revisionists, who had pioneered and popularized the Jewish army concept between 1940 and 1942, could justifiably feel proud that the birth of the Jewish Brigade was due in part to their political spadework.[29]

As the U.S. presidential election season heated up, Jewish Democrats countered rumblings of grassroots Jewish dissatisfaction with Roosevelt by pointing to another gesture from the administration: FDR's announcement that about one thousand European refugees, most of them Jews, would be brought to a temporary safe haven in upstate New York. There were only a few murmurs of criticism from Jewish activists who regarded the safe haven plan as too little, too late.[30]

Governor Dewey, for his part, could not be persuaded that a serious pitch for Jewish votes was worth his while. The Dewey campaign declined an offer by the Revisionists to assist in a six-month campaign of newspaper ads, radio broadcasts, mass mailings, and public rallies seeking Jewish votes for Dewey in New York by highlighting the weakest spots in FDR's Jewish record, including the Bermuda failure, the delay in creating the War Refugee Board, the administration's reluctance to quickly abolish Vichy anti-Semitic legislation after the Allies liberated North Africa, and Roosevelt's opposition to congressional resolutions favoring a Jewish Palestine.[31] Unable to secure Republican collaboration in the pursuit of Jewish votes for Dewey, the Revisionists issued their own election-eve "Open Letter" to FDR—in the form of a newspaper ad—strongly criticizing the president for promising to aid Zionism "if re-elected." Why wait until after election day, the NZOA demanded to know. "A President in office does not have to wait for election in order to carry out his promises." The ad was secretly authored partly by Benjamin Akzin, although at the time he was an employee of the War Refugee Board.[32]

Dewey's last chance to win any meaningful portion of the Jewish vote probably vanished when his vice presidential running mate, John Bricker, denounced the safe haven camp at upstate Oswego, New York, on the grounds that the refugees were not the "palefaced women and frail children" that had been depicted in the media but rather seemed to be "writers, lawyers, artists and intellectuals generally." Bricker's remarks about the refugees came shortly after another unpleasant controversy in which Bricker at first accepted, and only later disavowed, an endorsement from Gerald L. K. Smith, one of America's most prominent anti-Semitic agitators.[33] The Bricker controversies were a reminder to the Jewish community that a significant part of the Republican Party was still in the hands of those with whom Jews were the least comfortable, politically, socially, and culturally. Roosevelt might not be the Messiah, and some of his positions on Jewish issues might have left something to be desired, but when the alternative was the likes of John Bricker, it is not surprising that the vast majority of Jewish voters cast their ballots for FDR in November 1944, just as they had in the three previous presidential elections. Roosevelt's vague promise to support Zionism had worked, Republican activist George Sokolsky remarked. "The promise has performed its full mission: it collected votes."[34]

Amid the turmoil of the presidential election season, the Bergson group ignited a fresh dispute that engulfed the Jewish community in bitter acrimony. Bergson purchased the former Iranian Embassy building in Washington, D.C., and at a dramatic May 18 press conference proclaimed it the headquarters of a new "Hebrew Committee of National Liberation." Bergson declared that his committee, patterned on the various wartime European governments-in-exile, was the authentic representative of Palestine Jewry and those stateless European Jews hoping to immigrate to the Holy Land. This was a direct challenge to the authority of the World Zionist Organization and the Jewish Agency, which considered themselves the sole legitimate representatives of the *yishuv*.

To make matters even more complicated, Bergson used the occasion of the Hebrew Committee's creation to unveil his rather unorthodox personal perspective on the question of Jewish identity. Bergson announced that the new committee would distinguish between "Hebrews" and "Jews." It would apply the term "Hebrews" to Jewish residents of Palestine and stateless European Jews whom Bergson expected would soon immigrate to Palestine, while "Jews" would connote a religious preference with no implications of nationality and would refer only to American and other Diaspora Jews outside Europe. Bergson imagined that such a formal separation of Palestinian and European Jews from their American brethren would put an end to anti-Zionism among American Jews. He assumed that once American Jewish identity was formally defined as only religious rather than national, American Jews would no longer fear that the creation of a Zionist state would arouse anti-Semitic accusations of "dual loyalty." Bergson also believed that he had finally demonstrated to his critics that even though he was a foreigner, he was sensitive to American Jews' concerns about their place in American society.

The "Hebrews" gambit flopped. It satisfied nobody and enraged almost everybody. Non-Zionists and anti-Zionists were not mollified. They knew it would take more than linguistic sleight-of-hand to convince non-Jews that American Jews had no connection to a Jewish state. Mainstream American Zionist leaders, who were an integral part of the WZO and the Jewish Agency, were outraged by Bergson's challenge to their authority. They were also horrified by the "Hebrews" theory, since it undermined the basic Zionist tenet of international Jewish solidarity. A torrent of denunciations rained down upon the Bergson boys, and a number of those who had supported the Committee for a Jewish Army or the Emergency Committee to Save the Jewish People of Europe hurried to announce their resignations from the Bergson camp. Lillie Shultz of the American Jewish Congress took advantage of the tumult to persuade Freda Kirchwey, publisher of the *Nation,* to refuse all future advertisements from Bergson.[35] "We are the first to concede that Mr. Bergson's group, with its sensational publicity, contributed considerably at one time to awakening public opinion in this country to the urgency of the immediate rescue of Europe's Jews," the editors of the Independent Jewish Press Service declared, "[but] you cannot artificially disclaim centuries' old relationships consisting of a thousand ties, cultural, religious, ethical. . . . The last we heard from Europe was that the Jews there were still Jews. Those seeking their way out of the ghettoes and those who died on the barricades are known to themselves and to the world as Jews. . . . The Jews of Europe will be tragically surprised on the day of liberation to find that they have been turned into another people."[36]

None of the criticism fazed the unflappable Bergson. "He would retreat and lick his wounds, and the next day he would be ready for the next round," Ben-Ami recalled.[37] From May 1944 on, the word "Jew" virtually disappeared from the Bergsonites' vocabulary. In their press releases, advertisements, and newsletters, the Jews in Europe became "Hitler's Hebrew victims," the Jews in Palestine were "the Hebrews of Palestine," and the Irgun Zvai Leumi underground was "the Hebrew resistance." Congressmen who remained sympathetic to Bergson likewise embraced the linguistic shift, introducing resolutions urging the Roosevelt administration to "rescue the Hebrews from their Nazi persecutors." The use of the term "Hebrews" in this sense in the 1940s was not, however, quite as jarring to the ear at that time as it would seem in retrospect. Some Americans were accustomed to using the terms "Hebrew" and "Jew" interchangeably, since "Hebrews" was the word used to describe the Jews in many parts of the Bible. Indeed, American Jews who served in the U.S. Army had the letter "H," for "Hebrew," stamped on their identification tags to indicate their religion. Some American Jews, especially those associated with Reform Judaism, had employed the term "Hebrew" to refer to themselves or their institutions in order to downplay what they saw as negative images associated with the word "Jew"; the national association of Reform temples, for example, named itself the Union of American Hebrew Congregations. This popular blurring of the terms "Hebrew" and "Jew" obscured the radical nature of Bergson's position, so that the media continued to give his activities generous coverage, rather than dismiss him as a crackpot, as the mainstream Jewish leadership had hoped.

A year after the Hebrews theory was introduced, Bergson tried another unorthodox tactical maneuver, again without success. His goal was no longer the creation of a "Jewish" state, Bergson announced in 1945, but rather merely a "democratic commonwealth" where members of all religions would have equal rights. He was interested only in creating an American-style democracy in the Middle East, not establishing an ethnocentric or theocratic Jewish country. Bergson imagined that his new platform would be easier for the American public—and government—to swallow. This was, of course, semantics; independence for Palestine was widely understood to mean that there would be a huge, immediate influx of Holocaust survivors that would turn the new country into a de facto Jewish state.

The British, for their part, were not fooled. "The strategy here is presumably to secure the Palestinian State first and then capture it by Jewish immigration," the British Embassy correctly noted. As for Americans, the

Bergson declaration was really unnecessary. The terms "Jews," "Hebrews," and "Palestine" had become so intertwined in the vocabulary of the media, Congress, and public discourse as to mean virtually the same thing. The details of what kind of state the Jews would have, or whether they would consider themselves Jews or Hebrews, were immaterial to the average American. Thus while Bergson's call for a "democratic commonwealth" aggravated mainstream Zionists (Revisionists, too), public sympathy for his activities did not appreciably diminish as a result. Even the British Embassy, which dubbed Bergson "a Semitic Himmler," grudgingly acknowledged that there remained "a fairly considerable public which is still impressed by him and continues to subscribe handsomely to the Hebrew Committee's funds."[38]

The strident Jewish infighting that accompanied the "Hebrew Committee" controversy erupted at the worst possible time for the Jews who were still alive in the Nazi inferno. On March 19, 1944, the Germans occupied Hungary, the last country on the European mainland with a large Jewish population that had been largely untouched by the Holocaust. Mass confiscation of Jewish property and forced ghettoization proceeded throughout April. Nationwide deportations of Hungarian Jews to Auschwitz began on May 15 and continued for nearly two months; over 400,000 perished. Only the Jews of Budapest were spared—temporarily. Unlike previous stages of the Holocaust, the catastrophe in Hungary was widely reported in the Western media as it was unfolding. From his vantage point on the staff of the War Refugee Board—a position secured thanks to his relationship with Senator Claude Pepper—Benjamin Akzin repeatedly put forward the idea of Allied air strikes on the Auschwitz death camp and the railways leading from Hungary to Auschwitz. The World Jewish Congress, the Orthodox Vaad Ha-Hatzala, officials of the Jewish Agency in Europe and in Palestine, and other Jewish organizations likewise privately urged the Allies to bomb the death camps or the connecting railroad lines. Adamant that the U.S. military not devote any of its attention or resources to refugee matters, the War Department rejected the proposals without even studying their feasibility.[39]

The response of mainstream American Jewish leaders to the Hungarian crisis was less vigorous than what might have been expected in view of the information that was available about what was happening in Hungary. Many in the Jewish leadership had been mollified by Roosevelt's establishment of the War Refugee Board, in January, and his announcement, in June, that about a thousand refugees from Hitler would be granted emergency haven in the United States. Others were busy throwing darts at Bergson; time and energy that could have been devoted to advocating rescue measures was expended on combating the dissidents.

For Netanyahu and the Revisionists, the "Hebrews" flap posed a unique dilemma. Did they dare risk impeding the valuable work Bergson was doing by joining in the condemnations? Until the "Hebrews" affair, the NZOA and the Bergson committees had coexisted more or less amicably, with both sides satisfied at the division of labor that left Bergson dealing with rescue matters while the Revisionists focused on Palestine. Events sponsored by the Emergency Committee to Save the Jewish People of Europe were announced in the NZOA newsletter, and Bergson's most enthusiastic congressional ally, Senator Edwin Johnson (D-Colorado), even addressed a March 18 dinner organized by the Revisionists to commemorate the founding of the Jewish Legion.[40] But the "Hebrews" announcement created a new and serious fissure in the Zionist right. Already quietly smarting from the Bergsonites' competition, and restless over Bergson's reluctance to criticize the British administration in Palestine, NZOA leaders saw the "Hebrews" declaration as proof that the dissidents had lost their senses. Netanyahu wrote that Bergson and his cohorts were now no better than "the assimilationists of the type of Lessing Rosenwald [a prominent anti-Zionist] . . . they are worse than the American Jewish Committee [whose members were generally either non-Zionists or anti-Zionists]."[41] The notion that American Jews, unencumbered by embarrassing ties to Palestine or European Jewry, could live safely in the Diaspora clashed with the classic Zionist maxim that persecution was inevitable wherever Jews reside outside their national homeland. "The sword of Damocles hangs over the Jews everywhere," Netanyahu warned, "and it may descend upon them unexpectedly even in places where they feel secure."[42]

Within the U.S. Revisionist rank and file, opinion was divided on how to respond to the "Hebrews" affair. Chicago Revisionist leader Moshe Steiner pleaded with Netanyahu for restraint. "Our members feel that there is still some possibility of getting together with 'the boys,'" especially since the Bergsonites' positions are "of Revisionist origin," he urged the New York leadership.[43] Hoping to avoid a rift with Bergson's allies in the NZOA, and cognizant of the contributions the Bergson group had made in arousing American public sympathy for a Jewish army and European Jewry, Netanyahu and his colleagues decided "that it would be better not to be too harsh in our criticism." The resolution they presented at the NZOA national convention in June, which won a large majority, stated only that the Revisionist movement was "neither organizationally nor ideologically nor politically connected with this group and is not responsible in any way for the activities of its organizations." Even that was too much for a handful of pro-Bergson NZOA activists, who responded by breaking away from the national movement to form their own Zionist-Revisionist Organization of America. Although not formally affiliated with Bergson, the new Zionist-Revisionist group would work closely with the Bergsonites in the years to follow.[44]

Vladimir (Ze'ev) Jabotinsky (1880–1940), founder of Revisionist Zionism. Photo courtesy of the Zionist Archives.

Rabbi Louis I. Newman, president of the Revisionist Zionist movement in the United States during the 1930s. Photo courtesy of the Newman family.

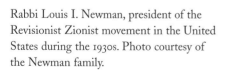

Lieutenant Colonel John Henry Patterson, famed lion hunter, commander of the Jewish Legion, and Jabotinsky supporter. Photo courtesy of the Zionist Archives.

Rabbi Baruch Rabinowitz, one of the Jabotinsky movement's lobbyists in Washington, D.C., delivering a speech at a rally, circa 1943. Photo courtesy of Baruch and Malka Robbins.

Benzion Netanyahu, executive director
of the Revisionist Zionist movement
in the United States from 1941 to 1948.
This photograph was taken shortly
after he arrived in America in 1940.
Photo courtesy of Benzion Netanyahu.

Eliahu Ben-Horin, a veteran activist in the U.S.
Revisionist Zionist movement who later became a
senior aide to American Zionist leader Abba Hillel
Silver. Photo courtesy of the Zionist Archives.

Peter Bergson (*center,* dark suit) and colleagues holding a press conference in
Washington, D.C., in May 1944. Photo courtesy of Harry L. Selden.

Harry L. Selden, director of the American
League for a Free Palestine (1945). Photo
courtesy of Harry L. Selden.

Ben Hecht (*right*) showing former U.S. senator Guy Gillette the manuscript of
A Flag Is Born (1946). Photo courtesy of the Zionist Archives.

The SS *Ben Hecht*, which militant American Zionists purchased to bring European
Jewish refugees to Palestine in 1947, in defiance of British immigration restrictions.
Photo courtesy of the Zionist Archives.

European Jewish refugees aboard the SS *Ben Hecht* on their way to Palestine in 1947. Photo courtesy of the Zionist Archives.

WHO are the real TERRORISTS?

With rage in their breasts—having failed to provoke Palestine Jewry into a civil war—the British have sent 100,000 troops, armed in full war regalia, to roam the country-side, the cities and villages of the Holy Land. Innocent men, women and children are being beaten up and homes ransacked under the pretext of suppressing violence.

With the help of rigid military censorship in Palestine, *American public opinion is being hoodwinked.* Acts of desperation by Jewish men and women—provoked by illegal military measures and deportation of Jewish refugees to concentration camps—are magnified. Acts of brutal terrorism by British military are glamorized.

A veritable barrage of photographs is being directed to this country, which depict the "poor British" in Palestine as martyrs. Why are not photographs permitted to reach these shores showing the clubbing of survivors of Nazi massacres, the shooting of a four-year-old Jewish girl and the wounding of her older sister who came to her rescue? Neither have we seen photographs of a cyclist shot to death while riding on a peaceful errand, or of the wanton destruction of Jewish homesteads by military patrols in peaceful settlements.

$400,000,000 has to date been spent on the maintenance of 100,000 troops in Palestine "for the sake"—in the words of Winston Churchill —"of a senseless, squalid war against the Jews." This money could profitably be used to provide the necessities of life to the British people at home!

⊕

The Zionist Organization of America has pledged its continued help to the stream of Jewish immigration into Palestine. It fights on all fronts to secure justice for the Jewish people and safeguard its rights to a Jewish Palestine before the United Nations.

☙

ZIONIST ORGANIZATION OF AMERICA

Regions of Manhattan, Brooklyn, Bronx, Westchester and Long Island

THERE IS ROOM FOR 100,000 TROOPS IN PALESTINE, BUT NO ROOM FOR 100,000 JEWISH REFUGEES!

The American public and the United Nations must be informed of the true facts. We intend to do so, but we need your help

The Zionist Organization of America is the acknowledged major instrumentality of American Jewry for the upbuilding of Jewish Palestine. It asks you to join its forces fighting for Jewish survival.

Enroll today as a member.

Zionist Organization of America
41 East 42nd Street
New York 17, New York

Gentlemen:
    I wish to enroll as a member of the Z. O. A. and thereby join actively in the fight for Jewish survival by adding my voice in support of the Zionist case before the United Nations.
    Enclosed is $5.00 as my annual membership dues.

NAME ....

ADDRESS ....

CITY ....
Please make checks or money orders payable to Zionist Organization of America.

Advertisement by the Zionist Organization of America that appeared in the *Nation* on April 12, 1947. Courtesy of the Zionist Archives.

THE *New Palestine*

Voices in the Yishuv
by J. L. Teller

British Gestapo
by DVA

Jewish Education in America
by Daniel Frisch

The Mufti's Coup
by Mark Krug

•

A Voice From the Past
by M. M. Ussishkin

•

The Sin
by Jacob Picard

JEWS IN THE ARAB WORLD
by CECIL ROTH

SOVIET JEWS — OR JEWRY
by JACOB LESTCHINSKY

Vol. XXXVI   OCTOBER 4, 1946   No. 24

New Palestine, published by the Zionist Organization of America, compared the Palestine Jewish underground fighters to the patriots of the American Revolution. Courtesy of the Zionist Archives.

Revisionist Zionist activist Abraham Zweibon in front of his East New York store, where he and his wife, Sylvia, hid weapons before shipping them to the Palestine Jewish underground. Photo courtesy of Emanuel Zweibon.

Advertisement by the Palestine Resistance Fund that appeared in the *New York Post* on April 16, 1947. The illustration is by Arthur Szyk. Courtesy of the Zionist Archives.

Rabbi Baruch Korff, leader of the militant Political Action Committee for Palestine, meeting with members of Congress in 1947 to deliver petitions calling for Jewish statehood. *Left to right:* Senators William Langer, Irving M. Ives, and Arthur Capper, Representative Sol Bloom, and Rabbi Korff. Photo courtesy of Brown University Library.

Rabbi Baruch Korff greeted by his father upon his return from France, where he had been imprisoned because of his ties to the Palestine Jewish underground. Photo courtesy of Brown University Library.

Rabbi Baruch Korff hoisting the Israeli flag at his Boston headquarters moments after Israel's creation was announced. Photo courtesy of Brown University Library.

7 • A Powerful New Alliance

The increasing prominence of the Revisionists and the emergence of Abba Hillel Silver as a major figure in the battle over the 1944 Republican Party platform illustrated the realignment of the political forces in the American Jewish community that was under way. During the early years of the war, American Zionists had been generally united in support of the policies of Stephen Wise and his allies; those favoring a more activist approach were a small minority in the Jewish community. But in 1943 and 1944, grassroots Jewish outrage over the European massacres and Britain's Palestine policy catapulted Abba Hillel Silver to Zionist leadership and stimulated support for the Revisionist groups as well. The one-two punch delivered by Silver and the Revisionists at the Republican convention dramatized the shifting balance of power in the community. Now the Silver faction of the mainstream, with its newfound Revisionist allies, was arrayed against a Wise faction of "moderates" whose numbers and influence were rapidly diminishing.

In his heart, Wise had never really accepted Silver's ascent. When Silver was appointed co-chair of the American Zionist Emergency Council in the summer of 1943, Wise privately vowed: "I shall show my fellow-Zionists now that I am not to be shelved, I am not to be displaced; that I will exert my authority as the Chairman of the [AZEC]."[1] Throughout Silver's first year at the AZEC, the tensions between the two co-chairs mounted steadily. Personality differences, disagreements over strategy, and their unresolved struggle for leadership of the Jewish community combined to make peaceful coexistence between the two increasingly impossible. Typical of their conflicts was a dispute over arrangements to meet Secretary of State Edward Stettinius in the summer of 1944. In January of that year, the AZEC had attracted substantial congressional support for a pro-Zionist resolution, only to see the initiative killed by the insistence of the War and State Departments that such a resolution would harm the war effort by inflaming the Arab world against the Allies. By summertime, with the war's end in sight, Silver was anxious to start pressing the administration to withdraw its objections. Wise, by contrast, hesitated to take any action that might annoy the president, and Nahum Goldmann assured the British Embassy that he (Goldmann) and Chaim Weizmann regarded the resolution as "an error" since it might "embarrass the Allied governments."[2]

In early August 1944, Silver urged Wise to secure an immediate appointment for the two of them to see Stettinius. Wise, who was summering at Camp Willamette in picturesque Lake Placid (upstate New York), asked Stettinius to meet them on August 29.[3] Silver complained bitterly to Emanuel Neumann about Wise's latest "stunt": "He suggested the date of the 29th to Mr. Stettinius because he plans to attend the [AZEC] meeting in New York [City] on the 28th. This will save him an extra trip from Lake Placid! The Zionist Movement in these critical war times must conform with the lecture schedule and the vacation schedule of Dr. Wise."[4] Wise and Silver did, however, manage to join hands in opposition to two congressional initiatives by the Hebrew Committee and the NZOA. In August 1944, Bergson induced his closest congressional allies, Senator Elbert Thomas and Representative Andrew Somers, to introduce a resolution calling on the United States to pressure England to create "mass emergency rescue shelters" in Palestine for Jewish refugees. The measure won the initial support of, among others, House majority leader John W. McCormack and Silver's old friend Senator Robert Taft—until Wise and Silver strenuously objected, on grounds that the resolution wrongly portrayed Palestine as a temporary haven rather than a Jewish national homeland. They successfully lobbied to bury the Bergson resolution before it could come to a vote.[5]

Several weeks later, Netanyahu convinced Taft to sign a letter publicly criticizing President Roosevelt's stance on Palestine. Much to Netanyahu's surprise and delight, Taft personally escorted the Revisionist leader to the offices of four other senators to secure their signatures on the letter as well. But then Taft woke Netanyahu with an early-morning phone call the day the statement was to be released, instructing him to postpone it until Taft could discuss the matter with Silver. The next day, Taft called back to say the statement would have to be shelved. "I have never seen Rabbi Silver so upset," the senator told Netanyahu. "He feels the statement will do more harm than good, that it will antagonize the President rather than influence him." Taft said he was "perplexed" by Silver's attitude, but the senator was unwilling to risk making an enemy of his old friend and ally.[6]

Silver now prepared to forge ahead with his own political action campaign, beginning with the resurrection of his own pro-Zionist congressional resolution. Such resolutions, Isaiah Berlin of the British Embassy noted, "even if they were mere expressions of goodwill and no more," were useful "to inhibit [administration] officials from going too far, for fear of being attacked by name in Congress and in the press."[7] Silver's resolution, which had been stalled since January, gained new life in October when the War Department, assessing the latest changes for the better on the war front, withdrew its earlier objections to the resolution. Silver's congressional allies began arrangements to hold hearings on the resolution while Silver pressed the State Department to drop its opposition. Wise and Nahum Goldmann, however, quietly assured Secretary of State Stettinius that they would accept further postponement of the resolution. Unbeknownst to Silver, they even lobbied key congressmen to put off consideration of the matter. When Silver, accompanied by Senator Robert Wagner, visited Stettinius on December 2, the secretary of state displayed a confidential telegram he had just received from Wise, asserting that American Jewry would not be unhappy if the resolution were postponed. The resolution was buried, and recriminations were soon flying fast and furious within the deeply divided American Zionist leadership. The struggle reached its climax at back-to-back meetings of the ZOA Executive Committee and the AZEC on December 19 and 20.

Wise's followers, led by Goldmann, who was now serving as the Jewish Agency representative in Washington, blasted Silver for being too aggressive in his efforts on behalf of the resolution:

What we are doing here is what Revisionists have done for 20 years. It is exactly Revisionist tactics. Revisionists are very good Zionists. There has never lived in the world a better Zionist than Vladimir Jabotinsky, the incarnation of passion and devotion to Zionism, but if we would have adopted his tactics we would never have had 600,000 Jews in Palestine; we would have remained with resolutions, protests, and emotional outbursts of the so-called Jewish masses and would never have achieved the little or the much that we have achieved in Palestine.[8]

If Netanyahu and his comrades had heard Goldmann's assessment, they would no doubt have agreed that Silver had, in effect, adopted Revisionist tactics. Silver's idea of the AZEC was, in a sense, Revisionism without the

Revisionists. He was trying to lead the mainstream to embrace the ways of the activists: using electoral leverage to secure Jewish aims; seeking allies for Zionism in both parties, regardless of his comfort with the parties' stands on other issues; pressing the Zionist agenda even over the objections of the White House and the State Department; insisting on nothing less than full Jewish statehood. Silver had risen to co-chairmanship of the AZEC because he had widespread grassroots backing for this activist agenda.

Silver's support among the grassroots did not avail him that frigid week in December 1944, for Wise's allies still enjoyed a majority in both the ZOA hierarchy and the organizations that made up the AZEC. Reprimanded by the ZOA and facing dismissal at the next day's AZEC session, a furious Silver announced his resignation.[9]

State Department officials watched these developments with barely disguised glee. Wallace Murray, the director of the State Department's Office of Near Eastern and African Affairs and a firm anti-Zionist, reported to Secretary of State Cordell Hull that the administration's role in killing the resurrected Palestine resolution "attracted comparatively little attention among Zionists." He cited the small volume of critical mail received on the topic as well as the "fairly light" coverage by the media. "The most likely explanation for the comparative absence of adverse comment," Wallace told the secretary of state, "is undoubtedly the split within the Zionist leadership, notably the difference of opinion between Rabbi Wise and Rabbi Silver resulting in the resignation of [Silver]." With Silver out of the way, the State Department could breathe much easier.[10]

Foggy Bottom's joy was short-lived. Silver's departure was soon followed by a repeat of the events of the summer of 1943. Once again, there was a tidal wave of grassroots demands for a more activist leadership. In the face of increasingly detailed revelations about the extent of Nazi atrocities, as well as Britain's refusal to change its Palestine immigration policy despite the official expiration of the White Paper in May 1944, American Zionists from coast to coast bombarded the ZOA leadership with letters demanding Silver's return. The Jewish press was filled with calls for reconciliation with the Silver group. Enthusiastic ovations greeted Silver at Zionist rallies. "The house literally rose to its feet and cheered" at the mere mention of Silver's name, Pierre van Paassen found when he spoke in favor of Silver's approach at rallies in Washington and New York in January 1945. Van Paassen conferred privately with local Zionist activists in Brooklyn and reported to Silver that they were "boiling with indignation."

They want to sweep the administration into the ash can. I think they will. The Jews are sick and tired of appeasement and whispers and dark hints. Their kinsmen are dying in Europe. The White Paper is in force. Tomorrow the British will tell us: there are no Jews clamoring to enter Palestine. The Jews are dead. Hitler killed them. Before this argument is advanced they want action. And they feel that you ought to lead them. They are waiting for word from you. They are deeply stirred.[11]

A worried Nahum Goldmann confided to State Department officials that the rising tide of Jewish anger in the United States, Europe, and Palestine was such that "Dr. Weizmann and the other moderates" in the leadership of the world Zionist movement "might be ousted in favor of Rabbi Silver and other advocates of a stronger policy." Goldmann estimated that "at least 70% of American Zionists" were "backing Rabbi Silver strongly and it was not at all certain that the extremists would not prevail." He mentioned that there had recently been "much talk" of allowing the Revisionists to rejoin both the World Zionist Organization and the American Zionist movement, "as Rabbi Silver desired." Goldmann noted that while he had blocked the Revisionists' entry, there was no telling how long he would prevail.[12]

If the contents of Goldmann's frank discussion at the State Department had leaked out, it would have provided both Silver and the Revisionists with plenty of ammunition. "For five years and more," Goldmann recalled at the meeting, he, Weizmann, and Wise had acceded to a request by the administration that they "urge their people to follow a policy of moderation and not to expect a solution of the Palestine question along Zionist lines before the end of the war in Europe." Goldmann boasted that he and his colleagues "had succeeded to a notable degree in imposing a policy of restraint upon the Jews of the world" and had "persuaded [our] people to accept in a disciplined manner the terrible misfortunes which had been visited upon world Jewry in the last few years." Now, with England still refusing to offer any concessions whatsoever on Palestine, it was possible that the leadership of the Zionist movement "would pass to those not averse to violence." Goldmann pleaded with the State Department officials to convince the British to make some kind of a gesture, lest the "moderate" faction in the Zionist movement be voted out.[13] Goldmann could read the writing on the wall. By the summer of 1945, a Zionist "Peace Committee" worked out a new deal that returned Silver to co-chairmanship of the AZEC and also awarded him chairmanship of the powerful ZOA Executive Committee. American Zionism would never be the same.

The Revisionists, for their part, continued and intensified their public political action efforts. Newspaper advertisements were still the medium of choice for communicating the NZOA's message to America; ads denouncing the British and demanding Jewish statehood appeared in the *New York Times, New York Post, Washington Post, Boston Globe, Philadelphia Inquirer,* and elsewhere. During the spring of 1945, the Revisionists also regularly sponsored paid broadcasts on major New York City radio stations. A speech by Senator Brewster at an NZOA dinner was aired on WMCA; an address by Colonel Patterson was broadcast on WHN.[14]

The bulk of the spring, however, was taken up by preparations for the forthcoming founding conference of the United Nations in San Francisco. Although denied formal observer status at the conference, the American Revisionist leadership decided to send a delegation to press the Palestine cause nonetheless. Netanyahu was dispatched to Washington beforehand for several intensive weeks of recruiting senators to take part in the NZOA's planned propaganda effort at the UN gathering.[15] Then it was back to New York for the long train ride to the West Coast alongside Major William Friedman, a Jewish War Veterans leader and NZOA vice president, who was serving as acting chairman while Mendelsohn mended fences with the South African wing of the Revisionist movement. Hours before their departure, Netanyahu was informed that the secretary they had hired in San Francisco was unavailable. His wife, Cela, replaced her. The Netanyahus and Friedman were met in San Francisco by Professor Abraham S. Yahuda, a brilliant, if eccentric, Egyptologist who had once lived in Spain; Netanyahu thought he would be useful for lobbying the Spanish-speaking delegates at the UN conference.

The NZOA delegates energetically "worked the floor" at the conference, cornering delegates in the meeting rooms, in the lobby, often in the hotel bar, typically devoting fifteen exhausting hours daily in a frantic effort to influence postwar Allied policy on the Middle East. Their message was simple: take the Palestine Mandate away from England and give it to the UN for five years, during which time there would be unrestricted Jewish immigration, followed by Jewish statehood.[16] They reinforced their private lobbying with a publicity barrage centered on their release of a letter signed by twelve U.S. senators calling for a Jewish state and asking the conference to admit an official delegation representing Palestine Jewry. Because of his earlier success in establishing relationships with the senators, Netanyahu was able to quickly recruit them, by telephone from San Francisco, to sign the statement.[17]

Delegates to the conference faced the occasionally bewildering spectacle of being wooed by three different Zionist factions. Netanyahu's Revisionists were urging that the Palestine Mandate be taken away from the British. Mainstream Zionist representatives urged that England keep the Mandate with the understanding that it would permit Jewish immigration and the evolution of a Jewish national home, as originally promised in the 1917 Balfour Declaration. Bergson and his aides, who also lobbied vigorously in San Francisco, urged the delegates to endorse Jewish resistance against the British and recognize the Hebrew Committee of National Liberation as the voice of Palestine Jewry. Bergson also pressed the Yugoslavian representatives at the conference to place the former mufti of Jerusalem, Haj Amin el-Husseini, on their country's list of wanted Nazi war criminals because of Husseini's wartime recruitment of Yugoslavian Muslims for an all-Muslim division of the SS; shortly afterward, Yugoslavia placed the mufti on their wanted list. Jewish Agency representative Eliahu Epstein, watching Jabotinsky's disciples in action at the San Francisco conference and witnessing their reception by the local Jewish community, reported back to his colleagues that "the dissident groups have apparently gained some hold on Jewish opinion." He was especially troubled at the militants' ability to "attract to their cause groups of people who have previously been indifferent to Zionism and non-Jews of high social and political position."[18]

Ultimately, neither the Jabotinskyites nor the establishment Zionists made much headway in San Francisco. The United States and Great Britain were still in the process of formulating their postwar approach to the Palestine quandary and were therefore not about to permit the San Francisco conference to reach decisions that might tie their hands. Rejecting any specific consideration of Palestine, the UN's Committee on Trusteeships dealt in general terms with the guidelines for postwar Allied control of colonies and mandate territories. The Revisionists and mainstream Zionists alike, alarmed at the inclusion of language they feared would further restrict UN intervention in England's rule over Palestine, lobbied, with only partial success, for adjustments in the wording. Still, Netanyahu regarded the outcome of the conference as something of a victory, since there had been no explicit endorsement of continuing the British Mandate.[19]

While international attention was focused on San Francisco, behind-the-scenes developments in Washington were shaping events in ways that would soon have a major impact on the Zionist struggle. Treasury Secretary Henry Morgenthau, responding to pressure from mainstream Zionists and Jabotinskyites, lobbied Acting Secretary of State Joseph Grew on the future of Holocaust survivors residing in Allied Displaced Persons (DP) Camps in Europe. Citing reports of severe overcrowding and deteriorating health conditions in the Allied refugee camps, Morgenthau persuaded Grew to send an investigatory committee, headed by former U.S. immigration commissioner Earl Harrison, to examine the DPs' plight. Harrison's report recommended, most notably, the immediate admission of 100,000 DPs into Palestine. President Harry Truman and his political advisers, nervously eyeing the upcoming New York City mayoral election, saw Harrison's proposal as a way for the president to score political points by embracing a humanitarian gesture while at least temporarily avoiding taking a definitive stand on the stickier question of Palestine's future. Much to London's consternation, Truman endorsed the Harrison proposal. British foreign minister Ernest Bevin privately complained to his colleagues that the increasing influence of Jewish voters on the Truman administration was making it harder for England to decide long-term policy on the Arab-Jewish question.[20]

Worried that the growing American Zionist agitation over Palestine "was poisoning British relations with the United States government in other fields," Bevin proposed in October that the United States and Britain cosponsor a committee to examine the DP problem as well as Palestine. This was an expansion of an earlier plan for an exclusively British investigation that was to consider only the DPs' situation in Europe; in deference to America's intensifying interest in the subject, Bevin agreed to expand the committee's terms of reference to include Palestine. "The propaganda in New York has destroyed what looked to me a few weeks ago as a reasonable atmosphere in which we could get Jews and Arabs together," Bevin complained to the British ambassador, Lord Halifax; now there was no choice but to involve the Americans and bring Palestine into the equation. Much to London's annoyance, U.S. secretary of state James Byrnes, citing the "intense and growing agitation about the Palestine problem in the New York electoral campaign," insisted that the announcement of the creation of the Anglo-American Committee of Inquiry be postponed until after the November 6 New York mayoral election, lest it "inflame" Jewish voters and turn them against the Democratic candidate. It was a graphic reminder to the British government that American Zionist protests were having an increasing impact on the considerations of American policy makers. British officials expressed bewilderment at the growing intrusion of domestic politics into Anglo-American discussions about the Middle East, but from the point of view of the Truman administration it was potentially a matter of political survival. As Truman later pointed out to the American delegation to the Anglo-American Committee of Inquiry, "never before in the history of the White House had there been such a tremendous volume of mail as that dealing with the displaced persons." Truman knew that every such letter represented the sentiments of many more voters who had not bothered to write but would surely cast ballots on election day. The administration's sensitivity to Jewish protests, and the strains it was causing in American-British relations, demonstrated that American Zionists, mainstream and militants alike, were on the right track. Their rallies, newspaper advertisements, letter writing, and congressional lobbying were significantly increasing the pressure on Britain regarding Palestine.[21]

Meanwhile, back on American Zionism's domestic front, the NZOA leadership was grappling with the still-unresolved problem of unity within the ranks of the world Revisionist movement. With the London and New York branches still at odds over where the international headquarters should be situated, and South Africa wavering, the rivals agreed to settle their differences at a conference in London under the auspices of the Palestine Revisionists. At the same time, the New Yorkers were particularly intent on pressing for a decision to reenter the WZO. Ten years had passed since Jabotinsky had led his movement out of the WZO, a decade in which the Jewish world as Jabotinsky knew it had been devastated. In 1935 he had broken ranks with a Zionist movement that hesitated to criticize British policy in Palestine, refused to openly call for a Jewish state, and endorsed extreme measures, including violence, against Revisionists during the period of the Arlosoroff crisis. Ten years later, the world Zionist leadership, shaken by the catastrophe of the Holocaust and England's unyielding stance on Palestine, championed Jewish statehood and gave its blessing to the Haganah to join the Irgun and its splinter group, the Lohamei Herut Yisrael (Lehi), in the United Hebrew Resistance Movement's armed rebellion against the British Mandate authorities. The shift in mainstream Zionist attitudes gave the NZOA powerful ammunition in its quest for reentering the world Zionist movement.

Abba Hillel Silver, still hoping to bring the Revisionists into the Zionist mainstream, noted with satisfaction the new possibility of the Jabotinsky-ites' reentering the WZO, which would enable them to enter the AZEC as well. The Revisionists appreciated Silver's friendly attitude and were delighted that he had usurped Stephen Wise as leader of the mainstream

Zionists. The Revisionists also enjoyed the irony of Wise and his colleagues attacking Silver with "the usual attributes which were once hurled against the Revisionists with regard to discipline, etc." Mendelsohn, Colonel Patterson, and Major Friedman held a friendly consultation with Silver before sailing to London for the international Revisionist gathering. Joseph Schechtman, in his first major role as part of the NZOA leadership, accompanied the delegation to London. Netanyahu stayed behind to complete his doctoral dissertation, on medieval Jewish philosophy, at Dropsie College in Philadelphia.[22]

Before international Revisionist unity could be achieved, the London delegates had to deal with the nettlesome problem of divisions within the American branch. Bergson group activist Johan Smertenko, representing the pro-Bergson Zionist-Revisionist Organization of America, showed up at the conference and demanded to be seated as an accredited delegate. The NZOA representatives were furious at the appearance of the "paper organization," which they saw as little more than "a tool to confuse the public and create the impression that the Hebrew Committee [of National Liberation] has some backing."[23] Intensive negotiations between the two camps produced a surprisingly speedy resolution: several officials of the Zionist-Revisionist group would be given senior positions within the NZOA in exchange for the dissolution of their splinter group.[24] The broader question of the Revisionists' relations with the WZO was not so easily resolved. After a vigorous debate, the London Revisionist conference opted to leave the matter in the laps of the individual branches; after each country's Revisionist movement held its own convention and voted, the international movement would decide.

With elections for delegates to the 1946 World Zionist Congress less than ten months away, the NZOA leaders returned to New York and immediately began organizing their next convention. A formal decision by the convention in favor of joining the WZO was needed before the U.S. Revisionists could compete for seats in the Zionist Congress. In the midst of a fierce January winter, NZOA activists from around the country assembled at New York's Hotel Edison to decide the fate of their movement. Several prominent delegates, including Jabotinsky's widow, Johanna, opposed entering the WZO. Netanyahu delivered the pitch for unity with the Zionist mainstream. With the major differences between the Revisionists and the American Zionist establishment evaporating, the NZOA now faced a clear choice, he argued: remain "a back door party" on the fringes of Zionism, or enter the WZO, influence its policy, and perhaps play a role in changing its leadership. "Either we remain a small insignificant group, fighting from the back, and seclude ourselves," he pleaded, "or we go with the current, push the current, and finally we ride the current." Skeptics called the WZO's recent trend toward militancy an illusion and warned that the Revisionists might be rendered toothless once confined by the movement's discipline. But Netanyahu's argument carried the day. By a two-to-one margin, the delegates endorsed "going with the current" by rejoining the world Zionist movement and participating in the World Zionist Congress elections.[25]

London was not pleased by the latest developments. With Zionist unity achieved, the British Embassy warned, "the stage is set for a renewal of the battle [for public opinion], with conservative and radical forces joined." The Zionists could be expected to exercise pressure on the Republicans and Democrats alike in advance of the 1946 congressional elections, and there was a real possibility "that this new pressure campaign will have more success than its predecessors." To make matters worse, a new danger had arisen, the British Embassy warned London: postwar discrimination in the United States against Jews in employment and schooling could provoke American Jewish immigration to Palestine on the order of "several thousand a year," with as many as "a million and a quarter to a million and a half potential immigrants" waiting in the wings.[26]

In preparation for the forthcoming Zionist elections, the NZOA reunited with the earliest Revisionist splinter group, the small Jewish State Party. Their joint list of candidates for the elections, known as the "United Zionists-Revisionists," would be headed by the Jewish State Party chairman, Meir Grossman. Their campaign slogan: "Vote for a militant, outspoken and courageous Zionist policy!" Devoted, articulate, and well liked by the various factions in the movement, Grossman soon emerged as the obvious choice to succeed the exhausted Morris Mendelsohn as leader of the NZOA itself.[27] At an April 7 conference in New York, the NZOA renamed itself the United Zionists-Revisionists of America (UZRA) and elected Grossman president, with Schechtman as chair of the policy-making Political Committee and Netanyahu continuing as executive director.

During the weeks leading up to the World Zionist Congress elections, the UZRA sponsored a series of campaign ads in the Yiddish press and the *New York Post*, and Betar teens blanketed New York's boroughs with election literature. Netanyahu and his colleagues had good reason to expect they would receive a significant number of votes. Events abroad during the weeks before the election seemed to confirm the Revisionists' pessimistic warnings of British intransigence. On April 27, British soldiers angry over a Jewish underground attack rioted in the Jewish towns of Netanya and Be'er Tuvia, smashing stores, beating up passersby, and daubing anti-Semitic slogans on walls. On May 1, the Anglo-American Committee of Inquiry released its report, recommending perpetuation of British rule; the one aspect of the report pleasing to the Zionists, a call for the immediate immigration of 100,000 Jewish refugees to Palestine, was rejected by the British. Then, on the day before the Zionist elections, June 29, the British conducted nationwide arrests, seizing senior Jewish Agency leaders and nearly three thousand others they deemed possible supporters of Jewish terrorism. In the course of the sometimes brutal "Black Sabbath" raids, four Jews were killed and eighty injured.

Yet when the ballots were counted, the U.S. Revisionists had captured just eight thousand votes, about 4 percent of the total. Abba Hillel Silver's ZOA list won the largest bloc, 31 percent; the Labor Zionists and Hadassah received about 23 percent each; the Religious Zionists won 14 percent. In view of the UZRA's late entry into the campaign and its limited budget, the final result was deemed satisfactory by Netanyahu and his aides.[28] No doubt one of the reasons for the Revisionists' meager showing was the fact that Abba Hillel Silver's agenda was nearly as militant as that of Netanyahu and company. Many potential Revisionist voters, who would not have cast their ballots for a Zionist establishment headed by Stephen Wise, felt comfortable with the activist approach of Dr. Silver.

Although the American Revisionist delegation was small, the mood at the Zionist Congress itself was as activist as Jabotinsky's followers could have hoped. The crucial vote came over England's invitation to the Zionists to take part in another conference with Arab representatives. An activist faction led by Abba Hillel Silver and David Ben-Gurion opposed the British proposal, while WZO president Chaim Weizmann favored it. When the delegates rejected the proposal, 171 to 154, they were in effect voting no-confidence in the Weizmann administration. Weizmann promptly resigned, and the delegates put the movement's governing power in the hands of the activists by electing Ben-Gurion chairman of the Zionist Executive and Silver chairman of the newly formed American Section of the Jewish Agency.

Amidst the turmoil of the Zionist Congress elections and the dramatic change in leadership of the world Zionist movement, Abba Hillel Silver and the American Jabotinskyites were simultaneously campaigning against a proposed American loan of $3.75 billion to Great Britain for postwar reconstruction. Silver, appearing as the featured speaker at a June 11 rally for

Palestine in Madison Square Garden, urged American Jews to ask their congressmen whether Britain could be trusted to repay the loan in view of its "shocking record of broken pledges" concerning the Jewish national home. His appeal produced an avalanche of letters to Congress urging linkage between the loan and the admission of 100,000 DPs to Palestine. Benzion Netanyahu and his colleagues denounced the loan at Revisionist rallies and in letters to congressmen. Former Bergson activist Baruch Korff, now head of his own Political Action Committee for Palestine, combed Capitol Hill, rounding up 177 senators and representatives to sign a newspaper ad headlined "Kill That Loan!—Lest You Forsake Your Conscience"—an impressive show of militant Zionism's strength in Washington, although the lobbying cost the Korff committee its tax-exempt status.[29]

A worried Ambassador Halifax reported to London that in the Senate, Senator Taft was working to link the loan to a change in England's Palestine policy. In the House, Congressman Emanuel Celler led a spirited fight against the loan, seeking to broaden the opposition by raising questions not only about British policy in Palestine but also the terms of the loan and England's ability to repay it. "I don't place my opposition to the loan on the narrow grounds of British perfidy and failure to keep her promises to the Jews," Celler declared. "There are numerous other reasons for opposition." In a series of speeches, press conferences, and articles, Celler questioned the 1.62 percent interest rate (as compared to the 4 percent charged "when a GI borrows anywhere," he pointed out), the loose wording concerning how the money might be used ("escape clauses, weasel words and abracadabra," he called it), and the danger that other countries would demand similar loans ("there is a long queue of representatives from many nations holding out hands to us").[30] Even Congressman Sol Bloom, chairman of the House Foreign Affairs Committee, who ordinarily adopted the State Department's line on Middle East matters, initially opposed the loan because of the Palestine situation but was persuaded by Stephen Wise to withdraw his opposition.[31]

Fearing that the Jews would be blamed for postwar suffering in Britain if the funds were denied, Wise publicly endorsed the loan. "Noisy Jewish disapproval of the Loan" would make it appear as if "we [have] become Jews resident in America rather than American Jews"—that is, loyal to Jewish interests above American interests, Wise worried. He knew that his position was at odds with many in the Jewish community: "Zionistically I took my life in my hands," he later noted, referring to the widespread anti-loan sentiment among American Zionists. Even Wise's colleague Carl Alpert, formerly editor of the ZOA journal *New Palestine*, publicly accused

Wise of "betraying his people by endorsing the British loan."[32] Nevertheless, egged on by the White House, Wise pressured Bloom to read aloud Wise's endorsement of the loan during the congressional hearings. When presidential aide David Niles was slow to arrange the insertion of Wise's endorsement in the *Congressional Record,* Wise pressed him to hurry in order to "counteract" what he called the "Silver mischief" and "the Revisionists' telegram to all the members of Congress against the loan."[33] Celler watched bitterly as the loan won approval—he was especially angry at "the defection of his Jewish colleagues and of some of the Zionist leaders," Akzin reported to Silver—but he understood that the publicity surrounding the fight had surely dealt another important public-relations blow to London's psyche.[34]

In Silver's view, Wise's lobbying—undertaken "in clear disregard" of the AZEC's position on the loan—played a crucial role. Prior to Wise's intervention, "passage of the loan was definitely in doubt," Silver told the 1946 ZOA convention. "Enough of our friends had rallied to our side in addition to those who were opposed to the loan on other grounds to make the postponement of [approval] very likely," but then Wise "came forth as the champion of the loan in the name of Americanism, [which] demoralized and scattered our friends in Congress." After all, Silver pointed out, "They could see no sense in voting against an Administration measure to help the Zionist cause when a Zionist leader himself stepped forth as its champion. We have a genius for kicking ourselves in the face."[35]

Meanwhile, the escalating conflict in Palestine, combined with the plight of hundreds of thousands of Holocaust survivors languishing in DP camps in Europe, was stimulating grassroots support for the U.S. Revisionist movement. Every facet of organizational activity brimmed with newfound energy. For the first time, the UZRA had its own internal newsletter and a speakers bureau, not to mention new chapters in Manhattan and the Brownsville section of Brooklyn and nuclei in Boston, Philadelphia, and Pittsburgh. A new chapter was also initiated at Yeshiva College (today the undergraduate division of Yeshiva University) after a standing-room-only lecture by Netanyahu, who, as the son of an Orthodox rabbi, was sufficiently versed in biblical and Talmudic literature to make good use of the suitcase full of books he brought to the event. Young Moshe Arens (who would one day become Israel's Defense Minister) carried the luggage.[36]

UZRA publications bore all the telltale signs of a burgeoning, spirited activist movement. There were enough young people involved that a new

UZRA front group, the National Jewish Youth Council, could host its own Labor Day weekend get-together at Lake Hopatcong. There were enough members in the UZRA's East New York chapter alone that it could hold its own Oneg Shabbat celebrations and produce its own mimeographed newsletter, the *New Zionist*.[37] There were enough young adults in the movement that the newsletter's "Congrats" column was overflowing with news of UZRA members becoming engaged, getting married, and giving birth—including belated congratulations to the Netanyahus on "the birth of a son who is now old enough to apply for membership to Betar (5 months)." That son, Jonathan, named after John Henry Patterson and Netanyahu's father, the late Rabbi Nathan Mileikowsky, would grow up to become the hero of the famous Israeli raid that freed Jewish hostages at Entebbe airport in 1976.[38] By 1947 the UZRA had its own Women's Division, the National Jewish Youth Council was holding packed weekly meetings, the Bronx division was so large that it set up a separate Bronx Youth chapter, and full chapters had been established in New Haven, Boston, Pittsburgh, and Houston thanks to the efforts of Haim Lubinski, a former Bergson activist who toured the United States in early 1947 to organize new Revisionist groups and revitalize older ones that had withered, such as Chicago, Detroit, and Newark.[39]

As the UZRA intensified its Washington activity, however, the potential for new conflicts with the Zionist establishment arose. By early 1947, Abba Hillel Silver's activist leadership of the AZEC had moved the Zionist mainstream to the point where most of the differences between the UZRA and the AZEC had vanished, and the UZRA was admitted to the AZEC without difficulty. Netanyahu and Schechtman, who represented the UZRA at AZEC meetings, maintained cordial relations with the other Zionist representatives. Part of the reason for the calm at the surface, however, was that Silver and his colleagues did not realize that behind the scenes, the Revisionists were breaching the AZEC's cardinal rule.

Although member-organizations of the AZEC were free to pursue their own agendas, they were precluded from establishing contacts with officials of the Truman administration. Congressmen could be approached, but the White House, the State Department, and the Pentagon were off-limits. Just as the Jewish Agency in Palestine regarded itself as the only body authorized to negotiate with the British, Silver and his closest colleagues in the AZEC leadership regarded negotiations with the U.S. administration as their private domain. The Revisionists did not set out to violate this understanding, but an incident in late 1946 changed their minds. In the course of a debate at an AZEC meeting at which Netanyahu was present, Silver expressed exasperation over the apparent ineffectiveness of his recent meetings with State Department officials and suggested that there was no point in further meetings. If that were the case, Netanyahu reasoned, why shouldn't other Zionists seek their own meetings?[40]

An opportunity for the militants to meet with a senior State Department official unexpectedly presented itself in early 1947, when Netanyahu was introduced to Congresswoman Frances Bolton at a cocktail party. Fascinated by the militant Zionist agenda, Bolton offered to arrange a meeting between a Revisionist representative and Loy Henderson, a devout anti-Zionist who directed the State Department's Office of Near Eastern and Africa Affairs and played a major role in shaping Foggy Bottom's Palestine policy. Although meeting Henderson would breach AZEC's rules, Netanyahu decided that it would be justified in view of the desperate situation in Palestine and the DP camps and the diplomatic stalemate over the future of the Holy Land.[41]

The mainstream Zionists' emphasis on humanitarian issues such as the Holocaust and the homelessness of the DPs would never win over senior U.S. officials, Netanyahu believed; he preferred arguments appealing to American fears of Soviet expansion. Over dessert at Mrs. Bolton's Washington, D.C., townhouse, Netanyahu told Henderson that although Washington and Moscow were allies for the moment, U.S.-Soviet tension was bound to resurface. The Middle East, with its oil resources and strategic significance, was the most likely flashpoint for conflict between the superpowers. The British would soon depart Palestine, leaving a vacuum that the Russians would try to fill. The Arabs would be too weak to stop them; the Soviets "would cut through the Arabs like a knife through butter." The Jews, by contrast, if properly armed by the United States, could provide a pro-America buffer against Soviet aggression in that vital region.[42] Although Netanyahu did not make a convert out of Henderson, their discussion did open doors for him and a Revisionist colleague, Zvi Kolitz, to meet with General Dwight D. Eisenhower, chief of staff of the U.S. Army. Eisenhower, in turn, arranged for them to speak with General Lauris Norstadt (later chief of NATO). The Revisionist representatives also met with outgoing secretary of state Dean Acheson; his successor, Robert Lovett; U.S. Navy admiral F. P. Sherman; General John Hildring, assistant secretary of state for the Allied-controlled areas of Europe; and the United States representative to the United Nations, Senator Warren Austin. Rumors about the meetings reached Abba Hillel Silver by summer's end. Netan-yahu, given assurances that Silver would not seek the Revisionists' expul-sion from the AZEC, briefed him on his Washington activities and was pleasantly surprised to discover that Silver regarded the Revisionists' effort as a helpful complement to mainstream Zionist lobbying.[43]

8 • A Flag Is Born

On a sunny April morning in 1944, the mailman brought a particularly intriguing envelope to the Manhattan headquarters of the American League
for a Free Palestine (ALFP), a group recently established by Peter Bergson
to rally public support for the Jewish revolt against the British. The delivery
was a membership card signed by Mrs. Alice Brandeis, widow of the famed
jurist and Zionist leader, together with payment of her annual membership
dues. Mrs. Brandeis was just one of many celebrities who were attracted to
Bergson's committees, but the controversy that exploded over her affiliation
with militant Zionism illustrates the ongoing rivalry between the mainstream Zionists and the Jabotinskyites.

Mrs. Brandeis was no stranger to the Bergson activists; the previous year,
she had joined the Emergency Committee to Save the Jewish People of
Europe.[1] Her earlier affiliation with the Emergency Committee had indeed
troubled the mainstream Zionist leaders with whom Mrs. Brandeis normally associated. But her decision to join the ALFP, along with the prospect of the hallowed Brandeis name being used on behalf of Jews waging
war against the British while the British were still fighting the Nazis, was
the straw that broke the camel's back. Mainstream Zionist officials had frequently approached politicians, intellectuals, and rabbis who had endorsed
the Bergsonites and pressured them, sometimes successfully, to sever their
connection, with the militants. Now they would take aim at Alice Brandeis.[2]

Hadassah board member Jeannette Leibel was the first to sound the
alarm. Upon hearing of Mrs. Brandeis's connection to the ALFP, Leibel,
recalling an earlier attempt to persuade the Zionist leader's widow to resign
from the Emergency Committee, asked her Hadassah colleague Denise
Tourover, "Do you think you should make another 'educational' visit? . . .
The use of her name in conjunction with the [ALFP] would do considerable damage and would attract a great many others to that group. So please
do something." After winning a promise from Mrs. Brandeis's aide, Miss

Kropp, to intercept any mail from the Bergsonites and "to communicate with me before Mrs. Brandeis does anything other than what she KNOWS to be accepted by us," Tourover assured Leibel that there was no need to pay Mrs. Brandeis a visit right away, especially since she was really too busy to do so: "I am training a new maid—there is a wedding in the family next week, incoming guests, etc. etc."[3]

When the "Hebrew Embassy" controversy broke in mid-May, however, Herman Shulman of the AZEC immediately began pressuring Tourover to persuade Mrs. Brandeis to formally repudiate the Bergson group, desiring to "secure from her not a routine letter, but the kind of letter which can be publicized if necessary." Leibel wanted no more delays. "I am sure you know your job in this respect as we all do," she wrote Tourover, "but this is just an 'in case.'" Tourover promptly paid an "educational visit" to the Brandeis residence on May 27 and emerged with Mrs. Brandeis's signature on a letter to Bergson—Tourover had come with the draft already prepared—that sidestepped the question of her signature on the membership card, simply asserting that "the use of my name [on ALFP letterhead] is completely unauthorized." While Bergson's attempts to secure an appointment with Mrs. Brandeis were rebuffed, the letter of repudiation was published in the *New York Times*—"brief, to the point, and effective," exulted the AZEC's Arthur Lourie.[4]

"Astounded" by the *Times* article, ALFP executive director Alex Wilf produced the smoking gun: a copy of Mrs. Brandeis's signed ALFP membership form. A startled Denise Tourover admitted to Robert Szold, longtime Zionist activist and Brandeis confidante, that "the signature on the card is really Mrs. Brandeis'," but Tourover refused Bergson's request for a retraction and "informed [Mrs. Brandeis] to refuse to accept all telephone calls" from the militants. Wilf then gave the Brandeis signature card to the *New York Times*, which published a follow-up story that enabled both sides to claim partial victory: the ALFP was cleared of the charge of fabricating the signature, while the establishment rejoiced in her public dissociation from the Bergsonites.[5]

The problem for the Jewish establishment was that Mrs. Brandeis was just one of a slew of celebrities who were attracted to one or more of Bergson's groups. Mainstream Jewish groups did not have the resources to contact every big-name Bergson supporter, nor did they have the ability to win over more than a handful of those whom they did contact. During the final months of World War II and especially during the first years after the war, a wide range of legislators, intellectuals, and entertainers were moved to embrace the militant Zionist agenda by the horrors of the Holocaust and the inspiring image of modern-day Maccabees fighting for Jewish freedom against the British. Even an ostensible rival such as *New Palestine* editor Carl Alpert realized that the ALFP's work was having "a profound effect on the American public."[6]

Typical of the ALFP's extraordinary success in attracting the support of major personalities from Washington to Hollywood was a June 1944 two-page spread in the *New Republic* featuring over two hundred signatures, including twenty U.S. congressmen, actresses Stella Adler and Jane Wyatt, film producer David O. Selznick, conductor Leonard Bernstein, concert manager Sol Hurok, sculptor Jo Davidson, and sportscaster Bill Stern, among others. Numerous other celebrities became ALFP supporters in the months and years to follow, including comedian Carl Reiner, Harpo Marx of the Marx Brothers, actor Vincent Price, who chaired the ALFP's annual dinner in Los Angeles, and rising young political stars such as Hubert Humphrey, then mayor of Minneapolis.[7] While some of these VIPs lent only their names to the cause, others played a more active role. Paul O'Dwyer, an attorney and Irish-American activist (and brother of New York City's mayor), and Adam Clayton Powell, an African-American congressman, exhibited particular enthusiasm. In his memoirs, O'Dwyer recalled standing with Powell backstage at an ALFP rally in Madison Square Garden in 1948 and watching in frustration as an elderly former British major, obviously inexperienced at public speaking, made an ineffective appeal for funds: "Powell became impatient and whispered to me, 'This guy's blowing it. Paul, I think this calls for a Baptist minister and an Irish revolutionary. You handle that microphone over there and I'll handle this one.' In unison we rose and in unison we took the microphones gently away from the major. We collected $75,000 from the crowd that night."[8] An FBI agent sent to monitor the event gave his superiors a somewhat lower estimate of the amount raised, $55,000, although either figure was a considerable sum for that era. The FBI man dourly noted that Powell stated in his speech that "spies were present here from Ten Downing St. as well as spies from the office of Loy Henderson of the State Dept."[9]

Staffed by the same coterie of activists who had so successfully made the rescue issue into a political headache for the Roosevelt administration, the ALFP employed much the same tactics as Bergson's Emergency Committee: public rallies, congressional lobbying, and a blizzard of newspaper ads. The response of grassroots American Jews to the ALFP's activity was enthusiastic. Public events drew large audiences; advertisements attracted a slew of donations; activists hit the pavement in search of contributions. A typical member of the ALFP's small army of volunteers was Doris Baer, part-time secretary and passionate Zionist, who spent her spare time going door-to-door in her Brooklyn neighborhood, soliciting signatures on an ALFP petition with the stipulation that each signatory was required to contribute one dollar; the signatures, and the contributions, were plentiful.[10]

Donations sometimes came from unusual sources. Sy Dill, a teenage volunteer in the ALFP's Manhattan headquarters, recalls the arrival of a $25,000 check from reputed mobster Meyer Lansky.[11] Another underworld figure, Mickey Cohen, approached Ben Hecht to find out "what's what with the Jews fighting in Palestine." Cohen then offered to host "a party where you can raise some dough" for the Irgun. An attempt by Haganah supporters to persuade Cohen to divert the money to their group failed when Cohen learned that the Haganah had "squealed" on the Irgun to the British—a severe offense in the eyes of a gangster.[12]

Cohen held his party at Slapsy Maxie's Cafe in Los Angeles, where Hecht addressed an audience of "a thousand bookies, ex–prize fighters, gamblers, jockeys, touts and all sorts of lawless and semi-lawless characters—and their womenfolk." Dissatisfied with the initial round of pledges, Cohen ordered his bodyguard to go onstage and demand a doubling of their gifts. "Tell 'em it's for Jews ready to knock hell out of all the bums in the world who don't like them. Go on—tell 'em." The bodyguard complied, "roaring inarticulately over the microphone." Then Cohen "came to the edge of the stage and stood in the floodlights. He said nothing. Man by man, the 'underworld' stood up and doubled the ante for the Irgun." They raised $200,000 that night. On other occasions, Cohen sent his men to stand guard outside ALFP meetings in southern California to make sure that opponents of the Irgun did not attempt to disrupt the proceedings.[13] Cohen's associates in St. Louis agreed to follow his lead in helping the Irgun only after Baruch Rabinowitz promised that their fund-raiser would be attended by the boxer Barney Ross, who in their eyes was the living symbol of Jewish toughness. After his exploits in the boxing ring and some well-publicized heroics on the battlefield against the Japanese, Ross joined the ALFP and spoke at league rallies from coast to coast, including the St. Louis event, "which raised a good deal more" than the $100,000 that the mobsters had initially promised Rabinowitz they would collect.[14]

While the ALFP's fund-raising network was in high gear, so was its creative political action team. In the summer of 1946, Guy Gillette and Harry Selden set out on a carefully choreographed, well-publicized, and highly critical "fact-finding" tour of the Holy Land. After losing his bid for reelection to the Senate, Gillette had recently assumed the presidency of the ALFP, much to the chagrin of the British Embassy in Washington, which reported back to the Foreign Office that Gillette "has proved impervious to repeated representations on the part of reputable Zionists, who have tried to enlighten him as to Bergson's real nature and motives."[15]

Gillette and Selden reached their destination in Jerusalem, the King David Hotel, just hours after the Irgun had blown up the wing that housed British military headquarters. Their taxi driver sped away, anxious to get home before the start of the 6 P.M. curfew, while the former senator and his Zionist companion stood amidst the rubble, suitcases in hand, watching relief workers dig bodies from the smoking ruins. Gillette and Selden hitched a ride to the Eden Hotel in an open-backed lorry used for carting debris from the scene of the blast. In the Haifa harbor, they had a firsthand look at ships used to deport illegal immigrants to British detention camps on Cyprus. With less than a foot separating the stacks of wooden planks on which the prisoners slept, the boats were nothing less than "slave ships," Gillette announced in a press release. "The African ships I read about as a boy were something I would not believe to be repeated in the 20th century."[16]

Gillette and Selden also met the British high commissioner for Palestine, Sir Alan Cunningham, who confirmed the visitors' worst fears about British intransigence. Cunningham bluntly told them his job was to "maintain a balance between the Arab and Jewish communities" rather than to implement the original Balfour Declaration pledge to facilitate the creation of a Jewish national home.[17] Gillette and Selden faced additional disappointments during their tour. Their request to visit imprisoned Jewish underground fighters was denied by the British, and a plan to meet with members of the Irgun High Command had to be scrapped because of heavy British police surveillance of the American visitors. A particularly jarring moment for Selden came when the vehicle in which he was traveling was stopped by British soldiers at a roadblock outside Jerusalem. When the woman sitting next to Selden reached over to hand a soldier her identification papers, her tattooed Nazi death camp number became visible. As the soldier reached over to take the papers, Selden could see that he had a tattoo of his own: a swastika.[18]

When Gillette returned to New York at summer's end, the Bergsonites were startled to find that he had come back "a converted revolutionary . . . his eyes blazed as he told us his experiences in Palestine." The former senator had always been strongly supportive of the militant Zionist cause, but seeing the Jewish-British conflict firsthand filled him with a renewed sense of commitment and urgency. Almost immediately upon his return, Gillette flew to Los Angeles to address a "Force the Gates of Palestine" dinner sponsored by the ALFP's West Coast Division, which had recently landed James Roosevelt, eldest son of the late president, as its chairman. From there, Gillette went on to address three radio audiences in Chicago and mass meetings in Philadelphia and New York.[19]

Meanwhile, Selden staged a dramatic press conference in New York, at which he unveiled the first message from Irgun Zvai Leumi leader Menachem Begin to the American public. "People of the United States of America," Selden read aloud, "you who cherish freedom, you who have sacrificed your lives for it ever since your country was born, help us so that we too may be free. Embattled Palestine needs your help."[20] Then it was off to Mexico, as part of a delegation including Congressman Andrew Somers, Stella Adler, and Rabbi Baruch Rabinowitz, to rally support south of the border for the Palestine revolt. Selden aptly summed up the problem militant Zionists were creating for London: "Britain can't fight the resistance when she is forced to fight it not only in Palestine, but in the United States, France, England, Latin America and elsewhere." When Selden returned home, he immediately threw himself into the preparations for a huge "Salute to the Palestine Resistance Fighters" at Carnegie Hall. The rally attracted an audience of more than two thousand and plenty of media coverage.[21]

Selden also organized coast-to-coast screenings of *Last Night We Attacked,* a stirring eighteen-minute film showing the exploits of the Irgun, narrated by journalist Quentin Reynolds. Leo Halpert, a fugitive Irgun activist who had been smuggled out of Palestine to avoid arrest, sometimes delivered Zionist pep talks prior to screenings of the film, using the nom de guerre "Amichai."[22] The movie ran into trouble in Pennsylvania, where members of the State Board of Censors objected to its explicit appeal for funds to fight the British. After a special screening for the attorney general, the deputy attorney general, and the chief of the state police, the censorship board voted to eliminate a segment near the film's end referring to "the backing of our allies in America" and urging viewers to "Send us your support, America, and we will continue to attack until Palestine is free." That language was ruled "Not Proper and in the judgement of the Board tends to corrupt morals." Despite the censorship problems in Pennsylvania, the movie was an effective tool in spreading the message of militant Zionism and attracting donations for the cause.[23]

An even more powerful tool for the cause was the ALFP's production of *A Flag Is Born,* a play written by Ben Hecht in the summer of 1946.[24] It was set in a European cemetery. Two elderly and ailing Holocaust survivors on their way to Palestine, Tevya and Zelda, pause to rest there on the eve of the Sabbath. In the midst of his prayers, Tevya has a series of visions in which he encounters sages, heroes, and kings from the Jewish biblical past. Their conversations serve as Hecht's platform to survey the lessons of Jewish history, the need for a Jewish state, and the cruelties of British rule in Palestine. The bridge between past and future is provided in the form of David, a distraught young Treblinka survivor who stumbles into the cemetery during the final part of the play. Tevya and Zelda die, but David is inspired to join the Palestine Jewish underground in its war against the British. In the play's dramatic final moments, David delivers a stirring Zionist speech and marches off to fight for Jewish freedom in the Holy Land, holding a makeshift Zionist flag fashioned from Tevya's tallit.

Luther Adler, star of the Yiddish theater, was chosen to direct *A Flag Is Born.* He cast his famous half-sister, Celia Adler, as Zelda, and another Yiddish theater veteran, Paul Muni, as Tevya. Quentin Reynolds was picked as the narrator. For the role of David, Hecht and Adler chose an up-and-coming twenty-two-year-old Adler protégé by the name of Marlon Brando. According to his memoirs, Brando's interest in *Flag* was kindled by "what we were beginning to learn about the true nature of the killing of the Jews and because of the empathy I felt for the Adlers and the other Jews who had become my friends and teachers and who told me of their dreams for a Jewish State."[25] Luther's sister, Stella Adler, had taken a leadership role in three of Bergson's groups, the Committee for a Jewish Army, the Emergency Committee to Save the Jewish People of Europe, and the ALFP; Luther was also active in the league.[26] Brando's motives were not entirely political; he was also attracted by the prospect of working with Paul Muni, whom he described as "the only actor who ever moved me to leave my dressing room to watch him from the wings." As a gesture of solidarity with the Zionist cause, Brando and the other cast members performed for the minimum actors guild wage. Later, Brando volunteered to appear as the guest speaker at showings of *Last Night We Attacked* around the country.[27]

The actors rehearsed at a "bare studio" above Al and Dick's Restaurant on West 54th Street. Between rehearsals for *Flag,* Brando relaxed at Hecht's suburban Nyack, New York, home, where Zionist activists and sympathetic celebrities—among others—regularly crossed paths. "Around me in Nyack the Palestinian underground crackled constantly," Hecht later recalled. "Russian and British spies pattered through the house and eavesdropped at the swimming pool where the Irgun captains were wont to gather for disputation." On one occasion, Hecht, Brando, and the other guests "eased the political tensions of the household" by squaring off in a rain-drenched celebrity baseball match.[28]

At one point in *A Flag Is Born,* Brando's character delivers an impassioned, heart-rending speech accusing American Jewry of failing to pressure the Roosevelt administration to rescue Jewish refugees from Hitler. "Where were you, Jews? Where were you when six million Jews were being burned to death in the ovens? Where were you?" Brando demanded, beginning in a quiet voice and growing louder as he repeated the question. The accusation "sent chills through the audience," Brando recalled. At some performances, "Jewish girls got out of their seats and screamed and cried from the aisles in sadness, and at one, when I asked, 'Where were you when six million Jews were being burned to death in the ovens of Auschwitz?,' a woman was so overcome with anger and guilt that she rose and shouted back at me, 'Where were *you*?' . . . At the time there was a great deal of soul-searching within the Jewish community over whether they had done enough to stop the slaughter of their people—some argued that they should have applied pressure on President Roosevelt to bomb Auschwitz, for example—so the speech touched a sensitive nerve." Despite his limited knowledge of Jewish affairs, Brando had hit the nail on the head. The postwar revelations of the full details of the Nazi atrocities, combined with remorse over the American Jewish community's failure to protest more vocally during the Holocaust, had intensified Jewish passions over Palestine. In this atmosphere, perhaps it was no surprise that Hecht elicited such an enthusiastic response when he stepped onstage to appeal for donations at the end of the opening-night performance of *A Flag Is Born.* "Give us your money," he said, "and we will turn it into history." They did give, and Hecht kept his promise.[29]

Hecht originally planned a four-week run for *A Flag Is Born* on Broadway before taking it to other cities, but the show's immense popularity persuaded him to extend its stay at the Alvin Theater on 52nd Street.[30] He later extended it again, eventually running for a full ten weeks. Officials of the British Consulate in New York were annoyed to note the "crowds" that were "flocking" to see Hecht's play. Several months later, however, they were pleased to discover that, "in sharp contrast" to the reception accorded *A Flag Is Born*, an anti-British film marketed by mainstream Zionist groups attracted sparse attendance because it was "dull" and badly produced. The cynical British Consulate staff found the film's lukewarm reception surprising in view of the fact that the movie industry "is to a considerable extent in the hands of co-religionists."[31]

Flag's timing could not have been better. Throughout the summer and autumn of 1946, British-American tensions over Palestine were approaching the boiling point, and *Flag* contributed its share to the charged atmosphere. By presenting the Palestine conflict in simple, dramatic images that ordinary Americans could easily understand and remember, *Flag* broadened American public antagonism toward England and sympathy for the Jewish revolt. The British, for their part, did plenty to facilitate that antagonism. In June, Foreign Minister Bevin infuriated the American Jewish community when he asserted that Truman administration officials were pressing for the admission of DPs to Palestine only because "They did not want too many Jews in New York." Nobody had yet forgotten Bevin's statement the previous November that "if the Jews, with all their sufferings, want to get too much at the head of the queue, you have the danger of another anti-Semitic reaction through it all." His new slur seemed to confirm Jewish suspicions that Bevin was not merely cold to Zionist aspirations but an anti-Jewish bigot as well, provoking a torrent of denunciations from the media, Congress, and the Jewish community and injecting even more passion and outrage into American Zionist protests. Even the British ambassador in Washington, Lord Halifax, feared that Bevin had gone too far with his remark about more Jews in New York, and thought that London might have to now make some gesture to mollify its critics. "Your criticism of New York has, of course, not only hit the nail on the head but driven it woundingly deep," he wrote the foreign minister.[32]

American Zionist protests, British intransigence on Palestine, and the American political calendar were on a collision course. Midterm congressional elections were just a few months away, and many of President Truman's aides were increasingly worried that resentment over the administration's reluctance to confront the British on Palestine would spill over into support for Republican candidates. These political concerns spelled doom for the Morrison-Grady plan, a proposal drawn up in the summer of 1946 by British and American envoys that would have divided Palestine into semiautonomous Jewish and Arab provinces under continued British rule. Both London and the State Department pressed fervently for U.S. adoption of the plan, and at a July 30 cabinet meeting an exasperated Truman complained of the Jews that "Jesus Christ couldn't please them when he was here on earth, so how could anyone expect that I would have any luck?" Yet while he was personally convinced the Morrison-Grady plan was "really fair," Truman was increasingly sensitive to the volume of Zionist protests and their potential electoral impact. Henry Wallace, now secretary of commerce, had warned him in a private telephone conversation the previous day that Abba Hillel Silver had been "working with the Republicans" to whip up sentiment on Palestine, and Truman brought with him to the cabinet session "a sheaf of telegrams about four inches thick" that had been received from Zionist protesters. The meeting ended with Truman opting to reject Morrison-Grady, in deference to Wallace's warning that the plan was "political dynamite." Wallace later noted in his diary: "I emphasized the political angle because that is the one angle of Palestine which has a really deep interest for Truman."[33]

London harbored no doubts that this was yet another instance of Zionist pressure preventing the Truman administration from acquiescing in Britain's Palestine policy. The new British ambassador in Washington, Lord Inverchapel, informed Bevin that Truman's rejection of the Morrison-Grady plan was "solely attributable to reasons of domestic politics," reminiscent of the administration's insistence on delaying the 1945 announcement of the Anglo-American Committee of Inquiry until after that year's New York mayoral election. Based on a talk with the State Department's Loy Henderson, Inverchapel told Bevin that since Stephen Wise was a Democrat and Abba Hillel Silver a Republican, "Neither therefore could afford to compromise without the certainty that the other would at once derive political benefit from his decision. With both leaders thus solidly opposed to the joint recommendations the administration dared not take the risk of antagonising the powerful Zionist lobby in an election year."[34]

Soon Inverchapel had more disappointing news: despite England's request that the United States seal the borders of its occupation zone in Germany to prevent the entry of more DPs from adjoining regions—which London feared would increase the pressure to admit them to Palestine—the Truman administration refused to take such action because of the likelihood of American Jewish backlash. The worried ambassador also warned Bevin of unpleasant political fallout from Britain's announcement that it would deport to Cyprus all Jewish DPs who reached Palestine illegally. Because the Zionists "are so strong in this country and exercise so great an influence on domestic politics," Inverchapel urged London to consider making gestures needed to appease Jewish sentiment, such as inviting Jewish leaders to send a delegation to see the Cyprus detention camps for themselves. London rejected the proposal for fear of creating a precedent of American Jewish involvement in Britain's Palestine policies, but it was clear that American Jews were, in fact, already deeply involved. Nowhere was their role more apparent—and more disconcerting to the British—than in Truman's decision to issue a statement on the eve of Yom Kippur, barely a month before the midterm congressional elections, for the first time implying U.S. support for the creation of a Jewish state. Secretary of State Dean Acheson privately admitted to Inverchapel that Truman decided to take this step because he had learned that New York governor Thomas Dewey, the likely Republican presidential candidate in 1948, was about to make a pro-statehood speech of his own. Truman's statement did not have the desired effect; the Republicans swept the elections, gaining control of the House and Senate for the first time in nearly twenty years. From Britain's perspective, the conclusion of the election campaign did not signal relief from the problem of Jewish electoral pressure influencing America's Middle East policy. In the two years leading up to the 1948 presidential election, both parties will be "promising the Zionists the moon" in order to secure Jewish support, Inverchapel warned Bevin.[35]

Into this volatile mix leaped the irrepressible Ben Hecht with his blend of drama and politics, not to mention his knack for making headlines and aggravating British officialdom. *Time* magazine called *A Flag Is Born* "colorful theatre and biting propaganda," while *Life* complimented its "wit and wisdom." Not surprisingly, the British press had a different view. The *London Evening Standard* expressed horror that large audiences were going in droves to view what it called "the most virulent anti-British play ever staged in the United States."[36] Judah Magnes, the outspoken pacifist and chancellor of Hebrew University, inadvertently drew even more attention to the play when he publicly charged that its proceeds bought guns for Jewish terrorists and appealed to Eleanor Roosevelt to withdraw her name from the list of its sponsors. That drew predictably colorful retorts from the sharp-tongued Free Palestine activists. Hecht called Magnes's denunciation "the sort of the thing that comes from Jews in fancy dress with frightened brains." Former senator Guy Gillette sarcastically declared that "the statement that the League gives money for the 'purchase of arms for terrorist groups' would imply that we are sending money to the British government—I was in Palestine, and the only terror I saw there was perpetrated by the occupation troops on the Hebrew population."[37]

After completing its Broadway run, *Flag* went on the road. Brando turned down the lead role in the forthcoming film *Gentleman's Agreement* to go on the tour. The play was staged in Chicago, Detroit, Philadelphia, Boston, and at the National Theater in Washington, D.C., where it unexpectedly became the focus of a controversy over racial discrimination. The play hit the road just as Hecht and thirty-two other prominent playwrights and dramatists were announcing they would no longer permit their works to be performed at the National and other Washington theaters that discriminated against African Americans.[38] The Washington engagement was quickly withdrawn and rescheduled for the Maryland Theater in nearby Baltimore. To accommodate members of Congress whom the ALFP expected to attend the Washington performance, arrangements were made for a special train car to bring the congressmen to Baltimore. Eighteen U.S. senators and an assortment of foreign diplomats were scheduled to attend, according to a league spokesman.[39]

In making the switch from Washington to Baltimore, ALFP activists struck an important symbolic blow against racial discrimination. But as it turned out, the controversy was far from over. Baltimore's Maryland Theater did not bar African Americans, as Washington's National Theater did—but, unbeknownst to the Bergsonites, it did restrict them to the balcony, which bigots nicknamed "nigger heaven."[40] Alerted by local NAACP activists, the Free Palestine leaders fashioned a kind of "good cop–bad cop" strategy. Just hours before the first curtain, the Bergsonites went to the Maryland Theater management with a plea and a warning: rescind the seating discrimination or face an angry NAACP picket line. The date was February 12, Lincoln's Birthday; protesters invoking the memory of the Great Emancipator "would have a particular news value," they emphasized.[41] While management was mulling over that demand, the Bergsonites added a threat of their own: Professor Fowler Harper, former deputy to Interior Secretary Harold Ickes, prominent legal expert, and ALFP activist, intended "to personally test this discriminatory ruling by taking two colored persons as his guests to tonight's performance"—Mrs. Dovey Roundtree, a civil rights activist and former Women's Army Corps captain, and Mary Johnson, a secretary at ALFP headquarters in New York.[42]

The pressure succeeded. The Maryland Theater management agreed to recognize the league as the "lessee of the theatre" for the duration of the run, making its ticket agents ALFP employees and subject to whatever seating policy the league chose to adopt. Ten to twelve African Americans attended the opening-night performance of *A Flag Is Born* and, in the words of a black weekly newspaper, "were seated indiscriminately, some holding orchestra and box seats, without untoward results."[43] Exuberant NAACP leaders hailed the "tradition-shattering victory" won by the alliance of black and Zionist activists against theater discrimination, and used that victory to help pave the way for the desegregation of other Baltimore theaters in the months and years to follow.[44] The Maryland Theater battle of 1947 was a rare instance in which militant Zionism and the black civil rights struggle intersected, giving the Irgun's American supporters an opportunity to use their considerable talent on behalf of another cause they supported. "I am proud that it was my play which terminated one of the most disgraceful practices of our country's history," a beaming Ben Hecht declared after the opening performance in Baltimore.[45]

From a financial point of view, *A Flag Is Born* was tremendously successful. According to the ALFP, the play brought in a sum approaching $1 million in ticket revenues and post-performance donations. Related events brought in additional funds; for example, a New York dinner in honor of Paul Muni in October 1946 raised $74,000 in a single evening. Part of the money raised by the *Flag* project was used to purchase a ship for the purpose of ferrying Holocaust survivors to Palestine in defiance of British immigration restrictions.[46]

The boat, a 400-ton former yacht known as the SS *Abril*, set sail for France on December 27, 1946, with a twenty-one-man crew, most of them American volunteers, seven from Brooklyn. Six hundred Holocaust survivors came aboard at Port de Bouc, where the ship was renamed the SS *Ben Hecht*. The voyage came to an abrupt end on March 8, 1947, when the *Ben Hecht* was intercepted by the British just ten miles from the Palestine shore. The refugees were taken to a detention camp in Cyprus, while the crew members were jailed at the Acre Prison, south of Haifa.

While *Ben Hecht* radio operator David Kaplan languished behind bars with his comrades, his mother, Mrs. Esther Kaplan, was transformed from Brooklyn housewife to political dynamo. Mrs. Kaplan's diary of her whirlwind two-week campaign for her son's freedom affords a fascinating glimpse of how grassroots Zionist activists helped influence American Jewry and Congress and contributed to the struggle for Jewish statehood. Like the ripples that emanate from the spot in a pond where a pebble is dropped, each meeting, mailing, or protest that Mrs. Kaplan initiated left its imprint on those who rallied to her side, those whom she lobbied, and beyond.

"Our home was converted into a beehive of activity," she later recalled. "We borrowed typewriters and friends came and worked assisting in sending out petitions. Aunt Pearl came, made pots of vegetable soup and sandwiches to feed the helpers." Participating in a struggle that was at once political and personal undoubtedly impressed upon these volunteer activists the urgency of the Zionist cause more than an article in the morning newspaper or a thirty-second spot on a moviehouse newsreel ever could. Every friend or neighbor who trooped to the Kaplans' house on a cold March night to stuff envelopes or went door-to-door with petitions calling for David's release was establishing a personal connection to the Jewish fight for freedom. The struggle against the British was no longer an abstract conflict thousands of miles away. This was their neighbor's son, a boy they knew—perhaps their own son's former schoolmate or their former newspaper delivery boy—jailed for helping the Irgun try to smash the British blockade of Palestine. A war was on, and they were suddenly part of it, from the neighbor who typed up letters of protest to the aunt who ladled out soup to keep the activists working overtime.

The same may be said of the numerous local and national political officials who found Mrs. Kaplan at their doorstep. Probably they had heard the Zionists' arguments, and felt some sympathy for the Jews' suffering under the Nazis—but how could Zionist speeches about the Jewish right to establish a state or even newspaper photos of emaciated DPs compare to the impact of meeting, in person, the distraught mother of a young American jailed for trying to bring Holocaust survivors to the Holy Land?

Within forty-eight hours of the beginning of their campaign, the Kaplans and their friends had galvanized a network of local sympathizers into action. Volunteers canvassed the heavily Jewish Williamsburg neighborhood, collecting food and clothing for the prisoners—"Response magnificent," Mrs. Kaplan noted in her diary. The leaders of the Kaplans' synagogue, Young Israel of Brooklyn, agreed to hold a protest assembly at the synagogue to rouse public consciousness, and asked the dozens of other Young Israel synagogues around New York City to petition their elected officials regarding David's imprisonment. An emergency meeting of executive directors of groups belonging to the Brooklyn Jewish Community Council resolved to join the campaign. The Women's League of one of the city's largest yeshivas, Torah Vodaath, handed out three hundred flyers about the *Ben Hecht* crew at a public meeting. Each synagogue that was contacted, each person who was handed a leaflet, each Brooklyn Jewish organization that sent a mailing to its members, in turn generated additional letters and phone calls to the White House, members of Congress, and others. The focus was on the imprisoned crew of the *Ben Hecht,* but the cumulative effect of such protests was to impress upon public officials the depth of Jewish communal opposition to British rule in Palestine. On the eve of a year that would include a presidential race as well as numerous congressional contests, the intensification of Jewish voters' anger over Palestine could not be easily ignored.

Mrs. Kaplan proceeded to Washington, armed with letters of introduction from Harry Shapiro of the AZEC and Sidney Marks of the Zionist Organization of America. With Abba Hillel Silver at the helm of the American Zionist movement, mainstream Zionist groups like the AZEC and ZOA were increasingly sympathetic to the Irgun and more than willing to lend Mrs. Kaplan a helping hand, despite her son's affiliation with the rival Bergsonites. She needed all the help she could get; Mrs. Kaplan was a novice on Capitol Hill, and almost immediately she felt like a fish out of water. "Night of doubt and misgivings and fears," she jotted in her diary on her first night in Washington. "Can't control tremblings, heart aches so. . . . During night stood at window, prayed and begged for guidance—didn't know which way to turn, where to go." She spoke with the Washington staff of the ALFP upon her arrival in the capital but decided not to have them accompany her so that her appeal for the *Ben Hecht* prisoner would be seen as a strictly humanitarian, rather than political, effort.

Thanks to contacts facilitated by the ALFP, the AZEC, and the ZOA, Mrs. Kaplan managed to secure appointments with numerous leading congressmen or their staffs, including Republican senator Irving Ives and aides to Democratic senator Robert Wagner, both of whose support she won, in part by claiming to each that the other had already pledged his backing. She also met with senior aides to House majority whip John McCormack and all of the U.S. representatives from Brooklyn, among whom she found the Irish Americans to be the most sympathetic. "Irish, sympathetic, hates British, will definitely help," Kaplan noted in her diary after her meeting with Congressman John J. Rooney (D-New York). In some instances, her reputation preceded her; when Mrs. Kaplan met with Representative Leo Rayfiel (D-New York), she was pleased to be told that he had already received petitions bearing hundreds of signatures from her supporters back home. Congressman Hugh Scott of Philadelphia even delivered a speech on the House floor about the imprisonment of the *Ben Hecht* crew.

By Friday afternoon, Mrs. Kaplan was emotionally and physically exhausted. "Rainstorm, windy, miserable cough and chills. . . . Entered Rabbi's home late, tired, wet from rain and greatly discouraged. Greeted at door with friendly welcome by [Rebbetzin] Esther Pruzansky and Deborah, 5 years old. 'Gut Shabbos, please come in and join us.' What a welcome, warm, genuinely sincere! I could see the candles burning in the dining room, white Shabbos tablecloth gleaming, the challahs covered, the wine decanter. . . . Deborah already made a prayer for me over the candles—'Come Sabbath Queen, bless our guest Mrs. Kaplan.' . . . I'm crying as I write this." Rabbi Pruzansky also provided a key political contact: he introduced her to Benjamin Pollack of the Justice Department, assistant to Attorney General Thomas Clark, who was deeply moved by Mrs. Kaplan's plight. Pollack offered Kaplan advice on how to most effectively speak with politicians, and volunteered to contact leading members of the Senate Foreign Relations Committee and Foreign Affairs Relations Committee on her behalf.

Many of the congressmen contacted either by Mrs. Kaplan or by her supporters telephoned or telegrammed the State Department, the White House, the British Embassy in Washington, or the American consul general in Jerusalem to urge the release of the *Ben Hecht* crew. Within days, there was good news: the British had decided to deport the crew members to the United States, and the U.S. attorney general had decided to refrain from bringing any criminal charges against them. The last thing the British needed was a fight with Congress over the imprisonment of American citizens; the last thing the Truman administration needed, on the eve of an election year, was to prosecute a group of young men regarded as heroes by Jewish voters.

The militant Zionists' political effort in the United States was composed of many small battles like the *Ben Hecht* episode, which focused on a particular point of controversy but at the same time contributed to the broader struggle. The fight to free David Kaplan and his comrades educated and galvanized grassroots Jews to become more deeply involved in the Palestine cause. The members of Congress who intervened on behalf of the *Ben Hecht* crew became more personally acquainted with the Zionist struggle and more likely to join in subsequent efforts. The Truman administration was reminded anew of the Jewish community's intensifying desire for the United States to press Britain to change its Palestine policies. And every telegram or phone call that the British received from a congressman about the *Ben Hecht* contributed further to the general pressure on England to withdraw from Palestine altogether. How many more black eyes could the British endure before they would throw up their hands in despair and quit?[47]

9 • The Guerrilla Rabbi

Yet another Jewish nationalist splinter group contributed to the Jabotinsky movement's impact in America: the Political Action Committee for Palestine. The PACP was the handiwork of Baruch Korff, an energetic young Orthodox rabbi from Boston who had honed his Washington diplomatic skills while lobbying for U.S. rescue action in 1943 and 1944 as a representative of the Bergson group and the Orthodox activist group known as the Vaad Ha-Hatzala.

At the end of 1945, Korff visited Benjamin Akzin at the American Zionist Emergency Council's Washington office with surprising news: he had decided to formally break with the Bergson boys because he was convinced they were diluting their political message in order to attain "power and prestige." Korff intended to establish his own Zionist group, which—Akzin reported to Silver—would "cooperate with us discreetly and coordinate his work with us." Akzin let Korff use the AZEC mimeograph machine to reproduce the announcement.[1]

Korff's inner circle consisted of a handful of Revisionists who found the New Zionist Organization of America too moderate and a handful of ex-Bergsonites who had trouble getting along with Bergson. Not surprisingly, the PACP's publicity tactics were strikingly reminiscent of Bergson's. Making good use of his contacts in the Orthodox community, Korff led hundreds of rabbis (six hundred according to the *New York Times;* over a thousand according to the *New York Daily Mirror*) in a march on Washington timed to coincide with an official visit to the capitol by British prime minister Clement Attlee. "The rabbis, many of them elderly and with flowing beards, seemed timid and mild-mannered, obviously unaccustomed to demonstrations," one reporter noted. "Young organizers of the march gave them directions and frequently tugged at their sleeves" as they visited the British Embassy, Capitol Hill, and the White House to dramatize their demand for free immigration to Palestine, followed by Jewish statehood.

The warmest reception was from congressional leaders, who sympathized with the Zionist agenda and were well acquainted with Rabbi Korff from his earlier lobbying forays. The rabbis were disappointed to be met at the White House by presidential secretary Matthew Connelly, rather than President Truman. Still, the march generated considerable media coverage, focusing negative attention on England's Palestine policy, annoying the visiting British prime minister, and dramatizing the groundswell of pro-Zionist sentiment in the American Jewish community.[2]

Korff's other activities were equally headline-grabbing. The PACP rented out Madison Square Garden and, before a capacity crowd of fifteen thousand, staged an anti-British pageant called *That We May Live*, accompanied by strongly pro-Zionist speeches by House majority leader John W. McCormack and Senator James Mead of New York. Korff and his colleagues also regularly sponsored large newspaper advertisements with dramatic headlines such as "Jewish Blood vs. Arab Oil!" in which they attempted to redefine the parameters of the Palestine conflict in the starkest language possible.[3]

A particularly well choreographed stunt was former congressman Joseph Clark Baldwin's "mission" to London and Jerusalem. A maverick New York Republican, Baldwin had recently been denied his party's renomination, leaving him free to become the PACP's administrative chairman. Baldwin's friendly relationship with President Truman may not have endeared him to his Republican colleagues, but it helped him secure a letter of introduction from the president to take with him when he assented to Rabbi Korff's request to stage a highly publicized visit to England and Palestine at the end of 1946. Within days of Baldwin's arrival in London, Korff authored a full-page advertisement, which appeared in the *New York Post* and elsewhere, reporting to the American public about Britain's "tyrannical" policies in Palestine. Then, immediately upon the conclusion of Baldwin's visit to the Holy Land, Korff sent a telegram, over Baldwin's name, to Irgun leader Menachem Begin, saying that he was "in the midst of preparing my report to the President and the Congress of the United States" and asking Begin to halt guerrilla operations against the British until the report was complete. The idea was to make Baldwin look moderate—"to rehabilitate Baldwin among the Anglophiles in anticipation of his report," as Korff later explained—and to give Begin a chance to explain his cause to the American public, since the media would inevitably quote his response to the former congressman. The strategy worked like a charm. And less than a day after the telegram was sent, the British provoked an international incident by publicly whipping a teenage Irgun member. The British action made the PACP seem reasonable when it announced that while the appeal to Begin had been made on the assumption that there would be no British provocations, the public flogging now made Irgun retaliation inevitable and to some extent even understandable.[4]

Korff employed a similar strategy in the composition of Baldwin's official report of the visit. "The report was deliberately so constructed as to be at variance" with the positions of the PACP, "lest it be dismissed in official circles for its 'extremism.'" "Still," Korff noted, "his recommendations shamed the maximum demands of the Jewish Agency." The Baldwin report called on England and the United States to recognize Palestine "as an independent democracy of which homeless European Jews shall be considered citizens." It differed from the PACP line by proposing that Transjordan be granted independence in exchange for Arab recognition of a Jewish state in the rest of Palestine. As soon as Korff finished writing Baldwin's report, he wrote a PACP press release criticizing the report for offering to relinquish the Jewish claim to Transjordan. The criticism was intended to demonstrate that Baldwin was not a puppet of the PACP but rather had visited London and Jerusalem with an open mind and returned with his own conclusions.[5]

To publicize the plight of imprisoned Irgun fighters, Korff convinced Senator William Langer (R-North Dakota), with the backing of Senators Robert Wagner (D-New York) and Arthur Vandenberg (R-Michigan), to send the PACP's Rabbi J. Howard Ralbag as their official representative to Palestine in 1947 to survey the prison conditions of the Irgun men.[6]

"A state of war exists in Palestine today."

So began Rabbi Ralbag's grim fifteen-page report to Senator Langer. "Everywhere I turned there were barricades of barbed wire, armored cars roaming the streets, and British patrols, armed to the teeth, marching and countermarching in every direction of the compass." Because of the harsh British rule, the Holy Land had degenerated into "a land without liberty, without personal freedom, without civil rights." It was, in short, "a reign of terror" comparable to that found in "the Hitler regimes in occupied Europe prior to their liberation by the Allies." Ralbag witnessed "scenes of wanton cruelty and naked force" during an anti-terror raid in which Jews were taken to prison detention camps that he called "newly prepared ghettoes." He reported "indescribable scenes of terror and human suffering" as British soldiers violently dragged refugees from a captured ship to waiting police vans. The rabbi visited the devastation and rubble of Jerusalem's King

David Hotel, still partly in ruins as a result of the massive Irgun bomb attack the previous July. Then he walked over to the nearby prison where the British had jailed seventy Jewish underground fighters, mostly from the Irgun and Lehi (better known as the Stern Group).

The prisoners' cells, Ralbag found, were "dilapidated and unsanitary," overcrowded, and poorly ventilated, with a single bucket in the middle of the floor serving as a toilet. There were agonizingly long waits for medical assistance, which was dispensed by a woman with no medical training who had to be stoked with *baksheesh* (a bribe). Food was inferior and served only in small quantities; baths were only once weekly, with insufficient water; religious rites, correspondence, and visitors were all severely restricted. Ralbag painted a bleak picture that reinforced the senators' suspicions about British misbehavior in the Holy Land. His visit undoubtedly strengthened their resolve to press for a British withdrawal from Palestine.[7]

Korff's relationship with Senator Langer illustrates the important role played by the lobbyists of the Zionist right in keeping the Palestine issue high on the agenda of the U.S. Congress, and at the same time using their relationships on Capitol Hill to gain publicity for the cause of Jewish statehood. Langer, a feisty, independent-minded Republican who was first elected to the Senate in 1940, was known for oratory "of the roaring, desk-pounding and arm-waving type."[8]

Langer's interest in Jewish issues did not stem from any electoral concerns. North Dakota during the 1940s had a Jewish community numbering barely three thousand—less than one-tenth of one percent of American Jewry. A Jewish businessman from back home once pointed out to Langer that his record on issues of Jewish concern "has made a lot of converts in Fargo who possibly did not vote for [you] in the last election but would in the next."[9] He may have been correct, but even a large Jewish vote for Langer in North Dakota would not mean much. Langer embraced Jewish issues out of genuine heartfelt sympathy for Hitler's victims and a simple conviction that it was unjust for England to prevent Jewish statehood.

Langer became associated with the Bergson group activists even before Korff became their director of rescue activities in late 1943. When Senator Scott Lucas took the Senate floor to blast Bergson's "Cruel Mockery" advertisement in the *New York Times* after the Bermuda refugee conference, it was Langer who rose to the Bergson group's defense. Bermuda, not Bergson, was the problem, Langer declared; as for Lucas's pledge to report to the Senate about Bermuda's accomplishments, Langer shot back: "I am looking forward to this address with the greatest impatience." Five months later, on the day Bergson staged his march of the rabbis in Washington, Langer urged his colleagues to endorse the rabbis' demand for a U.S. government rescue agency. And he paused to recall that five months had passed since Senator Lucas's promise. "Where is the report?" he demanded to know. There was no reply.[10]

After Korff shifted his attention to the Palestine issue and created the PACP in 1945 and 1946, he knew to which members of Congress he could turn for sympathy. Langer was at the top of the list. Korff and his colleagues provided the North Dakotan with a steady stream of letters, memoranda, and newspaper clippings about the British and the Arabs. They made sure, for example, that Langer saw a copy of an October 1945 *New York Times* report that an Egyptian newspaper had blasted "ignorant American Congressmen" and had declared, "You have not participated—nor your country—in the liberation of Palestine and her people have no obligation to you." Langer himself had not fought in World War I—he was serving as attorney general of North Dakota at the time—but the PACP reminded him that many Americans "fought in the war that liberated Palestine—as well as the Arab lands. You saw your American comrades bleed and die in a war in which the Arab leaders double-crossed both sides when they weren't actually fighting the Allies—just as they did in this war. Will you accept this affront?" The PACP also made sure to point out that, in view of the dominant British colonial control of much of the Arab world, "nothing appears in the Arab press which does not meet with official British sanction"; in other words, it was not just the Arabs who were slapping America in the face, but London as well.[11]

Langer's office correspondence files testify to the persistent lobbying of the various Revisionist factions. The files bulge with letters and telegrams about Palestine from constituents in North Dakota, concerned citizens in other parts of the country, and various interest groups. During the crucial period between 1943 and 1948, appeals from the Revisionist factions and the Bergson committees outnumbered correspondence from mainstream Zionist organizations by a margin of nearly four to one.[12] The militants recognized the need to combine their political talk with a personal touch. On one occasion after Langer delivered a stirring pro-Zionist speech on the floor of the Senate, Bergson sent Langer a box of expensive cigars—the perfect gift for a man whom the *New York Times* would one day recall in these terms: "Visitors to the Senate could spot Mr. Langer by the cigar he always chewed. It was never lit and always still in the cellophane wrapper." When

December rolled around, Rabbi Korff made sure to send the senator his personal best wishes for a merry Christmas and a happy new year.[13]

Langer soon emerged as one of the U.S. Senate's sharpest critics of England and most enthusiastic backers of the Jewish revolt. When the Bergsonites rented Madison Square Garden to stage a "public trial" of Britain's Palestine policy, Langer agreed to serve as a sponsor. When a handful of Jewish militants—including Stern Group leader and future Israeli prime minister Yitzhak Shamir—escaped from their British detention camp in Eritrea only to be arrested in neighboring Ethiopia, Langer cabled Emperor Haile Selassi to set them free. When the assassins of Lord Moyne faced execution, Langer signed a telegram calling for commutation of their sentence on the grounds that the "background of agony, despair and death of millions of Hebrews in Europe and continued sufferings of survivors in that inferno constitute sufficient reason for leniency."[14]

Despite protests by mainstream Zionist groups, Langer never shied away from closely collaborating with the Revisionists. He was, the British Embassy complained, a "habitual 'signer'" of militant Zionist advertisements. He added his name to their letterheads. He delivered speeches based on their drafts. When British complaints resulted in an IRS investigation of the Bergson group's tax-exempt status, it was Langer to whom they turned for help.[15]

Rabbi Korff's biggest splash came with his "Exodus by Air" plan to parachute thousands of young Jews into Palestine in defiance of England's immigration restrictions. Dramatic PACP newspaper ads featured a staged photo of a young parachutist cradling a Torah scroll in one arm. The advertisements threatened to "parachute into the Holy Land to supervise personally the D-day Exodus maneuvers" unless the United Nations "solves the problem of immigration and a Jewish homeland." According to Korff, the PACP purchased an airplane and "several hundred" parachutes, assembled "about 50 pilots, engineers, meteorologists, navigators and radio men," and was on the verge of launching the "exodus," when fate intervened in the person of the French police. While meeting in Paris with Jewish militants from Palestine to plan the parachuting, Korff became involved in a scheme to dump thousands of Stern Group leaflets from a plane flying over London. One of the conspirators, however, was a police informant, and Korff and four of his comrades were arrested just before they boarded the plane.

The arrests took place just before Rosh Hashanah, the Jewish new year's day, in September 1947. Although under normal circumstances five suspects awaiting interrogation in such a case would not be allowed any contact with one another, Korff insisted on his right, as a clergyman, to lead the others in High Holiday prayers. The five of them, together with an unsuspecting local Jewish criminal defendant, were taken to the prison chapel under the watchful eye of two French guards. In the guise of conducting the services, Korff, to the tune of a traditional Rosh Hashanah melody, lectured the "worshippers" in Hebrew on how to answer the questions of their French police interrogators. Each of the five took a turn on the podium, swaying piously as he offered suggestions on how to coordinate their stories. At one point, Korff even managed to persuade the guards to temporarily wait outside the chapel on the grounds that certain prayers could not be recited if "non-believers" were present. The French detectives who questioned Korff and his friends later that week were stymied by the suspects' perfectly coordinated responses.

At the same time, Korff, with his keen eye for publicity, launched a hunger strike, and the French authorities were more than a little embarrassed by the numerous U.S. newspaper reports about the American rabbi starving in a French prison. The media coverage, combined with protests by several of Korff's congressional allies, led to the defendants' release and confirmed the young rabbi's status as an international political celebrity. The British could only watch in frustration as the guerrilla rabbi escaped punishment and returned to the United States to resume agitating against London's policies.[16]

10 • Explaining the Jewish Revolt to America

Abba Hillel Silver returned to the helm of American Zionism in the summer of 1945 determined to infuse American Jewry with an activist spirit. Among his first steps in remaking the American Zionist movement were to place two of the most talented American Revisionists in senior positions on the American Zionist Emergency Council staff.

The first was Benjamin Akzin. With the war ending and the most important of the War Refuge Board's work completed, Akzin was ready to return to the world of Zionist politics—but not Bergson's brand. Akzin was not impressed by Bergson's January 21, 1945, letter complaining that "you, being an American politically, would without a moment's hesitation answer the call of your local draft board but you, being a Zionist leader, do not recognize the existence of any moral draft board that has the right to call upon you."[1] Akzin was convinced that both the Bergsonites and the Revisionists were too small, and too militant, to make a significant impact; he was determined to "bore from within," as he put it—to enter the mainstream so as to maximize his impact. Akzin was actually hired by the AZEC in Silver's absence, but his request to work in the powerful and influential Washington, D.C., bureau had been blocked by a wary Nahum Goldmann. The Revisionist Akzin "must be watched," Goldmann warned. Akzin was temporarily confined to a lesser role, in the New York office, where he soon found that the old-line AZEC leaders "resented" him and gave his political advice "more than a skeptical reception." Silver, upon his return to the AZEC helm in September 1945, overrode Goldmann's objections and installed Akzin as the new director of the D.C. office.[2]

Akzin was back in familiar territory, meeting with many of the same congressmen, congressional aides, foreign diplomats, and journalists whose acquaintance he had made during his months as a lobbyist in 1940. The terrain had scarcely changed, nor had the thrust of the propaganda—by 1945, the arguments made by the AZEC no longer differed significantly from those of the Revisionists—but there was one crucial difference. Now, when Akzin urged administration officials to pressure the British, he was not speaking on behalf of a small segment of the Jewish community, but rather could confidently assert that he was "representing the feelings of the vast majority of the Jewish citizens in this country." The administration might ignore the Revisionists; it could not ignore the AZEC.[3]

Silver's second Revisionist addition to the AZEC hierarchy was Eliahu Ben-Horin. The long years of poverty and frustration as the leader of a small opposition faction in the Zionist world had taken their toll on Ben-Horin. "I have neither energy nor patience left to go on 'opposing' indefinitely," he confided to Akzin in November 1944. The time had come to try influencing events from the inside. Although enjoying some success as a freelance writer, Ben-Horin was delighted when Silver offered him the opportunity to join the AZEC staff; now he could work to reverse the Zionist establishment's "old ways of political complacency and submission"—from within.[4] He was retained in the autumn of 1945 to handle contacts with VIPs, author AZEC literature and material for the AZEC newsletter *Palestine*, and advise Silver on political affairs. Ben-Horin was routinely dispatched to represent AZEC at meetings with U.S. and British officials and prominent journalists, not to mention international Zionist gatherings.[5]

In one of his first missions, Ben-Horin was sent by Silver in October 1945 to seek the support of former president Herbert Hoover for a Jewish state. Ben-Horin was pleasantly surprised to hear that Hoover was less interested in issuing a general endorsement of Jewish statehood than he was in promoting the idea of resettling Palestinian Arabs in Iraq in order to make room for a Jewish state—the same idea that Ben-Horin and the NZOA had advocated, via the short-lived American Resettlement Committee for Uprooted Jewry, in 1943.[6] Ben-Horin reported back to Silver on Hoover's suggestion. Despite the expanding workload imposed on the AZEC by the mounting warfare in Palestine and the intensifying diplomatic struggle surrounding the future of the Holy Land, Silver considered the project sufficiently worthwhile to authorize Ben-Horin to spend the bulk of the next two months helping Hoover promote and publicize the plan.

The idea of a Palestine-Iraq population transfer made perfect sense to Hoover, an engineer by profession who instinctively sought economic solutions for political problems. During the autumn of 1945, against the backdrop of Holocaust survivors in DP camps and boatloads of refugees being turned away from Palestine by British patrols, Ben-Horin helped Hoover draft a public statement proposing Iraq as the solution to the Palestine problem. The Hoover declaration, released in the form of a statement to the press on November 18, gained only limited media attention and was never given serious consideration by the Allies.[7] But the role of the AZEC in support of Hoover further demonstrates the extent to which the political mood in the American Zionist leadership had hardened. When the project came before the AZEC leadership for discussion, Silver lobbied strongly for the AZEC to "unofficially take the initiative" to help organize a group of prominent non-Jews, headed by Hoover, to promote the Iraq plan. For tactical reasons, the American Zionist leaders were careful not to explicitly endorse or promote the Hoover plan, but Ben-Horin was permitted to place an editorial in the AZEC's journal *Palestine* that referred favorably to Hoover's scheme.[8] The revelations of the Holocaust and the hardening British stance in Palestine were pushing the Zionist leadership to embrace views that they once denounced as Revisionist extremism. Ben-Horin now had plenty of reason to feel comfortable within the Zionist mainstream.

The addition of Akzin and Ben-Horin added a whole new flavor to the work of the AZEC. Intimately familiar with both Eastern Europe (where both were born) and Palestine (where Ben-Horin had lived), and still true in their hearts to the uncompromising Zionist ideology they learned at Jabotinsky's knee, Akzin and Ben-Horin exuded a particular sense of urgency about Jewry's plight and the need for activists to change the course of history. It was Silver who initiated and led the remarkable transformation that American Zionism underwent during the immediate postwar years, and his senior aides such as Emanuel Neumann and *New Palestine* editor Carl Alpert also played key roles. Now Akzin and Ben-Horin, their militancy tempered by the requirements of Jewish establishment protocol, would play a crucial role in guiding and articulating Silver's powerful vision.

The influence of Akzin and Ben-Horin soon became apparent in the AZEC's attitude toward Jewish underground military actions against the British Mandate authorities. The established Zionist organizations had been loath to defend Jewish violence against the British while World War II still raged, and while the Jewish Agency was denouncing the Irgun as treasonous. But all that changed in the summer and autumn of 1945. The new British government, led by Prime Minister Clement Attlee and Foreign Minister Ernest Bevin, dashed Zionist hopes by announcing a postwar continuation of England's tight immigration restrictions on Palestine. The Jewish Agency and its militia, the Haganah, responded by joining the Irgun and Stern Group in the United Hebrew Resistance Movement against the

British. Violence against the Mandate authorities suddenly became legitimate in the eyes of the mainstream Zionist movement. And Ben-Horin and Akzin were perfectly situated to shape, articulate, and sustain the AZEC's new view of Jewish militancy.

Shortly after taking up his position in the AZEC's New York headquarters, Ben-Horin reported to Akzin, in Washington, about a dramatic shift in Jewish public opinion. In response to the latest events abroad, even "the most mild and pacifist" among active New York Zionists "speaks of converting the whole Zionist enterpri[s]e into an army camp and organized rebellion."[9] Just as Ben-Horin and Akzin were assuming senior positions in the Zionist mainstream, developments in Europe and Palestine were making the Zionist mainstream ripe for their influence.

Adding fuel to the fire was a constant barrage of news reports about British abuses in Palestine. American Zionists read about British soldiers overreacting to Jewish protests in Tel Aviv on November 14 (1945), leaving three Jews dead and thirty-three wounded. On November 26, ten thousand British troops and policemen mounted a brutal search for Jewish fighters believed to be hiding in the Plain of Sharon, resulting in eight more Jewish deaths and seventy-five injured. Long curfews, harsh searches, collective fines, confiscation of private property, and mass detention of innocent civilians became standard British policy in response to the Jewish rebellion. It was no wonder Ben-Horin and Akzin were finding an increasingly receptive audience among mainstream Zionists for their efforts to encourage stronger AZEC criticism of the British.

Another important source of information about Palestine for American Zionist leaders was Ben-Horin himself, who was dispatched to the Holy Land by the AZEC in 1946 for a firsthand survey of the situation there. He returned full of praise for the Irgun, reporting to a meeting of AZEC officials that the Irgun had attracted "a great deal of sympathy" among Palestine Jewry and "is in a state of daily growth."[10] Ben-Horin and Akzin could feel proud of their role in the spadework that led to the near-unanimous passage of a resolution endorsing the "resistance" movement that was fighting "the oppressive British regime," at an AZEC emergency conference in Washington in early 1947.[11] Nor was it a coincidence that Palestine businessman and Labor Zionist Yosef Zinger found, during his visit to the United States in 1947, "many, many supporters of the [Irgun]" in the Jewish community.[12]

The efforts by Ben-Horin and Akzin to move the AZEC toward embracing the Jewish revolt against the British came precisely when the U.S.

Revisionists were themselves launching an all-out campaign to rally American support for the Palestine Jewish underground. Many of the emissaries who had come to America with Jabotinsky in 1939 and 1940, and who subsequently became the leaders of the NZOA and the Bergson committees, were representatives of the Irgun and had identified themselves as such during their first months of activity in the United States, before they realized that potential supporters might be alienated by that knowledge. The Irgun men who were now hurling homemade bombs at British military posts were the American Revisionists' ideological kinsmen, sometimes even their own friends or relatives.

During the early months of the revolt, while the war in Europe was still raging, the U.S. Revisionists had been somewhat equivocal in their view of the Irgun's actions. With the American and British armies still fighting side by side against Hitler, even the most nationalist-minded of American Zionists were reluctant to defend the killing of British soldiers by Palestinian Jews. The NZOA's internal newsletter, trying hard to balance the conflicting emotions in the movement, declared in March 1944 that Jewish attacks against the British "can neither be condoned nor condemned by us."[13] After Jewish militants assassinated Lord Moyne, the senior British official in the Middle East, in Cairo in November 1944, the NZOA was more explicit in distancing itself from the deed. "The New Zionist Organization has never advocated nor supported any acts of terror in Palestine," NZOA president Mendelsohn announced. Yet when the two accused assassins went on trial, the U.S. Revisionists publicly praised them as "patriots and fighters for freedom" and vigorously denounced the British judges for censoring the defendants' political statements.[14] The Bergsonites circulated an appeal against the imposition of the death penalty, signed by two dozen congressmen and Zionist activists, while the splinter Zionist-Revisionist Organization (the Bergson sympathizers who had split from the NZOA in 1944) set up a special "Committee for the Asirai-Zion [Prisoners of Zion]" to lobby against the execution. The committee dispatched a delegation of rabbis, including NZOA board member Rabbi J. Howard Ralbag, to the Egyptian Embassy in Washington to plead for clemency.[15]

The varied reactions of NZOA chapters outside New York to the Moyne assassination provide additional evidence of the divisions in the movement during those early months of the revolt. The Detroit chapter's statement about the Moyne killing fell far short of a condemnation, while the Midwestern Division of the NZOA, in Chicago, explicitly condemned the assassination and urged Palestine's Jews to confine themselves to nonviolent political methods. Yet even the Chicago condemnation emphasized that the British were to blame for provoking extreme Jewish reactions by implementing policies "more in accord with the methods of the Nazis than of a democracy." This tactic of shifting the moral responsibility for the violence from the Irgun to British provocations would soon become the hallmark not only of the NZOA's response to the Jewish revolt, but the Zionist establishment's response as well.[16]

Once the war ended, however, American supporters of the Palestine underground quickly shed their hesitations about endorsing the Irgun's actions, and the postwar revelations about the full extent of the Holocaust galvanized them to openly embrace the Palestine revolt. When eighteen Irgun and Lehi men were sentenced to death by a British court in 1946, the NZOA publicly appealed to Acting Secretary of State Dean Acheson to intervene. When President Truman condemned the Irgun bombing of the British military headquarters in Jerusalem's King David Hotel, the NZOA condemned *him* for not including in his condemnation any mention of "British acts of oppression against the Jewish community." The NZOA did not temper its statements even after the World Zionist Organization suspended six U.S. Revisionists from the WZO Executive for having violated WZO discipline by raising money for the Irgun.[17]

The U.S. Revisionists were especially successful in harnessing grassroots Jewish anger at the British execution of Irgun fighter Dov Gruner in 1947. Channeling communal outrage into political action, the NZOA staged a series of memorial-protest meetings that attracted crowds of unprecedented size, in cities where they previously had little or no presence. Some 1,000 people were on hand for the New Haven meeting; 1,200 attended in Pittsburgh. In Chicago there were enough participants to hold three separate meetings in different parts of the city, while 1,000 were turned away after an overflow crowd of more than 3,000 packed the Manhattan rally, which was addressed by Gruner's sister and Barney Ross, the most famous Jewish boxer of the era. Rabbi Louis Newman, who spoke at the rally despite his official position as United Nations observer for the (anti-Irgun) Central Conference of American (Reform) Rabbis, called Gruner "another Nathan Hale." The Boston gathering was addressed by local Betar leader Moshe Arens; the next day, Arens led a takeover of the city's British Consulate.[18]

A particularly colorful episode was the invasion of the British Consulate in Manhattan by fifty young Revisionists and Betar members protesting the Gruner execution. Consul General F. E. Evans sarcastically described to Foreign Minister Bevin how, after seizing a section of the offices, the militants "burst into a series of Hebrew songs in tones that would have done credit to the Don Cossack choir . . . [but] their harmonies failed them when it came to singing the American national anthem." The staff immediately called the police, but "some 18 minutes elapsed before the main body of constabulary arrived," a sure sign to Evans of collusion between the police and "the Jews," as he referred to them. During those anxious minutes, "a valiant lady member of my staff, Mrs. Fountain, armed with the long pole used for opening and closing windows, sought to repel a photographer from the newspaper *PM* (now virtually a Zionist house-organ)" who had stationed himself on the balcony. "Our Mrs. Fountain not only ejected the photographer, but slammed the window in his face!" Evans reported triumphantly. The chief police officer's "sycophantic" appeal to the demonstrators to leave infuriated the consul general. Evans detected a connection between the behavior of the police and a ceremony, elsewhere in Manhattan that same afternoon, at which the acting mayor had greeted crew members of the SS *Ben Hecht*, the American League for a Free Palestine boat that had recently tried to bring refugees to Palestine. "I cannot but regard it as a significant, if not a sinister, coincidence," Evans wrote Bevin, "that, at the moment when this official encouragement was being given to a group of conspirators against British authority, the New York police were showing such notable reluctance to take drastic action against another similar group of conspirators against the representative local office of the British Government." Evans concluded his report by wondering "whether Judaism is, as now, to be regarded as a militant would-be national movement founded on race, or as an inoffensive and respectable religion divorced from any nationality issue, as hitherto it has contented itself to be in the United States."

Two aspects of Evans's report are noteworthy for their broader implications. First, the quick assumption of collaboration between the police and the protesters, based on the flimsiest of evidence, is indicative of the extent to which the barrage of Zionist rallies, newspaper ads, and the like had succeeded in fostering a sense of siege and isolation among British officials in the United States. That was an important propaganda success. Second, Evans's patronizing reference to Judaism, considering it "respectable" only if it were "divorced from nationalism," is indicative of the mind-set among British officialdom that was partly responsible for stoking Jewish anger.[19]

In the wake of the execution of Gruner and other Jewish underground fighters in the late spring of 1947, the Revisionists found the American

Jewish community more receptive than ever to their appeals. Local committees were set up around the country, under the auspices of the UZRA's new Asirai Zion Fund, to publicize the cause while raising funds for the families of imprisoned Irgun fighters. (The British Embassy in Washington, which sometimes had trouble distinguishing between the Revisionists and the Bergsonites, mistakenly believed the new prisoners' committee was established by the Bergson group.)[20] Veteran Revisionist activists Dr. David Bukspan and Dr. Eliezer Shostak (who would later serve as Israeli minister of health) were brought from Palestine for a successful speaking tour for the Asirai Zion groups, as was Max Seligman, a prominent attorney who defended captured Irgun soldiers. The fund's activity was publicly endorsed by a committee of notable sponsors, including one of the most prominent Orthodox rabbis in the United States, Leo Jung, and Rabbi Louis Newman, who had been out of the Revisionist limelight for years.[21]

Ordinary seasonal distractions do not seem to have put a significant damper on the activities of the Irgun's American supporters during the tumultuous summer of 1947. News of the ongoing Jewish-British battles in Palestine, the hanging of Irgun fighters and counter-hanging of British soldiers, the dramatic voyage and capture of the SS *Exodus,* and the visit to Palestine of the UN's Special Committee on Palestine kept emotions at a fever pitch in the American Jewish community. Activists were highly motivated to mobilize, and the community increasingly welcomed them with open arms. "Summer months may create a lull in other organizations, but ours is geared to War!" declared the Palestine Resistance Committee (PRC), the latest Jabotinskyite creation—but this one was a joint Bergsonite-Revisionist effort. "There is a war being fought in Palestine today. There are no vacations for us." The PRC had its own Bronx chapter, named after David Raziel, one of the Irgun's first commanders, which "in spite of enervating weather and vacation plans" spent the summer "canvassing their neighborhoods with literature, collecting funds from friends and neighbors and conducting open air meetings."[22] The PRC's campus arm, the Intercollegiate Council for Palestine Resistance, reportedly raised $2,000 with its "Show Boat on the Hudson" evening. The council also assembled an interfaith team of college basketball stars to play a series of benefit games at Catskills resort hotels to raise money for the revolt against the British. The largely Jewish summer hotel circuit was in those days heavily traveled by ad hoc teams made up of college athletes as well as up-and-coming professional basketball players—including the young Wilt Chamberlain—who often worked as busboys during the day, then played for extra cash as the evening's entertainment. Italian-American college stars Vince Verdeschi and Lou Rossini, who grew up and played basketball in New York City alongside many Jewish friends and neighbors, sympathized with the struggle for a Jewish homeland and readily agreed to join fellow stars Lionel Malamed and Richard "Chubby" Sherman to help the Irgun as part of the PRC's interfaith team.

The most striking aspect of the Revisionists' campaign to win American public sympathy for the Palestine militants was their sophisticated use of carefully selected symbols, images, and phrases designed to make Jewish violence in Palestine more comprehensible to American audiences. "It's 1776 in Palestine" became the rallying cry as the NZOA and ALFP Americanized the Irgun's revolt by constantly referring to the American Revolutionaries in their newspaper advertisements, press releases, op-ed essays, radio broadcasts, public meetings, and protest rallies. Officials at the British Embassy, keeping an ever-watchful eye on the militant Zionists, found the 1776 analogy especially irritating—the product of "great and sometimes wilful ignorance," they asserted.[23]

"A revolutionary war is going on in Palestine," wrote Ben Hecht in one of his fiery broadsides. "The few survivors [of the Holocaust] . . . are making history in the same way as the Maquis, the Partisans, the Irish rebels and the American revolutionists."[24] Harry Selden of the ALFP minced no words: "But for an accident of time and place, Dov Gruner [the Jewish militant scheduled to be hanged by the British] might have been fighting in 1776 for American liberty and Nathan Hale might have been hanged in 1947, a martyr to Hebrew Freedom . . . they fought a common oppressor."[25] A brigade of Americans who volunteered to join the Irgun was named the "George Washington Legion," while a group that organized boycotts of British goods and services was dubbed the "Sons of Liberty Committee," in imitation of the colonial American boycotters of the same name.[26] British officials privately mocked the Revisionists' call for a boycott of British insurance companies as "presumably the most painless way of taking action," but they could not hide their anxiety at the prospect of a substantial Jewish boycott movement.[27]

Dr. Judah Magnes, the Hebrew University chancellor and outspoken Jewish pacifist, got an earful when he denounced Hecht and the ALFP for supporting "Jewish terrorism." The league's leaders fired back with a press release quoting the pure American rhetoric of one of their prominent non-Jewish supporters, former senator Guy Gillette: "Our forefathers started shooting redcoats when the matter of a tea tax was involved. The Hebrews in Palestine have taken a lot more than taxation without representation." The press release concluded by quoting Thomas Jefferson's memorable phrase, "Resistance to tyranny is obedience to God."[28]

For those who doubted the ability of a small Jewish guerrilla force to defeat the British army, Menachem Begin's American backers pointed to England's record. "Britain has capitulated in similar conflicts with the American colonies," one NZOA ad reminded readers of the *New York Post*. "She will capitulate in her ignoble extermination campaign against the Jewish people."[29] An ALFP broadside in the *New Republic* seconded the point: "We have no doubt as to the outcome—Great Britain never won a war against a people fighting for freedom."[30] The use of more subtle terminology reinforced the image of Begin's men as modern-day Nathan Hales. The pro-Irgun newspaper ads regularly referred to them as "patriots" and described their aim as the establishment of "a democratic Hebrew Republic"—phrases whose similarity to American Revolutionary rhetoric was more than coincidental.[31]

Ancillary aspects of the American Revolution likewise surfaced in the propaganda of the militant Zionists. "Just as the British stirred up the Iroquois [Indians] to fight the [American] colonists, so today they are stirring up the Arabs," ran one argument. Another described "the Hessians who were the British mercenaries" in the 1770s as "knightly gentlemen" in comparison to the "Arab mercenaries inspired by the British" in the Holy Land.[32] The willingness of some Zionist leaders in Palestine to collaborate with the British reminded Ben Hecht of the Revolutionary era, too:

> Respectability and wealth never lined up with a revolution—or a fighting minority. The American Revolutionary Army under George Washington went a long time without shoes, guns or food. The respectable and wealthy American colonists preferred British admiration to liberty and freedom. They thought it was bad taste to fight for such things—against the British, of all people. And they proved their respectability by playing informer to the British. You can see how little respectability has changed since 1776.[33]

Even Hecht himself was utilized to further the analogy. The publicity for Hecht's play, *A Flag Is Born*, pointed out that every "great issue in history has produced literary figures equal to the cause"; the American Revolution had its "Tom Paines and Jeffersons. . . . Ben Hecht is in this tradition."[34]

This line of argument was soon picked up by others in the Jewish community. After the British hanged Dov Gruner, the New York Board of Rabbis—representing the city's Orthodox, Conservative, and Reform rabbinate—declared: "Had the Thirteen Colonies lost their bitter struggle against British tyranny, Washington, Jefferson and their associates would have suffered similar deaths."[35]

Before long, such analogies were seeping into general American public discourse as well. "Many Americans feel sympathetic to the fight that the Jews are carrying on in Palestine. They feel that in some respects it is like the fight the American colonies carried on in 1776," wrote former vice president Henry Wallace in the *New Republic* (of which he was then editor). I. F. Stone, the Washington editor of America's other major liberal weekly, the *Nation,* concurred. The Jews who had taken up arms against the British in Palestine "are no more gangsters than were the men of Concord or Lexington," he wrote.[36] That two of America's most prominent political commentators publicly defended the Palestine Jewish revolt by comparing it to colonial America's own rebellion against England was testimony to the success of the militant Zionists' information campaigns on behalf of the Jewish rebels.

Whether they realized it or not, Begin's American Jewish cheerleaders, by using symbols and phrases that hearkened back to earlier periods in American history, were following in the footsteps of traditional mainstream American Zionist educational techniques. American Zionists had always justified Zionism in American terms. The Jewish refugees settling in Palestine reminded Richard Gottheil, president of the Federation of American Zionists in 1902, of "the Puritans [who] fled from persecution." The Zionist pioneers "are building the new Judea even as the Puritans built a new England three hundred years ago," declared his colleague, Bernard Rosenblatt, in 1907. "Hederah and her sister colonies are . . . the Jamestown and the Plymouth of the new House of Israel."[37]

Louis Brandeis, the great "Americanizer" of post–World War I Zionism, reveled in such comparisons. Brandeis's enthusiastic fusion of Zionist activities and American symbolism played a vital role in making American Jews feel that their nationalist sentiments were acceptable, particularly during World War I and the immediate postwar period, when nativism was running at a fever pitch and Theodore Roosevelt was thundering against "hyphenated Americans." Brandeis spoke of "the Jewish Pilgrim Fathers" in Palestine, working in "the Colonies," in a region that most closely resembled "a miniature California."[38]

The tension between the Jewish pioneers and local Arabs provided more grist for the analogy mills. The Federation of American Zionists' official *Course in Zionism* (1915) saw no need to worry about Arab violence, since the Zionists had their *Shomrim*, armed guards who "have all the accomplishments of Western cow-boys, [and] are rugged, efficient, fearless."[39] If there were occasional Arab attacks, Brandeis thought, that was inevitable, for the American pioneers "who found the Massachusetts Bay Colony [likewise] had to protect themselves against the Indians." Arab assaults gave the Jews a chance to demonstrate their "mettle" and polish their "manhood, courage, and ability to look out for themselves" (the very qualities Brandeis most admired in Americans).[40] Just as the early American settlers were not deterred by Indian attacks, neither would the Zionists abandon their work because of Arab attacks, reported Irma Lindheim, vice president of Hadassah, after visiting Galilee in 1922. The Jews reminded her of "those of the pioneer times of early New England, [who] went out each day, rifles in hand, to cut their fields into furrows, and plant crops for their subsistence."[41]

The Revisionists, the ALFP, Baruch Korff's Political Action Committee for Palestine, and the mainstream AZEC each contributed, in its own unique way, to the effort to explain the Palestine resistance to the American public. The NZOA, Korff, and the Bergsonites openly supported the Jewish revolt. The mainstream Zionist leadership used a different approach that was no less important. While not explicitly justifying Jewish violence, the American Zionist leadership's public statements—often crafted in part or whole by Ben-Horin or Akzin—implicitly rationalized the militants' behavior by focusing hostile attention on the English as the real cause of the Palestine trouble. When the British commanding officer in Palestine, Lieutenant General Gordon MacMillan, described a captured Irgun fighter as a "gangster," an editorial in the AZEC journal *Palestine* fired back: "There are gangsters in Palestine, but they may be found among the soldiers under General MacMillan's command."[42] Abba Hillel Silver told the 1946 Zionist Organization of America convention that "only Fascist Italy and Nazi Germany could offer parallels to such barbarism" as Britain was practicing in Palestine.[43] "Who Are the *Real* Terrorists?" asked the headline of a full-page ZOA ad in the *New Republic*. The ZOA's answer, of course, was the British, whose "illegal military measures and deportation of Jewish refugees to concentration camps" had "provoked acts of desperation by Jewish men and women."[44]

Ezekiel Leikin, who joined the ZOA national staff in 1946, found that

"ZOA leaders were quietly supportive of the underground groups, especially of the Irgun, and contributed funds for its operations." Leikin was himself a veteran Revisionist who had been hired by Benzion Netanyahu in 1946 to organize NZOA chapters around the country. When the Revisionists ran short of funds and let Leikin go after only a few weeks, Abba Hillel Silver snatched him up and set him to work organizing the ZOA's midwestern districts—another indication of the extent to which differences between the Revisionists and the mainstream were vanishing. Leikin's continuing sympathy for the Irgun, including his praise of Irgun martyr Dov Gruner in the letters column of the *Chicago Daily News* in 1947, did not faze his superiors at the ZOA. It did, however, prompt several attempts by the local chapter of Bergson's Hebrew Committee of National Liberation to recruit him to their ranks.[45]

Akzin made good use of the condemn-but-understand approach to the Irgun in his private meetings with VIPs. He told the U.S. ambassador to London in early 1947 that while the AZEC "deplored" the Jewish underground's violence, the British were to blame for "deliberately provoking and goading them into such acts." Using the Irgun's actions as a political pressure point, Akzin confided to the ambassador—and asked him to pass it along to London—that while "from time to time, we are able to restrain them, the longer the British provocation, the more difficult it is to stop these misguided groups." Ben-Horin did likewise in a July 1946 meeting with Lord Inverchapel, the British ambassador to the United States; he told him that the Haganah—then engaged in all-out guerrilla warfare against the English in Palestine—was "legitimate" and its deeds understandable, in view of the Mandate authorities' "Nazi-like practices."[46]

By frequently utilizing phrases that compared British behavior to that of the Nazis, the American Zionist leadership implicitly suggested that the violent resistance of the Jews to the British was as understandable as had been Jewish resistance to the Nazis. A British law permitting searches without warrants was cited as evidence that "it is difficult to detect the difference between the laws of [Nazi] Germany and the lawlessness of Britain." Abuse of Palestinian Jewish civilians by British soldiers constituted "a Nazi pogrom." The Palestine Mandate administration was described as "a virtual Gestapo regime." The seizure of boatloads of unauthorized Jewish immigrants and their deportation to "concentration camps" in Cyprus was "patterned on the Nazi practice," declared Henry Monsky, leader of the American Jewish Conference. By portraying Begin's revolt as a Jewish war against Nazi-like oppressors, the mainstream Zionist leaders lent an important helping hand to the militant Zionists' campaign on behalf of the Palestine fighters.[47]

The increasingly passionate tone of AZEC statements was also facilitated by Abba Hillel Silver's own private sympathy for the Irgun rebels. "Dr. Silver and Emanuel Neumann were clearly sympathetic to the Irgun in private conversations," *New Palestine* editor Carl Alpert later recalled.[48] Irgun leader Menachem Begin, who met Silver during the latter's visit to Palestine in late 1947, heard from him "words of encouragement for our struggle instead of the usual denunciations of the 'dissidents.'" According to Begin, Silver assured him that "American public opinion was sympathetic to the fighters because they too had to fight the British by extra-legal means." Begin's description of attempts by the Jewish Agency to stamp out the Irgun shocked and infuriated Silver.[49] At the conclusion of their talk, Silver gave Begin a code name to use if any Irgun emissary should ever want to see him in the United States: "Dr. Bloch."

Two months later, Dr. Silver received a call from "Dr. Bloch" and hurried to meet the Irgun representative, Shmuel Katz, in a midtown hotel. Katz, who spent about forty-five minutes with Silver that day, was "astonished by the warmth" Silver displayed when they met. According to Katz, Silver made it clear that he "wholeheartedly favored" the Irgun's actions, but when Katz asked him to seek an AZEC grant for the underground, Silver declined. He had "no hope" of winning a majority for such an allocation, Silver said, so the result "of his even raising the proposal in the committee would only be a loss of influence." Nahum Goldmann, for his part, recalled years later that Silver "was more sympathetic [than Goldmann] to [the Jewish underground's] activities and often condoned them," although Silver was careful to condone them only in private.[50]

Silver and his colleagues received their share of criticism for their attitude toward the Palestine Jewish underground. The Haganah's U.S. support group, Americans for Haganah, accused Silver of failing to take any "strong steps" against pro-Irgun groups, and complained about the "strongly pro-Irgun elements" present "in the leadership of Zionist organizations in America."[51] An editorial in the *Reconstructionist* in 1946 chided Silver for failing to specifically condemn Jewish terrorism in his address to that year's ZOA national convention.[52] Nahum Goldmann—who at one point had called for arming Jews in Palestine to "wipe out" the Jewish underground—chastised Akzin for "justifying" Jewish terrorism.[53]

Silver's opponents within the mainstream Zionist groups sometimes defied the national Zionist movement's policies. Ignoring the national AZEC's position, the Chicago branch of the AZEC tried, unsuccessfully, to pressure the Chicago Revisionists to stop praising the Irgun and to withdraw their cosponsorship of appearances by Irgun attorney Max Seligman. "Never before have I heard of any such thing as prohibiting opposition or forbidding people who think differently to criticize their leadership," an outraged David Bukspan shot back.[54] Likewise, a lecture by Benzion Netanyahu in New Haven, sponsored by local Revisionists—one of whom was Netanyahu's brother, Connecticut steel merchant Matthew Mileikowsky—was disrupted by a local ZOA leader shouting that the Palestine militants were "no better than Chicago gangsters." Outbursts of this nature were not uncommon at lectures by Revisionist spokesmen.[55]

Ultimately, however, the harsh accusations hurled at Silver over the Irgun missed the real point: the tide of U.S. Jewish opinion had turned in favor of Jewish militancy. It was not that Silver was guilty of "Revisionist tactics" (as Goldmann put it) or "American Irgunism" (in Wise's memorable phrase). Silver had not changed; American Jewry had. Silver, Netanyahu, Bergson, and the Revisionists whom Silver brought onto the AZEC staff accurately reflected the militant mood that had overtaken the Jewish community in response to events abroad. When a moderate such as Henry Monsky (president of B'nai B'rith and the American Jewish Conference) could declare that British policy toward Holocaust survivors was "patterned on the Nazi practice," and Wise himself could privately concede that the British were "almost conducting a veritable pogrom against the Jews of Palestine," there could be no doubt: the entire community had shifted in its views, with Silver's generation of young militants in the lead, leaving behind the more cautious elements represented by Wise.[56]

How successful was the campaign to Americanize the Jewish revolt? The polling data from the late 1940s is not sufficiently detailed to determine American public attitudes toward Jewish guerrilla activity specifically. Attitudes toward several related issues, however, are clear. Surveys indicate that the U.S. public's support for the creation of a Jewish state increased between 1945 and 1948. Twice as many—and later, three times as many—Americans sympathized with the Jews as with the Arabs. Only 7 percent thought that the British were treating the Jews better than the Arabs, while more than five times that number believed that the Arabs in Palestine were receiving better treatment. Of the 58 percent of Americans who said (in early 1946) that they "have followed the news about the disorders in Palestine," just 12 percent blamed the Jews, while 33 percent said that the British were to blame (10 percent blamed the Arabs; the rest had no opinion).[57]

The primary factors that encouraged the spread of such attitudes are readily apparent. Revelations about the full extent of the Holocaust generated sympathy for Zionism. So did the continuing plight of Holocaust survivors in Europe's DP camps. Energetic grassroots lobbying by hundreds of local ZOA and AZEC branches certainly contributed to fostering understanding of Zionist aims.

Yet the violent behavior of the Jewish forces in Palestine would have surely undermined American public sympathy for the Zionist cause, if not for the efforts of the Jewish underground's American friends. The one-two punch of militant Zionists justifying Jewish violence in American terms and mainstream Zionists focusing negative attention on Britain as the provoker of Jewish violence helped buttress U.S. public support for Zionism against the erosion that would otherwise have been caused by the stream of news reports about Jews killing British soldiers. The Jewish battle against the British, recast to resemble a reincarnation of America's own battle against England, helped redefine American public perceptions of the conflict in Zion.

British officials in Washington and London eyed the Irgun's American sympathizers with growing consternation. The impact of militant Zionist agitation on U.S.-British relations had to be considered, the embassy warned Foreign Minister Bevin: "Palestine is the only serious source of Anglo-American political friction at the present time. . . . The extreme Right and the extreme Left—pro-Russians and America firsters—can join hands with a miscellaneous collection of old opponents, such as the Irish Americans. India is now a broken reed. Palestine can take its place. . . . It is not safe to say that British policy towards Palestine can be based on the general assumption that United States opinion can be ignored."[58]

But what could be done? Frustrated embassy officials had long since adopted a policy of ignoring all letters from the Bergson committee ("these gangsters") and had instructed all consulates in the United States to refrain from having "any contact with these organizations."[59] The British Mandate government banned the printed version of *A Flag Is Born* from distribution in Palestine, along with Zionist books by William Ziff and Pierre van Paassen; but such acts of censorship only made the British seem draconian and increased sympathy for the Zionist militants.[60] The British tried banning movies with which Hecht had been involved, but Hecht found it flattering.

"An empire hitting at a single man and passing sanctions against him!" Hecht wrote. "There was something to swell a writer's bosom and add a notch to his hat size." The swelling subsided as Hecht found himself writing under pseudonyms for half his previous fee, but it never put a damper on his Zionist activity.[61]

The British also tried banning the militants themselves from England. After Bergson representative Johan Smertenko held a press conference in London at which he endorsed the Jewish revolt in Palestine, he was barred from reentering England, and British consuls in the United States were instructed to refrain from granting visas to members of any of the Jabotinsky factions. The Bergson committees, the Revisionists, the Betar youth movement (which the British Embassy in Washington regarded as "similar to the Hitler Youth"),[62] and their various fronts, offshoots, and affiliates all made the *non grata* list.[63]

Harsher action had been contemplated, as well. As early as the spring of 1944, the British Embassy had urged the U.S. administration to either draft Bergson or deport him, although embassy officials did not expect such action by the United States "in view of the influential friends who seem to be able to protect him." Nahum Goldmann met with State Department officials in May 1944 to recommend that Bergson be drafted or deported, pointing out to them that Stephen Wise "regarded Bergson as equally as great an enemy of the Jews as Hitler, for the reason that his activities could only lead to increased anti-Semitism." Similar action had been urged upon the State Department by Morris Waldman, executive director of the American Jewish Committee, a prominent Jewish defense agency founded in 1906 by wealthy German-born Jews who opposed Jewish nationalism and Zionism. (Ironically, Waldman and the American Jewish Committee regarded Goldmann with almost as much hostility as they did Bergson; Waldman denounced Goldmann to the State Department as "an alien" whose World Jewish Congress was proposing the "dangerous" notion of international Jewish solidarity.) Thanks to pressure from Bergson's allies in Congress, and the State Department's fear of "making a martyr out of Bergson," no action was taken.[64]

After Bergson took up temporary residence in Paris in late 1946, in order to establish a government-in-exile for Jewish Palestine, Britain pressed the Truman administration to prevent him from reentering the United States. According to British officials, Bergson's Paris office attracted "a number of doubtful characters" who met "for no well-defined purpose," and there was "strong suspicion" that the office was linked to the Jewish underground in

Palestine, but London preferred he be kept out of the United States on the grounds that "Bergson is likely to be less of a nuisance in France than anywhere else." The United States, preferring to avoid a public conflict over Bergson, denied the British request, and Bergson traveled back and forth between Europe and the United States repeatedly during the year preceding Israel's creation in May 1948.[65]

The Federal Bureau of Investigation, however, had its own reasons to keep an eye on the Bergsonites. Bergson "has been in the hair of [Secretary of State] Cordell Hull," one FBI official explained in an internal memorandum outlining the rationale for targeting the Zionist militant.[66] In addition to complaints from the State Department, there was pressure on the FBI from Congressman Sol Bloom, chairman of the House Foreign Affairs Committee, who warned—in a statement quoted prominently in FBI memoranda on the subject—that "if Kook [Bergson] were not deported from the United States, he would eventually provoke sufficient antagonism among the citizens of the United States to cause anti-Semitic pogroms."[67] In its search for ways to curb the Bergson activists, the FBI's primary focus was to determine whether the Hebrew Committee of National Liberation and the American League for a Free Palestine—which in the FBI's view were "for all practical purposes, interchangeable"—were providing funds to the Irgun Zvai Leumi. If so, it would mean that the Hebrew Committee had violated federal regulations concerning the registration of foreign agents, because the Hebrew Committee had registered itself as an agent of "the Hebrew Nation," rather than of the Irgun.[68]

Senior FBI officials would later describe the bureau's scrutiny of the Bergson group as "most extensive," and internal reports on the subject would eventually fill "an eleven-volume case file." The investigation bore all the indications of a serious inquiry. Mail to Bergson's headquarters in Washington was intercepted;[69] the trash of some Bergson activists was periodically examined;[70] and the FBI managed to persuade at least one person within Bergson's New York office to serve as a regular informant, providing them with personal information about key activists as well as copies of internal correspondence.[71] (The informant's statement that he "Fears bodily harm if called to testify re Irgun matters" no doubt reinforced the impression at FBI headquarters that they were dealing with a dangerous terrorist organization.)[72] On the other hand, the FBI's reports on Bergson contain a number of glaring gaffes which raise questions as to the quality of their surveillance, such as references to the 1943 Ben Hecht pageant "We Will Never Die" as "We Kill, Never Die."[73]

FBI agents devoted considerable energy to personal interviews with potential sources of information. They began by securing general background information on Jewish communal matters from what they called "persons in New York City who are familiar with Israelite matters."[74] They also interviewed numerous representatives of major Jewish organizations in search of information about Bergson's activities, with mixed results. For example, the Jewish Agency's Miami representative, I. R. Goodman, was "vehement in his denunciation" of the American League for a Free Palestine, describing it as "a racket" and alleging that its fund-raisers were pocketing the money they raised.[75] By contrast, when the FBI contacted Eliahu Epstein of the Jewish Agency's Washington office to discuss Bergson, they found him to be "very reluctant and apparently did not wish to speak at any length about the Bergson group."[76]

On the key question of the relationship between Bergson and the Palestine Jewish underground, the FBI's sources were equivocal. One informant reported that "he could not give any actual evidence as to the tie-up of the Irgun with [Bergson]," although he hastened to add that "he would state categorically in his opinion the actions of the Irgun and perhaps of the 'Stern Gang' were influenced by the Directors of the 'Hebrew Committee of National Liberation.'" Conversations between the FBI and representatives of Jewish organizations elicited similar suspicions but also a similar dearth of evidence. An official of the Anti-Defamation League "stated the HCNL is espousing the cause of the Irgun but he had no facts available to substantiate this statement." Likewise a representative of the American Jewish Congress remarked that he "had no evidence that the HCNL is active on behalf of Irgun but stated that in his opinion this connection is a fact because [Bergson and his colleagues] were all members of the Irgun at one time in Palestine."[77]

In addition to the FBI's ongoing scrutiny of Bergson, the bureau occasionally received unsolicited complaints from citizens offended by Bergson's advertisements or mailings. In one case, a complaint came from Congressman Thomas J. O'Brien, D-Ill., who reported that his name appeared in a 1948 list of "Congressional Sponsors" in an ALFP mailing, even though, he told the FBI, "he does not recall granting permission to use his name and he feels that if this group is using his and other names in this manner we should know about it and perhaps desire to conduct an investigation of the organization." In fact, O'Brien's name had been appearing on the ALFP's letterhead as one of its "Congressional Sponsors" since at least early 1946; it was a journalist's inquiry in 1948 that apparently motivated his change of heart and his approach to the FBI. The FBI agent who recorded O'Brien's complaint noted that "He asked that if an inquiry is made into the matter, his name not be used, remarking that there were some 25,000 people of Jewish extraction in his district which he has no desire to antagonize"—an indication of the extent of militant Zionist sentiment among grassroots Jews (or, equally significant, an indication of politicians' perception that such sentiment was prevalent).[78]

On the morning of March 19, 1945, teams of FBI agents swooped down on Bergson's New York and Washington offices. The agents had been given instructions to "begin simultaneously so that none of the [Bergson] groups will be forewarned." Their aim was to secure documents or other information concerning "the relations between these men and the terrorist groups in Palestine." The problem, however, was that while the regulations governing registered foreign agents permitted the FBI to inspect their records, in this case that would apply only to the Hebrew Committee, which alone among Bergson's groups was officially registered as representing a foreign entity. The FBI had not obtained any kind of court order permitting them to inspect the private documents of the other Bergson-created groups in which the FBI was interested, such as the ALFP and the Emergency Committee to Save the Jewish People of Europe. As a result, the investigating agents were instructed that, officially, "the permission of the custodians of the records of these groups will have to be obtained." This meant that the FBI team would have to give Bergson's office staff the impression that they were required to grant access to all their documents—without actually stating that there was such a requirement—so that the Bergsonites would be sufficiently intimidated to voluntarily surrender the desired records. How might this be accomplished? "It should be pointed out to them," the pre-raid instructions explained, "that the War Division of the Department of Justice has requested the [FBI] to examine the records of the HCNL under the provisions of the Foreign Agents Registration Act." No explicit mention of the other groups would be made, so as to leave the impression that the FBI agents were legally empowered to see whatever they wanted and that anyone refusing to let them do so might be in violation of the law. The agents were cautioned that "no official interrogation should be conducted of persons connected with the HCNL or its affiliates"—there was no legal basis for doing so—"However, any information volunteered in the way of explanation of financial transactions and activities should be carefully noted."[79]

The action did not go as smoothly as hoped. The agents who arrived at the New York office were initially granted permission by ALFP executive director Alexander Wilf to inspect the group's financial records, but after giving the matter further consideration, Wilf decided to request that the FBI agents provide "something in writing" explaining the justification and authorization for the visit. One of the agents quickly called headquarters to relay the request, and also to report Wilf's warning that he was "a personal friend of Attorney General Frances Biddle"; the agents "presumed that is who he would endeavor to call." Agent Conroy at headquarters instructed the investigating team to "try and go over everything, at least hurriedly, today as they may not get a chance to later."[80]

To make matters worse, Justice Department official Larry Knapp called Conroy later that day to complain that the agents searching Bergson's New York office had—apparently contrary to accepted practice—revealed Knapp's name as the person responsible for authorizing the action. As a result, Bergson had called Knapp personally to demand to know who had ordered the raids. Knapp refused to answer Bergson's questions, and called Conroy to remind him that agents should be careful not to "put any particular official on the spot" by revealing his identity to the targets of such raids. Tensions between the Justice Department and the FBI persisted in the months to follow, with Knapp at one point charging that with regard to information about Bergson, "the Bureau had always held out on the Department for some reason." Knapp cited as the most recent example the FBI's failure to tell the Justice Department about "the presence in this country of a confidential informant," evidently someone from Palestine who was giving information to the FBI about the Bergsonites.[81]

But the most serious blunder of the operation, from the point of view of the FBI's top brass, was that the investigating agents had examined only Bergson's financial ledgers. Angry internal memoranda from FBI director J. Edgar Hoover and his deputy, J. K. Mumford, reprimanded the supervisors of the investigation for failing to examine "written records such as correspondence and memoranda of this organization which would certainly have been of value in determining the scope of the activities of the HCNL." The raid had been "entirely inadequate and not in compliance with the Bureau's instructions." The supervisors were told to remind the investigating agents that "this case hinges" on proving a tie between Bergson and the Irgun. "I want you to be certain the men handling this case understand the objective of the investigation," Hoover admonished. "I shall expect that this matter will be handled immediately and continuously until a report is submitted." The agents returned to Bergson's New York office on April 7, only to be told by "the woman in charge" that she would not let them in without written authorization. After consulting with headquarters, the agents warned the woman that if she did not let them in "immediately," they would notify "the appropriate authorities for consideration of prosecutive action"; she relented.[82]

In the end, however, the FBI could not find the smoking gun. Hoping to find suspicious gaps in Bergson's financial records, the investigators examined "all 1944 vouchers and the bills or invoices attached thereto" as well as "all cancelled checks both as to payee and endorser," but were disappointed. "No discrepancies in the disbursement records were noted," the FBI's report found.[83] The FBI had been especially interested in the possibility that Bergson was funneling money to the Irgun through Hebrew Committee board member Theodore Ben-Nahum. Based on reports from informants, the FBI believed that Ben-Nahum had been "associated with some shady enterprises and dealings" and was the most likely of Bergson's confidantes to be serving as an Irgun agent.[84] But in scouring Bergson's records, the FBI could find "no transfer of funds abroad, nor payments to any organizations in which Theodore Ben-Nahum has an interest."[85] "The investigation failed to evidence any tieup in this country" between Bergson and the Irgun, the report concluded.[86] "No substantial or specific information of an evidentiary character was obtained with regard to a definite transfer of funds by the Hebrew Committee of National Liberation to terrorist groups in Palestine." In fact, according to Bergson lobbyist Baruch Rabinowitz, funds raised by the Bergsonites in the United States were indeed secretly transferred to the Irgun; the methods of transfer were simply so well concealed that the FBI could not uncover them.[87]

The FBI's other major area of investigation concerned whether or not the Zionist militants had any connections to Communism. Many of Bergson's campaigns had the distinction of being able to attract support from individuals at both extremes of the political spectrum. A columnist for the left-wing political journal *New Leader* remarked with amazement that one could find on Bergson's ads the names of "Mary Van Kleeck, leading Communist Party fellow traveller" and "Erwin Piscator, left-wing producer," alongside what he called "bitter Southern reactionaries" and "Big Business propagandists."[88] FBI director J. Edgar Hoover showed a particular interest in possible links between Bergson and Communism. As early as the spring of 1943, he authored a memo approvingly citing a remark by an American Jewish Congress official characterizing the Bergson activists as "a group of thoroughly disreputable Communist Zionists." According to Hoover, Ben

Hecht and six other prominent Bergson supporters qualified as "fellow travelers."[89]

One informant's report that someone in the Bergson group wanted to arrange a meeting between Bergson and U.S. Communist Party leader Earl Browder aroused interest at FBI headquarters, although no further information about the idea ever materialized.[90] Names of Bergson group officials were cross-checked with lists of Communists and fellow-travelers, and Bergson activist Alex Wilf was found "on the mailing list of Tom Paine School of Social Sciences, Philadelphia, a Communist dominated organization." A complaint to the Better Business Bureau against the Philadelphia-based Global Travel Service, by a woman who alleged she had been overcharged, attracted the FBI's attention because the company was owned by Maurice Rifkin, a leader of the Philadelphia branch of the American League for Free Palestine, and Global Travel was "the only organization in Philadelphia at that time through which packages could be sent to the Soviet Union."[91]

The fact that Bergson lobbyist Maurice Rosenblatt had been active in civil rights causes and left-wing politics provided additional grist for the mill. Internal FBI memoranda made much of the fact that "Rosenblatt and his Russian-born mother were registered members of the American Labor Party in 1940." Noting Rosenblatt's prewar involvement with the New York Coordinating Committee for Democratic Action, an FBI report remarked with some derision that "this Semitic Committee" compiled lists of pro-Nazi individuals and tried "to smear them through periodicals such as the *PM*." The report also asserted that the New York City Police Department "considers Rosenblatt a trouble maker."[92] In the end, however, the FBI's hunt for Communists under Bergson's bed proved unsuccessful. Despite allegations that "there were Communists infiltrating the [Bergson] Committee, there were no concrete indications of this," the FBI concluded; "None of its officers were known Communists." There were among the vice chairmen of the Emergency Committee to Save the Jewish People of Europe "a number of people who had been identified in liberal circles but who could not be considered Communists." In fact, FBI agents noted, the Communist Party USA's official newspaper, the *Daily Worker*, had repeatedly, and vehemently, denounced the Bergsonites.[93]

The FBI's investigation of Bergson quietly drew to a close in 1950, at which point the FBI finally realized that Bergson's committees had disbanded more than a year earlier.[94]

British diplomats abroad and policy shapers back home pondered possible new public-relations methods for combating the Jabotinskyite disciples, but invariably came up empty-handed. Full-page advertisements explaining England's point of view were ruled out because "the dollar expenditure involved would be incommensurate with the results." Ordinary correspondence and telephone conversations "are useful but do not reach a large audience." Private briefings for "reliable" journalists were of limited value because "most newspapers are now chary of accepting pro-British articles" concerning Palestine.[95]

The idea that attracted the most interest among British officialdom was pressuring the Truman administration to strip the militant Zionist groups of their tax-exempt status. A string of ALFP advertisements in the spring of 1946 stimulated British interest in the tax angle. The barrage began with an April 8 *New York Post* ad headlined "Another Treaty, Another Scrap of Paper!" It featured a graphic of a huge British hand crumpling the 1924 Anglo-American Convention on Palestine, a treaty that granted U.S. support for the British Mandate on condition that no changes be made in the Mandate without American consent. The State Department's minimalist interpretation of the treaty contended that its original intention was to protect commercial interests, not determine the country's political status or levels of immigration. Grumblers at the British Embassy were incredulous that "in spite of the correct interpretation given by the State Department to this convention, the Zionists assert it to have laid down that no change at all could be made in the mandate without the consent of the United States Government."[96]

Next came an April 17 full-pager in the *New York Times* that asked the public to "Give Us the Money . . . We'll Get Them There!" and, on April 29, a *New York Post* broadside describing "the underground railroad to Palestine." Both ads specifically asked for contributions to purchase ships to bring DPs to the Holy Land. "It costs $250 to move one concentration camp victim from Europe to Palestine," the ALFP explained. "With American dollars . . . the underground [will] buy or charter ships which will take them to Palestine, where the Resistance Forces prepare beachheads on which they land. This is their only chance." Suspecting that the Bergsonites were using the money for purposes other than illegal immigration, the Foreign Office instructed the British Embassy in Washington to "learn what view the competent United States authorities take of these activities." If the ALFP could not prove that the donations were used "for the ends claimed in the advertisement," the Foreign Office hoped, then the ads might constitute a criminal "conspiracy to defraud the American public."[97]

But by this time, Labor Zionists were only a shade better than Revisionists in London's view. From London's perspective, the Laborites were hardly distinguishable from their Revisionist rivals—after all, during 1945 and 1946 the Haganah had collaborated with the Irgun and it was continuing to sponsor illegal immigration. In October 1946, the National Committee for Labor Palestine, a U.S. Labor Zionist group, placed a full-page ad in the *New York Post* in which it presented itself as the true champion of illegal immigration in contradistinction to the ALFP. The Foreign Office immediately urged Foreign Minister Bevin, then visiting the United States, to speak to Secretary of State Byrnes about stripping the Labor group of its tax exemption. The Foreign Office warned that the funds raised by the National Committee for Labor Palestine, no less than the proceeds from *A Flag Is Born,* could wreak havoc with England's position in the Mediterranean: "As ships acquired in the United States will probably be Liberty Type, capable of carrying large numbers of immigrants, the effect on our dispositions in Palestine and Cyprus may be serious."[98] It hardly seemed to matter to London that a coalition of mainstream Zionist youth movements, including the Laborites, had recently sponsored a full-page ad in the daily *PM* to denounce the Irgun and the ALFP as violent "traitors." The ad claimed that the funds raised by the league might be used to purchase "molotov cocktails, machine guns and home-made flame throwers to blast the walls of a labor clubhouse" or rubber hoses with which to beat youths who were reluctant to join the Stern Group.[99]

The Haganah's official U.S. support group, Americans for Haganah, seemed to devote a considerable portion of its time to fighting the ALFP. It sent letters to VIPs on the league's board, urging them to resign, and circulated accusations that hinted at—but did not substantiate—allegations of financial misconduct by the Bergsonites. It even put pressure on Jewish storekeepers in Brooklyn to remove their pro-Irgun "pushkas," or charity collection boxes. A leaflet for public consumption claimed that the Americans for Haganah "Sound Truck Project" was using sound trucks to urge passersby to write to President Truman about Palestine, but a confidential internal report on the group's activities later described the sound trucks as intended to denounce the Irgun and thereby counter "the wide publicity achieved by the Irgun's counterpart in this country, the American League for a Free Palestine." The problem was that "the public was becoming confused" (a somewhat condescending term that opponents of Bergson often employed to explain grassroots support for militant Zionism), so "Americans for Haganah decided to launch a program of clarification." The sound trucks were dispatched to heavily Jewish neighborhoods, where they gave speeches "continuously from morning to night" to "inform the people of the treasonous and debilitating activities of the dissidents." Pressure from Americans for Haganah failed to dissuade conductor Leonard Bernstein and dancer Valerie Bettis from giving an ALFP benefit concert for wounded Irgun fighters, although they did convince opera stars Jennie Tourel and Robert Merrill and actor Henry Fonda to withdraw from the concert.[100] The irony was that no matter the intensity of the Labor Zionists' resentment of the ALFP, the British lumped moderates and militants together and lobbied to have all of their tax exemptions removed.

American supporters of both the Irgun and the Haganah had trouble living up to the promises they made in their newspaper advertisements about illegal immigration efforts. Between 1946 and 1948, ten ships purchased in the United States attempted to bring Holocaust survivors from Europe to Palestine. They carried more than thirty-two thousand people, about half of the total number of those who attempted to immigrate during that period. Nine of the ships were sponsored by the Haganah, and one by the Irgun (the *Ben Hecht*). All ten were intercepted by the British, and their passengers were interned, most in detention camps in Cyprus. Despite their capture, the voyages scored important public-relations victories for the Zionist movement by dramatizing the cruelty of Britain's refusal to permit desperate survivors of the Nazi genocide to reach their ancestral homeland.[101]

Each new round of militant newspaper ads roused the British to again seek action against the sponsors' tax status. British officials were aghast at the full-page advertisements that appeared simultaneously in *PM* and the *New York Post* in December 1946, announcing that the United Zionists-Revisionists, the ALFP, and various affiliates of each had joined together to establish the Palestine Resistance Committee for unified fund-raising on behalf of the Jewish underground's fight against "the British occupants and oppressors." It was the first joint activity by the Bergson committee and Netanyahu's group since the Jewish army campaign of 1941, and such Zionist unity could only spell more headaches for London. Officials at the British Consulate in New York feared "that H.M.G. will be influenced by all the pressure propaganda that the different Zionist bodies have been publishing at intervals in the New York press." Hoping to curb the militant Zionists' "abusive agitation and muck-raking," the consulate rushed copies of the ads to the embassy in Washington and the Foreign Office in London with a proposal for renewed action on the tax issue. Such outspoken support for anti-British violence warranted another call to Truman administration officials to determine if the ALFP was not "guilty of a serious infringement of the laws of the Country—if not indeed of international law," the consulate asserted. "It is certainly a breach of etiquette and of international good manners." The Foreign Office concurred; five days—and two more full-page ads in the *New York Post*—later, it instructed the embassy to again make "strong representations" to the United States about the militant Zionists' tax exemptions.[102]

While the increasingly irritated British waited for a reply from the U.S. administration, the militants fired their loudest salvo yet. Ben Hecht's "Letter to the Terrorists of Palestine" ran once in the *New York Herald-Tribune* and twice in the *New York Post* in May 1947. "Every time you blow up a British arsenal," Hecht declared, "or wreck a British jail, or send a British railroad train sky high, or rob a British bank or let go with your guns and bombs at the British betrayers and invaders of your homeland, the Jews of America make a little holiday in their hearts." Nahum Goldmann denounced the ad as "disgusting" and insisted to reporters that Hecht was "insignificant" in the Jewish world. Goldmann's hopes could not change political reality. It was Hecht who was the focus of the front-page *New York Times* story about the British protesting the Truman administration's failure to take action against the Zionist militants. And while Goldmann was inveighing against Hecht, popular syndicated columnist Walter Winchell was defending Hecht's ads for exposing the fact that the British had become "the Brutish" in their fight against "Palestinian patriots," who were no different from "our Minute Men." Winchell's sharp choice of words prompted angry editorials in four leading British newspapers, which denounced Hecht and Winchell as "a couple of damned fools" and wondered how Americans would feel if Englishmen tried to interfere in some aspect of American affairs. Retorted Winchell: "You tried the Palestine policy in America and got your answer in 1776." Tension between London and Washington was rising, exactly as Jabotinsky's disciples had hoped.[103]

Despite British anger over Hecht's "Letter to the Terrorists," Truman administration officials informed London that there were no grounds for a legal challenge to the militants' tax status. The president did, however, issue a brief public statement on June 4, urging "every citizen and resident" of the United States to refrain from activities that might "inflame the passions" in Palestine. Needless to say, the Zionist militants were not impressed. "Despite the fact that he is President, Truman is entitled to his opinion," a sarcastic Hecht told reporters.[104]

By June 1947 the British were beginning to realize there was virtually no hope for U.S. action against the militant Zionists' tax exemption. Numerous written and verbal protests had been made by the British Embassy to the State Department "concerning all forms of American aid for illegal immigration and terrorism," the embassy reported to the Foreign Office. "After 11 months no written reply had been received and all that could be extracted was an expression of regret that no legal means were open to the United States Government to prevent such activities." Even worse, "It has even been indicated [by the United States] that the withdrawal of tax exemption facilities would stir up more trouble than it would be worth." The embassy also relayed to Foreign Minister Bevin warnings from U.S. officials that if the administration clashed with American Zionists, U.S. aid to England might be the victim. The Americans suggested it "would be unwise to jeopardise the more important moves which were being made [by the United States] to assist [the British] in carrying their general economic and political burdens. . . . It is possible that in a close fight in Congress some damage might be done by Zionist supporters."[105]

Refusing to take no for an answer, the Colonial Office and the Foreign Office both pressed the British Embassy in Washington to seek independent legal counsel on what action might be taken. The advice the embassy obtained was less than promising. The militant Zionist organizations all seemed to be properly incorporated, so no basis existed to challenge the legality of their existence. The U.S. government could not be expected to agree with the British view that advertisements supporting anti-British violence constituted violations of international law, so there was no basis for action on that score, either. The tax-status question could be raised anew, although chances for success seemed doubtful. About the most the embassy could hope for, its lawyers advised, was compelling some of the Zionist factions to register as "foreign agents."[106]

Some British officials considered that angle worth pursuing, expecting that the taint of foreignness might harm the militants' efforts to attract public support. But the resources to be expended in such an effort had to be weighed against the reality of an American public mood that already turned sharply against London's Palestine policy. A good example of the futility of focusing on American Zionists' legal status was provided by the reactions to the Irgun's hanging of two British sergeants, in July 1947, in retaliation for the British execution of three captured Irgun fighters. The embassy reported to the Foreign Office that while the Irgun's action was condemned in the American press, the effect of that condemnation "has been blunted" by the news of British soldiers engaging in violent reprisals against Jewish civilians in Palestine. In many leading newspapers, the news of the hangings was "completely subordinated" to the news of the British reprisals. Abba Hillel Silver and other mainstream Zionist leaders had made things worse by issuing statements that, after condemning the Irgun hangings, concentrated on "strictures upon British policy which they held to be ultimately responsible for the present situation." The embassy was also receiving a steady stream of "hostile letters in which opposition to further U.S. aid to Britain is expressed." It was inevitable that the anti-British slant of the American press "must have its effect," and there was a danger that "should any public debate take place in the near future about aid to Britain, the waters might be muddied by those attacking Palestine policy as 'Nazi.'" When the British loan had been debated in 1946, the embassy recalled, "There was considerable Zionist opposition to the U.S. loan and we were much indebted then to the Zionist Rabbi Wise for his outright support—support which can hardly be expected from any prominent U.S. Zionist now." This, the embassy concluded, is "one factor in U.S. opinion on our economic problems which should not be forgotten."[107]

London had not forgotten it. Wearied by the military struggle in Palestine and the public-relations beating it was taking in the United States, fearful of losing American aid and facing growing discontent at home over casualties in the Middle East, the British in early 1947 began what turned out to be the process of leaving Palestine. In February, the British cabinet voted to submit the Palestine problem to the United Nations for its consideration, although London still hoped that its rule would continue. In May, the UN General Assembly appointed the United Nations Special Committee on Palestine (UNSCOP), to conduct an on-site investigation of the problem. The thirteen members of the committee, representing a variety of countries, heard testimony from Jewish, Arab, and British representatives in Palestine from June 16 to July 24. The crisis over the SS *Exodus* unfolded during the UNSCOP hearings, as did the British hangings of Irgun prisoners and Irgun retaliatory hangings of British soldiers. UNSCOP's final report, completed in August, recommended partitioning Palestine into separate Jewish and Arab states. This combination of military and diplomatic pressure compelled the exhausted British to formally return the Palestine Mandate to the UN in September 1947. The decades-long struggle for Jewish statehood at last stood on the verge of triumph, and Revisionist Zionists in the United States could justly claim credit, alongside the rest of the American Zionist community, for having contributed to the process that brought about Britain's departure, thus paving the way for the birth of the state of Israel.

11 • Guns for Zion

Immediately after the United Nations vote of November 1947, Arab violence erupted throughout Palestine. Determined to prevent a Jewish state of any size from coming into being, the Palestinian Arabs plunged the country into full-scale civil war, and neighboring Arab regimes threatened to invade if a Jewish state were declared. As the British began making preparations for their planned May 1948 withdrawal, the Jewish underground forces turned their attention to defending the *yishuv* against Palestinian Arab attacks and readying for the expected Arab invasion.

The Haganah had been planning for this eventuality for several years, and already had in place an extensive network of American sympathizers who had been organizing surreptitious shipments of weapons and other materials to Palestine.[1] The Revisionists' efforts in this regard had been sporadic, but now they were intensified in view of the looming war with the Arabs.

Part of the Irgun's American supply line was perfectly legal. During 1947 and 1948, Revisionist newspaper ads, literature, and newsletters openly solicited funds to be sent to Palestine for the explicit purpose of "purchasing and manufacturing arms" there. The money would also be used, the Revisionists promised, to buy "legally procurable materiel in this country, including medical supplies, binoculars, range-finders and other devices," which would be shipped to the Jewish underground. Revisionist fund-raisers canvassed Grossinger's and other popular resort hotels in upstate New York during Passover week, while Betar youths on a flatbed truck used a mobile amplified sound system to blare the message of "Fighting Zion" in New York City's Jewish neighborhoods and collect spare change for the cause.

Harry Green, a Marine Corps veteran from Kentucky, would stand in front of the parked Betar sound truck, holding up one end of a Zionist flag into which passersby were urged to throw their donations. "One of the boys would stand on the truck and scream his lungs out," Green recalled. "It was marvelous to watch people who really didn't have any money, somehow finding money to give." Between speeches, Green and his friends shouted slogans such as "Every dollar is a bullet in a rifle that has no bullets!" Green was later "pleasantly surprised to learn that the money we collected did go where it was supposed to go."[2]

The Revisionists also promoted the idea of holding a special third Passover seder, to be called a "Freedom Seder," with proceeds going to the Irgun. One such seder was staged at Manhattan's Paramount Restaurant in April 1948, for fifteen dollars per plate. Benzion Netanyahu's mailings pleaded with members to make appeals for donations to the Irgun at "every birthday party in your family, every social event in your friend's house." Maxim's, a fashionable Bronx nightclub, was persuaded to donate its premises for a card party to benefit the Irgun. The Revisionists' Bronx division, freshly renamed the Dov Gruner Revisionist Chapter, established a Burnside Avenue depot where volunteers collected clothing, medicine, food, tobacco, and other goods to be shipped to Palestine.[3]

Ben Hecht glowingly described the outpouring of grassroots support that greeted the Bergsonites' collections for the Palestine underground:

> I watched with awe as they rose out of their stores and work shops and came to our side. Jewish clerks and salesladies, garage workers, plasterers, elevator boys, Yeshiva students, policemen, garment workers, prize fighters, housewives; Jewish soldiers and sailors still in American uniforms, Jews from night clubs, tenements, farm lands, synagogues and even penthouses came boldly to the Irgun banner. . . . They poured their dollar bills and five-dollar bills into the Irgun coffers, and the coffers swelled with millions. They crowded our rallies and theaters. They cheered with joy and there was no more fear in them than in any other group of humans whooping for victory.[4]

But what the Irgun needed more than anything else was guns. And through an array of unorthodox methods, their American supporters got them.

The Interior Decorator

Zweibon's, a floor covering store at the corner of Sutter Avenue and New Jersey Avenue in Brooklyn's East New York neighborhood, provided an effective cover for Irgun smuggling. Proprietors Abraham and Sylvia Zweibon were veteran Revisionists, and Abe was a member of the NZOA's National Council; on occasion they placed advertisements for the store in *Zionews*.[5] A customer would never have imagined that inside the giant rolls of linoleum, the Zweibons regularly hid weapons and other military supplies en route to the Holy Land.

Today, East New York is a crime-ridden slum of burned-out storefronts and abandoned buildings on weed-covered lots, but during the 1930s, when the Zweibons first set up shop there, it was a bustling Jewish neighborhood. Nestled on the Brooklyn-Queens border, adjacent to the heavily Jewish Brownsville section, East New York offered an attractive option for young families in search of a semi-suburban alternative to the congested Lower East Side of their parents' generation.

A Betar activist in her native Lubin (Poland), Sylvia came to the United States as a teenager, in 1929, and promptly joined the fledgling Betar movement in America. She met Abe in the movement, and despite the hardships of sustaining their linoleum business and raising a family during the Depression years, both of them remained active Revisionists. One crisp autumn evening not long after the end of World War II, "a friend of a cousin of a friend" paid an unexpected visit to the Zweibons' Sutter Avenue store. The man, who gave only his first name, had known Sylvia from her Betar days in Poland. He himself had immigrated to Palestine, joined the Irgun, and had been dispatched to the United States to find "people we can trust" to aid in getting weapons to the rebels. Soon there was a steady stream of visitors to Zweibon's, mostly Jewish veterans of the U.S. Army.

Typically there were two or three such visitors each day, carrying small bundles. "Frequently, when they came in, we weren't sure if they were ordinary customers or bringing 'gifts' for the Irgun," recalled Sylvia. Those bearing the "gifts" would say, simply, "This is for you" and depart without another word. Toward the back of the store were rows of huge rolls of linoleum. The rolls in the rear were reserved for the Jewish underground. Guns, radios, walkie-talkies, and similar "donations" were stored in the center of each of the rolls; hundreds of pieces could fit at a time. Irgun emissaries would occasionally drop by with small groups of young Revisionists to pack the contraband into crates. A band of four Irgun packers once spent several days straight on the job, sleeping in the Zweibons' bedroom—"it was a small apartment"—and sharing dinner with them each evening. They were assisted by a Christian neighbor whom the Zweibons would hire for moving particularly large items to or from the store; he found the gun-packing operation "intriguing." When enough crates were full, a truck would be rented to bring the material to a New York dock for shipping to Palestine.

The quantities of weapons and related material stored by the Zweibons increased significantly as the Irgun's fight against the British intensified during the late 1940s. Eventually they were forced to rent a second storefront nearby, on New Jersey Avenue, to store the gun-stuffed linoleum rolls. Even the second store proved insufficient to handle it all; surplus weapons soon filled the basement of the Zweibons' vacation bungalow near Allenville, in upstate Ulster County.

The curious goings-on at the linoleum store were never discovered by the authorities, although Sylvia was frequently kept busy trying to distract friendly neighborhood police officers who dropped by to gossip while on their daily beat. On one occasion, she listened with barely disguised anxiety as a policeman spent nearly an hour describing in detail how he had delivered the baby of a woman who could not get to a hospital in time. On another occasion, when the Irgun men came to pack weapons, they brought the wrong kind of hydraulic lift and were compelled to move the heavy crates by hand. Through the window of the store, Abe fortuitously spotted a six-foot, four-inch Ukrainian-American neighbor of theirs, whom they affectionately called Big Bill, and enlisted his aid. Taken aback by the weight of the boxes, Bill bellowed, "What the hell do you have here, Abe, guns for Palestine?" An auxiliary policeman who could not join the regular police force because he had repeatedly flunked the requisite intelligence test, Big Bill flagged down two friends of his who happened to be passing by—uniformed policemen, both of whom helped load the crates of illegal Zionist guns onto the Irgun's truck.[6]

The Undertaker

On his way home from the hospital where his wife had just given birth to their first child, in early 1946, Lawrence Schwartz, the twenty-three-year-old son of a Lower East Side funeral home director, passed the famous New York Jewish eatery Ratner's, on Second Avenue. Ravenously hungry from the long hours spent at his wife's bedside, Schwartz stepped into the restaurant "just to grab a quick bite to eat." The last thing in the world he would have suspected was that he was being watched. As Schwartz left Ratner's, he was stopped by two burly young men who wanted to speak with him about "trying to get important goods to Palestine."

Having just been discharged from the U.S. Army, Schwartz was particularly wary of getting mixed up with lawbreakers, but the horrors of the Holocaust gnawed at his conscience and the Jewish fight for Palestine aroused instincts of pride. Schwartz let the pair accompany him as he walked the four blocks to his nearby apartment. He was intrigued to hear that the directors of two Ludlow Street funeral parlors, the Lurie Funeral Home and Harry Nieberg and Son, were already involved in the operation. A visit to Harry's son, Isaac, confirmed the outlines of the story. The younger Nieberg described the shortage of supplies among the Jewish fighters and persuaded Schwartz to lend a helping hand.[7]

Lawrence Schwartz became a central figure in an elaborate ruse. Approximately once every six weeks, from early 1946 through early 1948, a coterie of senior Revisionists, accompanied by their smartly dressed children, would arrive at the Schwartz funeral home. With faces as somber as real mourners, they would crowd around the hearse as the coffin was loaded—a coffin filled with weapons bound for the Irgun.[8] Instead of going to a cemetery, the hearse would be driven to a preselected Irgun arms depot. Warehouses in Yonkers, White Plains, the Bronx, and Brooklyn were utilized for that purpose. At 9 P.M. sharp, Schwartz would go to a public telephone near his house, where he would receive a call from an Irgun emissary known only as "Ari." The Irgun man would name a street corner where Schwartz should meet him. When they met, no words were exchanged, only a slip of paper with a destination on the piers at the Marine Terminal (Hoboken, New Jersey) or Bush Terminal (Brooklyn). Typically Schwartz would make two "runs" a night, careful to avoid taking the same route twice. When he arrived in his hearse at the gates, Schwartz would be escorted by two other cars to the pier, where he stood aside while others loaded the guns into three large, heavy crates, marked "Rhoade Islands Ltd, Greece," and draped with a *dekke,* the black cloth traditionally put on a Jewish coffin.

Different piers—dozens in all—were used each time. At Hoboken, no guards were in sight. At the Bush Terminal, according to Schwartz, there was always a guard who would wave them on through without questions; Schwartz believed "he must have been bribed." One night on Willoughby Street, approaching the Bush pier area, two police officers in a patrol car compelled Schwartz to pull over and demanded to know "How come we see you every night, passing here?" Schwartz, under strict orders to let the Irgun men handle potential problems, remained silent as two of his "escorts" hurried over to the patrol car, conversed quietly with the officers for a few moments, then waved as the police drove off.

The Rabbi

Oscar Bookspan was not the typical rabbinical student. As a youngster growing up in Boston he displayed a special knack for electronics, and after completing high school he earned a diploma in radio technology from Curtis Tech. Yeshivat Beis Yosef, in Brooklyn's Boro Park section, which Oscar entered in 1943, was not the typical yeshiva. Throughout the war years, the yeshiva directors helped young European Jewish refugees reach the United States by granting unearned rabbinical ordination and imaginary faculty positions to anybody over sixteen years of age so as to circumvent U.S. immigration restrictions that blocked entry to individuals deemed "likely to become a public charge." The attitude of the yeshiva administration was, in Oscar's words, "Bend the law to save a life." That may explain why the senior rabbis at Beis Yosef, although well aware of Oscar's connection to the militant wing of the Zionist movement, chose to look the other way. At a time when millions of Jews were being massacred, those Orthodox rabbis who were not particularly enamored of Zionism—because most Zionist leaders were non-religious and some even anti-religious—softened their opposition in the hope that a Jewish homeland, whatever its spiritual orientation, might serve the overriding priority of saving lives.

With his immediate family still in Boston, Oscar drew close to his nearest local relatives, his uncle and aunt, Samuel and Sophie Bookspan. Uncle Samuel ("Shmiel," his nephews and nieces called him), a member of the NZOA's National Council and an electrical contractor by profession, introduced Oscar to militant Zionism and guided him in using his knowledge of radio technology in the service of the cause. Every Tuesday evening, Oscar would join Samuel, Sophie, and a crew of senior Revisionists in the Bookspan dining room, on West 24th Street in Manhattan, for a hearty meal and conversation—in Yiddish—about the latest developments on the Zionist scene.

Late one evening, after the other guests had departed, Bookspan pulled Oscar aside and pressed a five-dollar bill into his hand. He needed Oscar to run an unusual errand, he explained; he wanted him to visit a certain store in lower Manhattan and purchase a black market rectifier tube, the kind needed by the Irgun for its radio receivers and transmitters. Because of the American army's wartime need for rectifier tubes, they could not be obtained legally. Uncle Samuel sent him to a particular section of Chambers Street, at the southern end of Manhattan, where a number of Jewish-owned stores were selling surplus army-navy goods, including assorted electronic items. Several of them had rectifier tubes for sale under the table for five dollars apiece—up from their prewar price of thirty cents. Since he himself was in the electrical business, Samuel could not risk having it become known that he was purchasing illegal equipment. Oscar was the perfect assistant; there was no need to worry that a Curtis Tech graduate would purchase the wrong tube or a defective one.

Soon Oscar was a regular customer on Chambers Street, purchasing not only rectifier tubes but also a wide array of other radio equipment not legally available, including sockets, condensers, and switches, as well as basic small hardware pieces that were legal but scarce in Palestine, such as hooks, nuts, and screws. A curious merchant who asked Oscar why he was constantly buying such materials, was so delighted to hear that they were "for *Eretz Yisrael*" that he began giving him parts for free. Other Jewish store owners insisted on giving Oscar steep discounts when they heard that his purchases were bound for the Holy Land. For more than a year, Oscar made the rounds on Chambers Street each week, then delivered the goods to Uncle Samuel for shipping to Revisionist colleagues in Philadelphia and Charleston, two port cities where the equipment was stowed in crates with false markings and transported to the Middle East.[9]

The Trial

A stray duffle bag in a Manhattan elevator led to one of the few captures of Revisionist gun smugglers. The U.S. Navy duffle, stuffed with weapons, was inadvertently left behind in a freight elevator on West 28th Street one April night in 1948 while young militants were transporting guns and ammunition from a truck in an adjoining alleyway to a fifth-floor loft. The forgotten bag was discovered the next morning by the building superintendent, who promptly notified the police.

The superintendent pointed them toward the fifth-floor offices of the Sondovitch export-import firm, a site that in recent weeks had been attracting an unusually large number of late-night visitors, many with audible European accents. The police raid on the loft netted "a huge pile of bundles" containing, among other things, 300 pistols, 100 rifles, 6 machine guns, 5 hand grenades, thousands of rounds of ammunition, and "a large number of knives." Herman Sondovitch, owner of the company, insisted he knew nothing of the arms cache—only that his vice president, Alexander Gurvitch, had given a Zionist group "permission to wrap food and clothing bundles" to send to Palestine. Gurvitch, a veteran Revisionist activist, was fortunate to be out of the country that week. The "Zionist group" in question was the Revisionist movement. Indeed, in October 1946, Netanyahu had authored a memo to members in the New York area, urging them to drop off bundles of "warm clothing" at the Sondovitch loft, to be sent to the fifteen thousand "naked and barefoot" Betarim and Revisionists who had survived the Holocaust and were about to face "a cold, cruel European winter" while they waited for permission to immigrate to Palestine.[10]

The two young men on the premises when the police burst in, Isaiah Warshaw and Joseph Untermeyer, were promptly arrested. Warshaw, a thirty-year-old watchmaker and member of the NZOA National Council since 1946, had just six weeks earlier been elected—along with Alexander Gurvitch, Moshe Arens, and nineteen others—to the governing Administrative Committee of the U.S. Revisionists. Friends later recalled Warshaw as "a real gentleman," widely respected in the movement and unusually idealistic.[11]

Untermeyer, nineteen, was the son of the prominent poet Louis Untermeyer and former judge Esther Untermeyer, national treasurer of the American League for a Free Palestine. Both parents were on hand when their son and Warshaw were arraigned the next morning before Magistrate Peter M. Horn of the Felony Court on charges of violating the Sullivan Law, legislation enacted to restrict the transportation of weapons. "Youth is outraged over the reversal of American policy and especially over the aid being given the Arabs who are in defiance of the United Nations," the elder Mr. Untermeyer told courthouse reporters. "I think the kids are actually supporting the United Nations and the cause of liberty everywhere." Mrs. Untermeyer offered to "serve any penalty my son might receive" if it emerged that "my own activities had influenced him in the fight for Hebrew liberation."[12]

Warshaw and Untermeyer were represented in court by attorney Paul O'Dwyer, brother of New York City's mayor and himself an enthusiastic supporter of the ALFP. He immediately turned the initial court hearing into a political forum, declaring that the Sullivan Law was inapplicable in this case because its purpose was "to prevent gangsterism," whereas "these guns were to be sent to Palestine to protect people in their homes." O'Dwyer denounced the U.S. arms embargo on Palestine, arguing that by defying the embargo, "the two defendants were only doing what every freedom-loving person should be doing." Judge Horn agreed to release Warshaw and Untermeyer in the custody of their attorneys and adjourn hearings until the following month while the FBI continued its investigation of the case.[13]

When the first pretrial hearing convened before Magistrate Frederick Strong on May 28, O'Dwyer quickly moved for dismissal of the charges. Comparing the Irgun gun smugglers to the patriots of the American Revolution, O'Dwyer asserted that the guns "were in transit to Israel and were bound to the people who were fighting for the liberty." No court, he said, "could declare it a crime to help people gain their freedom." While he agreed that "somebody should be indicted," it "should not be these two defendants, but rather Glubb and Abdullah and Bevin"—referring, respectively, to the British officer helping to lead the Arab forces against Israel; the king of Jordan; and the British foreign minister.

Judge Strong agreed that O'Dwyer's argument might have been persuasive "in Boston in 1776," but he did not consider it plausible in the context of the Sullivan Law. Instead, the judge seized upon the fact that presence of the defendants in the loft where the guns were found did not necessarily prove they had "exclusive possession" of the contraband. Over the loud objections of Assistant District Attorney Richard Denzer, Strong granted O'Dwyer's motion and threw out the case. Warshaw and Untermeyer were set free.[14]

The Refugee

By day, seventeen-year-old George Studley stuffed envelopes in the Manhattan office of the ALFP. By night, he packed weapons for the Irgun. Studley's appreciation of the urgency of the Jewish struggle for statehood was born of personal experience. Nine-year-old George, his brother Julien, and their parents fled their home in Belgium in 1940 literally as war raged around them. Some of the bridges they crossed were blown up just moments later by the clashing British and German armies. They spent a year in southern France—not yet occupied by the Axis—before securing a visa to Cuba. The family sailed from Marseilles to Morocco, then purchased passage on a Portuguese freighter from Casablanca to Havana. After two years in Cuba, George's father, who had been born in Poland, was able to arrange entry to the United States through the Polish immigration quota. Dozens of their relatives in Poland perished in Nazi death camps.

As the family struggled to rebuild their shattered life, the Studley brothers were naturally drawn to Zionism as the answer to Jewish homelessness.

Julien became active in the ALFP and began hosting meetings in his family's Manhattan apartment. George soon joined as well. In addition to his involvement in the day-to-day political activities of the movement, George took part in a week of military training exercises held on the Connecticut estate of ALFP vice president Nathan George Horwitt, a wealthy inventor. Marty Marden, a leader of the American wing of Betar, tutored the young activists in self-defense techniques, Zionist ideology, and pistol disassembly.

It was Marden who introduced Studley to the Irgun's American gun-smuggling network. Throughout 1948, George and other young ALFP activists were regularly dispatched to various sites in and around New York City to pick up weapons donated to the Palestine underground by Jewish war veterans and other sympathizers. The young couriers brought the guns to a rented garage on West 158th Street in Manhattan, where they were inspected, cleaned, and stored before being shipped to the Holy Land. It was at the garage, on a frigid November night, that disaster struck.

Close to midnight on November 24, Studley and four comrades drove up to the garage in a two-ton truck borrowed from Bergson sympathizers in New Jersey. At first glance, the crates in the back would not have aroused suspicion; only straw was visible through the narrow slits. But beneath the straw cover were 45 rifles, 75 pistols, 5 machine guns, 2,360 mechanisms for setting off hand grenades, and other munitions. It would have been an ordinary drop-off, similar to the many they had done before, except for one thing: somebody forgot the key to the garage padlock. As they argued and tried vainly to pick the lock, a sleeping neighbor was roused by the commotion and called the police. The officers who were handcuffing his cohorts did not see Studley—acting "in true spy fashion," he later recalled—hurriedly swallowing the pieces of paper in his wallet that bore the names and phone numbers of his Irgun contacts.

At the Amsterdam Avenue police station—where a Jewish sergeant only half-jokingly told Studley he could have avoided arrest if he had just "slipped a twenty" to the officers at the garage—Studley waited nervously for his father, who had been called from his Wednesday evening bridge game to bail his gun-smuggling son out of jail. The elder Studley arrived at the station "practically with his cards still in hand" and with his three bridge partners in tow. The five youths spent the night in jail before being arraigned on charges of conspiracy to violate the Sullivan Law. They were released on bail, with a court date fixed for December 9.

After his success in the Warshaw-Untermeyer case, Paul O'Dwyer was the natural choice to defend Studley and company at the December 9 hearing before Magistrate Vernon C. Riddick. O'Dwyer immediately launched into a political speech. The Sullivan Law was "meant to prevent gangsters from obtaining arms and ammunition, not to prevent people from defending their homes and hillsides," he declared. "If there is any conspiracy at all, that conspiracy exists within the State Department and—" Judge Riddick interrupted O'Dwyer and, with a wave of his hand, announced that he was dismissing the charges. Because he was still several months shy of his eighteenth birthday, Studley was technically a minor and so was required to attend juvenile delinquency classes for some months after the case was thrown out. It was a small price to pay.[15]

12 • Afterword: Bringing the Jewish Tragedy to the Fore

"Tumultuous cheering" greeted the motorcade that transported Irgun Zvai Leumi leader Menachem Begin, standing in an open car, through central Manhattan's Garment Center on a crisp autumn afternoon shortly after Thanksgiving 1948. Hunted by the British, reviled as a terrorist by some mainstream Jewish leaders, but hailed as a hero by many grassroots Jews, Begin was met by an overflow crowd of more than four hundred when the motorcade came to a halt at city hall, where he was enthusiastically welcomed by Mayor William O'Dwyer.[1] Over a thousand guests packed the Waldorf-Astoria Hotel for a banquet in Begin's honor.

Begin's visit to the United States was not without controversy. Before his arrival, Israeli ambassador Eliahu Epstein and the American Zionist Emergency Council's Arthur Lourie tried, behind the scenes, to persuade members of the Begin Reception Committee to withdraw their names.[2] Labor Zionist activist Harvey Avrutin pressed trade union leader Harvey Rosen, an associate of American League for a Free Palestine attorney Paul O'Dwyer, to urge O'Dwyer to "make a public exodus from the [reception] committee" on the grounds that Begin and the Irgun were "the most reactionary and anti-labor elements in Israel." The feisty O'Dwyer would not be intimidated: "The Irgunists are good boys, and they did a very intelligent job of chasing the British out of Israel," O'Dwyer retorted. "If Israel were to wait for freedom to come from the conference table, Harvey Rosen would be getting Social Security before the matter would come up for the second reading. To ask me to turn my back on the Irgunists would be like asking me to denounce the Irish Republican Army."[3]

At the same time, twenty-eight prominent Jews, including Albert Einstein, Hannah Arendt, and the Socialist intellectual Sidney Hook, signed a letter to the *New York Times* comparing Begin's movement to "the Nazi and Fascist parties," while the anti-Zionist American Council for Judaism appealed to the U.S. attorney general to investigate the legality of Begin's visit.[4] The U.S. Labor Zionists pressed the AZEC and the American division of the Jewish Agency to publicly condemn Begin in advance of his visit, but Abba Hillel Silver and Emanuel Neumann blocked the move. According to one of those who attended the AZEC discussion of Begin's visit, Silver said he "considers Beigin [*sic*] one of the great heroes of Israel and the Irgun has written one of its most glorious chapters."[5] Unable to secure a condemnation of Begin by the mainstream Zionist leadership, the frustrated director of Americans for Haganah publicly condemned the "silence" of the Zionist leaders: "Where are the voices of the leaders of the ZOA, the American Zionist Emergency Council and the American Section of the Jewish Agency? Surely it is for them—Rabbi Silver, Dr. Neumann and others—to explain to the American people the facts concerning Mr. Beigin [*sic*], his party and his American supporters. Silence can be taken for support unless the record is made clear."[6]

At the dinner itself, a brief reminder of the bitter quarrels of the preceding decade was provided by a handful of Hashomer Hatzair members, who showed up at Begin's banquet to distribute leaflets declaring that "Support for Mr. Beigin [*sic*] is support for gangsterism well-schooled in the tenets of the Nazi primer."[7] But the name-calling could not dampen the excitement and spirit of the evening. The banquet brought together an extraordinary cross section of leaders from the multitude of Revisionist factions: Ben-Ami, Rafaeli, Hecht, and Selden of the Bergson groups; Danzis, Bookspan, Kopelowicz, and Newman of the New Zionist Organization of America/United Zionists-Revisionists of America; and Korff, Giloni, and Rosen of the Political Action Committee for Palestine. Some attendees likened it to a family reunion.[8] Several of the most important members of the family, however, were absent that evening, having already set sail for the Jewish state they helped establish.

Benzion Netanyahu had returned to Jerusalem, where he would serve as editor of the prestigious *Encyclopedia Hebraica*. Later he would spend some years in the United States, teaching Jewish history at Dropsie College, the University of Denver, and Cornell University before returning to Israel permanently. His middle son, Jonathan (Yonatan), was killed while leading the rescue of Israeli airline passengers who were being held hostage by Arab terrorists in Entebbe, Uganda, in 1976. Benzion's youngest son, Benjamin, served as Israel's ambassador to the United Nations and then as deputy foreign minister before becoming head of the Likud Party in 1992 and then prime minister of Israel from 1996 to 1999.

Peter Bergson reassumed his original name, Hillel Kook, and together with Samuel Merlin returned to Israel shortly after its establishment. They arrived in the midst of a crisis over the *Altalena,* an Irgun ship bringing arms to Israel to use against the invading Arab armies. Ben-Gurion, in his capacity as acting prime minister, ordered the Haganah to sink the ship off the Tel Aviv coast, and Haganah gunners shot dead sixteen of the passengers as they swam for shore. Hundreds of Irgun members and Revisionist activists were then detained in a nationwide sweep, including Kook, who spent the summer of 1948 in an Israeli prison. Both Kook and Merlin ultimately won election to the First Knesset as representatives of Begin's Herut (Freedom) Party. During their first term in parliament, however, Kook and Merlin quarreled with Begin over a variety of ideological and personal issues, and soon they opted to withdraw from the political scene and return temporarily to the United States to pursue private business interests. Kook later went back to Israel, where he passed away in 2001. Merlin chose to remain in New York, where he passed away in 1996.

Benjamin Akzin, Eliahu Ben-Horin, and Joseph Schechtman temporarily continued their Zionist activities in the United States. During the first year following Israel's creation, Akzin continued his work at the AZEC, supplementing with occasional ghostwriting for the Zionist Organization of America.[9] He moved to Israel in 1949 and soon established himself as one of Israel's most distinguished academic figures. He taught government and constitutional law at Hebrew University, served as dean of its Faculty of Law, then became president of the University of Haifa and was awarded the Israel Prize in 1967. He died in 1985.

Eliahu Ben-Horin attempted, but failed, to secure a position with the new Israeli government; he believed political differences were the cause. While remaining temporarily with the AZEC, Ben-Horin agreed, at the urging of the Israeli Foreign Ministry, to revive the Hoover plan in early 1949 as a way of promoting the idea of permanently resettling Palestinian Arab refugees in the Arab countries. Working closely with Abba Hillel Silver and the Israeli ambassador to the UN, Abba Eban, Ben-Horin wrote articles, met with State Department officials, and lobbied fervently to have Hoover appointed head of a proposed U.S. agency on Arab refugee matters.[10] When the lobbying effort failed, Hoover lost interest in the undertaking and Ben-Horin moved on to other projects. He remained in New York, working in a variety of professions and writing occasionally for Jewish periodicals. He passed away in 1966.

Joseph Schechtman was hired by Abba Silver and the AZEC in early 1949 to organize a propaganda campaign advocating the resettlement of

Palestinian Arab refugees in the Arab countries.[11] Israeli Foreign Minister Moshe Shertok, the Israeli ambassador to the United States, Eliahu Epstein, and his counterpart at the UN, Abba Eban, helped plan the campaign.[12] Schechtman authored two detailed booklets, "Arab Refugees: Facts and Figures" and "Resettlement Prospects for Arab Refugees," which served as the American Zionist leadership's staple literature on the subject for years to come.[13]

In the midst of the political battles of the mid-1940s, Benzion Netanyahu paused to reflect on what he and his colleagues had accomplished. "We do not write history today," he told Emanuel Neumann of the AZEC, "but when the history of Zionism is written, I do not believe that anyone with a minimum of fairness and honesty will discount the activities of those who brought, under seemingly insurmountable obstacles and difficulties, the Jewish question and Jewish tragedy to the fore; who vigorously exposed and attacked British policy in Palestine in a manner and on a scale never before attempted; and who relentlessly pressed in many ways American public opinion and American leadership for intervention in that issue."[14]

By virtue of their willingness to take on unpopular issues and their talent at explaining those issues in American terms, the Revisionists had indeed helped in "bringing the Jewish question and Jewish tragedy to the fore"— that is, bringing it to the point where it became a matter of concern to the American mainstream. In order to see their agenda implemented, the Jabotinskyites had to first make that agenda relevant to the masses of American Jews, and then to Congress, the media, and the broader American public.

The Revisionist activists who arrived in the United States from Europe and Palestine between 1938 and 1940 knew little about either American Jewry or the American political system, but they learned quickly and made up for their inexperience with energy and determination. They soon discovered that a sizable segment of the American Jewish community as well as many prominent non-Jews were ready to support an activist movement on behalf of European Jewry and Jewish statehood. The Nazi persecutions and England's shutdown of Jewish immigration to Palestine galvanized a seismic shift in Jewish public opinion. When mainstream Jewish leaders such as Stephen Wise hesitated to take forceful action on critical issues, the Zionist maximalists filled the vacuum, with the enthusiastic support of a growing segment of the Jewish grassroots. Some mainstream leaders realized what was happening and urged the use of more forceful tactics, both to respond to the European crisis and to prevent the Revisionists from capturing the hearts of grassroots American Jewry. "They write very good advertisements, and we ought to compete with them," the ZOA's Louis Lipsky counseled his colleagues.[15] But Stephen Wise did not—or would not—recognize the changing mood in the Jewish community. He was understandably thrilled when his companion on a 1936 visit to Warsaw told him that a crowd of Jews was admiringly chanting "Stepan Weisz, Stepan Weisz!" as they passed by; one wonders how Wise would have responded had he known what Chaim Kaplan, chronicler of the Warsaw Ghetto's agony, wrote in his diary in June 1942 as Warsaw Jews awaiting deportation to the death camps wondered at the inaction of American Jewish leaders: "A joke is making the rounds. Rabbi Stephen S. Wise is helping. He has ordered the American Jews to say the memorial prayer for the departed souls of Polish Jewry. His foresight is accurate."[16]

Many prominent Jewish leaders of that era adhered to a "universalist perception" that tended to hamper their effectiveness in times of Jewish crisis, historian Henry Feingold has noted. "Stephen Wise's interest in the Jewish dilemma was often overshadowed by such preoccupations as the Sacco and Vanzetti case or the corruption in the Jimmy Walker administration of New York City during the New Deal or the progress of the newly formed Congress of Industrial Organizations. . . . His letters tell of his embarrassment at speaking in the Oval Office of the special crucible of the Jews when the entire world was in flames." By contrast, "groups like the [Orthodox] Agudath and the Bergson Boys, the latter composed primarily of Palestinian Jews, were much better able to imagine the disaster and propose solutions more appropriate for the specific Jewish need" because "both groups were not locked into the prevailing secular universalist perception. They wanted simply to save Jews qua Jews."[17]

Given their limited manpower and financial resources, however, the Revisionists often found themselves unable to press a particular issue with sufficient vigor to keep pace with the rapidly changing situation abroad. Many of their accomplishments thus fell into the frustrating category of "what might have been." Throughout the 1930s, Jabotinsky and his followers warned of impending disaster for European Jewry and called for "emergency evacuation," but they never had the means to evacuate the endangered masses. The Revisionists initiated the sending of boatloads of unauthorized immigrants from Europe to Palestine, but they had the resources to send only fifteen thousand or so before the eruption of World War II put a halt to virtually all *aliyah bet* efforts, Revisionist and non-

Revisionist alike. The American Revisionists did much of the propaganda spadework that popularized the idea of a Jewish army, but it was not until near the end of the war that the British finally assented to the creation of the Jewish Brigade. The Bergson boys took the rescue issue off the back burner; John Pehle of the War Refugee Board acknowledged in 1944 that "the Emergency Committee to Save Jews of Europe has rendered a significant service in calling to the attention of the American public the enormous tragedy that has befallen the Jews of Europe."[18] The Bergson group's public-relations savvy aroused substantial public and congressional sympathy, which, in turn, was used by Treasury Secretary Henry Morgenthau to persuade Roosevelt to establish the War Refugee Board—but only near the end of the war, when millions had already been murdered. The various Jabotinsky factions, together with the Revisionists who "bored from within" by joining and radicalizing the mainstream AZEC, made the Jewish revolt against the British palatable to the American public. Yet they never succeeded in garnering enough support to bring about the abrogation of the Truman administration's arms embargo against the newborn state of Israel.

Still, no recital of the Jabotinskyites' failings can obscure their accomplishments. Even if the pre–World War II *aliyah bet* had the potential to bring many more immigrants to Palestine, the fact remains that many thousands of lives were saved. The Jewish Brigade, although late on the scene, performed vital work organizing the illegal immigration of Holocaust survivors to Palestine, and the training that the brigade members received was put to good use when they joined the fledgling Israeli army.[19] Although the War Refugee Board was not created until near war's end, it saved an estimated 200,000 lives.[20]

The Revisionists' lobbying efforts also broke new ground for Zionism in Washington, planting the seeds for future political alliances between Jerusalem and Capitol Hill. Many mainstream Zionist leaders such as Stephen Wise were closely tied to the Democratic Party, especially its liberal wing, and were uncomfortable seeking relationships with Republicans or even conservative Democrats. In addition, Wise's vocal support for U.S. aid to Britain between 1939 and 1941 (the period when England was at war with Germany, but the United States was not) reduced his ability to reach out to those congressmen who opposed American intervention. The Revisionists, having no special relationships with the Democrats and having played no role in the early debates over U.S. intervention in Europe, found themselves better positioned to woo isolationist Democrats and conservative Republicans. They found considerable sympathy in quarters where more liberal

Jews seldom ventured. Netanyahu's pitch for support on the basis of the Jewish state's role blocking Soviet regional advances anticipated, by three decades, the approach that would cement relations between his Likud successors and Washington's Republicans.

These different strategies were born, in part, of the drastically different worldviews harbored by the moderates and the militants. Many Jewish leaders adhered to an optimistic worldview, in which they expected both superpowers would eventually be persuaded to sympathize sufficiently with the Jewish plight to facilitate the creation of a Jewish national home. Jabotinsky and his followers, by contrast, saw the world as a cruel place, where life and liberty were commodities that were not inevitable, but for which one had to fight with no holds barred. In Palestine that meant taking up the gun and the bomb against the British, while in Washington it meant waging political struggles with whatever methods proved most efficient, no matter how unorthodox. If a particular congressman might sympathize with Zionism, he was to be pursued, regardless of his position on other issues. If a politician or a diplomat might be influenced by exploiting his anti-Jewish prejudices—for example, by dropping hints about Jewish electoral power or Jewish influence in the media—so be it.

The militant Zionists' provocative and relentless propaganda efforts embarrassed London and intensified the pressure on England to withdraw from Palestine. Zionist activism also "put heart into the Jews of America," British Embassy official Isaiah Berlin estimated. "Consequently they remained unshaken by the opposition of powerful American political leaders [including some] among the President's trusted advisers." British officials anxiously monitored the emergence of this "mass enthusiasm in America," as Abba Hillel Silver rose to power, encouraging and articulating the new American Jewish mood, surrounding himself with some of the Revisionists' most talented activists, and working hand in glove with the Jabotinsky factions.[21] They were a powerful combination indeed, and their efforts undoubtedly contributed to the pressures that led to Britain's decision to leave Palestine, paving the way for the creation of Israel. Hard-hitting propaganda "could bewilder the enemy like a plague of locusts," Hecht correctly predicted. "It could confuse the enemy's home front, particularly a British home front as susceptible to phrases as to bombs. . . . It could never knock an enemy soldier down but it could sink the spirit of his home front—and its eagerness to keep him all shined up and shooting."[22]

Even the remarkable disunity that characterized American Jewry during the Hitler years did not wreck the community's political effectiveness. Rival groups, sometimes rivals within the same groups, delivered conflicting messages to the powers in Washington, diluting the community's influence. The AZEC's impact was diminished by the Wise-Silver battles. American Zionism as a whole suffered because of the rift between the mainstream groups and the Revisionists. Even the Revisionists were torn by the secession of the Bergsonites and others. Yet could it be that the very multiplicity of pro-Palestine organizations had some advantages as well? Determined to make their voices heard above those of their rivals, the various factions cranked up the volume of their activity to an almost deafening level. The torrent of newspaper advertisements, radio broadcasts, public rallies, and delegations to Washington from so many different groups demonstrated that a substantial number of American Jews were aroused. Since all of the protesters were making—or perceived to be making—similar points about rescue, immigration, and statehood, they effectively reinforced one another in the minds of the media, the White House, and the Congress.

The existence of multiple organizations also meant that creative individuals who might have found themselves stifled within the confines of a single mainstream organization instead enjoyed outlets for the fullest expression of their abilities and views. The talents of a Benzion Netanyahu, a Peter Bergson, or a Ben Hecht would likely have been underutilized in a traditional Jewish organizational setting. Free from the shackles of diplomatic niceties and watchful boards of directors, these maverick Zionists were able to experiment with new, bold, and often effective varieties of Jewish political activism. Unity is always ideal, but in a Jewish world where such noble ideals are seldom realized, Jabotinsky's followers managed to achieve far more for the rescue of European Jewry and the cause of Jewish statehood than either their supporters or their detractors ever believed possible.

Notes

Abbreviations

AHSP	Abba Hillel Silver Papers, The Temple, Cleveland
AJA	American Jewish Archives, Cincinnati
AJHS	American Jewish Historical Society, Waltham, Massachusetts
BAP	Benjamin Akzin Papers, MZ
BP	Brandeis Papers, Princeton University
CZA	Central Zionist Archives, Jerusalem
DTEP	Denise Tourover Ezekiel Papers, HA
FDRL	Franklin D. Roosevelt Library, Hyde Park, New York
FLP	Fiorello La Guardia Papers, New York City Municipal Archives
HA	Hadassah Archives, New York City
HMP	Harold Manson Papers, The Temple, Cleveland
JDB	*Jewish Daily Bulletin*
JTA	*Jewish Telegraphic Agency News Bulletin*
LC	Library of Congress, Washington, D.C.
MZ	Jabotinsky Institute, Metzudat Ze'ev, Tel Aviv
NA	National Archives, Washington, D.C.
NP	*New Palestine*
NR	*New Republic*
NYP	*New York Post*
NYT	*New York Times*
PRO	Public Record Office, London
PSGP	Palestine Statehood Groups Papers, Yale University
SGP	Solomon Goldman Papers, AJA
SWP	Stephen S. Wise Papers, AJHS
WLP	William D. Langer Papers, Department of Special Collections, Chester Fritz Library, University of North Dakota, Grand Forks

Chapter 1

1. Israel Posnansky, "January 1926–January 1935," *Our Voice* 2 (January 1935): 13.

2. Samuel Halperin, *The Political World of American Zionism* (Detroit: Wayne State University Press, 1961), 327.

3. Joseph B. Schechtman and Yehuda Benari, *History of the Revisionist Movement: Volume 1, 1925–1930* (Tel Aviv: Hadar, 1970), 414.

4. Michael Brown, "The New Zionism in the New World: Vladimir Jabotinsky's Relations with the United States in the Pre-Holocaust Years," *Modern Judaism* 9 (February 1989): 87.

5. Ibid.; Joseph Schechtman, *Fighter and Prophet: The Jabotinsky Story—The Last Years, 1923–1940* (New York: Thomas Yoseloff, 1961), 53.

6. Brown, "New Zionism," 87–88; Schechtman, *Fighter and Prophet,* 53.

7. Vladimir Jabotinsky, "Revisionism: The Essentials of Its Programme," *NP,* 19 Mar. 1926, 272–73, and 26 Mar. 1926, 296–98.

8. "Mr. Jabotinsky's Views" (editorial), *NP,* 19 Mar. 1926, 268.

9. Schechtman and Benari, *History of the Revisionist Movement,* 415.

10. "No Disagreement between American Zionists and Weizmann, Lipsky Tells Press Representatives," *JDB,* 11 Apr. 1926, 3; Shmuel Katz, *Lone Wolf: A Biography of Vladimir (Ze'ev) Jabotinsky,* vol. 2 (Barricade Books: New York, 1996), 992–93.

11. Schechtman and Benari, *History of the Revisionist Movement,* 415–16.

12. Ezekiel Leikin interview with the author, 18 July 1996.

13. Schechtman and Benari, *History of the Revisionist Movement,* 415–16.

14. Noted in "Order Sons of Zion Convention Discusses Revisionism," *JDB,* 22 June 1926, 3.

15. Brown, "New Zionism," 88; Schechtman, *Fighter and Prophet,* 52.

16. "Common Counsel Not Parties" (editorial), *NP,* 30 Apr. 1926, 400; Louis Lipsky, "An Open Letter to the Order Sons of Zion," *NP,* 28 May 1926, 493.

17. Schechtman, *Fighter and Prophet,* 53.

18. "Order Sons of Zion Convention Discusses Revisionism"; Schechtman and Benari (*History of the Revisionist Movement,* 419) report a vote of 99 in favor, 32 against.

19. Louis Lipsky, "The Chairman's Annual Message," *NP,* 9 July 1926, 6; "$7,500,000 Will Be Sought for Palestine Next Year, Zionist Convention Hears," *JDB,* 29 June 1926, 3, 7; "Zionist Convention Urges England to Active Cooperation in Rebuilding Palestine Homeland," *JDB,* 20 June 1926, 3, 5–6, 8;

"Zionists Oppose Strife in Palestine," *NYT,* 29 June 1926, 12; "Order Sons of Zion" in "The Convention Mass Meeting," *NP,* 9 July 1926, 20–22.

20. Schechtman and Benari, *History of the Revisionist Movement,* 421–22.

21. *Der Tog,* 20 Feb. 1926.

22. *Dos Yiddishe Folk,* 5 Mar. 1926.

23. Schechtman and Benari, *History of the Revisionist Movement,* 413.

24. "Vladimir Jabotinsky, Leader of Zionist Revisionists, Arrives in America," *JDB,* 28 Jan. 1926, 2.

25. Johan J. Smertenko, "The Case for Revisionism," *Menorah Journal* 12 (October–November 1926): 471–79; Emanuel Neumann, "Revisionism: A Rejoinder," *Menorah Journal* 12 (October–November 1926): 479–90; Johan J. Smertenko, "Revisionism to the Rescue: A Reply to Mr. Neumann's 'Rejoinder,'" *Menorah Journal* 12 (December 1926): 610–21.

Chapter 2

1. "The Revisionist Movement in America (Mr. Emanuel Nagler in Interview)," 1930, 4, 16-gimel/10, MZ.

2. Beth S. Wenger (*New York Jews and the Great Depression: Uncertain Promise* [New Haven: Yale University Press, 1996], 193–94 and 258 n. 132) suggests that the growth of Zionist youth groups during the 1930s indicates that "American Zionism did make significant inroads in the 1930s." The likely explanation for the growth in youth group memberships despite the Depression was the emotional impact of events in Europe and Palestine, combined with low membership dues, as compared to adult Zionist organizations. Halperin (*American Zionism,* 261–64) is more skeptical than Wenger as to the growth of the youth groups during the early 1930s, although there is no dispute that after the rise of Hitler in 1933, all Zionist groups experienced significant increases in membership, despite the continuing hardships of the Depression.

3. "The Revisionist Movement in America (Mr. Emanuel Nagler in Interview)," 1930, 1–2, 16-gimel/10, MZ.

4. "Statement by the Executive Committee of the League of Zionist Revisionists, September 14th 1929," 16-gimel/5, MZ.

5. "American Jews' Confidence in British Palestine Policy Thoroughly Shaken, Louis Lipsky Declares in London," *JDB,* 3 Sept. 1929, 5; "Wise Holds British Guilty on Riots," *NYT,* 16 Sept., 1929, 18; "$25,000 Straus Gift Sent to Palestine," *NYT,* 28 Aug. 1929, 4.

6. "Statement by the Executive Committee of the League of Zionist Revisionists, September 14th 1929," 16-gimel/5, MZ.

7. Noted in "The Revisionist Movement in America (Mr. Emanuel Nagler in Interview)," 1930, 4, 16-gimel/10, MZ.

8. Elias Ginsburg, "Zionists Have No Fascisti in Ranks, Says Member Here," *New York World*, 14 Sept. 1929, 6.

9. Twenty-seven letters from assorted politicians acknowledging receipt of the memorandum may be found in the file 16-gimel/7, MZ.

10. "Sham Parliaments" (editorial), *NP*, 28 Sept.–5 Oct. 1928, 207–8.

11. Fritz Loewenstein, "Democratic Rule in Palestine," *NP*, 28 Sept.–5 Oct. 1928, 214–15; A Political Correspondent, "The Legislative Council Again," *NP*, 28 Sept.–5 Oct. 1928, 215–16. For more on the Brith Shalom group, see Aharon Kedar, "'Brith Shalom,'" *Jerusalem Quarterly* 18 (Winter 1981): 55–85.

12. "Revisionists Demand Magnes Be Disciplined," *JDB*, 26 Nov. 1929, 8.

13. "Jewish Congress Repudiates Magnes's Statement; Scores Nullification of Balfour Paper," *JDB*, 25 Nov. 1929, 3; "Dr. Magnes Scored in Jewish Press," *NYT*, 22 Nov. 1929, 6; "Magnes Criticized by Jewish Leaders," *NYT*, 25 Nov. 1929, 10.

14. "A Protest Meeting against the Traitor of Mount Scopus," March 1931, F38/646, CZA; Wise to Mack, 27 Mar. 1931, 16-gimel/10, MZ.

15. "The Revisionist Movement in America (Mr. Emanuel Nagler in Interview)," 1930, 3, 16-gimel/10, MZ.

16. "In the Movement," *Our Voice* 1 (June 1934): 15.

17. "Minutes of the First Meeting of the Tel Hai Committee," 30 Dec. 1929, 16-gimel/5, MZ. The address listed on the Tel Hai letterhead, 32 Union Square, Manhattan, is identical to that of the U.S. Revisionist headquarters at that time.

18. The U.S. wing of Betar is mentioned for the first time in Posnansky to Zionist Organization of America, 15 Aug. 1930, F38/646, CZA.

19. "Zionist Groups Convene," *NYT*, 28 Dec. 1930, 24; "Zionists Score Weizmann," *NYT*, 30 Dec. 1930, 24.

20. "Vote Boycott on Britain," *NYT*, 31 Oct. 1930, 19.

21. Samuel Grand, "A History of Zionist Youth Organizations in the United States" (M.A. thesis, Columbia University, 1958), 110.

22. "Minutes of Administrative Committee Meeting of Zionist Revisionist Organization of America" [hereafter ZROA Minutes], 16 Feb. 1931, 2, 16-gimel/7, MZ.

23. ZROA Minutes, 26 Feb. 1931, 1, ibid.

24. Ginsburg to Jabotinsky, 10 Aug. 1935, F25/390, CZA.

25. Ibid.; Ginsburg to Jabotinsky, 11 Apr. 1934, F25/389, CZA.

26. ZROA Minutes, 6 Apr. 1932, 16-gimel/7, MZ.

27. ZROA Minutes, 23 Mar. 1931, 30 Mar. 1931, ibid.

28. Ginsburg to Jabotinsky, 11 Apr. 1934, F25/389, CZA.

29. Wise to Jabotinsky, 2 July 1930, Box 102, SWP.

30. Mack to Ginsburg and Posnansky, 8 Aug. 1930, F38/646, CZA.

31. Mordechai Danzis to Szold, 16 Oct. 1930, ibid.

32. "Two Visitors" (editorial), *NP,* 27 Feb. 1931, 51; Altman to Szold, 4 Mar. 1931, F38/646, CZA.

33. Minutes, 23 Mar. 1931, 1, 16-gimel/7, MZ; Danzis to Szold, 27 Mar. 1931, F38/646, CZA.

34. Leikin interview.

35. Szold to Wise, 28 Apr. 1934, Box 120, SWP; "60th Birthday of Dr. Stephen Wise," *Rassviet,* 15 Apr. 1934, translation in Box 102, SWP; E[lias] G[insburg], "The Stavsky Defense Committee," *Our Voice* 1 (June 1934): 10.

36. Elias Ginsburg, "The Red Terror in the White-Blue Land," *Our Voice* 1 (April 1934): 6–7.

37. Ginsburg to Jabotinsky, 10 Aug. 1935, F25/390, CZA; Ginsburg to Jabotinsky, 11 Apr. 1934, F25/389, CZA.

38. "The Peace Pact" (editorial), *Avukah Bulletin* 6 (November 1934): 1.

39. Ginsburg to Schechtman, 12 Nov. 1933, 16-gimel/7, MZ.

40. Vladimir Jabotinsky, "Yes, To Break," *Haint,* 4 Nov. 1932, 9.

41. Bulletin no. 1, 31 Jan. 1933, 16-gimel/10, MZ; "'Our Educators' in Palestine," 2, and Gabriel Preil, "Palestine under Histadruth Rule," 7–9, *Revisionist,* 1 July 1933, 16-gimel/10, MZ.

42. For a good survey of the status of Jewish workers during the 1920s and 1930s, see Henry L. Feingold, *A Time for Searching: Entering the Mainstream, 1920–1945* (Baltimore: Johns Hopkins University Press, 1992), 125–54.

43. Szold to Mrs. Wise, 1 Oct. 1930, Box 121, SWP; Weizmann to Wise, 9 Apr. 1925, Box 122, SWP; Jabotinsky to Mrs. Wise, 19 June 1930, Wise to Jabotinsky, 2 July 1930, Jabotinsky to Wise, 23 July 1930, Wise to Jabotinsky, 14 Oct. 1930, Wise to Huebsch, 4 Dec. 1930, Huebsch to Wise, 9 Dec. 1930, Wise to Knopf, 16 Dec. 1930, 22 Dec. 1930, and Jabotinsky to Mrs. Wise, 24 Feb. 1931, 25 May 1932, all in Box 102, SWP.

44. Wise to Baker, 17 Jan. 1934, and Wise to Danzis, 16 Dec. 1930, Box 102, SWP.

45. "Lipsky Back from Prague Tells of Congress and German Situation," *NP,* 20 Sept. 1933, 1.

46. Wise to Levinson, 3 Oct. 1934, Box 102, SWP.

47. Frankfurter to Wise, 12 Dec. 1934, Box 109, SWP.

48. Jabotinsky to Mrs. Wise, 18 Oct. 1934, and Wise to Jabotinsky, 29 Oct. 1934, Box 102, SWP.

49. "Why Zionists Cannot Support Jabotinsky and Revisionism: Excerpts of Address Delivered before the Free Synagogue at Carnegie Hall—Sunday Morning, March 10, 1935, by Dr. Stephen S. Wise," ibid.

50. "Jewish-Arab Amity Urged by Einstein," *NYT,* 21 Apr. 1935, sec. 2, p. 4.

51. "Don't Fall for Jabotinsky" (editorial), *Reconstructionist,* 11 Jan. 1935, 8; "Rabbis May Plead Guilty" (editorial), *Reconstructionist,* 22 Feb. 1935, 3–4.

52. Grand, "Zionist Youth Organizations," 117; Schechtman, *Fighter and Prophet,* 261.

53. Elias Ginsburg, "Is Revision-Zionism Fascist?" *Menorah Journal* 22 (October–December 1934): 190–206; Marie Syrkin, "Labor-Zionism Replies," *Menorah Journal* 23 (April–June 1935): 66–79.

54. Walter Laqueur (*A History of Zionism* [New York: Schocken, 1976], 360–64) describes Achimeir's followers as "a small group" who "were of no great political significance" and says that Achimeir "had a few admirers but his impact on the younger generation was strictly limited." Likewise, Anita Shapira (*Land and Power: The Zionist Resort to Force* [New York: Oxford University Press, 1992], 201) calls Achimeir's Brit Habiryonim group "an ephemeral movement whose membership did not encompass more than a few dozen isolated individuals." In 1935, Achimeir "emerged a broken man from his experience in prison and did not return to the helm of leadership of any group" (ibid., 202). Yaacov Shavit (*Jabotinsky and the Revisionist Movement, 1925–1948* [London: Frank Cass, 1988], 71) agrees that "Achimeir's faction disintegrated after 1933. Following [the Arlosoroff] trial, the Brit Habiryonim faded out of sight."

55. Alice Nakhimovsky, in "Vladimir Jabotinsky, Russian Writer" (*Modern Judaism* 7 [May 1987]: 171), argues that the "fascist" label has been unfairly perpetuated by historians who have erroneously ascribed to Jabotinsky sentiments expressed by one the characters in his novel *Samson.* In a related historiographical debate, Shlomo Avineri (*The Making of Modern Zionism: The Intellectual Origins of the Jewish State* [New York: Basic Books, 1981], 173–74) perceives similarities between Jabotinsky's views on race and those of European fascists, while Shavit (*Jabotinsky and the Revisionist Movement,* 113–14 and n. 9) argues that Jabotinsky's use of the term "race" must be understood in the context of conventional (not merely fascist) racial theories of that era, and also in relation to similar writings by other Jewish leaders.

56. "Unmask the Hypocrites!" (editorial), *Our Voice* 1 (June 1934): 1.

57. "'Our Educators' in Palestine" (editorial), *Revisionist,* 1 July 1933, 1.

58. "The Jewish Press" (editorial), *Revisionist*, 1 July 1933, 1.

59. Ibid.

60. "Tentative Statement of Program of the American 'B' Group, General Zionists," March 1935, F38/599, CZA.

61. Wise to Jabotinsky, 29 Oct. 1934, Box 102, SWP.

62. "Palestine Labor Movement Backed by 241 Reform Rabbis of Country," *JDB*, 27 Jan. 1935, 2.

63. *JDB,* 28 Jan. 1935, 1; Schechtman, *Fighter and Prophet,* 260; "The Jabotinsky Tour," *Our Voice* 2 (February 1935): 14.

64. Baruch Rabinowitz, "The Legacy" (unpublished autobiography), 49–50, 62–63, Baruch Rabinowitz Papers, privately held by the Rabinowitz family.

65. "Reception Committee (To Nov. 27th)," *Our Voice* 1 (December 1934): 13.

66. "Justice as Synonym of 'Class Concept'" (editorial), *Our Voice* 2 (January 1935): 5; "An Instructive Comparison" (editorial), *Our Voice* 2 (January 1935): 4. The periodical further charged that "In certain out of town places, methods of coercion have been employed. Threats to deprive physicians or some of their patients, storekeepers and professions of part of their clientele have been made." But it did not cite any specific sources for this information.

67. ZOA president Morris Rothenberg reported to the ZOA's annual convention in June 1934 that while "for the past five years there had been a continually descending ratio of membership," 1933 and 1934 brought "a complete reversal in the trend, so that we come to this convention with almost twice as many members as we had in 1932." The decision to reduce membership rates from six dollars to three undoubtedly helped boost the membership rolls. "Administration Report of the Zionist Organization of America and Survey of the Zionist Position," *NP,* 29 June 1934, 6.

68. For the Revisionists' role in the boycott movement, see untitled minutes of Second National Conference of the Zionist-Revisionists of America, April 6–8, 1935, 16-gimel/7, MZ; also see "Resolution Offered by the Zionist Revisionist Organization of America" [regarding the anti-Nazi boycott], [1933], ibid. For information on the new Revisionist chapters and other activities, see *N.Z.O. Bulletin* 1 (April 1936): 7–9. The Yiddish version was called *HaTzohar Bulletin.*

69. Jeremy Newman interview with the author, 9 June 1996; Louis I. Newman, *Biting on Granite: Selected Sermons and Addresses* (New York: Bloch, 1946); Fred Rosenbaum, *Architects of Reform: Congregational and Community Leadership Emanu-El of San Francisco, 1849–1980* (Berkeley, Calif.: Western Jewish History Center and Judah L. Magnes Memorial Museum, 1982), 87–105; David Polish, *Renew Our Days: The Zionist Issue in Reform Judaism* (Jerusalem: World

Zionist Organization, 1976), 161–62; Isaac Allen, Jacob de Haas, and Louis I. Newman, "Tentative Statement of Program of the American 'B' Group, General Zionists," F38/599, CZA.

70. Embassy to Halifax, 29 Sept. 1939, FO 371/23240, PRO.

71. Newman interview.

72. Syrkin, "Labor-Zionism Replies," 68, 71.

Chapter 3

1. Newman to La Guardia, 7 June 1937, File: Arabian Controversy, FLP.

2. Dabronsky to La Guardia, 7 June 1937, ibid.

3. "City Radio Broadcasts Arab Libels against Jews," *Morgen Zhurnal,* 7 June 1937, 3; "Zionist Organization on Municipal Radio Station to Answer Arab Libels," *Der Tog,* 8 June 1937, 2; "Zion Organization Will Be on Radio Station to Answer Arab Libels," *Forverts,* 8 June 1937, 2; Samuel Margoshes, "Arab Propagandists Invade New York," *Der Tog,* 8 June 1937, 1; "Arab Politicians in New York," *Der Tog,* 8 June 1937, 6; Kracke to La Guardia, 7 June 1937, File: Arabian Controversy, FLP.

4. "No. 1355—Resolution Condemning the Use of Station WNYC for the Spread of Political Propaganda and Racial Hatred," Resolutions of the Board of Aldermen, Municipal Archives and Research Center, New York City.

5. Estimates of Young Israel's strength in New York's boroughs are derived from the pamphlet *Young Israel: Its Aims and Activities,* published by the National Council of Young Israel, circa 1935 (Yeshiva University Library, New York). Although specific data on the residential patterns of interwar American Revisionists do not exist, Revisionist literature from that period indicates that whereas the movement had only one chapter in the Bronx and one in Manhattan, there were so many members of the Revisionist organization or its youth division, Betar, residing in Brooklyn that individual chapters were established in numerous Brooklyn neighborhoods, including Brownsville, Williamsburg, Boro Park, Flatbush, and East New York. See "In the Movement," *N.Z.O. Bulletin* 1 (March 1936): 33, 16/gimel/10, MZ; "In the Movement," *N.Z.O. Bulletin* 1 (April 1936): 6–7, 16/gimel/5, MZ; and *Zionews,* 20 Oct. 1940, 9.

6. Wise to Frankfurter, 22 Jan. 1937, Box 109, SWP.

7. Deborah Dash Moore, *At Home in America* (New York: Columbia University Press, 1981), 23.

8. Moses Rischin dubbed the Lower East Side and adjacent environs "Yiddish New York." See Rischin, *The Promised City: New York's Jews, 1870–1914* (Cambridge: Harvard University Press, 1962), 238.

9. Many sociologists erroneously predicted that suburbanization would lead directly to Jewish assimilation. See, e.g., Louis Wirth, *The Ghetto* (Chicago: University of Chicago Press, 1928).

10. Moore, *At Home in America;* Jeffrey S. Gurock, *When Harlem Was Jewish, 1870–1930* (New York: Columbia University Pres, 1979); Jenna Weissman Joselit, *New York's Jewish Jews: The Orthodox Community in the Interwar Years* (Bloomington and Indianapolis: Indiana University Press, 1990); Jeffrey S. Gurock, "The Orthodox Synagogue," in Jack Wertheimer, ed., *The American Synagogue: A Sanctuary Transformed* (New York: Cambridge University Press, 1987), 37–84.

11. Joselit, *New York's Jewish Jews*, 17, 19, 114–15, 135–36 and 142.

12. Kopelowicz to Levin, 10 May 1940, S-gimel/2/1, MZ.

13. Epstein family biography in *The Nordau Circle Testimonial Dinner in Honor of Beinish Epstein—May 5, 1963, Hotel Windermere.* Courtesy of Doris Baer.

14. Rabinowitz autobiography, 77.

15. "The Jewish National Labor Union in Eretz Yisrael," *N.Z.O. Bulletin* 1 (April 1936): 5.

16. Caricature, *N.Z.O. Bulletin* 1 (March 1936): 5.

17. Blanche B. Goldman and Mrs. Maurice M. Goldman to Kracke, 14 June 1937, Fabricant to Kracke, 14 June 1937, and Stroock to Kracke, 14 June 1937, File: Arabian Controversy, FLP; Wise to Kracke, 14 June 1937, Folder 5, Box 14, SWP; Statement by Commissioner F. J. H. Kracke, 15 June 1937, File: Arabian Controversy, FLP; "Anti-Jewish Bias on WNYC Is Denied," *NYT,* 16 June 1937, 16.

18. *Palestine Royal Commission Report* (London: His Majesty's Stationery Office, 1937), 390–91.

19. "Royal Commission Report Urges End of Mandate," *NP,* 12 July 1937, 1–2.

20. Newman to Wise, 30 July 1937, Stephen S. Wise Folders, Louis I. Newman Papers [hereafter LNP], AJA.

21. "Communists in Palestine" (editorial), *Jewish Frontier* 3 (June 1936): 9–10; "Italian-Arab Flirtation," *Jewish Frontier* 3 (September–October 1936): 9; "What Is Happening in Palestine?" (editorial), *Jewish Frontier* 3 (May 1936): 8–9.

22. Wise to Brandeis, 21 Sept. 1936, Reel 104, BP.

23. Wise to Weizmann, 26 Oct. 1936, Box 122, Reel 2400, SWP; Wise to Weizmann, 28 Oct. 1936, Box 4, Folder 19, Stephen S. Wise Papers, AJA.

24. "Why Ignore Transjordan?" (editorial), *NP,* 7 May 1937, 4. Jacob de

Haas, too, began leaning toward Arab resettlement as the solution in the wake of the 1936 violence. He counseled Jabotinsky that swift mass movement of European Jews to Palestine would overwhelm any Palestinian Arab opposition and make it "possible [to] talk of evacuating or restricting the Arabs." De Haas to Jabotinsky, 7 Oct. 1936, Reel 39, Jacob de Haas Papers, Zionist Archives, New York City.

25. "The Program at Buffalo" (editorial), *NP*, 18 June 1926, 556.

26. "Jewish Self-Restraint" (editorial), *NP*, 19 Nov. 1937, 4.

27. Wise to Mrs. Richard Gottheil, 6 July 1936, Box 109, SWP.

28. Wise to Mrs. Richard Gottheil, 3 Sept. 1937, ibid.

29. Halprin to Epstein, 13 July 1938, "Social Unrest between Jews and Arabs Series," Record Group 1, Hadassah Medical Organization, Box 55, Folder 5, HA.

30. William R. Perl, *The Four-Front War: From the Holocaust to the Promised Land* (New York: Crown, 1978), 16–17.

31. Dalia Ofer (*Escaping the Holocaust: Illegal Immigration to the Land of Israel, 1939–1944* [New York: Oxford University Press, 1990], 14 and 319–27) estimates that 17,240 illegal immigrants reached Palestine during 1938 and 1939, of whom about 12,000 were organized by the Revisionists. Perl (*Four-Front War*, 367–71) offers similar, but slightly higher, calculations. Exact numbers cannot be determined because additional ships reached Palestine with unknown numbers of passengers and because some other illegal immigrants reached Palestine by foot.

32. Lubinsky to "Judge" [evidently Felix Frankfurter], 25 Mar. 1939, F35/380, CZA.

33. "Irish Deputy Seeks Refugee Aid by U.S.," *NYT*, 3 Jan. 1939, 3; Yitshaq Ben-Ami, *Years of Wrath, Days of Glory: Memoirs from the Irgun*, 2nd ed. (New York: Shengold, 1983), 220–21; Alex Rafaeli, *Dream and Action: The Story of My Life* (Jerusalem: Achva, 1993), 110.

34. Ben-Ami, *Years of Wrath*, 216–17.

35. Lubinsky to "Judge" [evidently Felix Frankfurter], 25 Mar. 1939, F35/380, CZA.

36. Rafaeli, *Dream and Action*, 98.

37. Amos Bunim, *A Fire in His Soul: Irving M. Bunim, 1901–1980—The Man and His Impact on American Orthodox Jewry* (Jerusalem and New York: Feldheim, 1989), 44–45; Ben-Ami, *Years of Wrath*, 215.

38. Bunim, *Fire in His Soul*, 44, 110.

39. Ben-Ami, *Years of Wrath*, 215.

40. Ibid., 215, 220, 223.

41. Ibid., 220.

42. Ibid.

43. Wise to Frankfurter, 13 Dec. 1939, Box 109, SWP.

44. Allon Gal ("Brandeis' Social-Zionism," *Studies in Zionism* 8 [Autumn 1987]: 191–207) writes that in supporting Hashomer Hatzair, Brandeis "probably was attracted to the movement's firm anti-Revisionist stand." The key word is "probably"; Gal offers no additional evidence on this point. Again, with regard to Avukah, Gal asserts: "It *seems* [emphasis added] that he sided with the militant anti-Revisionist line of Avukah" (ibid.); the sentence has no footnote to back it up. In a later essay ("Brandeis, Judaism, and Zionism," in Nelson L. Dawson, ed., *Brandeis and America* [Lexington: University Press of Kentucky, 1989], 65–98), Gal again attempts to link Brandeis's sympathy for Avukah to that group's anti-Revisionism, and again fails to provide persuasive documentation.

45. For remarks by Brandeis regarding illegal immigration, see "Memorandum of Conference with Justice Louis D. Brandeis—Monday, July 31, 1939," SGP, and Brandeis to Szold, 23 May 1939, in Melvin I. Urofsky and David W. Levy, eds., *The Letters of Louis D. Brandeis, Volume 5 (1929–1941): Elder Statesman* (Albany: State University of New York Press, 1978), 619. For details of the Labor Zionist leaders' shifting and often ambivalent attitude toward illegal immigration, see Ofer, *Escaping the Holocaust,* 28–31, 223.

46. "Confidential Minutes of Z.O.A. Executive Held on Wednesday, May 10, 4 P.M., 1939, at the Commodore Hotel, New York City," Box 21, Folder 1, p. 4, SGP.

47. Landauer to Lauterbach, 3 Jan. 1940, S5/471, CZA.

48. Minutes of Emergency Committee for Zionist Affairs meeting, 4 Dec. 1939, Record Group 4, Folder 98, p. 4, HA; Memorandum, Israel Goldstein to Solomon Goldman, Louis Lipsky, Abba Hillel Silver, and Stephen S. Wise, 28 Nov. 1939, Box 12, Folder 11, SGP.

49. Memorandum, Goldstein to Goldman, Lipsky, Silver, and Wise, 28 Nov. 1939, Box 12, Folder 11, SGP.

50. "Wishful Thinking" (editorial), *Jewish Frontier* 6 (February 1939): 4.

51. Y. Greenberg, "Danger on the Right," *Hashomer Hatzair,* December 1939, 22–27.

52. "Statement Issued by Emergency Committee on Zionist Affairs," 5 Jan. 1939, 16-gimel/10, MZ.

53. Harry Louis Selden interview with the author, 6 June 1996.

54. Foreign Office to Colonial Office (H. M. Eyres), 20 Aug. 1940, FO 371/24567, PRO; Wright to Foreign Office, 12 Apr. 1945, FO 371/40398, with note by J. G. Donnelly, PRO.

55. Selden interview, 6 June 1996.

56. Memorandum, Goldstein to Goldman, Lipsky, Silver, and Wise, 28 Nov. 1939, Box 12, Folder 11, SGP; Minutes of Emergency Committee for Zionist Affairs meeting, 2 April 1940, Record Group 4, Folder 98, p. 3, HA.

57. Selden interview, 6 June 1996. Selden, for one, recalls receiving "literally dozens" of such letters, as well as reports that others associated with Bergson likewise endured a "deluge" of protests from Jewish establishment organizations.

58. Akzin to Norman, 2 Dec. 1940, 8/15-peh, BAP.

59. Embassy (Chancery) to Eastern Department, Foreign Office, 9 Jan. 1940, CO 733/426, PRO.

60. Memorandum, Goldstein to Goldman, Lipsky, Silver, and Wise, 28 Nov. 1939, Box 12, Folder 11, SGP.

61. Unsigned [Kopelowicz] to Akzin, 7 May 1940, Kopelowicz to Akzin, 10 May 1940, and Akzin to The Presidency, 9 May 1940, S-gimel/4/1, BAP. A reference to the *Chronicle* as the possible venue for an unspecified Revisionist "mock trial," in a discussion between Jabotinsky and his top aides, likewise indicates the close relationship between Akzin's newspaper and the movement. "Decisions of the Delegation," S-gimel/1/3, MZ.

62. *American Jewish Chronicle,* 20 June 1940.

63. Wise to Newman, 6 Dec. 1939, Stephen S. Wise Folder, LNP.

64. Selden interview, 6 June 1996; Montor to Rabinowitz, 1 Feb. 1940, copy provided to the author by Harry Louis Selden.

65. Emergency Committee for Zionist Affairs, "Revisionism: A Destructive Force" (New York: Emergency Committee for Zionist Affairs, 1940).

66. Ben-Ami, *Years of Wrath,* 321.

67. "Colonize for Whom?" (editorial), *Our Voice* 1 (July 1934): 1.

68. Naomi W. Cohen, *American Jews and the Zionist Idea* (New York: Ktav, 1975), 59.

69. Isadore Breslau, "Memorandum Re Committees," n.d., 2, P-507, Isadore Breslau Papers, AJHS.

70. Monty N. Penkower, "Ben Gurion, Silver, and the 1941 UPA National Conference for Palestine: A Turning Point in American Zionist History," *American Jewish History* 69 (September 1979): 66–75; Penkower, *The Jews Were Expendable: Free World Diplomacy and the Holocaust* (Urbana and Chicago: University of Illinois Press, 1983), 52–58. Menahem Kaufman believes that the

"turning point" did not come until after the United States entered the war in December 1941. See Kaufman, "American Zionism and United States Neutrality from September 1939 to Pearl Harbor," *Studies in Zionism* 9 (Spring 1988): 19–46.

71. Minutes of Hadassah National Board Meeting, 17 Dec. 1940, 1, HA.

Chapter 4

1. "How to Be a Guerrilla: 'Yank' Levy Preaches the Art He Has Practiced," *Life*, 17 Aug. 1942, 40–45; Committee for a Jewish Army "Memo," 5 Feb. 1942, 5, MZ.

2. "Memorandum on the Anglo-American Committee for a Jewish Army," 3, n.d., FO 371/31380, PRO.

3. "Comments," *Zionews*, 10 Jan. 1941, 1.

4. "Comments," *Zionews*, 29 Jan. 1941, 1.

5. Sim Rosenberg interview with the author, 2 Jan. 1996; Benzion Netanyahu interview with the author, 20 Mar. 1997; Eliahu Ben-Horin, *A Brick for the Bridge* (unpublished autobiography), 5, 41, 76a, Eliahu Ben-Horin Collection, MZ.

6. Netanyahu interview with the author, 26 June 1997.

7. Ibid.

8. Netanyahu interview, 20 Mar. 1997; Jacob Polieksin, "Michal Halperin: A Jewish Don Quixote," *Maccabaean* 32 (September 1919): 267–69.

9. "New Zionist Leader Heard by 5,000 Here," *NYT*, 20 Mar. 1940, 14.

10. Landauer to Shertok, 25 Mar. 1940, Z4/15297, CZA.

11. Kopelowicz to Levin, 10 May 1940, 5-gimel/2/1, MZ.

12. "Appalling Horrors" (editorial), *Opinion*, February 1940, 4.

13. "Nazis Machine-Gun All Jews in Town near Warsaw, Refugees Report," *JTA*, 8 Dec. 1939, 1; "Wars, Executions, Disease Wiped Out 250,000 Jews in Nazi Poland, 'White Book' Charges," *JTA*, 18 Dec. 1939, 1.

14. These particular phrases, although culled from somewhat later newspaper advertisements, are nonetheless typical of the Revisionists' Jewish army appeals throughout the war years. See "Hitler's Enemy No. 1 Must Be Our Ally No. 1" (advertisement), *NYP*, 31 Aug. 1943, 11; "Action, Not Pity, Can Save Millions Now" (advertisement), *NYT*, 8 Feb. 1943, 8.

15. Kopelowicz to Levine [*sic*], 5 Apr. 1940, 5-gimel/2/1, MZ.

16. ECZA Minutes, 2 Apr. 1940, Record Group 4, Folder 98, HA.

17. Kopelowicz to Levin, 5 July 1940, 5-gimel/2/1, MZ.

18. Ben-Horin to Nachmias, 26 Apr. 1940, 5-gimel/4/6, MZ.

19. Kopelowicz to Levin, 19 Apr. 1940, 5-gimel/2/1, MZ.

20. "Jews Planning Merchant Fleet," *Montreal Daily Star,* 21 Mar. 1940, 24; "Jewish Ships Will Defy Palestine Ban," *London Daily Mail,* 25 Mar. 1940, 8.

21. Margulies to Lourie, 22 Apr. 1940, and "Jewish Marine League Proposals—May 21, 1940," both in 2/1/n, MZ; Shumel Katz interview with the author, 18 Nov. 1996.

22. "A Report on the War-Time and Post-War Activities of the New Zionist Organization of America and the United Zionists-Revisionists, November 22, 1946," 1, 16-gimel/9, MZ.

23. Kopelowicz to "Abe" [Abrahams], 4 May 1940, 5-gimel/2/1, MZ.

24. Alon Gal (*David Ben-Gurion and the American Alignment for a Jewish State* [Bloomington and Indianapolis: Indiana University Press, 1991], 117) erred when he asserted that Jabotinsky's presence in the United States during the spring and summer of 1940 "did nothing to breathe life into the movement." At the same time, he is to be credited for pointing out that Jabotinsky's depression during that period was due in part to factors beyond longing for his spouse. Katz (*Lone Wolf,* 2:1768–69) indicates two additional factors: Jabotinsky's "sense of guilt from the very beginning over his visit to America because he had to leave [his wife] Joanna behind," and the eruption of stressful internal quarrels among the senior Revisionist activists in the United States.

25. Unsigned [Kopelowicz] to "Abe" [Abrahams], 3 May 1940, 5-gimel/2/1, MZ.

26. Kopelowicz to Levine [*sic*], 17 May 1940, ibid.

27. Netanyahu interview, 20 Mar. 1997.

28. Ibid.

29. Ibid.; "A Report on the War-Time . . . ," 1; Unsigned [Ben-Horin] to Akzin, 29 May 1940, 16/15-peh, BAP.

30. ECZA Minutes, 18 Dec. 1940, 30 Dec. 1941, and 9 Jan. 1941, CZA; "Palestine Asks Aid for Refugees on Ship," *NYT,* 21 Apr. 1939, 7.

31. Akzin to The Presidency, 11 May 1940, 5-gimel/4/1, BAP; Akzin to Newman, 20 May 1940, 5-gimel/4/7, BAP.

32. Akzin to Mrs. Gunther, 14 May 1940, 9/15-peh, BAP; Kopelowicz to "Abe," 4 May 1940, 5-gimel/2/1, MZ.

33. Kopelowicz to Abrahams, 25 June 1940, 5-gimel/2/1, MZ.

34. Akzin to The Presidency, 14 May 1940, 16/15-peh, BAP.

35. Akzin to The Presidency, 5 June 1940, 5-gimel/4/1, BAP. Akzin probably picked up the term "Society for Trembling Jews" from Eliahu Ben-Horin, who, in his *A Brick for the Bridge* (44), attributed authorship of the phrase to the British Zionist leader Lord Melchett.

36. Akzin to The Presidency, 15 May 1940, 4/5/4-gimel, BAP; Akzin to The Presidency, 4 June and 5 June 1940, 5-gimel/4/1, BAP; Kopelowicz to Levine [*sic*], 17 May 1940, 5-gimel/2/1, MZ.

37. Ben-Horin to Sperberg, 15 May 1940, 5-gimel/4/10, MZ.

38. Kopelowicz to Levine [*sic*], 17 May 1940, 5-gimel/2/1, MZ.

39. Abrahams to Kopelowicz, 19 May and 24 May 1940, ibid.

40. Akzin to The Presidency, 9 May and 28 May 1940, 5-gimel/4/1, BAP.

41. Akzin to The Presidency, 7 May and 13 May 1940, ibid. The only problem with the Lithuanian ambassador was linguistic: "I longed to talk Russian to him," Akzin recalled, "but he insisted on a rotten English which gave him obvious pain." Akzin to The Presidency, 13 May 1940, ibid.

42. For an earlier explanation by Wise as to his reasons for opposing mass emigration, see "Dealing Responsibly with Poland" (editorial), *Opinion*, November 1936, 4. For a fuller discussion of American Jewish responses to contacts between Jabotinsky and the Polish government during 1936 and 1937, see Laurence Weinbaum, *A Marriage of Convenience: The New Zionist Organization and the Polish Government, 1936–1939* (Boulder: East European Monographs/Columbia University Press, 1993), 94–99.

43. Akzin to The Presidency, 9 May 1940, 5-gimel/4/1, BAP.

44. Akzin to The Presidency, 13 May 1940, ibid.

45. Gerald P. Nye, "America, Jewry, and the War," *American Jewish Chronicle*, 20 June 1940, 5–6.

46. Akzin to The Presidency, 7 May and 9 May 1940, 5-gimel/4/1, BAP.

47. Akzin to The Presidency, 13 May 1940, ibid.

48. Akzin to The Presidency, 28 May 1940, ibid.

49. Akzin to The Presidency, 5 June 1940, ibid. Patterson relayed the contents of his conversation with Lothian to Justice Louis D. Brandeis, who repeated it to American Zionist Bureau director Isadore Breslau. A summary of it appears in Breslau to Wise, 10 June 1940, Box 107, Folder 2, Isadore Breslau Papers [hereafter IBP], AJHS.

50. Mathews to Abrahams, 28 May 1940, and Churchill to Abrahams, 24 May 1940, 5-gimel/2/1, MZ.

51. Akzin to Abrahams, 11 June 1940, ibid.; Akzin to The Polish Ambassador, 14 June 1940, 5-gimel/3/5, BAP.

52. Kopelowicz to *Jewish Standard* (Levin), telegram, 15 June 1940, 5-gimel/2/1, MZ.

53. Kopelowicz to Abrahams, 18 June 1940, 5-gimel/2/1, MZ; Ben-Horin to Lewis, 16 June 1940, 6/5/5-gimel, MZ; Akzin to Millar, 17 June 1940 (telegram), 5-gimel/3/5, BAP; "Zionist Leaders Here Frown on Jabotinsky Army Plan,"

JTA, 19 June 1940, 2–3. Wise may have been tipped off when Lieutenant Colonel Patterson innocently relayed the contents of his conversation with Lothian to Justice Louis D. Brandeis, who then forwarded it to Wise via American Zionist Bureau director Isadore Breslau. See Breslau to Wise, 10 June 1940, Box 107, Folder 2, IBP.

54. Samuel Merlin, quoted in Ben Hecht, *A Child of the Century* (New York: Simon and Schuster, 1954), 547.

55. Meyer W. Weisgal, "Events and Trends in American Jewry," *Congress Weekly*, 11 Sept. 1942, 18–20.

56. "A Misleading Slogan" (editorial), *NP*, 21 June 1940, 4.

57. "Zionist Leaders Here Frown on Jabotinsky Army Plan," *JTA*, 19 June 1940, 2–3.

58. Foreign Office to Lord Halifax, Washington, February 1943, FO 371/35031, PRO.

59. Breslau memorandum, "Lord Lothian 6/17/40," P-507, IBP.

60. Wise to Roosevelt, quoted in Stephen S. Wise, *Challenging Years: The Autobiography of Stephen S. Wise* (New York: Putnam, 1949), 225–26; Roosevelt to Wise, 9 June 1941, PPF 8084, FDRL.

61. Kopelowicz to Levin, 24 June 1940, 5-gimel/2/1, MZ.

62. Ben-Horin to Lewis, 16 June 1940, 6/5/5-gimel, MZ; Kopelowicz to Abrahams, 18 June 1940, 5-gimel/2/1, MZ.

63. Ginsburg to Keenleyside, 21 June 1940, Keenleyside to Ginsburg, 22 June 1940, Ginsburg to Keenleyside, 5 July 1940, and Akzin to Abrahams, 2 July and 5 July 1940, all in 5-gimel/2/1, MZ; Akzin to Ginsburg, 18 July 1940, 5-gimel/4/3, BAP.

64. Akzin to Abrahams, 26 July 1940, 5-gimel/2/1, BAP; Ginsburg to Shubow, 31 July 1940, 6/5/5-gimel, MZ; Ginsburg to Rossman, 31 July 1940, and Ginsburg to Weisbrot, 1 Aug. 1940, 5-gimel/2/4, MZ.

65. Rosenberg interview; Bernard Dworkin interview with the author, 8 Oct. 1999.

66. "Comments," *Zionews*, 28 July 1941, 1.

67. Ben-Ami, *Years of Wrath*, 244.

68. Kopelowicz to Abrahams, 6 Sept. 1940, 5-gimel/2/1, MZ.

69. Kopelowicz to Levin, 4 Dec. 1940, ibid.

70. Netanyahu interview with the author, 25 June 1997.

71. NZOA Presidency Minutes, 12 Aug. 1940, 16-gimel/5, MZ; Klinger to The Administrative Committee, 12 Aug. 1940, and Ben-Horin to Altman, 14 Aug. 1940, 5-gimel/2/5, MZ; Akzin to Abrahams, 18 Aug. 1940, 16-gimel/5, BAP.

72. NZOA Presidency Minutes, 4 Dec. 1940, 16-gimel/5, MZ; Ben-Ami, *Years of Wrath,* 238, 248.

73. "Rabbis Denounce Palestine Policy," *NYT,* 21 May 1939, 26; "Synagogues Offer Prayers for King," *NYT,* 11 June 1939, 39; "Firm Jewish Stand Urged by Newman," *NYT,* 16 June 1939, 18; "Niemoller Stand Praised by Rabbis," *NYT,* 2 July 1939, 8.

74. Newman interview; Netanyahu interview, 26 June 1997.

75. "The Convention," *Zionews,* 10 Jan. 1941, 6, MZ.

76. Levin to Kopelowicz, 7 Feb. 1941, 5-gimel/2/1, MZ.

77. "Comments," *Zionews,* 21 Apr. 1941, 3.

78. "Comments," *Zionews,* 29 Jan. 1941, 2.

79. "Comments," *Zionews,* 5 May 1941, 1–2.

80. Kopelowicz to Levin, 4 Dec. 1940, 5-gimel/2/1, MZ; Ben-Horin to Altman, 25 April 1941, 16-gimel/5, MZ; Presidency Minutes, 8 Apr. 1941, 5-gimel/1/3, MZ.

81. "Jews Reported Creating Fleet to Carry Exiles," *New York Herald Tribune,* 24 Mar. 1941, 10.

82. Presidency Minutes, 8 Apr. 1941, 5-gimel/1/3, MZ; Presidency Minutes, 12 Apr. 1941, 16-gimel/5, MZ; Presidency Minutes, 17 Apr. 1941, 5-gimel/1/3, MZ.

83. Joseph Beder, "Report of the Administrative Committee on Its Activities and on the State of the Organization from May 1st, 1941 to February 20, 1942," 16-gimel/8, MZ.

84. Kopelowicz to Beder, 2 June 1941, 16-gimel/3, MZ.

85. "Comments," *Zionews,* 7 Apr. 1941, 1; Akzin to "Kop," 9 Sept. 1941, 14/4/5-gimel, BAP.

86. "Report on Actions of N.Z.O.A. for Aug. 1942–June 1943," 16-gimel/2, MZ; "In the New Zionist Movement," *Zionews,* 15 Sept. 1941, 7; "In the New Zionist Movement," *Zionews,* 19 May 1941, 7.

87. "Jabotinsky Aviation School Officially Inaugurated," *Zionews,* 13 Feb. 1941, 4–5; "The Jewish Youth of America Wants to Fly," *Zionews,* 26 Feb. 1941, 4–5; "Keep Them Flying," *Zionews,* 2 Dec. 1941, 1; "A Mass Pilgrimage to Vladimir Jabotinsky's Grave," *Zionews,* 28 July 1941, 4; "First Anniversary of Jabotinsky's Death," *Zionews,* 11 Aug. 1941, 5; "Wings for a Jewish Army," *New York Journal-American,* 1 Dec. 1941, 11; "Jewish Youth Here Ready to Aid RAF," *New York Daily News,* 1 Dec. 1941; Dworkin interview.

88. "Graduate of Jabotinsky Aviation School Decorated for Heroism," *JTA,* 21 Apr. 1943, 4.

89. "Keep Them Flying" (pamphlet), 1/2-n, MZ; Moshe Brodetzky, inter-

view with the author, 22 Aug. 1998; Jenny Marden interview with the author, 7 Oct. 1999.

90. Netanyahu to Mirelman, 31 July 1942, 16-gimel/9, MZ.

91. Ben Ami, *Years of Wrath*, 242.

92. Netanyahu interview, 20 Mar. 1997.

93. "Jewish Army Rally Huge Success," *Zionews*, 30 June 1941, 6–7; "In the New Zionist Movement," *Zionews*, 28 July 1941, 7.

94. "Report on Actions of N.Z.O.A. for Aug. 1942–June 1943," 16-gimel/2, MZ.

95. Hecht, *Child of the Century*, 540–41.

96. Netanyahu interview, 25 June 1997.

Chapter 5

1. Netanyahu interview, 25 June 1997.

2. Jabotinsky to Dayag, 4 Sept. 1943 (Palestine Censorship file), FO 371/40129, PRO.

3. "A Zionist Army?" (editorial), *NYT,* 22 Jan. 1942, 16; "A Jewish Army" (editorial), *PM,* 23 Jan. 1942, 4.

4. "The New Zionism" (editorial), *NR*, 8 Mar. 1943, 303–4.

5. Henderson (Foreign Office) to Baker (Colonial Office), 28 Nov. 1945, CO 733/461/75872/14C, PRO.

6. F. B. A. Randall (British Consulate-General, New York) to A. S. Tandy (British Embassy, Washington, D.C.), 20 Mar. 1946, FO 371/52568, PRO.

7. Rabinowitz autobiography, 111–12.

8. For examples of Rabinowitz's typically whirlwind schedule, see Rabinowitz to Merlin, 19 June 1942, Rabinowitz to Merlin, 7 July 1942, "Report: June 19th–June 26th [1942]," and Rabinowitz to Bergson, 5 July 1943, all in Baruch Rabinowitz Papers, privately held by the Rabinowitz family.

9. Hadassah Minutes, 17 Dec. 1941, 75, HA.

10. "Army Plan Approved" (letters), *NYT,* 26 Jan. 1942, 14; Embassy to Foreign Office, 2 July 1942, FOR 371/31379, PRO.

11. Hadassah Minutes, 14 Jan. 1942, 103.

12. Hadassah Minutes, 28 Jan. 1942, 114.

13. Ibid., 113.

14. Hadassah Minutes, 5 May 1942, 228.

15. Lourie to Wechsler, 6 Jan. and 26 Jan. 1942, 1:6, PSGP.

16. "Nazis Execute 52,000 Jews in Kief; Smaller Pogroms in Other Cities,"

JTA, 16 Nov. 1941, 1; "Germans Impose Mass Death on Red Prisoners and Poles," *Life*, 23 Feb. 1942, 26–27.

17. Halifax to Eden, 13 Jan. 1943, FO 371/35031, PRO.

18. Ibid.

19. Penkower, *The Jews Were Expendable*, 16; *Foreign Relations of the United States—Diplomatic Papers: Volume 3, 1942* (Washington, D.C.: Government Printing Office, 1969), 549–50. Murray's 2 June 1942 memorandum on the subject to FDR is quoted in Joseph B. Schechtman, *The United States and the Jewish State Movement* (New York: Herzl Press, 1966), 50.

20. Ben-Ami, *Years of Wrath*, 248.

21. Halifax to Eden, 13 Jan. and 15 Jan. 1943, FO 371/35031, PRO; Netanyahu interview, 25 June 1997.

22. Ben-Ami, *Years of Wrath*, 284.

23. Hecht, *Child of the Century*, 516.

24. "A Report on the War-Time and Post-War Activities of the New Zionist Organization of America and the United Zionists-Revisionists, November 22, 1946," 3, 16-gimel/9, MZ.

25. Mendelsohn to Mirelman, 8 Sept. 1942, ibid.

26. Monty N. Penkower, *The Holocaust and Israel Reborn* (Urbana and Chicago: University of Illinois Press, 1994), 64.

27. Ben-Ami, *Years of Wrath*, 251.

28. Netanyahu interview, 25 June 1997; Mendelsohn to Villa, 2 Feb. 1943, and Katz to Mirelman, 10 Mar. 1943, 16-gimel/9, MZ.

29. Netanyahu interview, 25 June 1997.

30. Sharon Kay Smith, "Elbert D. Thomas and America's Response to the Holocaust" (Ph.D. diss., Brigham Young University, 1992), 59–60, 70, 79–80, 93.

31. Netanyahu interview, 25 June 1997.

32. Ibid.

33. Ibid.

34. "Campaign for Representation Launched," *Zionews*, 1 Dec. 1942, 3, 6, 26; "Zionists Demand National Status," *NYT*, 18 Nov. 1942, 17.

35. "European Jewish Holocaust Fails to Arouse Nations," *Zionews*, 1 Dec. 1942, 5; Netanyahu to Mirelman, 19 Nov. 1942, 16-gimel/9, MZ.

36. Hecht, *Child of the Century*, 518–19.

37. "For Sale to Humanity: 70,000 Jews, Guaranteed Human Beings at $50 Apiece" (advertisement), *NYT*, 16 Feb. 1943, 11.

38. "Down with Fascism Forever, Is Cry of 1943" (editorial), *National Jewish*

Monthly, January 1943, 145; "A People in Mourning" (editorial), *Jewish Spectator,* January 1943, 4–5.

39. "Rumor behind the News," *Hamigdal* 3 (April 1943): 14; "Tuesday to Be Day of Prayer for Jews," *NYT,* 6 Mar. 1943, 8; "Report on Attempts to Stage *We Will Never Die* in Kingston, Rochester, Buffalo, Baltimore, Gary, and Pittsburgh," 13:57, PSGP; Merlin to Ziff, 23 Apr. 1943, 1:8, PSGP.

40. Rafaeli, *Dream and Action,* 109.

41. Halifax to Eden, 25 May 1943, FO 371/35035, PRO.

42. "To the Gentlemen at Bermuda" (advertisement), *Washington Post,* 20 Apr. 1943, 10; *NYT,* 4 May 1943, 17.

43. "Memorandum for Mr. Ladd," 12 May 1943, from files of the Federal Bureau of Investigation made available to the author under the provisions of the Freedom of Information and Privacy Acts [hereafter FBI Files]. The "Cruel Mockery" advertisement also taught Bergson an important lesson in political manners. Since the ad appeared under the auspices of the Committee for a Jewish Army, Bergson saw nothing wrong in listing the committee's sponsors, including U.S. senators and representatives, even though he did not apprise them of the text in advance. Several U.S. senators, including Harry S Truman, immediately denounced Bergson and dissociated themselves from the ad, and Bergson was compelled to publicly apologize.

44. "Bermuda Conferees Agree to Another Conference," Independent Jewish Press Service, 30 Apr. 1943, 3; "Failure in Bermuda" (editorial), *Opinion,* May 1943, 4.

45. "Rumor behind the News," *Hamigdal* 3 (April 1943): 14; "Mass Action" (editorial), Independent Jewish Press Service, 12 Mar. 1943, 4-c.

46. Saadia Gelb, "The Conference to the Rescue," *Furrows* 2 (December 1943): 9–11.

47. "Annual Report to the Zionist Organization of America—47th Annual Convention, October 14–17, 1944, Atlantic City, New Jersey," p. 59, CZA 1753.

48. Pierre van Paassen, "Israel, You Are Being Betrayed!" *Zionews,* 1 Oct. 1942, 17.

49. Netanyahu interview, 25 June 1997; "Massacred by Foe, Ignored by Friend, a People Appeals to the Conscience of America" (advertisement), *NYT,* 23 Feb. 1943, 13.

50. Netanyahu interview, 25 June 1997.

51. *NYT,* 3 Jan. 1944, 12; *NYP,* 3 Jan. 1944, 21; *NYP,* 29 Feb. 1944, 8; *NYP,* 14 Mar. 1944, 35; *NR,* 23 Mar. 1944, 13; *NYP,* 9 May 1944, 19; *Washington Post,* 17 May 1944, 6; *NYP,* 18 July 1944, 17; *Chicago Daily News,* 18 July 1944, 13; *NYT,*

19 July 1944, 12; *Chicago Daily Sun,* 26 Nov. 1944, 11; *Der Tog,* 27 Nov. 1944, 8; *NYP,* 14 Dec. 1944, 18.

52. Halifax to Eden, 25 May 1943, FO 371/35035, PRO.

53. Unsigned [Netanyahu] to Mirelman, 12 June 1944, 16-gimel/9, MZ.

54. "Mr. Churchill, Drop the Mandate!" (advertisement), *NYT,* 18 May 1943, 15.

55. According to Eliahu Ben-Horin, "the owners of the paper, being assimilationist Jews, are of course more Catholic than the Pope," and insisted on softening the text of the NZOA's Churchill ad prior to its appearance in the *Times* (Ben-Horin to Patterson, 13 Apr. 1943, 16-gimel/1, MZ). However, according to Benzion Netanyahu, no changes were requested or made (Netanyahu interview, 25 June 1997).

56. "A Forgotten People" (editorial), *Reconstructionist,* 30 Apr. 1943, 3; "An Appeal for Zionist Unity" (editorial), *Reconstructionist,* 2 Mar. 1943, 5–6.

57. Wise to Goldmann, 4 Aug. 1943, Box 109, SWP; *Foreign Relations of the United States—Diplomatic Papers: Volume 4, 1943* (Washington, D.C.: Government Printing Office, 1969), 802–3; Murray to Hull, 16 Aug. and 17 Aug. 1943, and Murray to Long, 25 Oct. 1944, 867N.01/1908, NA; Morgenthau-Cohen-Weisgal talk, 4 Aug. 1943, Z5/387, CZA, and Goldmann to Wise, 5 Aug. and 8 Aug. 1943, Z5/1216, CZA, cited in Penkower, *The Holocaust and Israel Reborn,* 159, 162, and 173 n. 39.

58. Akzin to Monsky, 18 Jan. 1943, 8/15-peh, BAP.

59. Monsky to Sperber, 21 Jan. 43, 16-gimel/1, MZ; Levinthal to Akzin, 18 May 1943, 12/4/5-gimel, BAP; Isaac Neustadt-Noy, "The Unending Task: Efforts to Unite American Jewry from the American Jewish Congress to the American Jewish Conference" (Ph.D. diss., Brandeis University, 1976), 272–74.

60. Bromfield et al. to Hughes, 12 June 1943, and Keane to Hughes, 12 July 1943, Correspondence Files "E," Box 53, Langston Hughes Papers, Yale University Library.

61. Embassy (Hayter) to North American Department, 9 Sept. 1943, Foreign Office, FO 371/35038, PRO.

62. Akzin to The Presidency, 2 June 1940, 16/15-peh, BAP.

63. Murray Everett, "Inside and Out," *New Leader,* 8 Apr. 1944, 10.

64. This estimate is based on a combination of the slightly varying population figures listed in *Statistical Abstract of Palestine—1942* (Jerusalem: Palestine Government, 1942), 12; *General Monthly Bulletin of Current Statistics,* April 1943, 76; and *Report of the Jewish Agency for Palestine—1940* (Jerusalem: Jewish Agency for Palestine, 1941), 14.

65. Emanuel Neumann, "A Territorial Solution," *Palestine Review*, 10 Feb. 1939, 682–83; "Hapitaron Hasofi," *HaBoker*, 8 Feb. 1939, 2, 5. Netanyahu gave Jabotinsky a copy of his Zangwill book shortly after it appeared. Some years later, according to Netanyahu, Joseph Schechtman told Netanyahu that in mid-1939 Jabotinsky authored an article, in a Yiddish newspaper in Poland, entitled "A Talk with Zangwill," which, in discussing the book, seemed to express sympathy with Zangwill's view of the Arabs—a shift that surprised Schechtman, since Jabotinsky had never before advocated transferring Arabs out of Palestine. Schechtman ascribed Jabotinsky's shift to Netanyahu's influence (Netanyahu interview, 25 June 1997).

66. Resolutions of the NZOA Convention, Manhattan Center, February 21–23, 1942, as published in *Zionews*, 6 Mar. 1942, 8.

67. Another endorser of the Arab transfer idea was the former U.S. ambassador to the Soviet Union and France, William Bullitt, who unveiled his views on the subject at an April 1944 NZOA dinner. See William C. Bullitt, "A Constructive Solution," in *The American-British Convention on Palestine* (New York: New Zionist Organization of America, 1945), 25–30; "U.S. Urged to Face Palestine Issues," *NYT*, 24 Apr. 1944, 6.

68. Hayim Greenberg, "The Irresponsible Revisionists," *Jewish Frontier* 10 (November 1943): 6–8; Meir Grossman, "A Fair Solution of the Arab-Jewish Conflict," *Hamigdal* 4 (December 1943): 6–7, 9; Meir Grossman, "Extremism versus Realism," *Hamigdal* 4 (May 1944): 6–7. A passing reference to the resettlement committee's ad—but without specifically mentioning the ad or its sponsor—appeared in an essay by Dr. Israel Goldstein, president of the ZOA: "Zionist Discipline," *NP*, 21 Jan. 1944, 205. For a full discussion of American Zionist attitudes toward the transfer concept and the Palestinian Arab issue generally, see Rafael Medoff, *Zionism and the Arabs: An American Jewish Dilemma, 1898–1948* (Westport, Conn.: Praeger, 1997).

69. For details of Silver's ascent in 1943, see Marc Lee Raphael, *Abba Hillel Silver: A Profile in American Judaism* (New York: Holmes and Meier, 1989), 81–89.

70. British Foreign Office memorandum, "Palestine," 21 Aug. 1943, File: ABC 383. 7–28 January 1944, Box 396, Entry 421, RG 165, NA.

71. George V. Strong, "Memorandum for the Chief of Staff: Subject: The Arab-Jewish Controversy," 5 Aug. 1943, ibid.

72. For the full story of the proposed joint Anglo-American statement, see Penkower, *The Holocaust and Israel Reborn*, 145–76. Also see "Rumor Washington Urging Delay in American Jewish Conference," Independent Jewish Press Service, 16 Aug. 1943, 1; Ben-Ami to Bergson, 13 Aug. 1943, File 21/3/3: "Com-

mittee for a Jewish Army—New York: Formation of a Free Palestine Commit- tee and American League for a Free Palestine, Sept. 1943–1944," MZ; Morris D. Waldman, *Nor by Power* (New York: International Universities Press, 1953), 257–58, 262; Herbert Parzen, "The Roosevelt Palestine Policy, 1943–1945: An Exercise in Dual Diplomacy," *American Jewish Archives* 64 (April 1974): 33–35; and Neustadt-Noy, "Unending Task," 315–16, 320.

73. Rafaeli letter to the author, 21 Feb. 1996; Samuel Margoshes, "Zionist Ire at White Paper Boils in Geneva," *New York Herald Tribune,* 21 Aug. 1939, 1–2.

74. For the Bergsonites' self-perception as being in a position of weak- ness, see Fineman to Bergson, 8 Jan. 1943, 1:7, PSGP. For details of the nego- tiations, see "First Proposal Made by the Committee for a Jewish Army to the Emergency Committee on Zionist Affairs," 3 Dec. 1941, 1:5, PSGP; Lourie to Wechsler, 6 Jan. and 26 Jan. 1942, 1:6, PSGP.

75. Embassy to North American Department, Foreign Office, 14 Oct. 1943, FO 371/35040, PRO.

76. Silver's Confidential Washington Diary, entry for 11 Oct. 1943, 3–4, AHSP.

77. Selden interview with the author, 20 Feb. 1996.

78. For example, Manson to Montor, 30 Nov. 1943, Z5/919, CZA. Some of their tactics were quite creative. One of Silver's additions to the staff, Leon Feuer, once concocted a scheme to have a group of Jewish congressmen stage a fake hearing, with Bergson as the sole invited guest. If Bergson, suspecting a trap, failed to show up, that could be used against him. If he did show up, the congressmen would proceed to pepper him with embarrassing questions sup- plied by the AZEC, and the answers could be used to erode sympathy for the Bergson group on Capitol Hill. The meeting took place, but the proceedings were not as confrontational as Feuer had hoped. See Feuer to Silver, 10 May 1944, 12 June 1944, File: II-6, HMP. For more on their anti-Bergson activities, see AZEC Minutes, 5 June 1944, Z5/1208, CZA.

79. Silver to Netanyahu, 2 Nov. 1945, File 4-3-3, AHSP; Silver to Goldstein, 26 Jan. 1944, F38/559, CZA.

80. Lourie to Silver, 16 Dec. 1943, and Silver to Lourie, 23 Dec. 1943, File I-37, HMP.

81. The Stern Group, officially known as the Fighters for the Freedom of Israel (Hebrew acronym: LEHI), was a militant offshoot of the Irgun. Wise used the phrase "American Irgunism and ZOA Sternism" in a letter to the editor of the *National Jewish Post,* 16 Sept. 1946, Box 109, SWP. In the pub- lished version of the letter, however, the words "ZOA Sternism" were omitted; whether it was Wise who deleted them or the editor is unclear. "Rabbi Wise

Defends Nahum Goldmann, Jewish Agency, Charges Post Aiding U.S. Irgun Representatives," *National Jewish Post*, 11 Oct. 1946, 10.

82. Minutes, ZOA Executive Committee Meeting, 19 Dec. 1944, 109–10, F38/71, CZA.

83. Wise to Frankfurter, 19 May 1943, Box 109, SWP.

84. Zvi Ganin, "Activism versus Moderation: The Conflict between Abba Hillel Silver and Stephen Wise during the 1940s," *Studies in Zionism* 5 (Spring 1984): 92.

85. Neumann to Netanyahu, 14 Dec. 1944, A123/307, CZA.

86. Silver to Neumann, 16 Aug. 1944, A123/315, CZA.

87. Wise to Szold, 11 July 1946, Reel 2399, SWP; Wise to Frankfurter, 18 Oct. and 21 Oct. 1946, and Wise to Goldman, 29 Mar. 1944, Box 109, SWP. Ordinarily, one would assume that Wise did not mean to refer to a literal danger to his life; yet in 1944, Wise told John Pehle, executive director of the War Refugee Board, "that he had told his family that if he were found dead in the alley some night that they would know who did it and that he seriously felt that [Peter] Bergson might kill him." Morgenthau Diaries, Book 735, p. 60, FDRL.

88. Nahum Goldmann, *The Autobiography of Nahum Goldmann: Sixty Years of Jewish Life* (New York: Holt, Rinehart and Winston, 1969), 227.

89. Mendelsohn to Silver, 5 Oct. and 25 Oct. 1943, S5/681, MZ.

90. Netanyahu to Silver, 3 Nov. 1943, 16-gimel/11, MZ; Netanyahu interview, 25 June 1997.

91. Minutes of Hadassah National Board meeting, 22 Dec. 1943, HA.

92. Ibid.; Minutes of AZEC Meeting, 29 Nov. 1943, AHSP.

93. Minutes of AZEC Meeting, 29 Nov. 1943, AHSP.

94. Goldmann to Nathan, 8 June 1944, Z5/345, MZ.

95. Wise, Silver, Lipsky, and Goldmann to Shertok, 16 Nov. 1943, s5/777, CZA; Silver repeated this argument in AZEC Meeting Minutes, 13 Dec. 1943, AHSP.

96. Netanyahu to Akzin, 13 Jan. 1944, 8/15-peh, BAP; Akzin to "Kop[elo-witz]," 5 Apr. 1944, 14/4/5-gimel, BAP; Netanyahu to Katz, 25 Oct. 1944, 5/16-gimel, MZ; Text of cables in Hadassah Board minutes, 22 Dec. 1943, HA; Lourie to Silver, 6 Dec. 1943, File I-37, HMP; AZEC Minutes, 24 Feb. 1947, AHSP. For Silver's dismay at the delay in the Jewish Agency's endorsement of admitting the Revisionists in the autumn of 1946 (and an attempt by Emanuel Neumann to have them "provisionally admitted" even prior to the Agency's approval), see Wise to Goldmann, 11 Sept. 1946, Box 109, SWP. Doreen Bierbrier ("The American Zionist Emergency Council: An Analysis of a Pressure Group," *American Jewish History* 60 [September 1970]: 101) incorrectly states

that "the Revisionists joined the AZEC early in 1945"; the organization that was admitted was the small Jewish State Party, a group that had broken away from the Revisionists back in 1933 and, having no history of conflict with the established Zionist organizations, encountered no difficulties when it applied for membership in the AZEC in the spring of 1945. AZEC Minutes, 30 May 1945, AHSP.

Chapter 6

1. Irving Howe, *World of Our Fathers* (New York: Harcourt Brace Jovanovich, 1976), 393.

2. Melvin J. Lasky, "The Shame of a World," *New Leader,* 23 Oct. 1943, 2.

3. Oral History Interview with Irving Bunim, Yeshiva University Library, New York, 16–17, made available through the courtesy of Rabbi Moshe Kolodny, Agudath Israel Archives, New York.

4. Hecht, *Child of the Century,* 580–82; David S. Wyman, *The Abandonment of the Jews* (New York: Pantheon, 1984), 156; "My Uncle Abraham Reports . . ." (advertisement), *NR,* 22 Nov. 1943, 698.

5. Ben-Ami, *Years of Wrath,* 292.

6. Henderson (Foreign Office) to Baker (Colonial Office), 28 Nov. 1945, CO 733/461/75872/14C, PRO.

7. Shalom Wurm, "When the Leaders Fail," *Furrows* 2 (January 1944): 14–17.

8. Eri Jabotinsky, untitled memorandum, Dec. 9, 1943, File: Emergency Committee to Save the Jewish People of Europe, Serial 87—Jabotinsky, Eri, 1943–1945; 8/10/11, MZ.

9. Morgenthau Diaries, Book 694, p. 97, FDRL.

10. John Morton Blum, ed., *The Price of Vision: The Diary of Henry Wallace, 1942–1946* (Boston: Houghton Mifflin, 1973), 211, 265 n. 1.

11. Morgenthau Diaries, Book 694, pp. 195, 202, FDRL.

12. Ibid., Book 707, pp. 220–21.

13. For details of the circumstances surrounding Morgenthau's action, see Wyman, *Abandonment of the Jews,* 178–92.

14. The "nuisance" characterization appears in an editorial note in Bergson's publication, *The Answer* (12 Feb. 1944, 3).

15. Blum, *Price of Vision,* 313.

16. Ibid., 265 n. 1; T. R. B., "Washington Notes: Political Jitters," *NR,* 10 Apr. 1944, 500.

17. Unsigned to Sperber, 29 June 1944, 6/16-gimel, MZ; Netanyahu to

Klinger, 26 July 1944, 16-gimel/4, MZ; Pepper to Mendelsohn, 23 July 1944, Brewster to Mendelsohn, 11 July 1944, and Landon to Mendelsohn, 21 Aug 1944, 16-gimel/3, MZ.

18. Unsigned [Netanyahu] to Mirelman, 12 June 1944, 16-gimel/9, MZ.

19. Mendelsohn to Johannesburg, Hamashkif, Mirelman, and Standard (telegram), n.d. [June 1944], 16-gimel/11, MZ; "Republican Plank on Palestine Preceded by NZOA Political Campaign," *Zionews*, July 1944, 3.

20. Netanyahu interview, 26 June 1997. Luce was also friendly with Ben Hecht and the Bergson group. See Hecht to Luce, 9 July 1946, and Luce to Hecht, 11 July 1946, File: Public Service—Congressional Correspondence, June 1946 Heb—Hee, Clare Booth Luce Papers, LC.

21. Untitled editorial, *Zionewsletter* [London], 22 Sept. 1944, 7, 16-gimel/4, MZ.

22. For details of Silver's contacts regarding the Republican platform, see Raphael, *Abba Hillel Silver*, 108–15.

23. Netanyahu interview, 25 June 1997.

24. Raphael, *Abba Hillel Silver*, 112.

25. Ibid., 113.

26. Netanyahu interview, 25 June 1997.

27. "Spokesman for Zionism," *NZOA Bulletin*, 20 July 1944, 1, 16-gimel/1, MZ.

28. Neumann to Netanyahu, 20 Nov. 1944, and Netanyahu to Neumann, 4 Dec. 1944, A123/307, CZA; Mendelsohn to Walff, 28 June 1944, 5/16-gimel, MZ.

29. NZOA Press Statement, 20 Sept. 1944, 16-gimel/9, MZ. For a full analysis of the factors leading to the establishment of the Jewish Brigade, see Penkower, *The Jews Were Expendable*, 3–29.

30. Marie Syrkin, e.g., in "Free Port" (*Jewish Frontier*, July 1944, 6–8), charged that the shelter was "impressive neither as a practical measure of alleviation nor even as a gesture."

31. "Memorandum," n.d. [1944], 16-gimel/2, MZ; Mendelsohn to Landon, 7 Sept 1944, 16-gimel/9, MZ.

32. NZOA Press Statement and "We Regret, Mr. President!" (open letter), 1 Nov. 1944, 16-gimel/9, MZ; Netanyahu interview with the author, 25 May 2000.

33. Richard O. Davies, *Defender of the Old Guard: John Bricker and American Politics* (Columbus: Ohio State University Press, 1993), 100–101.

34. Quoted in "Zionism in the United States," *Review of the Foreign Press—Series N: The Near and Middle East*, 7 Feb. 1945, 22.

35. Shultz to Weisgal, 16 Aug. 1944, z5/868, CZA.

36. "Pete Bergson Gives Birth to a Nation" (editorial), Independent Jewish Press Service, 26 May 1944, 3A–5A. For a detailed exposition of the "Hebrews" theory, see Horon (pseud.), "The Hebrew Movement: An Outline," 12:40, PSGP.

37. Ben-Ami, *Years of Wrath*, 295.

38. A. H. Tandy, British Embassy, 10 Sept. 1945, "Memorandum on Jewish Affairs in the United States at the Termination of the World War," CO 733/463/75842/134, PRO.

39. Akzin to Pepper, 23 Jan. 1945, 17/15-peh, BAP; Akzin to Lesser, 29 June 1944, and John Pehle, "Memorandum for the Files," 24 June 1944, 16/15-peh, MZ; David S. Wyman, "Why Auschwitz Was Never Bombed," *Commentary* 65 (May 1978): 37–38; Oral History Interview with Irving Bunim, Yeshiva University Library, New York, 16, made available through the courtesy of Rabbi Moshe Kolodny, Agudath Israel Archives, New York.

40. For examples of NZOA groups selling tickets for the Emergency Committee's program about European Jewry, the "Show of Shows," see "Local Activities," *Bulletin of NZO*, 9 Mar. 1944, IV, 16-gimel/5, MZ.

41. Netanyahu to Mirelman, 19 May 1944, 16-gimel/9, MZ.

42. Netanyahu to Macy, 10 July 1945, 16-gimel/11, MZ.

43. Steiner to Netanyahu, 2 June 1944, 16-gimel/5, MZ.

44. *NZOA Bulletin*, 24 June 1944, 4–5, 16-gimel/1, MZ; Netanyahu interview, 25 June 1997; "NZO Refusal to Support Hebrew Liberation Committee Leads to Split in Party," *JTA*, 25 June 1944, 3.

Chapter 7

1. Wise to Goldmann, 4 Aug. 1943, Box 109, SWP.

2. Embassy to Foreign Office, 24 May 1944, FO 371/40131, PRO.

3. Silver to Wise, 18 Aug. 1944, A123/315, CZA.

4. Silver to Neumann, 22 Aug. 1944, ibid.

5. AZEC Executive Committee Minutes, 31 Aug. 1944, 11 Sept. 1944, in "AZEC Minutes—Executive Committee, 9/28/43–12/11/43," Box LX:4, Zionist Archives, New York City; Ganin, "Activism versus Moderation," 78–79; Wyman, *Abandonment of the Jews*, 253.

6. Netanyahu interview, 25 June 1997.

7. Isaiah Berlin, *Zionist Politics in Wartime Washington: A Fragment of Personal Reminiscence—The Yaacov Herzog Memorial Lecture* (Jerusalem: Hebrew University, 1972), 37.

8. ZOA Executive Committee Minutes, 19 Dec. 1944, CZA.

9. For background on the events leading up to Silver's resignation, see Raphael, *Abba Hillel Silver*, 118–34; Aaron Berman, *Nazism, the Jews, and American Zionism, 1933–1948* (Detroit: Wayne State University Press, 1990), 132–35; and Ganin, "Activism versus Moderation."

10. Murray to Hull, 19 Dec. 1944, *Foreign Relations of the United States—Diplomatic Papers, Volume 5, 1944* (Washington, D.C.: Government Printing Office, 1969), 651–52.

11. Van Paassen to Silver, 6 Jan. 1945, A123/103, CZA.

12. *Foreign Relations of the United States—Diplomatic Papers, Volume 8, 1945* (Washington, D.C.: Government Printing Office, 1969), 710–12.

13. Ibid., 711.

14. Mendelsohn to Villa, 2 Apr. 1945, 16-gimel/11, MZ.

15. Netanyahu to Levine, 2 Feb. 1945, 16-gimel/3, MZ.

16. "NZO Delegation to San Francisco," *NZOA Bulletin*, June 1945, 1–5; Netanyahu to NZO, New York [telegram], 23 May 1945, 16-gimel/5, MZ.

17. "Palestine as an International Ward Asked by World New Zionist Group," *NYT*, 17 May 1945, 9; "Senators Appeal on Palestine," *NYP*, 23 May 1945, 5.

18. "Note for the File" regarding the mufti (n.d. [1945]), Harry Selden Papers, privately held by the Selden Family; Harry Selden interview with the author, 7 Aug. 1997; Ganin, "Activism versus Moderation."

19. "Zionist Group Is Alarmed," *San Francisco News*, 21 May 1945, 4; Mendelsohn to Villa, 18 June 1945, 16-gimel/11, MZ; Netanyahu interview, 25 June 1997.

20. Foreign Office Minutes, 10 Sept. 1945, FO 226/277, PRO.

21. Michael J. Cohen, "The Genesis of the Anglo-American Committee on Palestine, November 1945: A Case Study in the Assertion of American Hegemony," *Historical Journal* 22 (1979): 186–207; Bevin to Halifax, 12 Oct. 1945, FO 371/45381, PRO; Halifax to Foreign Office, 27 Oct. 1945, FO 371/45382 PRO; Bartley Crum, *Behind the Silken Curtain: A Personal Account of Anglo-American Diplomacy in Palestine and the Middle East* (London: Victor Gollancz Ltd., 1947), 16.

22. Netanyahu to Jaglom, 30 Jan. 1945, 16-gimel/1, MZ; Patterson, Mendelsohn, and Friedman to Villa [telegram], 6 Aug. 1945, 16-gimel/11, MZ; Netanyahu to Mirelman, 4 Sept 1945, 16-gimel/9, MZ.

23. Netanyahu to Yahuda, 27 June 1945, 16-gimel/4, MZ.

24. Friedman and Schechtman to Netanyahu, 12 Sept. 1945, 16-gimel/11, MZ; "The London Conference," *NZOA Bulletin*, October 1945, 1.

25. "Report of the National Convention of the New Zionist Organization of America, Hotel Edison, January 5, 6, 1946," 16-gimel/9, MZ.

26. A. H. Tandy, British Embassy, Washington, D.C., "Memorandum on Jewish Affairs in the United States at the Termination of the World War," 10 Sept. 1945, CO 733/463/75842/134, PRO.

27. Leikin interview; "Why You Should Vote United Zionist-Revisionist!" (leaflet), 16-gimel/7, MZ.

28. Netanyahu interview, 25 June 1997.

29. Ibid.; "Kill That Loan!—Lest You Forsake Your Conscience" (advertisement), *NYT,* 10 July 1946, 12; Baruch Korff, *Flight from Fear* (New York: Elmar, 1953), 140–42; Akzin to Silver, 17 July 1946, 8/15/peh, BAP; Akzin to Shapiro, 7 Aug. 1946, 16/15/peh, BAP.

30. Halifax to Foreign Office, 3 Oct. 1945, FO 371/45380, PRO; Celler to Thackeray, 8 Mar. 1946, Subject File—British Loan: Correspondence November 1945–April 1946, Emanuel Celler Papers, LC; "Developing Opposition to the British Loan: Statement by Congressman Emanuel Celler," 12 Dec. 1945, ibid.

31. Akzin to Shapiro, 7 Aug. 1946, 16/15-peh, BAP. Ironically, just three years earlier, Bloom had privately denounced Wise (to Vice President Henry Wallace) as a "racketeer" and "troublemaker" (Blum, *Price of Vision,* 193–94).

32. Wise to Frankfurter, 11 July 1946, Box 109, SWP; Carl Alpert, "Another Zionist Munich," *Jewish Post,* 13 Sept. 1946, 6.

33. Raphael, *Abba Hillel Silver,* 141–42; Wise to David Niles, 18 June 1946, and Wise to Lady Eva Reading, 10 July 1946, in Carl Hermann Voss, ed., *Stephen S. Wise: Servant of the People—Selected Letters* (Philadelphia: Jewish Publication Society of America, 1969), 273–74.

34. Akzin to Silver, 17 July 1946, 8/15-peh, BAP.

35. "Our Battle for Jewish Statehood: Text of Political Addresses by Dr. Abba Hillel Silver—49th Annual Convention of the Zionist Organization of America, Atlantic City, New Jersey, October 25 to 28, 1946" (New York: Zionist Organization of America, 1946), 8.

36. David Krakow interview with the author, 3 Jan. 1996; Netanyahu interview, 26 June 1997.

37. *New Zionist,* [1946], 16-gimel/10, MZ.

38. *Bulletin of the Organization Committee of the United Zionists-Revisionists of America* [hereafter *Bulletin of the UZRA*], September 1946, 1–5.

39. "Organizational Activities," *Bulletin of the UZRA,* 31 Mar. 1947, 5–6.

40. Netanyahu interview, 25 June 1997.

41. Ibid.

42. Allen H. Podet, "Anti-Zionism in a Key United States Diplomat: Loy Henderson at the End of World War II," *American Jewish Archives* 30 (November 1978): 155–87; Netanyahu interview, 25 June 1997.

43. Department of State Memorandum of Conversation, "United Zionists Revisionists of America," with Saltzman, Hulick, Netanyahu, and Propes participating, 27 Oct. 1947, 800.4089/10-2747, NA; Netanyahu and Schechtman to Armour, 2 Mar. 1948, Netanyahu and Schechtman to Bohlen, 2 Mar. 1948, and Armour to Schechtman, 10 Mar. 1948, 867N.01/3-248, NA; Netanyahu interview, 26 June 1997.

Chapter 8

1. Selden interview with the author, 30 Aug. 1993; Leibel to Tourover, 28 Apr. 1944, Box 1, Folder 3, DTEP.

2. For early attempts at pressuring supporters of Bergson's first group, the Committee for a Jewish Army of Stateless and Palestinian Jews, see Kahn to Earle, 18 Apr. 1940, Box 1, Folder 4, PSGP. For Stephen Wise's efforts to convince would-be participants in the 1943 Emergency Conference to Save the Jewish People of Europe to withdraw, see Wyman, *Abandonment of the Jews*, 144. For Wise's pressure on Interior Secretary Harold Ickes to spurn the chairmanship of the Washington, D.C., chapter of the Emergency Committee to Save the Jewish People of Europe, see Wise to Ickes, [27] Dec. 1943, Box 1, Folder 10, PSGP. For details of AZEC's pressure on Wendell Willkie and Jewish members of Congress to distance themselves from Bergson, see Minutes of AZEC Executive Committee Meeting, 15 May 1944, AZEC Papers, CZA. For references to efforts to pressure American Liberal Party leader Dean Alfange and other ALFP supporters to withdraw, see Minutes of AZEC Executive Committee Meeting, 5 June 1944, AZEC Papers, CZA. For Nahum Goldmann's frustration at his inability to persuade Representative Rogers to drop out of the Bergson group, see Memorandum of Conversation with Nahum Goldmann, 19 May 1944, 867N.01/2347/PS/LC, NA. For the successful effort to woo actor Edward G. Robinson away from the Bergsonites, see Robinson's autobiography, *All My Yesterdays* (New York: Hawthorne Books, 1973), 176.

The possibility that the ALFP had somehow fabricated Mrs. Brandeis's endorsements may have seemed plausible to the established Jewish leadership because of a related flap concerning the Bergson group's full-page ad in the *New York Times* after the 1943 Bermuda refugee conference. The thirty-three U.S. senators whose names appeared in the ad had not been consulted specifically about its text; they had signed on, a year or so earlier, as endorsers of Bergson's campaign for the creation of a Jewish army to fight against the Nazis. Since the Bermuda ad was officially sponsored by the same Bergson group, the Committee for a Jewish Army of Stateless and Palestinian Jews, the senators' names duly appeared as part of the committee's list of supporters. Although only a few of the thirty-three senators publicly dissociated themselves from the Bermuda ad, the incident gave Bergson's critics plenty of ammunition. Jewish leaders no doubt believed they had a similar case of Bergsonite misrepresentation on their hands when, in April 1944, they first heard rumors of Alice Brandeis's association with the ALFP. *NYT,* 4 May 1943, 17; "Refugee Parley 'Ad' Criticized in Senate," *NYT,* 7 May 1943, 3.

3. Leibel to Tourover, 28 Apr. 1944, Box 1, Folder 3, DTEP. After Mrs. Brandeis became a member of the Emergency Committee in 1943, her name appeared on its letterhead (Selden interview, 30 Aug. 1993), a fact mentioned by Murray Everett in his *New Leader* column, "Inside and Out," 8 Apr. 1944, 10; Tourover to Leibel, 29 Apr. 1944, 2 May 1944, Box 1, Folder 3, DTEP.

4. Leibel to Tourover, 26 May 1944, Brandeis to Bergson (draft), 28 May 1944, Tourover to Leibel, 29 May 1944, Shulman to Tourover, 31 May 1944, and Lourie to Tourover, 5 June 1944, Box 1, Folder 3, DTEP; "Mrs. Brandeis No Sponsor," *NYT,* 3 June 1944, 15.

5. Wilf to Brandeis, 3 June 1944, Tourover to Feuer, 5 June 1944, Tourover to Szold, 5 June 1944, Selden to Brandeis, 6 June 1944, Tourover to Szold, 6 June 1944, Tourover to Leibel, 8 June 1944, Tourover to Szold, 8 June 1944, and Manson to Tourover, 19 June 1944, Box 1, Folder 3, DTEP; "Mrs. Brandeis Explains," *NYT,* 8 June 1944, 19.

6. Carl Alpert interview with the author, 28 Feb. 1997.

7. "Americans Answer a Call for Life and Liberation" (advertisement), *NR,* 19 June 1944, 812–13; "With the ALFP: Los Angeles Division News," *The Answer,* 21 Nov. 1947, 7; "Successful Rogers Dinner in L.A.," *The Answer,* 2 Jan. 1948, 7; Sy Dill interview with the author, 19 Mar. 1997; "Build Dov Gruner's Memorial" (advertisement), *NYP,* 18 Apr. 1947, 40; Micah Naftalin interview with the author, 14 Mar. 2000; Arthur Naftalin interview with the author, 14 Mar. 2000.

8. Paul O'Dwyer, *Counsel for the Defense: The Autobiography of Paul O'Dwyer* (New York: Simon and Schuster, 1979), 154.

9. New York FBI to Washington, D.C., FBI Headquarters, 14 May 1948, FBI Files.

10. Doris Baer interview with the author, 21 Nov. 1996.

11. Dill interview.

12. Rabinowitz autobiography, 197–98.

13. Hecht, *Child of the Century*, 610–12; Paul Gropman interview with the author, 7 Oct. 1999.

14. Rabinowitz autobiography, 193–95.

15. Chancery (British Embassy, Washington, D.C.) to the Eastern Department, Foreign Office, 6 Aug. 1945, FO 371/45599-X/M928, PRO.

16. *American League for a Free Palestine Private News Letter*, 12 Aug. 1946; Selden interview, 7 Aug. 1997.

17. *American League for a Free Palestine Private News Letter*, 8 Aug. 1946; Ben-Ami, *Years of Wrath*, 381; Selden interview, 7 Aug. 1997.

18. Ben-Ami, *Years of Wrath*, 381–82; Selden interview, 7 Aug. 1997.

19. *American League for a Free Palestine Private News Letter*, 23 Sept. 1946; Ben-Ami, *Years of Wrath*, 382.

20. ALFP press release, 9 Sept. 1946.

21. *American League for a Free Palestine Private News Letter*, 12 Sept. 1946; ALFP press release, 16 Nov. 1946.

22. Albert Liss interview with the author, 10 Apr. 1997; Leo Halpert interview with the author, 3 Sept. 1997. When ALFP staff member Paul Gropman organized showings of the film at hotels in the Catskills mountains during the summer of 1947, the speeches were given by a young Bergson-group militant who called himself "Zvi Ben-Ami." (Gropman interview.)

23. Minutes of the Pennsylvania State Board of Censors (RG-22), 20 Jan. 1948, Pennsylvania State Archives, Harrisburg.

24. For a discussion of the broader issues involved in the uses of pageantry by Jewish political groups during the 1930s and 1940s, see Stephen J. Whitfield, "The Politics of Pageantry, 1936–1946," *American Jewish History* 84 (September 1996): 221–51.

25. Marlon Brando with Robert Lindsey, *Songs My Mother Taught Me* (New York: Random House, 1994), 107.

26. For a comprehensive chart listing the leaders of the various Bergson groups, see "Board List 1946–1947," American League for a Free Palestine Collection, AJHS.

27. Brando, *Songs*, 108. Brando's sympathy for the Irgun was genuine, if short-lived, his ex-wife Anna Kashfi later wrote; "I think Marlon was sincere in this and other causes he later espoused. But sincerity for Marlon is like a signal flare—it shines intensely for a moment but is soon lost in the night." Anna Kashfi Brando and E. P. Stein, *Brando for Breakfast* (New York: Crown, 1979), 33.

28. Jerome Lawrence, *Actor: The Life and Times of Paul Muni* (New York:

Putnam, 1974), 291–95; Hecht, *Child of the Century,* 508–9. The account found in Charles Higham's *Brando: The Unauthorized Biography* (New York and Scarborough, Ont.: New American Library, 1987) appears to confuse the 1946 game with a celebrity baseball game organized by Hecht back in 1935.

29. Brando, *Songs,* 108; Maurice Rosenblatt interview with the author, 3 Feb. 1997.

30. *American League for a Free Palestine Private News Letter,* 8 Aug. 1946.

31. Consul-General, New York (Wright), to Embassy (Bromley), 11 June 1947, FO 371/61756, PRO.

32. Halifax to Bevin, 14 June 1946, FO 371/52529, PRO.

33. Blum, *Price of Vision,* 606–7.

34. Inverchapel to Foreign Office, 31 July 1946, FO 371/52548, PRO.

35. Inverchapel to Foreign Office, 14 Aug. 1946, FO 371/57693, PRO; Inverchapel to Foreign Office, 19 Aug. 1946, CO 733/467/76021/48/3, PRO; Notes of the Acheson-Inverchapel conversation, 3 Oct. 1946, 867N.01/10-346, NA; Inverchapel to Bevin, 22 Nov. 1946, FO 371/52571, PRO.

36. "Nation's Critics Acclaim 'A Flag Is Born,'" *The Answer,* 11 Oct. 1946, 7; Ben-Ami, *Years of Wrath,* 384.

37. ALFP press release, 5 Dec. 1946. As a former U.S. senator, Gillette was able to use his friendships on Capitol Hill to open doors for the Free Palestine League. See, e.g., Gillette to Taft, 11 Apr. 1947, Subject File: Palestine 1947, Robert A. Taft Papers, LC.

38. Liss interview. For details of the Chicago performance, see Walter Roth, "'A Flag Is Born' Pageant Sought to Establish Jewish State in Palestine," *Chicago Jewish History* 16 (Fall 1992): 1, 4–7; "Thirty-Three Dramatists Issue Wash. Boycott against Negro Theatre Exclusion in 'Fight to Finish' Racial Snarl," *Variety,* 20 Nov. 1946, 65.

39. ALFP press release, 16 Feb. 1947, copy in the possession of the author (courtesy of Joseph Hochstein); Donald Kirkley, "'A Flag Is Born' Opens Here Tonight; Viewed as Timely," *Baltimore Sun,* 10 Feb. 1947, 6.

40. Harry S. Ashmore, *Hearts and Minds: The Anatomy of Racism from Roosevelt to Reagan* (New York: McGraw Hill, 1982), 102.

41. "Pickets' Appearance Makes Downtown Theatre Hurriedly Open Its Doors," *Afro-American,* 22 Feb. 1947, 1; White to Mitchell, 13 Feb. 1947, NAACP Papers, LC.

42. Selden interview with the author, 3 Apr. 1997; "Pickets' Appearance . . ."; ALFP press release, 16 Feb. 1947.

43. "Pickets' Appearance . . ."; ALFP press release, 16 Feb. 1947; Mitchell to White, 13 Feb. 1947, NAACP Papers. For the reviewers' assessment of the Bal-

timore performance, see Donald Kirkley, "Worth Seeing," *Baltimore Morning Sun*, 9 Feb. 1947, 6; Donald Kirkley, "'A Flag Is Born' Opens Here Tonight; Viewed as Timely," *Baltimore Morning Sun*, 10 Feb. 1947, 14; Donald Kirkley, "'A Flag Is Born,'" *Baltimore Morning Sun*, 11 Feb. 1947, 16; Hope Pantell, "'A Flag Is Born' Opens at the Maryland," *Baltimore Evening Sun*, 11 Feb. 1947, 14.

44. "Color Bar Broken in Baltimore Theater" (NAACP press release), 14 Feb. 1947; White to American League for a Free Palestine, 13 Feb. 1947; Atwood to O'Neill, 11 Mar. 1947; "The Story Thus Far," *Baltimore Fellowship News*, March 1947, 9; all in NAACP Papers.

45. ALFP press release, 16 Feb. 1947.

46. *American League for a Free Palestine Private News Letter*, 3 Oct. 1946; Hecht, *Child of the Century*, 614.

47. Diary of Esther Kaplan, Archives of the Zionist Organization of America, New York.

Chapter 9

1. Akzin to Silver, 18 Dec. 1945, File 4-3-2, AHSP; Korff, *Flight from Fear*, 132.

2. "Capital Hints at Palestine Review on Plea Presented by 600 Rabbis," *NYT*, 13 Nov. 1945, 4; "1,000 Rabbis in March on Capitol," *New York Daily Mirror*, 13 Nov. 1945, 6.

3. "British 'Indicted' in Jewish Pageant," *NYT*, 6 Mar. 1946, 10; "Jewish Blood vs. Arab Oil!" (advertisement), *NYP*, 20 Apr. 1948, 28.

4. "God Save the King!—A Message from London" (advertisement), *NYP*, 19 Nov. 1946, 34.

5. Korff, *Flight from Fear*, 145–51; Gene Currivan, "Truce in Palestine Urged by Baldwin," *NYT*, 29 Dec. 1946, 16; Gene Currivan, "Aide of Baldwin Defends Flogging," *NYT*, 1 Jan. 1947, 17.

6. Rabbi J. Howard Ralbag interview with the author, 18 July 1996; Ralbag to Langer, 7 Nov. 1947, and Langer to Ralbag, 10 Nov. 1947, both in Box 180, File 8, WLP.

7. "Palestine Today: A Report to Hon. William Langer, Senator, N. Dak., from Rev. Dr. J. Howard Ralbag, Congregation Ohav Shalom, New York, New York" (17 pp.), Box 180, File 8, WLP.

8. "Senator Langer, 73, G.O.P. Rebel, Dead," *NYT*, 9 Nov. 1959, 1.

9. Goldberg to Langer, 12 Feb. 1944, Box 145, File 8, WLP.

10. Wyman, *Abandonment of the Jews*, 146, 153.

11. "Dear Mr. Senator," n.d. [November 1945], Box 145, File 7, WLP.

12. See Box 180, Files 7 and 8, Box 217, File 12, and Box 145, Files 7, 8, and 9, ibid.

13. Langer to Bergson, 3 Jan. 1945, Box 145, File 8, ibid.; "Senator Langer, 73, G.O.P. Rebel . . ."; Korff to Langer, 25 Dec. 1945, Box 145, File 7, WLP.

14. Ziff to Langer, 18 Dec. 1945, and Langer to Ziff, 19 Dec. 1945, Box 145, File 7, WLP; Langer et al. to Selassi, 1 Aug. 1947, Box 180, File 7, WLP; Private Secretary to His Imperial Majesty to Langer et al., 12 Aug. 1947, Box 180, File 7, WLP; Silver to Langer, 19 Jan. 1945, and Langer to Silver, 20 Jan. 1945, Box 145, File 8, WLP.

15. Embassy to North American Department, Foreign Office, 14 Oct. 1943, FO 371/35040, PRO; Rosenblatt to Langer, n.d. [1947], Box 217, File 12, WLP.

16. Korff, *Flight from Fear*, 9–23, 167–72; "Rabbi Held in Paris Weakens as He Fasts," *NYT*, 14 Sept. 1947, 32; "Nobody Brings Jews into Palestine" (advertisement), *NR*, 7 Apr. 1947, 48; "Our Defiance: 'Exodus by Air'!" (advertisement), *NYP*, 8 May 1947, 54; "Rabbi Says Hotel Has Ousted Him," *New York Sun*, 27 Aug. 1947, 8.

Chapter 10

1. Bergson to Akzin, 21 Jan. 1945, and Akzin to Bergson, 26 Jan. 1945, 16/15-peh, CZA.

2. AZEC Minutes, 6 Mar. 1945, 29 Oct. 1945, AHSP; Lourie to Akzin, 7 Mar. 1945, 16/15-peh, BAP; Goldmann to Weizmann, 19 Apr. 1945, Z4/14482, CZA; Akzin to Wertheim, 6 Dec. 1944, 9/15-peh, BAP; Akzin to Wise, Greenberg and Shulman, 29 May 1945, A401/13, CZA; Akzin to Neumann, 31 Jan. 1947, 8/15-peh, BAP. Unfortunately, Akzin's autobiography provides only a brief and superficial discussion of his AZEC years. Benjamin Akzin, *From Riga to Jerusalem: A Memoir* (Hebrew) (Jerusalem: Publishing House of the World Zionist Organization, 1989), 347–53.

3. Akzin to Henderson, 8 Feb. 1946, Subject File: Israel-Palestine—Correspondence Re," Loy W. Henderson Papers, LC.

4. Ben-Horin to Akzin, 10 Nov. 1944, 15 Nov. 1945, 7/15-peh, BAP. For a discussion of the Truman administration's concerns about the Jewish vote in 1945 and 1946, see Michael J. Cohen, *Truman and Israel* (Berkeley: University of California Press, 1990), 123–24, 141–45.

5. Emanuel Neumann first recommended to Silver that Ben-Horin be hired in November 1944, as soon as he learned that Ben-Horin was available, but Silver resigned from the AZEC shortly afterward, so the decision was delayed (Neumann to Silver, 28 Nov. 1944, A123/315, CZA). Ben-Horin to Akzin,

3 Sept. 1945, 7/15-peh, BAP; AZEC Minutes, 29 Oct. 1945, 5 Nov. 1945, AHSP; "Memorandum by Eliahu Ben-Horin, September 10, 1945," File 4/3/8, AHSP; Ben-Horin to Akzin, 2 Aug. 1946, A401/4, CZA. For Ben-Horin's meeting with a *New York Times* correspondent, see Ben-Horin to Shapiro, 29 Jan. 1947, File IV-11, HMP. For Ben-Horin's meeting with the editors of the *Christian Science Monitor,* see Ben-Horin to Shapiro, 3 Feb. 1947, File IV-11, HMP.

6. For the full story of the Hoover plan, see Rafael Medoff, "Herbert Hoover's Plan for Palestine: A Forgotten Episode in American Middle East Diplomacy," *American Jewish History* 79 (Summer 1990): 449–76.

7. For the complete text, see "On the Palestine Question" in Herbert Hoover, *Addresses upon the American Road* (New York: D. Van Nostrand Co., 1949), 16–17.

8. "The Hoover Plan," *Palestine* 2 (November–December 1945): 16; Medoff, "Herbert Hoover's Plan."

9. Ben-Horin to Akzin, 15 Nov. 1945, 7/15-peh, BAP.

10. "Report by Mr. Eliahu Ben-Horin, at a Meeting Held at the Office of the American Zionist Emergency Council, December 5, 1946, at 3:00 P.M.," File III-89, HMP.

11. "Report on the Participation of the United Zionists-Revisionists of America in the Extraordinary Zionist Conference Called by the Zionist Emergency Council at the Statler Hotel, Washington, D.C., on Monday, February 17th, 1947," 16-gimel/10, MZ.

12. Zinger to Meyerson [Hebrew], 17 Oct. 1947, and Meyerson to Zinger, 27 Oct. 1947, S25/2071, CZA.

13. "Blood, Sweat, Not Tears" (editorial), *Bulletin of NZO,* 9 Mar. 1944, 10/g/5, MZ.

14. NZOA press releases, 1 Nov. 1944, 17 Jan. 1945, 16-gimel/9, MZ.

15. "Appeal for Clemency," *The Answer,* February 1945, 10.

16. "Terror in Palestine Will Most Likely Continue" (Detroit NZOA press release), 26 Nov. 1944, 16-gimel/9, MZ; NZOA Midwestern Division press release, 11 Nov. 1944, 16/g/5, MZ.

17. "Truman Plan Opposed," *NYT,* 18 Aug. 1946, 7; "Alfange Blames Britain," *NYT,* 26 July 1946, 4; Julian Louis Meltzer, "Zionists Suspend Six Revisionists," *NYT,* 16 Dec. 1946, 10.

18. "Dov Gruner Memorial Meetings," *Bulletin of the UZRA,* [late April or early May 1947], 5–6, 16-gimel/10, MZ; "Jews Here Invited to Join Resistance," *NYT,* 22 Apr. 1947, 23; "PRC Mass Meeting Packs Doors in Tribute to Executed Heroes," *Freedom* 1 (November 1947): 1.

19. Evans to Bevin, 2 May 1947, FO 371/61753, PRO; Marden interview;

"Office of British Consulate Here Stormed by Group of Young Jews, *New York Sun*, 18 Apr. 1947, 1.

20. Chancery (British Embassy, Washington, D.C.) to Eastern Department, Foreign Office, FO 371/45599, PRO.

21. *Bulletin of the Organization Committee of the United Zionists-Revisionists* 1 (September 1946): 1; United Zionists-Revisionists press release, 9 May 1947, 16-gimel/10, MZ; Embassy (Chancery) to Eastern Department, Foreign Office, FO 371/61754, PRO.

22. "Palestine Resistance Committee in Action," *Freedom* 1 (August 1947): 8.

23. "Freedom Fights on Many Fronts," in *The Fight for Liberation and Nationhood: Special Report, 1947* (New York: American League for a Free Palestine, 1947), 9; "Z.O.A. Delegates: Shame!" (leaflet), American League for a Free Palestine, F38/566, CZA; Inverchapel to Bevin, "Jewish Affairs in the United States," 29 Nov. 1946, FO 371/52571, PRO.

24. "Gillette Denies Aid to Terrorists," *NYT,* 5 Dec. 1946, 39.

25. Harry Louis Selden, "Dov Gruner and Nathan Hale: Two Patriots," *The Answer,* 16 Apr. 1948, 18.

26. Ibid.; "Boycott Britain" (advertisement), *NYP,* May 24, 1948, 24.

27. F. B. A. Randall (British Consulate-General, New York) to Wright (British Embassy, Washington), 20 Mar. 1946, FO 371/52568, PRO.

28. "Gillette Denies Aid to Terrorists," *NYT,* Dec. 5, 1946, 39.

29. "This Is What Americans Think of You, Mr. Bevin!" (advertisement), *NYP,* Nov. 4, 1946, 50.

30. "There Will Be More Violence" (advertisement), *NR,* Dec. 16, 1946, 780.

31. "Build Dov Gruner's Memorial" (advertisement), *NR,* 5 May 1947, 48; "There Will Be More Violence" (advertisement), *NR,* 16 Dec. 1946, 780.

32. Quoted by Henry Wallace in "The Problem of Palestine," *NR,* 21 Apr. 1947, 12; also see Selden, "Dov Gruner and Nathan Hale," and Lester Cohen, "'Resistance to Tyranny Is Obedience to God,'" *The Answer,* January 1946, 2.

33. "Letter to the Terrorists of Palestine" (advertisement), *NYP,* 17 May 1947, 18. This particular advertisement caused an international diplomatic incident. See "Britain Prods U.S. to Stop Funds to Defy Palestine Law," *NYT,* 20 May 1947, 1.

34. "Ben Hecht's *A Flag Is Born*," in *The Fight for Liberation and Nationhood: Special Report, 1947,* 8.

35. "City's Rabbis Condemn Execution of Dov Gruner," *Jewish Examiner,* 25 Apr. 1947, 1.

36. Wallace, "The Problem of Palestine," 12; I. F. Stone, "Gangsters or Patriots?" *Nation,* 12 Jan. 1946, 35.

37. Richard Gottheil, "The President's Annual Message," *Maccabaean* 2 (June 1902): 323; Bernard Rosenblatt, "Palestine: The Future Hebrew State," *Maccabaean* 12 (June 1907): 235.

38. Louis D. Brandeis, "Democracy in Palestine" (New York: Provisional Executive Committee for General Zionist Affairs), Reel 84, BP; Brandeis to Hapgood, Dec. 31, 1914, in Melvin I. Urofsky and David W. Levy, eds., *Letters of Louis D. Brandeis, Volume 3 (1913–1915): Progressive and Zionist* (Albany: State University of New York Press, 1973), 393; Brandeis to Lubin, Sept. 19, 1918, and Brandeis to Alice Brandeis, 10 July 1919, in Melvin I. Urofsky and David W. Levy, eds., *Letters of Louis D. Brandeis, Volume 4 (1916–1921): Mr. Justice Brandeis* (Albany: State University of New York Press, 1975), 356, 417–18.

39. *A Course in Zionism* (New York: Federation of American Zionists, 1915), 69.

40. "Brandeis Resumes Active Interest in Palestine Cause; Joins with Warburg in Establishing Palestine Corporation," *JDB*, 26 Nov. 1929, 6, 7; Brandeis's address to the Palestine Economic Conference, Washington, D.C., Nov. 24, 1929, Reel 89, BP.

41. Irma L. Lindheim, *Parallel Quest: A Search of a Person and a People* (New York: Thomas Yoseloff, 1962), 138. For an interesting variation on this theme, see the letter from Elisha Friedman, a Zionist activist and longtime Brandeis confidante, in *NYT*, 16 Dec. 1945, sec. IV, p. 8. Urging support for a proposal by former president Herbert Hoover to resettle Palestinian Arabs in Iraq, Friedman compared the idea of Arabs trekking from Palestine to Iraq to the "hundreds of thousands of farmers from the New England states [who] went West to Ohio, Iowa, Oregon, abandoned poor soil and acquired fertile land." In Friedman's analogy, it was the Arabs, not the Jews, who were comparable to the American frontiersmen.

42. "Colonel Blimp in Palestine" (editorial), *Palestine* 4 (February–March 1947): 18.

43. "Our Battle for Jewish Statehood: Text of Political Addresses by Dr. Abba Hillel Silver—49th Annual Convention of the Zionist Organization of America, Atlantic City, New Jersey, October 25 to 28, 1946" (New York: Zionist Organization of America, 1946), 13–14.

44. "Who Are the *Real* Terrorists?" (advertisement), *NR*, 21 Apr. 1947, 48. A minority within the ZOA, including some on the editorial staff of *New Palestine*, seem to have been unhappy with justifications of Jewish violence in particular and Silver's more militant line in general. Akzin repeatedly complained to Emanuel Neumann about the editors' deciding, "out of sheer cussedness," to

relegate his articles to less-noticed pages. On at least one occasion, they altered an article of Akzin's in order to temper its sympathy for the IZL: in a December 1946 essay, Akzin described Jewish attacks on the British as "inevitable excesses" that have merely "added to the confusion"; the editors inserted two sentences declaring that such attacks "must be deeply deplored." Akzin to Neumann, 17 May 1946, 8/15-peh, BAP; also see Akzin's copy of his article "The 22nd Zionist Congress," from *NP,* 13 Dec. 1946, 7–10, with his markings on p. 8, in 29/15-peh, BAP.

45. Leikin interview; Ezekiel Leikin, "Confrontations between Israel and the U.S. Jewish Community," *National Jewish Post and Opinion,* 24 July 1996, 8. The hiring of Leikin by the Revisionists is noted in UZR National Council Minutes, 3 Apr. 1946, 1, 16-gimel/9, MZ.

46. Akzin to Shapiro, 28 Jan. 1947, 38/15-peh, BAP; Ben-Horin to Silver, 9 July 1946, A401/4, CZA.

47. "Legalizing Lawlessness" (editorial), *Palestine* 2 (November–December 1945): 3; "The Moral Price" (editorial), *Palestine* 4 (January 1947): 3; "British Gestapo Regime" (editorial), *Palestine* 4 (April–May 1947): 35; "Jews Here Assail Palestine Closing," *NYT,* 14 Aug. 1946, 3.

48. Alpert interview.

49. Menachem Begin, *The Revolt* (Los Angeles: Nash, 1972), 314–16, 346; Silver to Neumann, 15 May 1947, A123/207, CZA.

50. Goldmann, *Autobiography,* 228; Katz interview; Shmuel Katz, *Days of Fire* (Tel Aviv: Steimatzky's, 1968), 209–11. The brief mention of a similar conversation between Irgun representatives and Silver by Ben-Ami (*Years of Wrath,* 419) appears to refer to the Silver-Katz meeting.

51. "Aide Memoir—Strictly Confidential," n.d., Americans for Haganah, F41/118, CZA.

52. "The Convention of the Z.O.A." (editorial), *Reconstructionist,* 15 Nov. 1946, 3–4. Interestingly, however, the *Reconstructionist* itself had, in 1944, twice published editorials that, while condemning Jewish terrorism, blamed the British for provoking the Jewish attacks. An April 13 editorial charged that in view of Nazi persecution and British mistreatment, the crimes of the Jewish militants fell into the halachic category of "One is not held responsible for what he does when in pain": "Can one say as much for the misdeeds of the Palestine administration that has condemned to death at the hands of the Nazis great numbers of Jewish who might have escaped to their national home?" "Terrorism in Palestine" (editorial), *Reconstructionist,* 13 Apr. 1944, 5–6. On November 17, the editors asserted that the British government's mistreatment of Palestine

Jewry and refusal to let refugees enter the Holy Land was to blame for having "driven sons of a peace-loving people to acts of desperation and crime." "Lawlessness in Palestine" (editorial), *Reconstructionist*, 17 Nov. 1944, 6–7.

53. Netanyahu to Neumann, 12 Nov. 1944, A123/307, CZA; Akzin to Goldmann, 13 Feb. 1946, Z6/300, CZA.

54. Berman to Teitelbaum, 10 June 1947, and Bukspan to Berman, 17 June 1947, File 4-4-45, AHSP.

55. Herbert Setlow interview with the author, 24 Dec. 1995; Netanyahu interview, 26 June 1997.

56. "Jews Here Assail Palestine Closing," *NYT*, Aug. 14, 1946, 3; Wise to Gottheil, 8 July 1946, Box 109, SWP.

57. Charles H. Stember et al., *Jews in the Mind of America* (New York: Basic Books, 1966), 174–80; for more on American public opinion during the 1940s, see George H. Gallup, *The Gallup Poll: Public Opinion, 1935–1971* (New York: Random House, 1972).

58. Inverchapel to Bevin, 29 Nov. 1946, FO 371/52571, PRO.

59. Embassy to Consulates, 5 July 1945 [1944], and Embassy (Russell) to Reconstruction Department, Foreign Office, 5 Mar. 1945, FO 371/50972, PRO.

60. "Hecht Play Banned," *NYT*, 27 Mar. 1947, 22.

61. Hecht, *Child of the Century*, 606–7.

62. Wright (British Embassy, Washington, D.C.) to Baxter (Foreign Office), 4 Feb. 1946, FO 371/52568/HM07059, PRO.

63. Foreign Office to Embassy, 11 Dec. 1946, and Foreign Office to A. R. Judge (Home Office), 10 Dec. 1946, FO 371/52571, PRO; Charles E. Egan, "Britain Bars American Zionist Who Backs Palestine Terrorism," *NYT*, 20 Dec. 1946, 18.

64. Halifax to Foreign Office, 24 May 1944, FO 371/40131, PRO; Chancery (British Embassy, Washington, D.C.) to Eastern Department, Foreign Office, 6 Aug. 1945, FO 371/45599, PRO; Memorandum of Conversation with Nahum Goldmann, 19 May 1944, 867N.01/2347/PS/LC, NA; Department of State—Memorandum of Conversation (Waldman, Murray, Alling, Wilson), 10 Jan. 1944, 3:67, PSGP.

65. U.S. Embassy, London, to Secretary of State, Washington, 6 Mar. 1947, FBI Files.

66. Alden to Tamm, 23 May 1944, ibid.

67. Alden to Ladd, 24 Mar. 1945, ibid.

68. Ladd to Director, FBI, 22 Aug. 1951, 1–2, ibid.

69. FBI Washington, Report on Hebrew Committee of National Liberation, 1 May 1947, 30, ibid.

70. Ibid., 44.

71. Report by New York FBI Office, 24 October 1945, "Hebrew Committee of National Liberation—Registration Act Internal Security."

72. Ibid.

73. Buckley to Ladd, 23 May 1944, ibid.

74. FBI New York to FBI Washington, "HCNL Registration Act," 11 Sept. 1950, 2, ibid.

75. Report of the St. Louis, Missouri, office of the FBI, January 8, 1948, "American League for a Free Palestine—Registration Act," 2, ibid.

76. FBI Washington, Report on Hebrew Committee of National Liberation, 1 May 1947, 27, ibid.

77. Report: Hebrew Committee of National Liberation, 18 Apr. 1945, ibid.

78. FBI Memo for the Files, 16 Feb. 1948, and Hoover to O'Brien, 20 Feb. 1948, ibid.

79. Mumford to Ladd, 26 Sept. 1945, ibid.

80. J. Edgar Hoover, "Hebrew Committee of National Liberation," 18 Feb. 1946, ibid.

81. Ibid.

82. Ibid.

83. Ibid.

84. Philadelphia FBI Report: "Hebrew Committee of National Liberation," 1 June 1945, ibid.

85. Ibid.

86. J. Edgar Hoover, "Hebrew Committee of National Liberation," 18 Feb. 1946, ibid.

87. Baruch Rabinowitz interview with the author, 7 Jan. 2001.

88. Murray Everett, "Inside and Out," *New Leader,* 8 Apr. 1944, 10.

89. Hoover to Smith, 13 Apr. 1943, FBI files.

90. Internal Security Report, "Hebrew Committee of National Liberation," 25 Jan. 1945, 20, ibid.

91. FBI Philadelphia Report, June 1, 1945, "Hebrew Committee of National Liberation—Registration Act Internal Security," 2–3, ibid.

92. FBI New York Report, "HCNL Registration Act," 14 Mar. 1951, 8, 11.

93. Buckley to Ladd, 23 May 1944, ibid.; Memo from J. Edgar Hoover, "Hebrew Committee of National Liberation," 18 Feb. 1946, ibid.; Ladd to Tamm, 23 May 1944, ibid.; Internal Security Report, "Hebrew Committee of National Liberation," 25 Jan. 1945, ibid.

94. FBI New York Report, "HCNL Registration Act," 14 Mar. 1951.

95. Embassy to Foreign Office, 6 Aug. 1947, FO 371/61784, PRO.

96. Inverchapel to Bevin, 25 June 1947, FO 371/61756, PRO.

97. "Aide Memoire," 28 June 1946, FO 371/52569, PRO.

98. Foreign Office to United Kingdom Delegation to Council of Foreign Ministers (New York), 30 Nov. 1946, FO 371/52571, PRO.

99. Ironically, in 1940 a mob of left-wing Zionist youths had stormed a clubhouse in Herzliya and beaten to death a young Revisionist named Eliahu Shlomi. "Police Guard at Funeral," *Palestine Post,* 20 Aug. 1940, 2; "Curfew in Herzlia: Histadruth Members and Revisionists in Brawl," *Palestine Post,* 20 Aug. 1940, 2.

100. Leonard Slater, *The Pledge* (New York: Simon and Schuster, 1970), 96; Wahl to Stella Adler, 18 Mar. 1948, Wahl to William O'Dwyer, 18 Mar. 1948, Wahl to Emanuel Celler, 12 Apr. 1948, 18 Mar. 1948, Halpern to Stern, 26 Aug. 1948, and Wahl to William O'Dwyer, 18 Mar. 1948, F41/124, CZA; "Americans for Haganah: Current Activities Other Than Publicity," 16 Mar. 1948, F41/4, CZA; "Activities of Americans for Haganah: July 1947–December 1948 (Confidential)," 7–8, F41/5, CZA; Simons to Wahl, 17 June 1948, Litwak to Wahl, 25 June 1948, Wahl to Litwak, 25 June 1948, Wahl to Iucci, 25 June 1948, Wahl to Bernstein, 25 June 1948, and Bernstein to Wahl, 27 June 1948, F41/53, CZA; "Bobbie" to Selden, 30 June 1948 (courtesy of Harry Selden); "Bernstein Will Play for Irgun," *New York Star,* 1 July 1948; Rafaeli, *Dream and Action,* 163–64; Alexander Rafaeli interview with the author, 17 Apr. 1996; Humphrey Burton, *Leonard Bernstein* (New York: Doubleday, 1994), 180–81.

101. Joseph M. Hochstein and Murray S. Greenfield, *The Jews' Secret Fleet* (Jerusalem: Gefen, 1987), 171–73.

102. Sinclair (Consulate-General, New York) to Rundall (Foreign Office), 2 Dec. 1946, and Foreign Office to Embassy, 7 Dec. 1946, FO 371/52571, PRO; "There Will Be MORE Violence" (advertisement), *NYP,* 3 Dec. 1946, 32.

103. Foreign Office to Washington, 23 Apr. 1947, FO 371/61805, PRO; James Reston, "Britain Prods U.S. to Stop Funds to Defy Palestine Law," *NYT,* 20 May 1947, 1; "Hecht Views Decried by Two Jewish Groups," *NYT,* 5 June 1947, 17; "Zionists *Must* Choose . . . *Now:* Partition of Palestine and a Perpetual Ghetto OR the Jewish Republic with Freedom and Dignity," *NYP,* 3 Dec. 1946, 26; "Calls Hecht Insignificant," *NYT,* 5 June 1947, 17; Walter Winchell, "In New York," *New York Daily Mirror,* 22 May 1947, 10; "British Press Attacks Winchell, Hecht," *P.M.,* 26 May 1947, 7.

104. "Truman Urges End to Aid in Palestine Strife," *New York Herald Tribune,* 6 June 1947.

105. Embassy (Inverchapel) to Bevin, 25 June 1947, FO 371/61756, PRO.

106. Beith (Foreign Office) to Higham (Colonial Office), 12 Aug. 1947, FO 371/61757, PRO.

107. Embassy to Eastern Department, Foreign Office, 6 Aug. 1947, FO 371/61784, PRO.

Chapter 11

1. Slater, *The Pledge.*

2. Harry Green interview with the author, 11 Nov. 1993.

3. *Bulletin of the UZRA,* 15 Apr. 1948, 16-gimel/10, MZ; "The Dov Gruner Chapter," *Bulletin of the UZRA,* 1 Aug. 1948, 7, 16-gimel/10, MZ.

4. Hecht, *Child of the Century,* 609. Whether the "Irgun coffers" in fact "swelled with millions" or some more modest sum is not known, since no documentation was kept on such collections.

5. For example, on page 6 of the 17 Nov. 1941 issue.

6. Sylvia Zweibon interview with the author, 16 Mar. 1993; Emanuel Zweibon interview with the author, 23 Mar. 2000.

7. Lawrence Schwartz interview with the author, 14 Mar. 1993.

8. Ruth Salomon King interview with the author, 15 Mar. 1993.

9. Oscar Bookspan interview with the author, 7 July 1996.

10. Netanyahu and Propes to "Dear Member," 2 Oct. 1946, 16-gimel/7, MZ.

11. Rosenberg interview.

12. "Large Quantity of Arms in West Side Loft Found Being Hidden in Palestine Parcels," *NYT,* 28 Apr. 1948, 12; Selden interview with the author, 29 Mar. 1993.

13. "Court Paroles Two in Zion Gun Inquiry," *NYT,* 29 Apr. 1948, 16.

14. "Two in Arms Cache for Palestine Free," *NYT,* 29 May 1948, 2; O'Dwyer, *Counsel for the Defense,* 162–64.

15. Interview with George Studley, 14 Jan. 2000; Selden interview with the author, 15 Jan. 2000; Dill interview; "Police Get Five Men with Arms Truck," *NYT,* 25 Nov. 1948, 1; "Five Youths Seized with an Arsenal," *NYT,* 26 Nov. 1948, 1; "Five Youths Released in Munitions Case," *NYT,* 10 Dec. 1948, 7.

Chapter 12

1. "Former Irgun Leader Hailed in the Garment Center," *NYT,* 27 Nov. 1948, 5; Selden interview, 7 Aug. 1997; Liss interview; Setlow interview, 24 Dec. 1995.

2. Lourie to Epstein, 14 Oct. 1948, Epstein to Lourie, 14 Oct. 1948, and Epstein to Lourie, 19 Oct. 1948, 126/8, Israel Ministry of Foreign Affairs Papers [hereafter IMFA], Jerusalem.

3. O'Dwyer, *Counsel for the Defense,* 166.

4. "New Palestine Party" (letters), *NYT,* 4 Dec. 1948, 12; "Begin's Hosts Here Assail His Critics," *NYT,* 2 Dec. 1948, 14.

5. "Abe" [Harman] to Ben-Horin, 28 Dec. 1948, A300/27, CZA; Wahl to Rycus, 28 Mar. 1949, F41/9, CZA.

6. David R. Wahl, "The Beigin [*sic*] Saga," *Haganah Speaks,* 3 Dec. 1948, 1, 3.

7. "Welcome Mr. Beigin [*sic*]!" (leaflet), F41/125, CZA; Setlow interview with the author, 25 Nov. 1996.

8. List of Begin dinner attendees, F41/125, CZA; "Former Irgun Leader Sees Palestine Unity with Brotherhood among Jews and Arabs," *NYT,* 30 Nov. 1948; Selden interview with the author, 22 Nov. 1996.

9. Ben-Horin to Silver, 10 Mar. 1949, File 4-4-63, AHSP.

10. Ibid.

11. Untitled memorandum in the "Schechtman" file of the Nahum Goldmann Collection, 25 Feb. 1949, Z6/171, CZA.

12. Minutes, American Section, Jewish Agency Executive, 22 Mar. 1949, 6, Z5/25, CZA; Minutes, 1 Mar. 1949, Z5/22, CZA.

13. "Arab Refugees: Facts and Figures" (New York: The Jewish Agency for Palestine, 1948) and "Resettlement Prospects for Arab Refugees" (New York: The Jewish Agency, 1949); Lourie to Schechtman, 17 June 1947, and Lourie to Shertok, 27 June 1947, 2268/18, IMFA; Epstein to Schechtman, 18 May 1948, and Schechtman to Epstein, 20 May 1948, Joseph Schechtman Papers [hereafter JSP], MZ; Schechtman to Silver, 12 Sept. 1948, 88/2, IMFA; Epstein to Schechtman, 1 Oct. 1948, and Schechtman to Epstein, 9 Oct. 1948, JSP; Lourie to Hammer, 11 Oct. 1948, and Schechtman to Lourie, 2 Nov. 1948, 88/2, IMFA; Epstein to Schechtman, 3 Nov. 1948, JSP.

14. Netanyahu to Neumann, 4 Dec. 1944, A123/307, CZA.

15. Minutes, AZEC Executive Committee, 17 Apr. 1944, Z5/1208, CZA.

16. Wise, *Challenging Years,* 268; Abraham I. Katsh, ed., *Scroll of Agony: The Warsaw Diary of Chaim A. Kaplan* (Bloomington and Indianapolis: Indiana University Press, 1999), 347.

17. Henry L. Feingold, *Bearing Witness: How America and Its Jews Responded to the Holocaust* (Syracuse: Syracuse University Press, 1995), 245–46.

18. Pehle to Bergson, 30 Nov. 1944, File: Emergency Committee to Save the Jewish People of Europe, Box 7, War Refugee Board Papers, FDRL.

19. For a history of the brigade, see Morris Beckman, *The Jewish Brigade: An Army with Two Masters, 1944–45* (Rockville Centre, N.Y.: Sarpedon, 1998).

20. Wyman, *Abandonment of the Jews,* 285.

21. Berlin, *Zionist Politics,* 64.

22. Hecht, *Child of the Century,* 606.

Selected Bibliography

Jabotinsky, Revisionist Zionism, and the Irgun Zvai Leumi

Books

Begin, Menachem. *The Revolt.* Los Angeles: Nash, 1972.

Bell, J. Bowyer. *Terror Out of Zion: Irgun Zvai Leumi, LEHI, and the Palestine Underground, 1929–1949.* New York: St. Martin's Press, 1977.

Charters, David. *British Army and Jewish Insurgency in Palestine, 1945–47.* Houndmills and London: Macmillan Press, 1989.

Clarke, Thurston. *By Blood and Fire: The Attack on the King David Hotel.* New York: Putnam, 1981

Cornfield, Giveon. *Zion Liberated.* Malibu, Calif.: Pangloss Press, 1990.

Frank, Gerold. *The Deed.* New York: Simon and Schuster, 1963.

Gitlin, Jan. *The Conquest of Acre Fortress.* Tel Aviv: Hadar, 1962.

Golan, Zev. *Free Jerusalem.* Jerusalem: Sdan Press and the Historical Society of Israel, 1998.

Heller, Joseph. *The Stern Gang: Ideology, Politics, and Terror, 1940–1949.* London: Frank Cass, 1995.

Heller, Tzila Amidror. *Behind Prison Walls: A Jewish Woman Freedom Fighter for Israel's War of Independence.* Hoboken, N.J.: Ktav, 1999.

Hoffman, Bruce. *The Failure of British Military Strategy Within Palestine, 1939–1947.* Ramat Gan: Bar-Ilan University Press, 1983.

Katz, Doris. *The Lady Was a Terrorist.* New York: Shiloni, 1953.

Katz, Shmuel. *Days of Fire.* Tel Aviv: Steimatzky's, 1968.

———. *Lone Wolf: A Biography of Vladimir (Ze'ev) Jabotinsky.* 2 vols. New York: Barricade Books, 1996.

Levine, Daniel. *The Birth of the Irgun Zvai Leumi—David Raziel: The Man and the Legend.* Jerusalem: Gefen, 1991.

Marton, Kati. *A Death in Jerusalem.* New York: Pantheon, 1994.

Nedava, Yosef. *Vladimir Jabotinsky: The Man and His Struggles.* Tel Aviv: Jabotinsky Institute of Israel, 1986.

Perl, William R. *The Four-Front War: From the Holocaust to the Promised Land.* New York: Crown, 1978.

Sarig, Mordechai, ed., *The Political and Social Philosophy of Ze'ev Jabotinsky: Selected Writings.* Essex: Valentine Mitchell, 1999.

Schechtman, Joseph B. *Fighter and Prophet: The Jabotinsky Story—The Last Years, 1923–1940.* New York: Thomas Yoseloff, 1961.

———. *Rebel and Statesman: The Jabotinsky Story—The Early Years, 1880–1923.* New York: Thomas Yoseloff, 1956.

Schechtman, Joseph B., and Yehuda Benari. *History of the Revisionist Movement: Volume 1, 1925–1930.* Tel Aviv: Hadar, 1970.

Shamir, Yitzhak. *Summing Up: An Autobiography.* Boston: Little, Brown, 1994.

Shapiro, Yonathan. *The Road to Power: Herut Party in Israel.* Albany: State University Press of New York, 1991.

Shavit, Yaacov. *Jabotinsky and the Revisionist Movement, 1925–1948.* London: Frank Cass, 1988.

Tavin, Eli, and Yonah Alexander, eds. *Psychological Warfare and Propaganda: Irgun Documentation.* Wilmington: Delaware Scholarly Resources, 1982.

Weinbaum, Laurence. *A Marriage of Convenience: The New Zionist Organization and the Polish Government, 1936–1939.* Boulder: East European Monographs/Columbia University Press, 1993.

Zadka, Saul. *Blood in Zion: How the Jewish Guerrillas Drove the British Out of Palestine.* London: Braessey's, 1995.

Dissertations

Rosenblum, Howard Isaac. "A Political History of Revisionist Zionism, 1925–1938." Ph.D. diss., Columbia University, 1986.

Scholarly Articles

Avineri, Shlomo. "The Political Thought of Vladimir Jabotinsky." *Jerusalem Quarterly* 16 (Summer 1980): 3–26.

Elam, Yigal. "'Haganah,' 'Irgun,' and 'Stern,' Who Did What?" *Jerusalem Quarterly* 23 (1982): 70–78.

Eldad, Israel. "Jabotinsky Distorted." *Jerusalem Quarterly* 16 (Summer 1980): 27–39.

Engel, David. "The Frustrated Alliance: The Revisionist Movement and the Polish Government-in-Exile, 1939–1945." *Studies in Zionism* 7 (Spring 1986): 11–36.

Getter, Miriam. "The Arab Problem in the Ideology of Lehi." *Studies in Zionism* 1 (Spring 1980): 128–39.

Goldstein, Joseph. "Jabotinsky and Jewish Autonomy in the Diaspora." *Studies in Zionism* 7 (Autumn 1986): 219–32.

Gordon, Louis A. "Arthur Koestler and His Ties to Zionism and Jabotinsky." *Studies in Zionism* 12 (Autumn 1991): 149–68.

———. "The Unknown Essays of Vladimir Jabotinsky." *Jewish Political Studies Review* 9 (Spring 1997): 95–104.

Heller, Joseph. "The Zionist Right and National Liberation: From Jabotinsky to Avraham Stern." *Israel Affairs* 1, no. 3 (1995): 85–109.

Nakhimovsky, Alice. "Vladimir Jabotinsky, Russian Writer." *Modern Judaism* 7 (May 1987): 151–73.

Nicosia, Francis. "Revisionist Zionism in Germany: Richard Lichtheim and the *Landesverband der Zionisten-Revisionisten in Deutschland, 1926–1930*." *Leo Baeck Institute Yearbook* (1986): 209–40.

Rosenblum, Chanoch [Howard]. "The New Zionist Organization's Diplomatic Battle Against Partition, 1936–1937." *Studies in Zionism* 11 (Autumn 1990): 154–81.

Shavit, Yaakov. "Fire and Water: Ze'ev Jabotinsky and the Revisionist Movement." *Studies in Zionism* 2 (Autumn 1981): 219–36.

———. "Politics and Messianism: The Zionist Revisionist Movement and Polish Political Culture." *Journal of Israeli History* 6 (Autumn 1985): 229–46.

Sofer, Sasson. "The Concept of Revolt in Menachem Begin's Thought." *Studies in Zionism* 7 (Spring 1986): 97–109.

Tomaszewski, Jerzy. "Vladimir Jabotinsky's Talks with Representatives of the Polish Government." *Polin* 3 (1988): 276–93.

Tzahor, Ze'ev. "The Struggle between the Revisionist Party and the Labor Movement, 1929–1933." *Modern Judaism* 8 (1988): 15–25.

Weinbaum, Laurence. "Jabotinsky and the Poles." *Polin* 5 (1990): 156–72.

Zweig, Ronald. "The Political Uses of Military Intelligence: Evaluating the Threat of a Jewish Revolt Against Britain during the Second World War." In *Diplomacy and Intelligence during the Second World War*, ed. Richard Langhorne, 109–25. Cambridge: Cambridge University Press, 1985.

Jabotinsky's Followers in America

Books

Ben-Ami, Yitshaq. *Years of Wrath, Days of Glory: Memoirs from the Irgun*. 2nd ed. New York: Shengold, 1983.

Hecht, Ben. *A Child of the Century*. New York: Simon and Schuster, 1954.

Korff, Baruch. *Flight from Fear*. New York: Elmar, 1953.

O'Dwyer, Paul. *Counsel for the Defense: The Autobiography of Paul O'Dwyer.* New York: Simon and Schuster, 1979.

Rafaeli, Alex. *Dream and Action: The Story of My Life.* Jerusalem: Achva, 1993.

Rapoport, Louis. *Shake Heaven and Earth: Peter Bergson and the Struggle to Rescue the Jews of Europe.* Jerusalem: Gefen, 1999.

Dissertations

Feinstein, Marsha. "The Irgun Campaign in the United States for a Jewish Army." M.A. thesis, City University of New York, 1973.

Levine, Charles J. "Propaganda Techniques of the Bergson Group 1939–1948." M.A. thesis, University of Texas, 1974.

Saidel, Joanna Maura. "Revisionist Zionism in America: The Campaign to Win American Public Support, 1939–1948." Ph.D. diss., University of New Hampshire, 1994.

Scholarly Articles

Ansell, Joseph. "Arthur Szyk's Depiction of the 'New Jew': Art as a Weapon in the Campaign for an American Response to the Holocaust." *American Jewish History* 89 (March 2001): 123–134.

Baumel, Judith Tydor. "The Irgun Zvai Leumi Delegation in the U.S.A., 1939–1948: Anatomy of an Ethnic Interest/Protest Group." *Jewish History* 9 (Spring 1995): 79–89.

Brown, Michael. "The New Zionism in the New World: Vladimir Jabotinsky's Relations with the United States in the Pre-Holocaust Years." *Modern Judaism* 9 (February 1989): 71–99.

Gordon, Louis. "William B. Ziff, Sr., Jabotinsky And the Zionist Revisionists in America." *Jewish Spectator* 61 (Winter 1996–97): 27–28.

Medoff, Rafael. "Herbert Hoover's Plan for Palestine: A Forgotten Episode in American Middle East Diplomacy." *American Jewish History* 79 (Summer 1990): 449–76.

———. "The Influence of Revisionist Zionism in America during the Early Years of World War Two." *Studies in Zionism* 13 (Autumn 1992): 187–90.

———. "Jabotinsky's Campaign in America: A Previously Unpublished Interview" (with Oscar Kraines). *Journal of Israeli History* 15 (Summer 1994): 223–29.

———. "Menachem Begin as George Washington: The Americanizing of the Jewish Revolt against the British." *American Jewish Archives* 47 (Fall/Winter 1994): 185–95.

———. "Who Fought for the 'Right to Fight'? The Campaign for a Jewish Army, 1939–1944." *Journal of Israeli History* 18 (Spring 1997): 113–27.

———. "Why Mrs. Brandeis Endorsed the *Irgun:* An Episode in Holocaust-Era American Jewish Politics." *American Jewish History* 84 (March 1996): 29–38.

Rosenblum, Chanoch [Howard]. "The New Zionist Organization's American Campaign, 1936–1939." *Studies in Zionism* 12 (Autumn 1991): 169–85.

Roth, Walter. "'A Flag Is Born' Pageant Sought to Establish Jewish State in Palestine." *Chicago Jewish History* 16 (Fall 1992): 1, 4–7.

Saposnik, Arye Bruce. "Advertisement of Achievement? American Jewry and the Campaign for a Jewish Army, 1939–1944: A Reassessment." *Journal of Israeli History* 17 (Summer 1996): 193–220.

Whitfield, Stephen J. "The Politics of Pageantry, 1936–1946." *American Jewish History* 84 (September 1996): 221–51.

Wyman, David S. "The Bergson Group, America and the Holocaust: A Previously Unpublished Interview with Hillel Kook/Peter Bergson." *American Jewish History* 89 (March 2001): 3–34.

INTERNATIONAL RESPONSES TO THE HOLOCAUST, INCLUDING THE ROLE OF THE BERGSON GROUP

Books

Breitman, Richard and Kraut, Alan M. *American Refugee Policy and European Jewry, 1933–1945.* Bloomington and Indianapolis: Indiana University Press, 1997.

Berman, Aaron. *Nazism, the Jews, and American Zionism, 1933–1948.* Detroit: Wayne State University Press, 1990.

Bunim, Amos. *A Fire in His Soul: Irving M. Bunim, 1901–1980—The Man and His Impact on American Orthodox Jewry.* Jerusalem and New York: Feldheim, 1989.

Feingold, Henry L. *Bearing Witness: How America and Its Jews Responded to the Holocaust.* Syracuse: Syracuse University Press, 1995.

———. *The Politics of Rescue.* New Brunswick: Rutgers University Press, 1970.

Finger, Seymour Maxwell, ed. *American Jewry During the Holocaust.* New York: Holmes and Meier, 1984.

Friedman, Saul S. *No Haven for the Oppressed: United States Policy Toward Jewish Refugees, 1938–1945.* Detroit: Wayne State University Press, 1973.

Lookstein, Haskel. *Were We Our Brothers' Keepers? The Public Response of American Jews to the Holocaust, 1938–1944.* New York: Random House, 1985.

Lowenstein, Sharon R. *Token Refuge: The Story of the Jewish Refugee Shelter at Oswego, 1944–1946.* Bloomington: Indiana University Press, 1986

Medoff, Rafael. *The Deafening Silence: American Jewish Leaders and the Holocaust, 1933–1945.* New York: Shapolsky, 1987.

Penkower, Monty N. *The Holocaust and Israel Reborn.* Urbana and Chicago: University of Illinois Press, 1994.

———. *The Jews Were Expendable: Free World Diplomacy and the Holocaust.* Urbana and Chicago: University of Illinois Press, 1983.

Wasserstein, Bernard. *Britain and the Jews of Europe, 1939–1945.* Oxford: Clarendon Press, 1979.

Wyman, David S. *The Abandonment of the Jews.* New York: Pantheon, 1984.

Zuroff, Efraim. *The Response of Orthodox Jewry in the United States to the Holocaust.* Hoboken, N.J.: Ktav, 2000.

Dissertations

Smith, Sharon Kay. "Elbert D. Thomas and America's Response to the Holocaust." Ph.D. diss., Brigham Young University, 1992.

Scholarly Articles

Lowenstein, Sharon R. "A New Deal for Refugees: The Promise and Reality of Oswego." *American Jewish History* 71 (March 1982): 325–341.

Medoff, Rafael. "'Our Leaders Cannot Be Moved': A Zionist Emissary's Reports on American Jewish Responses to the Holocaust in the Summer of 1943." *American Jewish History* 88 (March 2000): 115–126.

Peck, Sarah E. "The Campaign for an American Response to the Holocaust 1943–1945." *Journal of Contemporary History* 15 (1980): 367–400.

Penkower, Monty N. "In Dramatic Dissent: The Bergson Boys." *American Jewish History* 70 (March 1981): 281–309.

———. "American Jewry and the Holocaust: From Biltmore to the American Jewish Conference." *Jewish Social Studies* 47 (Spring 1985): 95–114.

ALIYAH BET

Avriel, Ehud. *Open the Gates! A Personal Story of "Illegal" Immigration to Israel.* New York: Atheneum, 1975.

Halamish, Aviva. *The Exodus Affair: Holocaust Survivors and the Struggle for Palestine.* Syracuse: Syracuse University Press, 1998.

Hochstein, Joseph M., and Murray S. Greenfield. *The Jews' Secret Fleet.* Jerusalem: Gefen, 1987.

Ofer, Dalia. *Escaping the Holocaust: Illegal Immigration to the Land of Israel, 1939–1944.* New York: Oxford University Press, 1990.

Perl, William R. *The Four-Front War: From the Holocaust to the Promised Land.* New York: Crown, 1978.

Zertal, Idith. *From Catastrophe to Power: Holocaust Survivors and the Emergence of Israel.* Berkeley: University of California Press, 1998.

AMERICAN ZIONISM

Books

Adler, Cyrus. *I Have Considered the Days.* Philadelphia: Jewish Publication Society of America, 1941.

Barnard, Harry. *The Forging of an American Jew: The Life and Times of Judge Julian Mack.* New York: Herzl Press, 1974.

Bentwich, Norman. *For Zion's Sake: A Biography of Judah L. Magnes.* Philadelphia: Jewish Publication Society of America, 1954.

Berlin, Isaiah. *Zionist Politics in Wartime Washington: A Fragment of Personal Reminiscence—The Yaacov Herzog Memorial Lecture.* Jerusalem: Hebrew University, 1972.

Berman, Aaron. *Nazism, the Jews, and American Zionism, 1933–1948.* Detroit: Wayne State University Press, 1990.

Brandeis, Louis D. *Brandeis on Zionism: A Collection of Addresses and Statements by Louis D. Brandeis.* New York: Zionist Organization of America, 1942.

Brinner, William, and Moses Rischin, eds. *Like All the Nations? The Life and Legacy of Judah L. Magnes.* Albany: State University of New York Press, 1987.

Chernow, Ron. *The Warburgs.* New York: Random House, 1993.

Cohen, Michael J. *Truman and Israel.* Berkeley: University of California Press, 1990.

Cohen, Naomi W. *American Jews and the Zionist Idea.* New York: Ktav, 1975.

———. *A Dual Heritage: The Public Career of Oscar S. Straus.* Philadelphia: Jewish Publication Society of America, 1969.

———. *Not Free to Desist: The American Jewish Committee, 1906–1966.* Philadelphia: Jewish Publication Society of America, 1972.

———. *The Year after the Riots: American Responses to the Palestine Crisis of 1929–1930.* Detroit: Wayne State University Press, 1988.

Dash, Joan. *Summoned to Jerusalem: The Life of Henrietta Szold.* New York: Harper and Row, 1979.

Farrer, David. *The Warburgs: The Story of a Family.* New York: Stein and Day, 1975.

Feinstein, Marnin. *American Zionism, 1884–1904.* New York: Herzl Press, 1965.

Fineman, Irving. *Woman of Valor: The Story of Henrietta Szold.* New York: Simon and Schuster, 1961.

Friesel, Evyatar, ed. *Certain Days: Zionist Memoirs and Selected Papers of Julius Simon.* Jerusalem: Israel Universities Press, 1971.

Gal, Allon. *David Ben-Gurion and the American Alignment for a Jewish State.* Bloomington and Indianapolis: Indiana University Press, 1991.

————, ed. *Envisioning Israel: The Changing Ideals and Images of North American Jews.* Jerusalem and Detroit: Magnes Press and Wayne State University Press, 1996.

Ganin, Zvi. *Truman, American Jewry, and Israel, 1945–1948.* New York: Holmes and Meier, 1979.

Goldmann, Nahum. *The Autobiography of Nahum Goldmann: Sixty Years of Jewish Life.* New York: Holt, Rinehart and Winston, 1969.

Goren, Arthur A. *Dissenter in Zion: From the Writings of Judah L. Magnes.* Cambridge: Harvard University Press, 1982.

Haber, Julius. *The Odyssey of an American Zionist: Fifty Years of Zionist History.* New York: Twayne, 1956.

Halkin, Hillel. *Letters to an American Jewish Friend: A Zionist's Polemic.* Philadelphia: Jewish Publication Society of America, 1977.

Halperin, Samuel. *The Political World of American Zionism.* Detroit: Wayne State University Press, 1961.

Halpern, Ben. *The American Jew: A Zionist Analysis.* New York: Herzl Press, 1961.

————. *A Clash of Heroes: Brandeis, Weizmann, and American Zionism.* New York: Oxford University Press, 1987.

Hoffman, Leon S. *Ideals and Illusions: The Story of an Ivy League Woman in 1920's Israel.* New York: SPI Books, 1992.

Jaffe, Eliezer, D. *Letters to Yitz.* New York: Herzl Press, 1981.

Katzman, Jacob. *Commitment: The Labor Zionist Life-Style in America: A Personal Memoir.* New York: Labor Zionist Letters, 1975.

Kaufman, Menahem. *An Ambiguous Partnership: Non Zionists and Zionists in America, 1939–1948.* Jerusalem and Detroit: Magnes Press and Wayne State University Press, 1991.

Kleiman, Aharon. *American Zionism: A Documentary History.* 15 vols. New York: Garland, 1990.

Kolsky, Thomas A. *Jews against Zionism: The American Council for Judaism, 1942–1948.* Temple University Press, 1990.

Levin, Alexandra. *Henrietta Szold and Youth Aliyah: Family Letters, 1934–1944.* New York: Herzl Press, 1986.

Levin, Marlin. *It Takes a Dream: The Story of Hadassah.* Jerusalem: Gefen, 1997.

Lindheim, Irma L. *Parallel Quest: A Search of a Person and a People.* New York: Thomas Yoseloff, 1962.

Lipstadt, Deborah E. *The Zionist Career of Louis Lipsky, 1900–1921.* New York: Arno Press, 1982.

Lowenthal, Marvin. *Henrietta Szold: Life and Letters.* New York: Viking Press, 1942.

Mack, Julian W. *Americanism and Zionism.* New York: Zionist Organization of America, 1919.

Malone, Bobbie. *Rabbi Max Heller: Reformer, Zionist, Southerner, 1860–1929.* Tuscaloosa: University of Alabama Press, 1997.

Medoff, Rafael. *Baksheesh Diplomacy: Secret Negotiations between American Jewish Leaders and Arab Officials on the Eve of World War II.* Lanham, Md.: Lexington Books, 2001.

———. *Zionism and the Arabs: An American Jewish Dilemma, 1898–1948.* Westport, Conn.: Praeger, 1997.

Meyer, Isidore S., ed. *Early History of Zionism in America.* New York: Herzl Press, 1958.

Neumann, Emanuel. *In the Arena.* New York: Herzl Press, 1978.

Polier, Justine Wise, and James Waterman Wise, eds. *The Personal Letters of Stephen S. Wise.* Boston: Beacon Press, 1956.

Polish, David. *Renew Our Days: The Zionist Issue in Reform Judaism.* Jerusalem: World Zionist Organization, 1976.

Proskauer, Joseph M. *A Segment of My Times.* New York: Farrar, Straus, 1950.

Raider, Mark A. *The Emergence of American Zionism.* New York: New York University Press, 1998.

Raider, Mark A., Jonathan D. Sarna, and Ronald W. Zweig. *Abba Hillel Silver and American Zionism.* London: Frank Cass, 1997.

Rosenblatt, Bernard A. *Two Generations of Zionism.* New York: Shengold, 1976.

Rosenstock, Morton. *Louis Marshall, Defender of Jewish Rights.* Detroit: Wayne State University Press, 1965.

Raphael, Marc Lee. *Abba Hillel Silver.* New York: Holmes and Meier, 1989.

Schmidt, Sarah L. *Horace M. Kallen: Prophet of American Zionism.* Brooklyn: Carlson, 1997.

Scult, Mel. *Judaism Faces the Twentieth Century: A Biography of Mordecai Kaplan.* Detroit: Wayne State University Press, 1993.

Shapiro, David H. *From Philanthropy to Activism: The Political Transformation of American Zionism in the Holocaust Years 1933–1945.* New York: Pergamon Press, 1994.

Shapiro, Yonathan. *Leadership of the American Zionist Organization, 1897–1930.* Chicago: University of Illinois Press, 1971.

Shargel, Baila Round. *Lost Love: The Untold Story of Henrietta Szold.* Philadelphia: Jewish Publication Society of America, 1997.

———. *Practical Dreamer: Israel Friedlaender and the Shaping of American Judaism.* New York: Jewish Theological Seminary of America, 1985.

Silver, Abba Hillel. *Vision and Victory.* New York: Zionist Organization of America, 1949.

Slater, Leonard. *The Pledge.* New York: Simon and Schuster, 1970.

Stevens, Richard P. *American Zionism and U.S. Foreign Policy, 1942–1947.* New York: Pageant Press, 1962.

Strum, Philippa. *Louis D. Brandeis: Justice for the People.* Cambridge: Harvard University Press, 1984.

Urofsky, Melvin I. *American Zionism from Herzl to the Holocaust.* Garden City, N.Y.: Anchor Press/Doubleday, 1975.

———. *Louis Brandeis and the Progressive Tradition.* Boston: Little, Brown, 1981.

———. *A Voice That Spoke for Justice: The Life and Times of Stephen S. Wise.* Albany: State University of New York Press, 1982.

———. *We Are One!* Garden City, N.Y.: Anchor Press/Doubleday, 1978.

———, ed. *Essays in American Zionism—Herzl Year Book, Volume 8.* New York: Herzl Press, 1978.

Urofsky, Melvin I., and David W. Levy, eds. *Letters of Louis D. Brandeis, Volume 3 (1913–1915): Progressive and Zionist.* Albany: State University of New York Press, 1973.

———. *Letters of Louis D. Brandeis, Volume 4 (1916–1921): Mr. Justice Brandeis.* Albany: State University of New York Press, 1975.

———. *Letters of Louis D. Brandeis, Volume 5 (1929–1941): Elder Statesman.* Albany: State University of New York Press, 1978.

Voss, Carl Hermann. *Rabbi and Minister: The Friendship of Stephen S. Wise and John Haynes Holmes.* Cleveland: World Publishing, 1964

———, ed. *Stephen S. Wise: Servant of the People—Selected Letters.* Philadelphia: Jewish Publication Society of America, 1969.

Waldman, Morris. *Nor by Power.* New York: International Universities Press, 1953.

Weinstein, Jacob J. *Solomon Goldman: A Rabbi's Rabbi.* New York: Ktav, 1973.

Wise, Stephen S. *As I See It.* New York: Jewish Opinion Publishing, 1947.

———. *Challenging Years: The Autobiography of Stephen S. Wise.* New York: Putnam, 1949.

Zeitlin, Rose. *Henrietta Szold: A Record of a Life.* New York: The Dial Press, 1952.

Dissertations

Frommer, Morris. "The American Jewish Congress: A History, 1914–1950." Ph.D. diss., Ohio State University, 1978.

Grand, Samuel. "A History of Zionist Youth Organizations in the United States." M.A. thesis, Columbia University, 1958.

Kutnick, Jerome M. "Non-Zionist Leadership: Felix M. Warburg, 1929–1937." Ph.D. diss., Brandeis University, 1983.

Miller, Donald H. "A History of Hadassah, 1912–1935." Ph.D. diss., New York University, 1968.

Neustadt-Noy, Isaac. "The Unending Task: Efforts to Unite American Jewry from the American Jewish Congress to the American Jewish Conference." Ph.D. diss., Brandeis University, 1976.

Sandler, Bernard I. "The Jews of America and the Resettlement of Palestine, 1908–1934: Efforts and Achievements." Ph.D. diss., Bar Ilan University, 1979.

Scholarly Articles

Bierbrier, Doreen. "The American Zionist Emergency Council: An Analysis of a Pressure Group." *American Jewish History* 60 (September 1970): 82–105.

Ganin, Zvi. "Activism versus Moderation: The Conflict between Abba Hillel Silver and Stephen Wise during the 1940s." *Studies in Zionism* 5 (Spring 1984): 71–95.

Kaufman, Menahem. "American Zionism and United States Neutrality from September 1939 to Pearl Harbor." *Studies in Zionism* 9 (Spring 1988): 19–46.

Penkower, Monty N. "Ben Gurion, Silver, and the 1941 UPA National Conference for Palestine: A Turning Point in American Zionist History." *American Jewish History* 69 (September 1979): 66–75.

GENERAL HISTORIES OF ZIONISM

Adler, Joseph. *Restore the Jews to Their Homeland: Nineteen Centuries in the Quest for Zion.* Northvale, Vt.: Jason Aronson, 1997.

Avineri, Shlomo. *The Making of Modern Zionism: The Intellectual Origins of the Jewish State.* New York: Basic Books, 1981.

Ben-Zvi, Izhak. *The Exiled and the Redeemed.* Philadelphia: Jewish Publication Society of America, 1963.

Chertoff, Mordecai S., ed. *Zionism: a Basic Reader.* New York: Herzl Press, 1975.

Cohen, Mitchell. *Zion and State: Nation, Class, and the Shaping of Modern Israel.* New York: Basil Blackwell, 1987.

Gilbert, Martin. *Exile and Return: The Struggle for a Jewish Homeland.* Philadelphia: Lippincott, 1978.

Gorny, Yosef. *The State of Israel in Jewish Public Thought: The Quest for Collective Identity.* New York: New York University Press, 1994.

Halpern, Ben. *The Idea of the Jewish State.* 2nd ed. Cambridge: Harvard University Press, 1969.

Heller, Joseph. *The Zionist Idea.* New York: Schocken, 1949.

Hertzberg, Arthur. *The Zionist Idea.* Philadelphia: Jewish Publication Society, 1959.

Laqueur, Walter. *A History of Zionism.* New York: Schocken, 1976.

O'Brien, Conner Cruise. *The Siege: The Saga of Israel and Zionism.* New York: Simon and Schuster, 1986.

Penkower, Monty N. *The Emergence of Zionist Thought.* Millwood, N.Y.: Associated Faculty Press, 1986.

Sachar, Howard M. *A History of Israel: From the Rise of Zionism to Our Time.* New York: Knopf, 1979.

Shapira, Anita. *Land and Power: The Zionist Resort to Force.* New York: Oxford University Press, 1992.

Shimoni, Gideon. *The Zionist Ideology.* Hanover: Brandeis University Press/ University Press of New England, 1995.

Sofer, Sasson. *Zionism and the Foundations of Israeli Diplomacy.* New York: Cambridge University Press, 1998.

Sokolow, Nahum. *History of Zionism, 1600–1918.* New York: Ktav, 1969.

Vital, David. *The Origins of Zionism.* Oxford: Oxford University Press, 1975.

——. *Zionism: The Formative Years.* New York: Oxford University Press, 1988.

Index

of Jewish voting patterns, 105; established, 92; investigated by the FBI, 190, 193; loses supporters because of "Hebrew Committee" controversy, 113; rabbis' march in Washington, 97–98; relations with the NZOA, 116; rescue resolution in Congress, 105–6; role in establishing the War Refugee Board, 216; success in attracting celebrities, 93, 148, 154; widespread support for, 98

Emergency Conference to Save the Jewish People of Europe, 92, 97, 250n. 2

Epstein, Beinish, 8, 10, 17, 26, 30
Epstein, David, 30
Epstein, Eliahu, 137, 189, 212, 215
Epstein, Rabbi Hayyim Fischel, 30
Evans, F. E., 177
Exodus, 199

Federal Bureau of Investigation, 188–93
Federation of American Zionists, 181, 182
Feingold, Henry, 216
Feis, Herbert, 58
Fineman, Bernard, 39
Flag is Born, A, 154–56, 158–60, 180, 186, 195
Fonda, Henry, 196
Fountain, Mrs., 177
France, 1
Frankfurter, Felix, 21, 32, 36, 37
Friedenwald, Harry, 19
Friedman, Elisha, 258n. 41
Friedman, William, 136, 140
Furrows, 87

Galili (Krivoshein), Moshe, 33
Gavrilovitch, Oscar, 83
General Zionists, 24, 27
George Washington Legion, 179
Gerard, James W., 60
Germain, Louis, 89

Gillette, Guy, 71, 103, 152–53, 158, 179
Giloni, Morris, 213
Ginsburg, Elias, 8, 17, 20, 22, 57, 62, 65–66
Goebbels, Joseph, 74
Goldberg, Abraham, 10
Goldman, Solomon, 37, 38, 54, 99
Goldmann, Nahum, 76, 96, 99, 100, 132–33, 135, 171, 184, 185, 187, 197, 250n. 2
Goldstein, Israel, 38, 41, 87
Goodman, I. R., 189
Gottheil, Richard, 25, 18
Green, Harry, 201–02
Greenberg, Hayim, 95
Grew, Joseph, 138
Gropman, Paul, 252n. 22
Grossman, Meir, 18, 95, 141
Gruner, Dov, 43, 176–77, 179, 181, 183, 202
Gruszka, Sylwester, 62
Gunther, Frances, 34–35, 39, 41
Gunther, John, 34–35, 39
Gurvitch, Alexander, 207

Ha'am, Ahad, 2
Hadassah, 21, 25, 33, 44, 75, 100, 142, 148, 182
Haganah, 47, 49, 139, 151, 173, 183–84, 195, 201, 214
Haint, 20
Hale, Nathan, 176, 179, 180
Halifax, Lord, 77, 78, 86, 138, 143, 156
Halperin, Jeremiah, 48, 52, 79
Halperin, Yehiel Michal, 48
Halpert, Leo, 153
Halprin, Rose, 33, 75
Harzfeld, Avraham, 6
Ha-Shomer, 48
HaBoker, 94
Hamigdal, 87
Harper, Fowler, 159
Harrison, Earl, 138
Hashomer Hatzair, 20, 30, 213, 231n. 44
Hashomer Hatzair, 39
Hawkes, Albert, 108

Palestine labor issues, 20–21, 24; criticism of Judah Magnes, 15; first national convention, 16; names William Ziff its president, 40; opposition to Legislative Council proposal 14; organizational growth, 1930s, 16, 26; organizational problems, 1930s, 17; relations with the ZOA, 18–19; response to 1929 Palestinian Arab riots 12–14. *See also* New Zionist Organization of America; United Zionists-Revisionists of America

Zweibon, Abraham, 203–04
Zweibon, Sylvia, 203–04